The Frontier in Alaska and the Matanuska Colony

Matanuska tent city, summer of 1935. Courtesy of University of Alaska Archives.

THE FRONTIER IN ALASKA

AND THE MATANUSKA COLONY

Orlando W. Miller

University of Alaska Press
Fairbanks

University of Alaska Press
PO Box 756240
Fairbanks, AK 99775-6240

Originally designed by John O. C. McCrillis and set in Baskerville type.

Cover design by Dixon J. Jones, University of Alaska Fairbanks, Rasmuson Library Graphics. Cover illustration Matanuska Valley farm, nine miles from the town of Palmer. Photo by Don C. Knudsen from the Lulu Fairbanks Collection #96-A, P68-69-1446, Box 2, folder 99, Archives, University of Alaska Fairbanks.

Library of Congress Cataloging-in-Publication Data

Miller, Orlando W.

The frontier in Alaska and the Matanuska Colony / Orlando W. Miller.

p. cm.

Originally published: New Haven : Yale University Press, c1975.

Includes bibliographical references and index.

ISBN 978-1-60223-053-8 (pbk. : alk. paper)

1. Land settlement—Alaska—Matanuska River Valley. 2. Frontier and pioneer life—Alaska—Historiography. 3. Matanuska River Valley (Alaska)—Economic conditions. 4. Frontier thesis. I. Title.

HD210.M37M54 2009

979.8'3—dc22

2008049198

This publication was printed on acid-free paper that meets the minimum requirements for ANSI / NISO Z39.48–1992 (R2002) (Permanence of Paper for Printed Library Materials).

TO

M. A. M.

Contents

Preface

This book grew out of an unforeseen choice of subject for a doctoral dissertation. In New York in the fall of 1959, the chance sight of a magazine article on new settlers in Alaska reminded me of the publicity that had been given six months earlier to those self-styled Fifty-niners as they traveled to Alaska with the announced intention of escaping from crowded urban America to homesteads on the last frontier. Reports of their journey and newspaper references to "modern pioneers" recalled an earlier incident, the New Deal–sponsored Matanuska Colony of 1935, and the manner in which it too had been reported as a revival of frontier days and as a comforting assurance that Americans still preserved the pioneer spirit.

In 1959 there was available one account of the colony written by a geographer interested in techniques of planning group settlement, and, after my own research was finished and the manuscript completed, a short popular history of the colony, centered on personalities and anecdotes, was published.[1] However, there has been an abundance of journalistic pieces on the colony and many allusions to it in general writings on Alaska. Rarely has there been more than a passing (and too often misinformed) reference to the condition of agriculture and rural life in the 1930s, the New Deal rural rehabilitation and resettlement program, the conditions in the region from which the colonists were selected, or the economic and social changes that even then made pioneer settlement in the old style obsolete. In such mentions of the colony it has been assumed that it was a belated and, as it later proved, an inadequate attempt to "open up the country," to prove the practicality of agriculture in the territory, and to increase the population. These aims have been regarded as good in themselves, a duty owed by the nation to Alaska, although few Americans were then conscious of any desire to settle in Alaska or aware of any need for its unsettled space.

Early in the research it seemed to me that a straightforward narrative of the colony, a chronicle of land cleared, stumps pulled, wells drilled, cows milked, and debts contested, would be unsatisfying and would explain little. Neither the colony nor other settlement nor Alaska's whole development should be seen standing bare, without a longer and wider view of American history, the American frontier, and even frontiers elsewhere. At the same time, although one might shy at making important claims, this one aspect of Alaskan history seen in that broad setting might contribute to an understanding of America's frontier past.

The conditions that made possible the Matanuska Colony experiment and the events in the colony seemed to me perhaps less important than what colonists and others thought happened. Journalists, politicians, and boosters influenced the environment of ideas and attitudes in which the colony and Alaska were discussed. They ran through the vocabulary of frontierism, chanting words rarely used by those who have actually lived in frontier style. Colonists, federal officials, older Alaskans, and journalists all had pictures in their minds of what the frontier had been, what rural life should be, and what the colony could accomplish. Those images were touched lightly by reality. If the colony survived and succeeded, it was in a manner and for reasons that were not anticipated in 1935.

I have not piled up references to the large and important additions to the literature on the frontier and Frederick Jackson Turner that have appeared since 1965. I should like to think that I have reexamined and lightly revised the manuscript with the benefit of an additional period of observing Alaskan life, now stretching to a total of nineteen years.

The epilogue summarizes Alaskan conditions as they were in the early fall of 1973, but any such summary quickly falls behind events. The trans-Alaska pipeline was authorized by Public Law 93-153, 16 November 1973; in December the secretary of the interior withdrew 83.47 million acres of federal public land for possible inclusion in national parks, wildlife refuges, national forests, and wild and scenic river areas. The action was protested by Alaskan politicians, the press, and spokesmen for both white Alaskans and Alaska natives. In April 1974 Governor William A. Egan announced that the state would file a suit against Secretary of the Interior Rogers C. B. Morton because of the withdrawals. Work began on the access road to the northern segment of the pipeline and on a bridge across the Yukon. In March 1974 a new land-status map of the Department of the Interior showed none of the patches of yellow that in the 1972 edition of the map had indicated unreserved federal public land. By Public Land Order 5418, 25 March 1974, those remaining areas of public land were withdrawn from all forms of entry and reserved for "classification and public interest." Thereafter there would be no entries for homesteads, homesites, headquarter sites, or trade and manufacturing sites, and the era of unregulated settlement in Alaska had ended.

First among those to whom I must acknowledge indebtedness is the late Richard Hofstadter, whose student I was at two widely separated times. With one whose career had been interrupted and delayed by chance and hesitation, he was patient and understanding, and he offered his encouragement even at a range of 4,000 miles. The generous interest and close readings by Earl Pomeroy of the University of Oregon and Wilbur R. Jacobs of the University of California at Santa Barbara brought the manuscript out of hiding.

I wish especially to thank old settlers and original colonists in the Matanuska Valley who enlightened me in conversation or patiently answered my lengthy questionnaire. Other Alaskans, some now in their very old age, have served as examples of the pioneer type, although they have not known that they were being so used. Mr. James J. Hurley, then general manager of the Alaska Rural Rehabilitation Corporation, gave me full access to the ARRC records; Mr. Don L. Irwin shared knowledge gained by long experience in the valley as an official of the colony and of the agricultural experiment station, and Mr. George W. Gasser gave me the benefit of his fifty years of agricultural experiment work. Senator Ernest Gruening, as former director of the Division of Territories and Island Possessions and then territorial governor, and Colonel Lawrence Westbrook, former head of the Federal Emergency Relief Administration's Rural Rehabilitation Division, replied at length to my inquiries. I was also generously helped by the staff of the University of Alaska Library. Judy Metro of the Yale Press has been a most perceptive copy editor.

O.W.M.

College, Alaska
May 1974

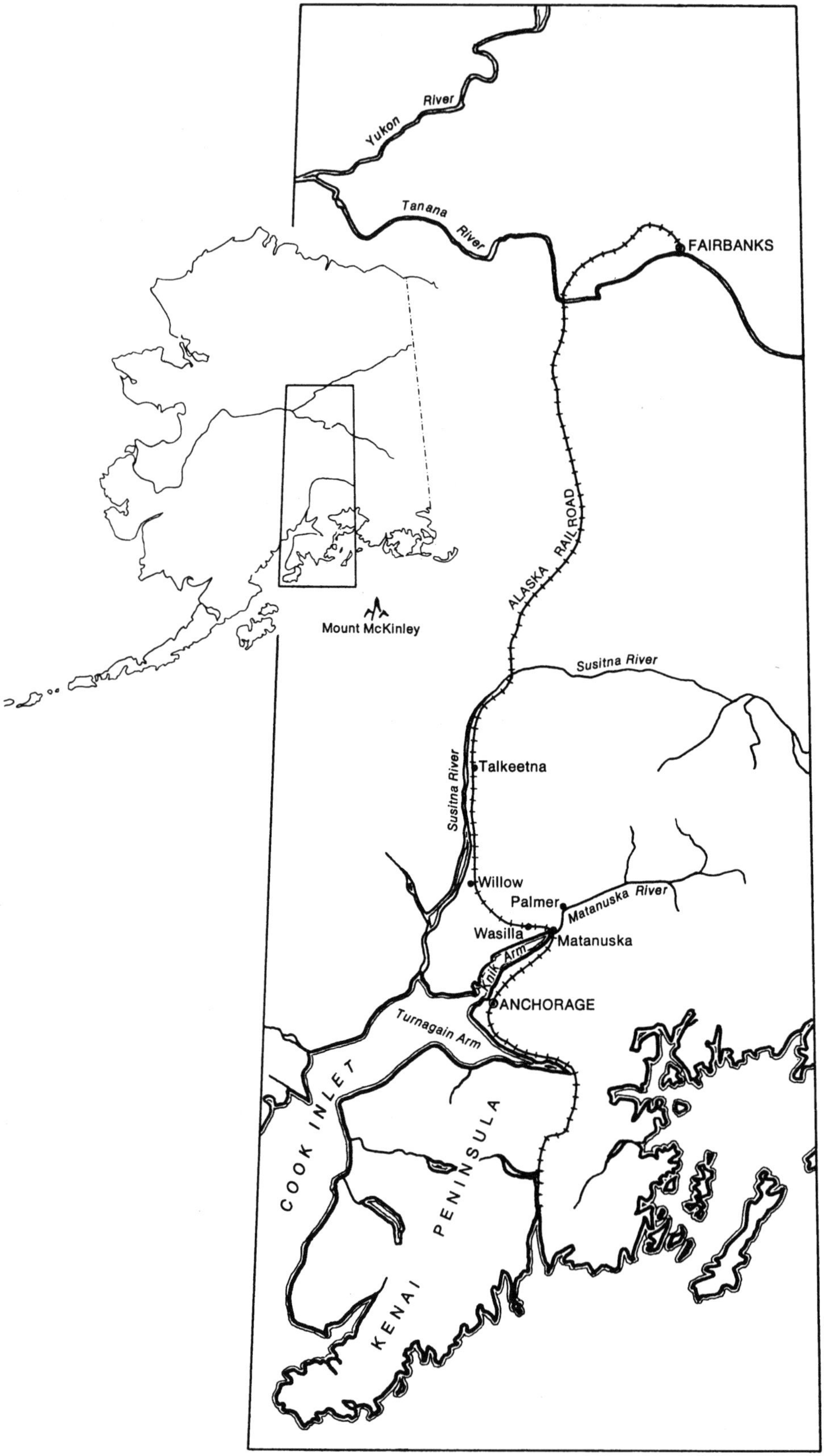

The Matanuska Colony area and the Anchorage–Fairbanks railbelt.

Introduction

On 23 April 1935 the *North Star*, chartered by the Federal Emergency Relief Administration from the Department of the Interior, sailed from San Francisco for Seward, Alaska, with the administrative staff and several hundred construction workers for the FERA's colonization project in the Matanuska Valley. On May 1 the army transport *St. Mihiel* sailed with the first of the colonists, and in the following weeks the two vessels shuttled between Alaska and San Francisco and Seattle with supplies, construction equipment, additional laborers, and a total of 202 colonists and their families. The *Anchorage Daily Times,* which for nearly a year had been reporting first the rumors and then the details of the colonization plan, found prose too thin to mark the arrival of the colonists and called on Whittier:

> I hear the tread of pioneers,
> Of thousands yet to be,
> The first low wash of waves
> Where soon shall roll a human sea.
> The elements of empire here
> Are plastic yet and warm,
> The chaos of a mighty world
> Is rounding into form.[1]

The *Daily Times* spoke for those Alaskans who believed that at last the settlement and development of the territory, long delayed by federal neglect and misinformed popular ideas about the region, were about to begin. The new federal interest in Alaska, the colony itself, and the accompanying publicity would end stagnation, and the small white population, much of it a changing, drifting group of occasional residents, would be enlarged by those attracted by the space to be filled, the land to be taken, and the resources waiting for use. Decades late, Alaska would experience the kind of frontier growth that had populated the western states.

Although Alaska boosters and newspapers in the territory and outside adopted the tone and vocabulary of frontier promotion, the Matanuska Colony did not originate in Washington's tardy realization that Alaska remained thinly populated and undeveloped. Like other New Deal resettlement projects, it was produced by the conditions of the depression era: the continuing unemployment that by 1934 or 1935 appeared chronic, the increased awareness of areas of deep rural poverty, the widely reported spontaneous back-to-the-land movement, a common faith in land settlement and small farming as alternatives to relief and guarantees of family security, a disillusionment with the city and industrialized civilization, an idealization of rural life, and a nostalgia for the vanished frontier and the opportunity associated with it.

In contrast to Alaskans, who were sure that the territory still offered pioneer opportunity, many other Americans saw no remaining frontiers and believed that the depression, or its severity, could be explained largely as the delayed result of the closing of the frontier. The booms of the world war and the 1920s had prolonged the careless optimism of the period in which a continent had been exploited, but by the early 1930s Americans felt hemmed in.[2] The economy had matured; there was no longer the outlet of free land in the West or the stimulus of new towns to be established, railroads to be built, mines to be opened, and forests to be cut. In the period of expansion the nation's population had soared, and each year's increase assured a larger market for agriculture and industry. Now immigration was all but shut off, the birthrate, although still high in rural areas, was declining in an urban nation, and the national industrial plant seemed overbuilt for a population approaching stability and eventual slow decline.[3]

In the best known and most explicit statement of the closed-frontier theory of the depression, Franklin D. Roosevelt rejected the mood of weariness and despair and affirmed his belief in America's possibilities. However, the tone of the rest of his speech, delivered at the Commonwealth Club in San Francisco on 23 September 1932, was grave.[4] New opportunity for ordinary men had been created and prolonged largely by the frontier and its abundant resources.

> Depressions could, and did, come and go; but they could not alter the fundamental fact that most of the people lived partly by selling their labor and partly by extracting their livelihood from the soil, so that starvation and dislocation were practically impossible. At the very worst there was always the possibility of climbing into a covered wagon and moving west where the untilled prairies afforded a haven for men to whom the East did not provide a place. So great were our natural resources that we could offer this relief not only to our own people, but to the distressed of all the world. . . .

Traditionally, when depression came a new section of land was opened in the West; and even our temporary misfortune served our manifest destiny.[5]

But as the frontier closed, concentrations of finance and industry increased; the habit of exploitation, tolerable in the past, continued in the name of industrialization until the country was well on its way toward economic oligarchy.[6] The main body of Roosevelt's speech hardly sustained his confident opening remarks.

A glance of the situation today only too clearly indicates that equality of opportunity as we have known it no longer exists. Our industrial plant is built; the problem just now is whether under existing conditions it is not overbuilt. Our last frontier has long since been reached, and there is practically no more free land. More than half of our people do not live on farms or on lands and cannot derive a living by cultivating their own property. There is no safety valve in the form of a Western prairie to which those thrown out of work by the Eastern economic machines can go for a new start. We are not able to invite the immigration from Europe to share our endless plenty. We are now providing a drab living for our own people. . . .

Our task now is not discovery or exploitation of natural resources, or necessarily producing more goods. It is the soberer, less dramatic business of administering resources and plants already in hand. . . . The day of enlightened administration has come.[7]

Adolf A. Berle, Jr., with some help from Rexford G. Tugwell, wrote the speech and was responsible for its content and somber tone.[8] Yet it seems likely that Roosevelt was comfortable making the references to the frontier, the West, free land, and the safety valve and that he found the closed-frontier explanation for the severity of the depression as familiar as if he had written it himself. In his last year at Harvard he had taken a course called "American History: The Development of the West" under Frederick Jackson Turner, who was then a visiting professor.[9] Although Roosevelt missed the first six weeks of the course while taking a Caribbean cruise with his mother and then busied himself editing *The Crimson,* working only casually in his courses,[10] Turner's classes, and the later recollection of them, probably reinforced ideas that he had absorbed without conscious thought.

Turner himself had found ready-made for him the idea of the importance of the frontier or free land in American development; it had been "in the air" for some decades before he published any of his essays, and, as the area of the best free land was reduced, there was in it and in his own interpretation a foreboding that his native optimism resisted.[11] Bidding farewell to the frontier in his essay of 1893, "The Significance of the Frontier in American History," repeating it in later essays, and looking for substitutes for the land and resources that had fostered democracy, equality, opportunity, and individualism, he trusted that ideals developed in the era of frontier settlement would be preserved in the period of increasing social control, cooperation, and government regulation of economic activity.[12] But there were repeated references, with the melancholy barely controlled, to an experience never to be relived. "The Western wilds, from the Alleghanies to the Pacific, constituted the richest free gift that was ever spread out before civilized man. . . . Never again can such an opportunity come to the sons of men. It was unique, and the thing is so near us, so much a part of our lives, that we do not yet comprehend its full significance."[13]

The unique frontier experience, never to be repeated, was mentioned by others in almost the same language,[14] and frontier historians following Turner wrestled with the problem of the consequences of the closing of the frontier and the disappearance of free land. Like him, they rather inconsistently hoped to find the best of frontier democracy and opportunity preserved in the new era by habit, legislation, and social control. However, some reconsideration of the pioneer past was necessary, and the appraisal, in language that would be heard again in the New Deal period, was not entirely favorable: "These habits—over-confidence, recklessness, waste, disregard for law—we Americans of the new era recognize as evils which must be inhibited. We have come, indeed, to a time of larger social control. The democracy of the public-land era was individualistic; the democracy of the new time is to be a socialized democracy."[15]

It was a common notion in Turner's day that the successive waves of frontier settlement recapitulated, and offered for study, the stages of development of the Old World. Lee Benson has explored the apparent influence on Turner of Achille Loria, the Italian economist who referred to the American frontier, gave a version of the safety-valve thesis, and was quoted and paraphrased by Turner.[16] There was deep pessimism in the idea of an inevitable movement toward European conditions of crowding and limited mobility and opportunity, a pessimism found in what has been called Turner's "closed-space" doctrine and in Halford J. Mackinder's influential discussion of the significance to the world of four hundred years of geographic expansion, ending about 1900.[17] Similarly, Arthur M. Schlesinger echoed Turner in referring to the end of the four hundred years of expansion and the presumable restriction of opportunity accompanying the return of a high man-to-land ratio.

Years later, looking back at the Great Depression Walter P. Webb, who ascribed much of the shaping of his thought indirectly to Achille Loria through Lindley M. Keasbey, Webb's onetime teacher and Loria's translator, put the end of the great world frontier at about the start of the depression, when the man-to-land ratio again reached the level of the year 1500 in western Europe.[18] Persisting high unemployment in a period of partial recovery seemed to confirm the belief that the end of the frontier in some way explained the depression.[19] This theory later gained the support of a group of stagnation economists, chiefly Alvin H. Hansen. Like Webb, Hansen referred to the closing of world frontiers, the scarcity of new territories and resources for exploitation, but he was less concerned about the crowding of once open space than about the falling rate of population growth that had in the past assured constantly increasing markets and had stimulated investment.[20]

Other writers offered confused comment: with the end of frontiers, the surplus population would find refuge on the land, which they would treat more carefully than in the past; the five million surplus population in agriculture or on poor land should be guided to migrate toward the urban fringes, there to await industrial reemployment; a movement back to the land or to the village, despite the existing surplus population on the land, carried hope for the future because it would slow or reverse the drift to the city and the lower urban birthrate; and the great problem was not technology or increased productivity, but the difficulty in a stabilized and aging population of training mature workers for new employment.[21]

While the frontier was so often mentioned, its leading historian was for the first time in the 1930s subjected to sustained and vigorous criticism. Turner's frontier interpretation of American history, which had been generally accepted with only occasional and mild qualifications, was found at many points to have weak foundations; it was overstated, couched in cloudy language, neglectful of cultural and other inheritances from the East and Europe, narrowly geographical in its determinism, and blind to the significance of such influences as urbanization and industrialization.[22] Yet after some years of such attacks there seemed to be no general rejection of Turner by American historians, and many of the objectors appeared content to accept as much of Turner's thesis as lay beyond their specific reservations.[23]

There was little indication that news of the historians' battles reached far beyond their own ranks. The idea of the frontier was in the air, as it had been thirty or forty years before, and those who used the passing of the frontier to explain the depression or to justify New Deal legislation did not, except for Governor LaFollette of Wisconsin, find it necessary to mention Turner.[24] Nor were references to Turner needed by conservatives who, in opposing the New Deal, appealed to the American frontier heritage and to pioneer individualism and self-reliance.[25] As several years of depression renewed the popular interest in rural life and created a rather self-conscious nostalgia for it, the persistence of older patterns of life in isolated areas was sometimes offered as reassuring evidence that America remained unchanged by the crisis.[26] The durable and self-reliant farmer, even in patched overalls, remained the most independent of men. In prosperity he enjoyed little of the ease and luxury of the cities; in hard times he worried about the mortgage, but he always enjoyed the shelter of his own home and the plentiful food he produced, and others thought him the better for escaping the softening effects of urban life.

Romantic and literary agrarians, usually living in the city, professional agriculturists speaking for farm groups, and farmers themselves saw agriculture as the most basic and necessary of occupations, the real and original source of wealth. If the national welfare did not depend solely on the farmer as producer, then it rested on his ability to buy and consume the products of urban industry. But more important than producing and consuming, farming was a way of life in harmony with nature and God, a mode of living to which the mercenary spirit and urban artificiality were foreign.[27] Even farmers in depressed agricultural communities, and their sons and daughters who moved to the city in search of jobs, habitually expressed their love of the land and their belief in the superiority of rural life.[28] After years of the "farm problem" in an increasingly urban nation, a historian of American agriculture could write in 1936:

> The real American farmer—the farmer of tradition and of daily observation everywhere in the northern states and over great areas of the South, we cannot too often repeat—is in the truest sense a free man. His essential character remains unchanged by the vicissitudes of "hard times," either those of the late nineteenth century or those of the present generation. . . .
>
> As opposed to the great city's mad pursuit of wealth and the things an excess of wealth has made fashionable, the small city, town, village, and the countryside, dominated up to now by a rural psychology, still retain the old primal American virtues; a sense of human values, neighborliness, morality, and religion. The country people are not yet generally blasé, but reflect that buoyant spirit which comports with genuine independence, creative activity,

and self-respecting industry. The farmers, from this point of view, are the hope of the nation's future as they have been the chief dynamic force of our country's past.[29]

Such sentiments, common and little changed over several generations, explain the appearance of a back-to-the-land movement in the period following or even overlapping the era of the most rapid disposition of public lands. A return to the land was suggested as a remedy for urban unemployment in the depression of the 1890s, as a correction for the supposedly dysgenic effect of urban life, as an opportunity to be offered veterans of World War I, and as an escape from the ugliness of postwar urban civilization.[30] After 1929, as the depression deepened, the earlier romantic agrarians and other advocates of land settlement made new converts, to whom it appeared obvious that a place in the country, a patch of land, a few chickens, and a vegetable garden offered at least security and even some advantages over city life. The actual refugees from the city moved in with relatives, bought old farms if they could manage it, built shacks on a few acres, or squatted on vacant land.

After 1930 it appeared that the long movement from country to city had been halted, even reversed, and that the farm population was again increasing. Later population studies showed that only in 1932 had there been a net rural population gain by migration; the rest of the change was explained by the damming of the normal movement from farms and by a twist of definition that made a farmer of a rural resident who had lost his usual employment. Nevertheless, for a time the country seemed a refuge. Reports on the back-to-the-land movement frequently assumed that urban employment would not be fully restored even it there should be an industrial recovery and that thousands or even millions of city workers would have to find rural employment.[31] Guides and handbooks were published for those who had some funds remaining and could buy or rent a rural home and a few acres of land, and one writer, Charles M. Wilson, whose desire to sell an article outweighed good sense, announced that there was land for the taking and provided a map of the western public lands where depression victims could homestead and ride out the depression.[32] There were warnings that even skillful and established farmers were facing great difficulties and that a rural farm and home offered security chiefly to those who had an assured income from another source.[33] As the back-to-the-land movement was taken up by politicians, businessmen, and publicists, who saw in it a partial answer to the problem of unemployment or a method of making the jobless less visible, Russell Lord commented, "Hardly a week goes by but some new leader of public opinion discovers the space between cities as a God-given dump for the unemployed."[34]

Franklin D. Roosevelt, who was no late discoverer of rural life, in his campaign speeches and messages as Governor of New York touched on matters that continued to occupy his mind after he became president: the drift to the cities had gone far enough: urban prosperity had not been shared by rural people; some abandoned farm land was probably not good enough to be restored to cultivation; and land studies should be made to determine the adequacy of farm lands currently under cultivation, the best use for different types of land, and the possible advantage of returning some inferior farm lands to forest. Early in the depression, in a speech at Cornell University, he suggested that the slow decay of rural areas could be stopped if some of the attractions of the city were extended to the country. At the same time he anticipated passages in the later Commonwealth Club speech and the mature-economy view of the depression:

> There is necessarily a limit to the continuance of the migration from the country to the city, and I look in fact for a swing of the pendulum in the other direction. Things all point that way. Industrially the United States has made not only the greatest strides in history in this generation, but perhaps has come to the period when industrial expansion will slow up. In other words, many economists are seriously questioning whether we have not for the time being reached the saturation point of industrial production calling for a period of digestion for a number of years to come.

He contrasted the plight of the city unemployed with the enviable security of rural people:

> How happy is the family today located on a farm in New York State and able to say every day as they get up in the morning and as they go to bed at night, "We at least have no fear of starvation. We may not be getting very rich, but at least we are able to go on with our lives without suffering and without drastic change."[35]

In the next few years Roosevelt repeatedly returned to the themes of the improvement of rural life, the establishment of light industry in country towns, land-use studies, reforestation, flood and erosion control, family security on the land, and the back-to-the-land movement as a corrective for the past prolonged migration to the cities.[36] In the spring of 1932 he ordered the New York Temporary Emergency Relief Administration to place as many families as it could on subsistence farms, to pay their rent, and to supply them with tools and seed. Later he boasted that 244 families had been settled in that way, but the number was a minute part of all the families in need. Because commercial farmers were uneasy at the prospect of added competition, Roosevelt called the plan a thrifty method of taking care of those on relief and denied that it was a sponsored back-to-the-land movement. Nor did he offer the idea of such settlement in his presidential campaign later that year.[37]

Roosevelt shared the sentimental American attachment to farming, or to the idea of farming as a way of life. Tugwell later described Roosevelt's beliefs as "an echo of utopian notions out of the past—the idea that men are better off close to nature and working with their hands on their own acres. This was an old weakness with Eleanor and Franklin and was shared by Louis Howe. They were amateurs. It would require some disappointing experience with homesteads to dispel the illusion."[38] Considering the new land put into production during World War I, changes in diet, the development of synthetic fibers, the past overcapitalization of farms, and the inability of farmers to meet their debts with incomes reduced by lower farm prices, it was foolish to suppose that any important movement to the farms was a possibility.

To argue in such a situation for a return to the land made no sense; it would not make much more sense in the depression years to argue that the unemployed could be cared for in this way. But to Franklin it seemed axiomatic that in the country they would have shelter at least and, if they would work, something to eat. It was not that simple, as he was to learn at some cost. But he resisted the lesson for a long time.[39]

Lessons in the difficulties of returning to the land were taught first by the career of the Division of Subsistence Homesteads and then by the activities of the Division of Rural Rehabilitation of the FERA, the Resettlement Administration (RA), and the Farm Security Administration (FSA).[40] In 1932 and 1933, at the peak of interest in the back-to-the-land movement as a relief measure, a half dozen congressional bills for the encouragement of the movement to the land died or were rejected, but a brief addition to the National Industrial Recovery Act, Section 208, Title II, authorized $25 million for the president's use for "aiding in the redistribution of the overbalance of population in industrial centers." The funds were to be used through agencies the president might create, under regulations he might impose, "for making loans for and otherwise aiding in the purchase of subsistence homesteads." From that came the Division of Subsistence Homesteads, directed at first by M. L. Wilson under Secretary Ickes and the Department of the Interior. Its accomplishments were disappointing. The projects were expensive, delayed by changes in the plan and by administrative confusion, and of benefit to only a discouragingly small number of the unemployed. The division alienated those who wanted local rather than federal control of projects, aroused the antagonism of spokesmen for the larger commercial farmers who were chiefly interested in higher farm prices, and shocked those who had expected a thrifty substitute for relief. Although its original purpose had appeared to be the relocation of urban families on small tracts, the Division of Subsistence Homesteads created some projects for full-scale farming or for stranded rural residents. The city dwellers selected for urban fringe communities were not the jobless and destitute, but those whose modest family incomes, supplemented by the product of an acre or two of land, would allow them to make the payments on their homesteads. The miximum income was supposedly $1,200 a year, but in practice some selected homesteaders had annual incomes of $1,600—well above the level of poverty by depression standards.

With the important exception of the greenbelt towns built by the RA,[41] the other New Deal resettlement programs were intended primarily to aid rural rather than urban victims of depression—or, more precisely, to aid residents of the open country or of rural villages in stagnating areas where poverty was older than the depression and would not be relieved even by general industrial recovery. Although resettlement officials sometimes allowed themselves to voice anti-urban and romatically agrarian sentiments,[42] they were usually realistic and matter-of-fact in recognizing that there was already a surplus of farm population and that few city people could be transplanted to the country. After the federal government entered directly into unemployment relief, the activities of the FERA and the relief census of October 1933 for the first time made clear the details and magnitude of the relief problem. Twelve and a half million persons, by no means including all who were in need, were dependent on relief. Although the city relief rate was higher than the rural rate, that was partly due to the timing of the census during the late harvest season. The very high relief rate for urban Negroes distorted the city rates; if whites alone were considered, the rural relief rate was higher than the urban.[43] The stereotype of rustic security and contentment bore little resemblance to the homespun poverty described in reports on rural life in the 1930s. The poverty of a million farm families and of many dwellers in small communities where mining, lumbering, and other rural industries had failed appeared largely the result of pioneer optimism, individualism, unregulated settlement, and carefree exploitation of resources.

During the 1920s some agriculturists and land economists had begun to suggest that continued expansion of agricultural acreage might be unwise and that the nation needed no more farmers, especially on poor land. A land utilization conference sponsored by the Department of Agriculture in 1931 recommended national inventories of land and resources, the retirement of submarginal land, and the licensing and regulation of land development.[44] From the reports in the 1930s of federal, state, local, and private agencies concerned with rural problems, population movements, relief, and land use, came a picture of abused land, uprooted families, rural slums, and deep poverty. In compressed form, the details were these:

Seventy-five to one hundred million acres of eroded or misused land should be withdrawn from cultivation and restored to forest and grass or put to recreational or other use. About five million people would have to move in order to complete that land retirement, and because neither they nor their land produced much, their withdrawal from agriculture would have little effect on commercial production. Rural poverty and poor and depleted land were concentrated in six "problem areas"—the eastern and western cotton belts, the Appalachian–Ozark area, the short grass/winter wheat and short grass/spring wheat areas, and the Great Lakes cutover region. The long decline of the rural population in relation to the urban had halted after 1930 and had been reversed. The farm population in 1930 was 30.2 million, in January 1935, 32.8 million, and none of the increase was needed. In past good times, the poorest farm areas, with the highest rate of population increase, had sent people to the cities, but since 1930 the increased farm population had clustered in those poor areas. Later studies showed that the apparent increase in the number of farms, supposedly caused by a back-to-the-land movement, was misleading. It resulted largely from a change in definition by which a rural resident on a few acres became a farmer by default when his normal industrial occupation disappeared. Only in 1932 had there been a net surplus of city-to-farm movements, but high fertility and the closing of opportunity in the city had raised the rural and farm population.

Poverty was most severe in the areas of part-time and subsistence farming, the substitute so often urged in place of industrial employment. In the problem areas were twenty-three of the twenty-nine counties of the United States that had more than 36 percent of the total population on relief. One county in northern Michigan showed, after intercensus population adjustment, approximately 70 percent of the population on relief, and in one Kentucky county the average per capita rural-farm income from all sources was $67 a year. In many parts of the problem areas, thin, scattered settlement made necessary costly services for a small population—the operation of rural schools, the transportation of school children, and the maintenance of little-traveled county roads—and these were provided while revenues declined, more property became tax delinquent, and the chief beneficiaries of the services commonly paid no taxes and were supported either by relief or by payments made to them for operating the services only they used. The poverty of the problem areas had resulted from unwise settlement practices of the past, with government policies more or less responsive to popular demands reinforced by promoters' boosterism. Unwise settlement had been complicated by sharecropping, exploitation of the soil, the dry farming of natural grassland, the decline of mining and lumbering as supplemental employments, and the popular habit of stubbornly affirming "faith in the country."[45]

The program of rural rehabilitation, resettlement, and community building conducted after February 1934 by the Division of Rural Rehabilitation of the FERA and then by the RA and the FSA did little to change the condition of most of the rural poor. Viewed optimistically, it could offer an alternative to indefinitely continued relief, preserve some self-respect, and provide a place on the land for those who were most comfortable there and who were perhaps unfitted for positions in crowded city industry.[46] But the program remained a makeshift. Unlike the romantic agrarians, Rexford Tugwell saw clearly that rural self-sufficiency was not part of the mainstream of American life and that such an arrangement was for the few:

There are many persons who are happier in a simple existence, living largely through their own efforts in a self-sufficient way . . . . We had it once in America, and there are those who feel that we lost something valuable in our departure from it . . . . The proportion of our population which likes to lead semi-independent lives with some acres to guarantee their own subsistence and with supplementary opportunities for income from industry may be larger than we suspect. The cultural level of such living, too, may be raised by education and handicrafts and other home industries. As a whole, however, I am inclined to believe that such settlements will function merely as small eddies of retreat for exceptional persons and that the greater part of our population will prefer to live and work in a more active and vigorous main stream of a highly complex civilization.[47]

Although the resettlement projects were always more widely publicized, the rehabilitation of established farm families was by far the more important activity. Expert guidance and loans for seed, fertilizer, livestock, tools, and equipment were intended to bring a decent level of self-support. The modesty of the goal is indicated by the standard farm plans used in the north central states which assumed that improvements would raise the average family to an annual gross cash income of $1,000, from which the family would live, meet farm operating expenses, and make payments on the loans.[48]

When compared with the rehabilitation program, the resettlement projects were small. A study of such projects, including those established by the Division of Subsistence Homesteads and the suburban communities of the RA, shows 10,938 family units in ninety-nine settlements.[49] But in addition to the families in the several kinds of rural communities and cooperative farms, there were other families individually resettled in existing farm areas under a so-called infiltration program. Counting such settlement, slightly more than 35,000 families were relocated.[50]

The FERA resettlement colony in the Matanuska Valley of Alaska was only one of many projects in what proved to be a minor program of the New Deal, but it received a disproportionate share of attention. It was remote from any important center of population or established agriculture—to outsiders the setting appeared an almost untouched wilderness—and nowhere else could a new community of two hundred small farms be expected to have so great an effect on the economy. The publicity and the frontier atmosphere at first excited the colonists; journalists took the opportunity to exercise their vocabularies of frontier jargon, and Alaskans welcomed the colony as a step toward ending their isolation. The too-high expectations made disappointment more keen when the colony made only halting progress and discontented families left the project. Although Alaskans and others continued to speak and write of a frontier awaiting modern pioneers, what accelerated Alaskan development was increased military activity, not the colony or other settlement. The wartime boom rescued the colony and stimulated Alaska, as it restored prosperity to agriculture outside and improved the position of the rural poor or removed them from public attention.

1

Alaska before the Matanuska Colony

Alaska in the early 1930s, just before the start of the Matanuska colonization project, had changed little since the gold rush days. The remote villages and most of the towns were clusters of log houses, and commercial buidings sometimes presented false fronts of finished lumber over the original logs. Although coal was avilable for fuel, the sight and pleasant smell of woodsmoke were common, and it had not been many years since the Northern Commercial Company at Fairbanks supplied the town with electricity from a woodburning power plant. The idea of Alaska popular outside,* and in Alaska too, a compound of Jack London, Rex Beach, and Robert W. Service, was not entirely mistaken. The southeastern panhandle lived by fishing and canning and the hardrock gold mining at Juneau and Douglas. In the rest of Alaska, the Westward as Alaskans called it, the small population scattered over a tremendous area lived by fishing in coastal areas and by mining, trapping, and trading elsewhere. Bush pilots flying light planes had since the mid-1920s begun to replace dog teams and river travel. The completion of the Alaska Railroad had brought the outside a little nearer and, by reducing river traffic, had contributed to the decline of some of the Yukon and Tanana villages. The total population of the territory, little more than 60,000, was composed largely of town dwellers, even though most of the 30,000, Indians and Eskimos lived in villages too small to be classified as urban. Only four towns had populations over twenty-five hundred, but the eight or ten largest communities, the centers of transportation, mining, and fishing, included nearly half the white population.

Only a minority of white Alaskans lived in real isolation, depending on themselves and the resources of the wilderness, but even in the towns there were reminders that Alaska was different. In Anchorage and Fairbanks the newspapers recorded the annual cycle of activity in fishing and mining, greeted miners returning in the spring, and in the fall regretted their departure and their export of earnings outside. In

* "Outside" is used in Alaska (and Canada) in a special way. In the sparsely populated bush the "outside" may be any considerably settled place anywhere else, Anchorage, for example. But usually in Alaska it is used to mean the other states.

Fairbanks the *Daily News-Miner* reported the arrivals and departures of the riverboats, in September announced the last sailings before the freeze-up, and carried the local news of the scattered interior villages and the mining camps, with gossipy information about who had worked what claims. The caribou herd in its fall migration crossed the highway only a few miles north of Fairbanks; a bear was shot on First Avenue; and after one spring breakup a trapper was found strangled with one of his snares, a suicide because he had been injured and alone. The Northern Commercial Company extended credit to miners, prospectors, and trappers and accepted their gold and furs as deposits against future purchases, sometimes uncertain for years whether a rarely seen customer was alive or dead. There were radio stations, motion picture theaters, and many of the conveniences known elsewhere, but the towns remained openings in the bush—only here and there scratched after more than sixty years of American settlement.

With approximate knowledge of how other American frontiers had developed, and in the belief that in the normal course of things the territory should already have followed a smilar pattern, many Alaskans were by the 1930s convinced that federal neglect and mismanagement, combined with the influence of outside interests (mainly the canneries' lobby), explained Alaska's stagnation. The most substantial work on Alaska available in the early 1930s—other than the history by H. H. Bancroft, which carried the account only to 1884—was that by Jeannette Paddock Nichols, which both confirmed the popular belief in neglect and predicted a different future: "The development of Alaska's resources will be of benefit not only to Alaskans but those not resident in the territory. Above all it will give opportunity for the settlement of this northern region, which is a boon to the American people who are still land hungry." Twenty years later Alaskan discontent was summed up in Ernest Gruening's *The State of Alaska,* a vehement denunciation of federal policy toward the territory and a sustained argument for statehood. The section headings indicate the tone of the book: The Era of Total Neglect, The Era of Flagrant Neglect, The Era of Mild but Unenlightened Interest, The Era of Indifference and Unconcern.[1]

It is true that for seventeen years after its purchase Alaska had no legal government but was under the extralegal and haphazard rule first of the War Department and then of navy and customs officials. It was true also that the general land laws had not been applied; that the 1884 Organic Act was inadequate; that the provision for town sites and trade and manufacturing sites was made only in 1891; that the

Homestead Act was applied only in 1898 and then with an eighty-acre limitation and without the surveys that would have made it effective; that there was no delegate to Congress until 1906; and that territorial organization was not granted until 1912. All this irritated and inconvenienced those who were already in Alaska, but the great complaint was that no more had come, that there had been no large-scale migration to Alaska. The nearly static population of the territory was regarded as shameful, as proof in itself that the American pioneering urge had been frustrated.

After the United States in 1867 acquired a territory in which the fur trade had been dwindling and Russian commercial activity stagnating for thirty years or more, and where there were fewer than seven hundred Russians and about two thousand Creoles, American occupation for some years caused no great change. The native Indian and Eskimo population continued to decline, many of the Russians chose to return to Russia, and a few hundred Americans engaged in trading or trapping, prospecting, and fishing. The largest enterprise, the twenty-year lease to the Alaska Commercial Company of the Pribilof Island fur sealing, had no effect on the rest of Alaska. After the establishment of two canneries in 1878, salmon fishing increased, and after 1880–81 hardrock gold mining in the Juneau district increased the white population there. Through the next fifteen years a succession of placer discoveries in the interior brought a few hundred stampeders to one mining area after another and took steamboat traffic up the Yukon River and into Canada and up such Yukon tributaries as the Tanana and Porcupine. The great Klondike strike of 1896 brought early stampeders from outside in 1897 and 1898. An estimated 100,000 men started for the Klondike, almost all taking one of the routes through Alaska, but many turned back or stayed only briefly. The later stampedes in Alaska took some of the same men, with new recruits, to the Forty Mile district, Nome, Fairbanks, Iditarod, and a dozen other mining areas. Everywhere, after the first rush, placer mining tended to become concentrated in fewer hands and to be dominated by those who could afford costly equipment, and from each district in turn many of the miners were drawn to new discoveries.

The short season for salmon fishing, the few weeks of cannery operation, and the limited season for most placer mining brought Alaska a seasonally fluctuating population, and even many of the year-around residents drifted from one location to another or were Alaskans for only a few years before returning outside. The numbers, composition, and sex ratios of the Alaskan population tell the story of hesitating development to 1930:[2]

	Total population	Native (Indian & Eskimo)	Non-native (white & other)	White males per 100 white females
1880	33,426	32,996	430	—
1890	32,052	25,354	4,298	865.8
1900	63,592	29,542	30,450	852.9
1910	64,356	25,331	36,400	500.1
1920	55,036	26,558	28,228	282.1
1930	59,278	29,983	29,045	227.8

SOURCE: George W. Rogers and Richard A. Cooley, *Alaska's Population and Economy*, vol. 2, *Statistical Handbook* (Juneau: Division of State Planning, 1962), tables P-3 and P-5.

As their attempts at agriculture failed, the Russians in Alaska had remained dependent on food imports, and for thirty years after the American purchase the reports of unfavorable conditions by travelers and officials gave little reason to suppose that there would ever be any important development of Alaskan farming.[3] Yet travelers also frequently reported the surprising discovery that vegetables and some other crops would actually grow.[4] With the gold rushes and the possibility of an increasing population, agriculture in Alaska was no longer regarded as a fascinating oddity. In 1897, supported by a congressional grant of $5,000, three special agents traveled through and reported on southeastern Alaska, the south central region, Kodiak, the Alaska Peninsula, and the Yukon Valley.[5] Although they cautiously mentioned difficulties—the lack of land laws, rough terrain, excessive moisture in the southeast, short growing seasons, bogs and peaty soils, uncertainty of markets, and problems of transportation—the investigators reported a variety of crops that could be grown, the supposedly rich soil in sections of the panhandle, and the vegetable gardening and even cattle raising already undertaken. The report urged the establishment of experiment stations and pointed out the benefits to the existing and expected white population and to the natives, who "are susceptible of civilization and elevation by contact with superior races." One of the investigators suggested the encouragement of settlement on small plots by men who would engage in mixed fishing, lumbering, and farming:

All this would be for the purpose of settling the country with a hardy race of fishermen and others used to the water, from which we may secure seamen for the merchant marine and Navy and at the same time we will develop our fishing and other resources in that country.

We will establish there a great civilization. The native races are fast passing away and ceasing to be a social or economic factor, and the time is ripe for the introduction of Anglo-Saxon races and institutions.[6]

The three-man report struck one note that was to be endlessly repeated in discussions of Alaska for the next sixty years—a comparison of Alaska's latitude, area, climate, soil, resources, and population with those of Scandinavia, Finland, northern Scotland, Iceland, and northern Russia.[7] Writing when the rush of prospectors of the summer of 1898 still lay some months in the future but expecting that there would be a great increase in the permanent as well as transient population,[8] the authors of the report made their comparisons in order to indicate what development of Alaskan agriculture might follow the appearance of markets and improved transportation. Later, for the promoters of Alaska, the comparison with Scandinavia became one of the standard means of lamenting the American failure to do as well with Alaska.

Following the recommendations of the report, which was endorsed by the secretary of agriculture, experiment stations were authorized for Alaska. However there was no territorial organization or land-grant agricultural college through which the program would operate, as in other territories and states. A station was opened in the summer of 1898 at Sitka, then still the capital, in spite of its limited areas of tillable soil and the excessively wet climate. It was directed by Charles Christian Georgeson, then forty-seven years old and about to begin a thirty-year career in Alaskan agricultural experiment work and in publicizing Alaskan farming possibilities.

In his native Denmark, C. C. Georgeson had studied agriculture, and after coming to the United States in 1873 he received his B.S., M.S., and later Doctor of Science degrees from Michigan State College of Agriculture. He had edited a farm journal in New York and had been a professor of agriculture in Texas, Kansas, and for four years at the Imperial University in Tokyo. As a special agent of the Department of Agriculture he had studied the dairy industry in Denmark and had then been appointed special agricultural agent in Alaska.[9] His training and experience and his following years of work in Alaska lent authority to his optimistic estimates of the territory's agricultural potential.

Before the work of the experiment station was more than started, Georgeson published an account of Alaskan farming based only on his summer work of 1898 at Sitka and on some supplemental work at Skagway. In it he quoted enthusiastic comments of a few small gardeners and pointed to the growth of agriculture as the hope for the natives of Alaska and the basis for the general development of the territory. Speaking of the great wealth in fish, furs, minerals, and forests that waited investment and development, he explained that

> the greatest drawback to the development of all these resources has been the fact that the Territory has so far had no agriculture. . . . The white population of the Territory is dependent upon the farmers of the States for maintenance, but what this means can scarcely be realized by those who are not familiar with the conditions. The fact that each of the many thousands of men who go there, to prospect, for instance, has to carry with him tons of provisions, not only increases the cost of the trip by the expense of the transportation of these supplies, but also adds materially to the hardships and dangers. The cost of board in the camps on the Yukon is some indication of what lack of agriculture means in the development of Alaska. In Dawson and other places $2.00 to $2.50 will pay for only a frugal meal. It stands to reason that if the means to support life can be produced within the boundaries of the Territory all the other resources will become more valuable.[10]

In 1899 another station was opened at Kenai, although there were no roads and all development in the area depended on irregular water transportation. That station was closed in 1908, but others were established. The river freight and passenger traffic to the gold fields seemed to indicate that the Yukon basin would be the site of permanent settlement. In 1900 Georgeson surveyed the site of an experiment station across the river from the village of Rampart, within one hundred miles of the Arctic Circle. In the short summers, through periods of almost continuous daylight, grains, root crops, vegetables, and berries were raised successfully, but the development of the area never came, the peak of river traffic passed, and the village dwindled; in 1925 the Rampart station was closed for lack of an appropriation. Another station at Copper Center lasted from 1903 to 1909, but there too the expected settlement failed to appear, and only one of six grain crops was successful. After 1907 a station was maintained at Kodiak for livestock experiments, but the cattle fell off cliffs, sickened and died of impaction from eating too much dead, wet grass, and the remainder had to be removed when in 1912 the eruption of Mount Kenai one hundred miles away covered the range with eighteen inches of volcanic ash. After two years the cattle were returned, but half the herd was then found to be tubercular. After treatment, the sound cattle were removed to Matanuska.[11]

The two other experiment stations, Fairbanks established in 1907, and Matanuska, in 1917, continued to operate after the others were closed when experiment work in Alaska was cut from the Department of Agriculture budget in 1931. For one year the Alaska Railroad supported the two stations, and then in 1935 they were taken over by the Alaska Agricultural College and School of Mines.[12]

C. C. Georgeson, directing all the experimental work at the various stations until 1928, was a most enthusiastic publicist for Alaskan agriculture. By 1902 he was carrying the good news of Alaska to a wider audience. During the preceding five years, he wrote, the prediction that Alaska would become a great and powerful state had become simply a common-sense view, an obvious conclusion based on the resources of the territory and the high order of agricultural possibilities. He estimated that Alaska could furnish 320-acre homesteads to 200,000 families and could support a population of at least three million. To prove his case he cited the example of Finland, a country less than one-fourth Alaska's size, without Alaska's wealth in mines and fisheries, with fewer agricultural advantages, but with a population of more than 2.6 million.[13] The failure of settlement he attributed to the difficulty in obtaining land title. To locate on unsurveyed land, a settler had to buy soldier's additional homestead entry script at $5 to $15 an acre and then pay a surveyor's charges, making a farm on wild land in Alaska as expensive as one in almost any developed state.[14] Under the regulations then in effect, changed in 1903, a homesteader had an 80-acre limit, which Georgeson thought too small for the stock-raising that he expected to be the leading form of Alaskan agriculture.[15]

The extremes to which enthusiasm could push writers on Alaska is illustrated by an article on the vegetable gardens planted by members of the International Polar Expedition at Point Barrow in 1881–83. Telling of the seeds that were planted within two hundred yards of the Arctic Ocean, in soil that thawed to a depth of three to nine inches, and of how, in the continuous Arctic summer sunlight, vegetables germinated, matured, and were harvested in twenty-seven days, the author describes the quick growth of the wildflowers and earth-hugging plants of the tundra and called Alaska's northern coastal area "nature's garden . . . the most extensive, the least cultivated, the most productive of any on the American continent."[16]

A critic warned that Georgeson's enthusiasm might be misleading and pointed out that Alaskan farmers had high production costs. To succeed, Alaskan agriculture would have to compete at the price levels of efficient agriculture in California, Oregon, and Washington, plus the cost of transportation to Alaska.[17] However, the information and advice prepared by Georgeson for intended settlers in Alaska conveyed, more effectively than any criticism, an impression of the difficulty of agricultural settlement and the endless labor required of pioneer settlers.[18] Except for some grazing areas on river and tidal flats and lower mountain slopes, all agricultural land required slow, laborious clearing. Trees had to be felled and the logs skidded away. Stumps had to be removed with grubbing hoe and ax, or sometimes with fire. The larger stumps might be pulled with chain and block and a team of horses or oxen, but the majority of settlers who had no work animals had to use heavy, homemade windlass arrangements turned with a twenty- or thirty-foot pole. Slashing, felling, and skidding, stump pulling, windrowing debris, and burning stumps and roots did not end the labor. A blanket of dense, springy moss, often two- to three-feet thick and laced with roots of trees and low, creeping bushes, had to be removed. Sometimes it could be burned where it was, but normally it was too wet and had to be cut and chopped, piled to dry, and then slowly burned while the pile was repeatedly turned to expose still wet moss.[19]

Having cleared a few acres, the new farmer would find that his land required several years of cultivation before it would produce satisfactory crops, and even then heavy fertilization was needed for good results. The acidity of the soil made applications of lime at the rate of five hundred pounds per acre desirable, but lime was imported and costly. Barnyard manure was scarce where farm animals were few, and for settlers in coastal regions Georgeson recommended the application of seaweed at the backbreaking rate of thirty tons per acre.[20]

Despite such exaggerated predictions of settlement and population growth as Georgeson's estimate of a possible population density of thirty per square mile, or a three-hundred-fold increase,[21] Alaska continued to be the home of 25,000 to 30,000 natives, who were increasingly degraded where they were in regular contact with whites and who were elsewhere little changed in their hunting and fishing economy. An approximately equal number of whites followed the occupations offered by the few towns or lived by prospecting, independent mining, working in the mines for wages—seasonally in the interior placer mines, almost the year around in the hardrock mines—fishing, working in the canneries during the salmon run, hunting, trapping, trading, wood cutting, and freighting on the rivers or the few wagon roads and holing up for the winter. Many white men could hardly be classified by occupation, since they were hunters, traders, trappers, or prospectors in turn or at once. For the footloose and independent, it was still possible to reduce the need for cash income to the little necessary for ammunition, the replacement of traps and a few simple tools, and coffee, sugar, bacon, flour, and beans. Until the early 1920s at least, the restrictions on hunting were so few that game alone could supply most of the food requirements of isolated prospectors or trappers, and some cash from the sale of game meat could be picked up besides.[22]

In the two areas that eventually became the centers of what agriculture Alaska developed—the Tanana and Matanuska valleys—some small farming and gardening followed mining and transportation. After the discovery of gold in 1902 in the hills north of the Tanana and Chena rivers and the appearance of new mining camps such as Ester, Cleary, and Chatanika, the new town of Fairbanks became the center of additional prospecting and of transportation and supply for the interior gold fields.[23] Local gardeners and farmers began to produce some vegetables and potatoes for the town and camps and hay and grain for the horses used in freighting. At the same time the liberalization of the homestead regulations in Alaska, allowing entry on unsurveyed land and increasing the maximum size of entries from the substandard 80 acres to 320, was described by the governor as the foundation of Alaska's future prosperity and an attraction that would soon bring thousands of farmers from the Middle West to Alaska.[24] However, in a few years the larger acreage limit did not seem wholly a blessing. Although later Alaskan boosters complained that the standard quarter-section homestead was too small for Alaska, in 1913 the first territorial legislature regarded 320 acres as too much and believed that requiring one-eighth of a homestead claim to be cleared and cultivated imposed an almost impossible task. The legislature memorialized Congress, asking that the size of entry be reduced to 160 acres, or even 80, and that the cultivation requirement be reduced to one-twentieth of the claim.[25]

Even by 1904 the Fairbanks district had drawn enough stampeders to depopulate some of the older placer mining areas, and the mayor of the new town estimated the white population of the district at eight thousand.[26] Ten years later a Department of Agriculture survey of Alaska repeated Georgeson's estimate of 100,000 square miles of land fit for agriculture and grazing and listed the Tanana Valley as a primary area for future farm settlement. The chief ground for optimism was that the high cost of freight from outside acted as a protective tariff and gave the local farmers an advantage; however, there were difficulties with the weather and costly land clearing, and local freight rates were high enough to prevent farmers from disposing of their products at markets only one or two hundred miles away.[27] One inflated estimate placed the number of homesteaders in Alaska in 1917 at fourteen hundred,[28] but there were few enough actual farmers so that those around Fairbanks, for example, were all known by name.

The Fairbanks experiment station, established in 1907, demonstrated the possibilities for farming in the region and distributed to farmers the seed for hardy strains of vegetables and grains.[29] Photographs of the well-tended experiment station fields, crops, and livestock were used for years in official reports and in other articles, usually with the implication that the pictures showed simply "a typical Alaskan farm."[30] Until the 1920s a large part of what Alaskan farmers produced supplied the need later filled by coal, oil, and gasoline—fuel for transportation. Raising hay and grain for horses kept a number of farmers occupied. One stage line from Fairbanks to Valdez kept 175 horses for its coaches, wagons, and sleds,[31] and in 1920 there were over 1,000 horses used in hauling, compared to only 385 horses used on Alaskan farms.[32] In the 1920s as trucks, cars, and the Alaska Railroad replaced horses, a part of the already small Alaskan agricultural market disappeared.

In south central Alaska, the Cook Inlet region had been known since the Russian period, but few white men had penetrated inland until prospectors began exploring the area in the 1880s. A handful of traders and settlers were in the country by 1890, and George W. Palmer kept a store at Knik Arm after the late 1880s. The discovery of placer gold in 1896, the following minor stampede, and the system of rough trails between the scattered diggings brought some population to the region between Cook Inlet on the south and the Talkeetna Mountains in the north, the Matanuska River in the east and the Susitna in the west. Small vessels brought supplies for the mining camps into Knik Arm, and, as quartz mining followed the placer diggings and as the mining population grew to several hundred, the village of Knik became a community of some importance by Alaskan standards. A post office was established there in 1905; by 1910 Knik's population was 118 and the population of the Matanuska Valley was about 500. By 1914 Knik had several stores and roadhouses, a school, a church, and a population of 250.[33] After the stampede to the new gold fields in the Iditarod region far to the west, an overland winter trail was opened from Seward, on the east coast of the Kenai Peninsula, through Knik to the Iditarod country, a trail made necessary by the winter closing of the water route through the Bering Sea and the Yukon River. The Alaska Road Commission improved the trail until it was passable even in summer by foot traffic and pack horses. The 508 miles of trail through the wilderness were dotted with roadhouses, but Knik, 144 miles from Seward and 364 miles short of Iditarod, was the only sizable settlement.[34]

A few of the early settlers in the Matanuska–Susitna region and the upper Knik Arm area had done a little gardening and farming from about 1898, and the experiment station at Sitka sent seeds and asked reports on their efforts.[35] Until about 1914 settlement in the region was limited to a few homesteads and to gardening and potato growing by men who looked upon their tracts as occasional residences between periods of employment in mining, trapping, freighting, and prospecting. Most of them were bachelors, accustomed to life in sparsely settled regions and familiar with the techniques necessary for living by a mixture of occupations. The type persisted after more intensive settlement of the region began. Years later the general manager of the Alaska Railroad explained to the secretary of the interior one reason for the creeping progress of agriculture:

> Farming in Alaska has not progressed as well as it should owing to the fact that the majority of the so-called farmers are old, broken-down prospectors, most of whom are single men. They have no cows and no poultry and in many cases these prospectors acquire a homestead only for the purpose of putting up a shack where they could live during the winter months, as the cost of living in hotels in the towns was too high.

The coal-lands leasing law of 1914, after the eight years of closure of coal leases, aroused some additional interest in the region and brought a few more homesteaders,[37] but it was the congressional authorization in the same year for the building of the Alaska Railroad that caused the rush of new settlement. The act empowered the president to

> designate and cause to be located a route or routes for a line or lines of railroad in the Territory of Alaska not to exceed in the aggregate one thousand miles, to be so located as to connect one or more of the Pacific Ocean harbors on the southern coast of Alaska with the navigable waters in the interior of Alaska and with a coal field or fields so as best to aid in the development of the agricultural and mineral or other resources of Alaska, and the settlement of the public land therein.[38]

After the route was finally established, the Alaska Engineering Commission, created under the Department of the Interior to build the railroad,[39] established a division point camp on Cook Inlet at Ship Creek, a camp that became Anchorage, a raw, booming construction town. By 1917 there was a population of five to six thousand people where two years before there had been none.[40]

In their soil reconnaissance of Alaska, Hugh H. Bennett and Thomas D. Rice estimated that there were about one thousand acres cleared in the Matanuska Valley and perhaps five hundred being cultivated, and they calculated that the region, together with the Kenai Peninsula could support ten thousand 160-acre farms, or an agricultural population of fifty thousand.[41] To promote the settlement of the region, and at the same time to create additional freight business for the railroad, the Department of the Interior in 1916 designated a Land and Industrial Commission to publicize Alaskan resources and development, to supply information to prospective settlers, to encourage development of agriculture, and to aid in the development of markets for farm products. Andrew Christensen of the General Land Office was made head of the commission with headquarters at Seward. In 1916 the commission reported three to four hundred homesteaders in the Matanuska and Susitna valleys, all busy clearing land and preparing to supply the growing market with potatoes and vegetables. In the whole region along the line of the railroad north of Seward there were an estimated five hundred to one thousand settlers. In 1916 the townsites of Matanuska and Wasilla were laid out by the commission, and from that time the older settlement of Knik began to wither until in a few years it was deserted.[42]

In his report for 1917, Governor J. F. A. Strong spoke with satisfaction of the gradual increase in the territory's permanent population, largely through the increase in farming in the Tanana and Matanuska valleys, and of the growth of the agricultural market since the start of construction on the Alaska Railroad. He mentioned also the cooperative action of Matanuska farmers in building a potato storage house, the agricultural fairs at Sitka, Fairbanks, and the new town of Anchorage. But at the same time the governor mentioned the decline in gold mining because of the shortage of labor and fuel, the high price of supplies and equipment, and the wartime boom in copper mining both in Alaska and outside. By estimating the white population of 1917 as "not much in excess of 50,000," he implied continued growth since 1910, when the white population of the territory had been 39,025. But his successor, Governor Thomas Riggs, Jr., lamented the loss of population and predicted that by the end of 1918 there would be hardly 18,000 whites left in the territory as Alaskans went into the army or found jobs in war industries or shipyards. He then added an optimistic note:

It is reasonable to suppose, following the declaration of peace, that men drawn from the more settled and staid portions of the United States and thrown into the atmosphere of adventure and outdoor life will not be content to settle down to their former humdrum existence of the factory, office, or farm, but that they will seek a wider horizon and greater possibilities here than offered by their return to former occupations.[43]

In the next few years, Governors Riggs and Scott C. Bone reported the disastrous influenza epidemic of 1918, floods at Seward, Juneau, and Nenana, and a fire in the business district of Fairbanks. The census of 1920 showed a decline in population from 64,356 to 55,036. But with sufficient determination some grounds for optimism could be found. As it seemed in official reports, the remaining population of the territory was solidly committed to life in Alaska. The 100,000 square miles of agricultural and grazing land beckoned to settlers. In 1920 the first flour mill in Alaska was opened at Fairbanks by the Tanana Valley Agricultural Association, and in 1922 the mill turned thirty-five tons of wheat into flour. The local wheat yield was nearly twenty bushels per acre. There were sixty-two active farmers in the Fairbanks district, and many inquiries came from prospective settlers outside. By 1922 the Alaska Railroad was all but completed, with only the Tanana River bridge at Nenana and the change of the Nenana–Fairbanks section from narrow to standard gauge still to be finished. Even before completion, freight and passengers were moving over sections of the railroad, and its effect on Alaskan growth was confidently awaited.[44] Governor Bone, in his report for 1923, announced that the year had been Alaska's most successful, not because of growth of population or influx of industry, but because the territory's greatest need—to be known to the outside world—had been met by the publicity given to President Harding's visit to Alaska.[45]

However, in spite of the modest rush of homesteaders to several areas along the railroad, in 1920 there were only 364 farms and 5,736 improved acres. The average size of farms, 249 acres, had increased partly because much of the homesteading had been done before 1916, while the maximum entry was 320 acres, and because at least 22 fox farms were included in the total. The average improved acreage per farm was 15.8 acres, about half of what it would have been had the minimum homesteading requirement for clearing and cultivation been met.[46] In 1923, in the areas that were advertised as the chief agricultural regions—the Fairbanks district and the Anchorage and Matanuska districts—there was a total of 90 farmers with 22,127 acres, but only 1,421 acres were cultivated.[47]

Commenting on the general stagnation of the territory and telling what it called "The Low-Down Truth of Alaska," the *Fairbanks Daily News-Miner*[48] recalled past boasting of the supposed twenty thousand population in the Fairbanks area and argued that the population had not dwindled because of federal bureaucracy but because those who had struck it rich had left the territory and the drifters and "grafters" had disappeared with the gambling dens and dance halls. The newspaper repeated the list of the advantages of the region—the rich coal deposits, the hardly touched placer and lode gold, the 100 million acres of unoccupied land in the Fairbanks Land District (roughly the whole interior region north of the Alaska Range), the thirty thousand acres near Fairbanks surveyed and not filed on, and half of all surveyed land still unoccupied after twenty years. It repeated the agrument that too much of Alaska's food needs came in from outside and deplored the fact that half the settlers who had taken land in the Tanana Valley had left and that no more than half those who remained would put in a crop that year.

The obvious contrast between the small production of Alaskan farms and the volume of food imports to the territory seemed an invitation to farm settlement. The Department of the Interior calculated that the region served by the Alaska Railroad, the so-called railbelt, annually imported $2 million worth of farm and dairy products that could be produced locally, and it estimated that with feeder roads being constructed in the railbelt there was room for two hundred additional farmer-settlers a year.[49] However, the population along the 471 miles of railroad was small. The three places that could be called towns—Seward, Anchorage, and Fairbanks—had a total population in 1930 of only 5,207, and both Anchorage and Fairbanks were smaller than they had been in their boom days.

The management of the Alaska Railroad shared with territorial officials, chambers of commerce, and the staffs of the experiment stations an interest in promoting the growth of the territory through settlement. That had been the announced object of the construction of the railroad; in fact, the railroad, which ran regularly at a loss, could not be efficiently or profitably operated until larger population and production increased freight revenues. It was frequently suggested that the railroad could actively recruit settlers. In 1927 a Mrs. Arthur J. Downes of Anchorage suggested to Noel W. Smith, then general manager of the railroad, that displays at county fairs, chautauquas, and reunions in the States might effectively promote settlement because "there are many young men who have grown up on farms, youths from the sturdy stock which has successfully colonized America, educated and practical farmers, many of whom are ready and financially able to stock farms for themselves and to whom free land in a growing country should appeal." Smith replied that the Alaska Railroad had neither funds nor authority to take up active colonization.[50] However, he was interested in the possibility of attracting the settlement of such religious groups as the Mormons or Mennonites. He praised their stable, self-contained communities and discussed the possibility of such settlement with H. W. Alberts, chief agronomist of the experiment station, and H. M. Myers, editor of the *Lapeer County Press* in Michigan, who was familiar with some Mennonite farm groups.[51] Governor George A. Parks was also interested in that possibility and told Charles D. Garfield of the Seattle Chamber of Commerce that he had discussed the idea with officials in Washington.

> I believe that in some of the eastern states, especially some of the colonies where there are religious sects, the districts have become over-populated for the reason that the original farms have been divided and subdivided to provide places for the children. . . . It seems to me that there must be some bond that will hold people together and in most instances before, these schemes have been successful the bond has been one of religion. . . . I believe that if we could present the situation to the people in some of the crowded districts and offer them some inducements we could get them to come to the Territory.[52]

Although nothing came of the discussion of colonization at the time, Smith received from G. W. Gasser, formerly in charge of the experiment station at Rampart and in 1927 a professor at the Alaska College of Agriculture and School of Mines, a plan for colonizing three or four regions of Alaska. Each region would have a cluster of twelve to fifteen homesteads organized around an agricultural village, and the settlements would be aided by a loan from the territory, supervised by the faculty of the territorial college, and organized chiefly for dairy farming.[53]

In 1928 Smith was succeeded as general manager of the railroad by Otto F. Ohlson, who continued the search for some means of stimulating settlement, and who had firsthand knowledge of the colonizing activities of American railroads. An energetic, quick-tempered man, always referred to as "Colonel" since he had directed military railroads in France during World War I, he had been a telegrapher in his native Sweden and later in South America, India, and the United States. After service with the Pennsylvania Railroad, he had risen from telegraph operator for the Northern Pacific Railroad in 1901 to directing superintendent in 1928. Although by Ohlson's period with the Northern Pacific the great boom in railroad land sales had ended, he was aware of it and saw a renewed colonization opportunity in Alaska. At once he wrote and distributed through the Department of the Interior a mimeographed pamphlet setting forth the agricultural and other attractions of the territory and pointing to similarities between Alaska and the Scandinavian countries.[54] In a letter to Secretary of the Interior Ray O. West, he argued that the only prospect of eliminating the railroad's persistent deficit lay in expanding the industry and agriculture of the interior, and he referred to the colonizing experience of American and Canadian railroads as a precedent for similar activities by the Alaska Railroad. He estimated that the railbelt in the Matanuska and Tanana valleys would accommodate "at least" fifteen hundred families on farms and give them a good living.[55]

In January 1929 the Alaska Railroad opened a branch office in Chicago to develop traffic and to promote the tourist trade and immigration. In April M. D. Snodgrass, until then in charge of the experiment station at Matanuska and the railroad's unofficial answerer of inquiries about Alaskan farming and settlement,[56] was appointed traveling representative of the railroad; he was to visit prospective settlers in the States and to make arrangements for their settlement in Alaska. In 1930 *Alaska, The Newest Homeland,* an enlarged and illustrated version of Ohlson's pamphlet, was prepared by Snodgrass with the help of the experiment station staff. In the next four or five years it was revised several times and was distributed in agricultural areas in the States. At the same time the railroad sent out posters for display in post offices and placed advertisements in farm area newspapers.[57]

Although the railroad could not give settlers direct financial help, it offered special rates for the movement of household goods and farm machinery, and Ohlson and Snodgrass negotiated with steamship lines and railroads in the States for special settlers' rates and got the approval of the Interstate Commerce Commission for the arrangement. In addition Snodgrass helped settlers find desirable homestead locations, and he and others connected with the railroad found jobs for settlers or their wives as railroad employees, road-commission laborers, mining-camp cooks, and the like.

Ohlson was so impressed by the comparison of Alaska with Scandinavia and Finland that he developed a kind of ethnic-latitudinal theory of pioneer settlement. He directed Snodgrass to look for no settlers in California, since experience in that climate would unfit them for Alaska, and he assumed that persons of north European descent would make the best Alaskan farmers. In the summer of 1929 he ordered two hundred of the colonization pamphlets sent to the Swedish vice-consul in Seattle and described to him the fine gradations of racial adaptation to northern settlement:

> We are endeavoring to interest the hardier races such as Swedes, Norwegians, and Finlanders, to settle in the Tanana Valley, which lies exactly in the same parallel degrees as do Sweden, Norway, and Finland, for we believe these races would do much better in that region, while for the Matanuska Valley we propose to interest the Dane, German, Hollander, and Swiss, as this region is better adapted to dairy farming because of its more moderate climate, although there is, of course, no objection to the northern races settling in this region.[58]

The composition of the Alaskan population gave some support to Ohlson's views of adaptability to the north. As early as 1874 a committee representing Icelanders in Wisconsin visited Cook Inlet and Kodiak Island and reported favorably on the prospects for settlement. The Alaskan white population declined between 1910 and 1920 from 36,400 to 27,833, with the foreign-born numbering 17,974 and 11,597. In 1920 there were 364 farms in Alaska, 2 owned by Indians, 1 by a Negro, 201 by native-born whites, and 160 by foreign-born whites, or twice the proportion to the general population. All but 18 of those 160 farmers came from Canada or northern Europe, 76 of them from Scandinavia or Finland.[59] In addition, studies of land settlement in other northern areas showed a remarkable ability of Scandinavian and Finnish settlers to succeed where others failed,[60] and Finns especially had demonstrated a consistent pattern of settlement in areas that seemed to offer few agricultural advantages but approximated conditions in Finland—or Alaska: glaciated terrain, many lakes and streams, cool climate, podzol soils, muskeg and wet lands, and coniferous and birch forests.[61]

The idea that there was a special racial adaptation to settlement in the north was not Ohlson's alone. The settlers for the Matanuska Colony were taken from the northern counties of Michigan, Minnesota, and Wisconsin not only because of depression in the cutover region or because of similarity of climate. Preference was given to people of north European stock "because of its hardihood and pioneering abilities, proved and tested during colonization of the northwestern United States."[62] Ten years later, after World War II, Harold Ickes said, in renewing his campaign for the settlement of Alaska, "The thousands of potentially fine pioneers who could, if given the chance, help to settle Alaska, are living now in northern Europe."[63]

The advertisements in forty-five farm newspapers and the distribution of the information bulletin brought inquiries from prospective settlers. In July 1929 Snodgrass reported to Ohlson that there had been 592 inquiries, that he had sent form letters and bulletins, and that he had by then visited thirty-seven intended settlers. By autumn Ohlson estimated that there had been 2,000 requests for information.[64] The would-be settlers were advised that they should arrive in Alaska with some equipment, chickens, and a cow. More important, they should have at least $2,000 to $2,500 to carry them through to the time when the homestead would begin to support them. However, Snodgrass reported, "A number of people tell me that they would never be able to come to Alaska if they wait until they have the amount of capital we recommend, and when I find they are real pioneer stock, know how to meet such conditions, I recommend that they come and look the country over."[65]

The settlement plan seemed to be growing and succeeding. Snodgrass reported his swings through the western and midwestern states, and between times he busily performed such tasks for settlers as searching for bargains in dairy cattle and arranging for their shipment.[66] The railroad's purchasing agent and office manager at Seattle, J. R. Ummel, met settlers arriving on the coast, arranged their passage to Alaska and the shipment of their goods, and acted as advertiser of the settlement program.[67] However, there were difficulties. In the middle of one trip through a dozen states, Snodgrass reported, "General hard times throughout the country has [*sic*] caused a number to postpone their making the trip this spring."[68] Many of those who were willing to move to Alaska were unable to sell their crops or their farms at prices that would make the trip possible. By early 1933, settlers were finding it even more difficult, and many of them had exhausted their funds by the time they arrived in the railbelt and had settled on a homestead.

Although the Alaska Railroad office continued to send out copies of *Alaska, The Newest Homeland* and to answer requests for information, it suspended the aggressive campaign for settlement and ended Snodgrass's trips. In the summer of 1934, in the early period of growing interest in a plan for government colonization, Ohlson summed up the railroad's work. About 110 settlers had come, but some had returned home after looking around and others had stayed only a year or two because they had been unable to find work with the railroad or road commission or in the mines. After settlement by several hundred homesteaders in the early period of the railroad building in 1915–16, 172 had remained long enough to receive patents. Some later homesteaders and the approximately 110 settlers attracted by the railroad program were added, but in 1934 there were only 117 occupied farms in the valley and the lower railbelt, the total cleared acreage was small, and most of the occupied homesteads were not actually farmed.[69]

As the depression deepened outside, Alaska felt some of the effects of the hard times. In 1933 the copper mines employed 143 men whereas they had employed 570 in 1929. The value of the fish catch declined and wages were low. Even in 1933 there was some increase in gold mining, but wages, which had been as high as $13 a day plus board in some specialties, had declined, and there were some hundreds of men prospecting for themselves who would normally have been employed at regular wages in the mines. Under the Emergency Reforestation Act of 31 March 1933, about 325 men had been put to conservation work, and local welfare programs and some federally sponsored public works took care of others.[70] Gold mining, normally most attractive in depression periods, was stimulated by the rising federal price for gold. As the price of gold rose, and until it was stabilized at $35 an ounce, the Fairbanks newspaper regularly carried a banner headline announcing the day's gold price: "Gold per Ounce Is Priced by United States Treasury Department Today at $33.15."[71]

In 1934 the outlook was brighter. Governor John W. Troy reported that public works and relief for the unemployed had carried them through the winter and enabled them to start the mining and fishing season in good condition. He repeated his earlier recommendation that the federal government stimulate the exploitation of Alaska's resources in order that the territory might develop as a refuge from the "overpopulation of congested areas" in the States.[72] The rise in the price of gold aroused hope of even greater gains, and mining lobbyists were reported working for a doubling of the old price of $20.67 an ounce.

The *Anchorage Daily Times* exulted that Alaska was rising to its opportunities and that the stream of precious metal would make the territory "blaze with prosperity."[73] The economy was still colonial and extractive. The exports from the territory, mostly fish, furs, and gold, annually averaged from one and a half times to twice the value of imports, and in 1935, for example, the largest single Alaskan import, valued at $5 million in a total of $32 million, was tin cans for packing the salmon catch.[74]

By the mid-1930s, Alaska had changed outwardly only a little since the early days of the salmon fisheries and the gold rushes. However, the old belief that the territory would inevitably follow the pattern of growth of past frontiers had been weakened. Boosters reaffirmed their faith in the attractions of Alaska, but increasingly the hope for development was centered on federal policies. In 1935 no one could quite duplicate the breathless anticipation of an earlier booster:

> In the years yet to be her great forests will deliver their wealth; her mines will surrender their riches; her seas will give up their abundance; her hospitable soil will yield of its marvelous productivity; her verdant fields will be harvested; her cereals will be ground into flour without which neither prince nor pauper can live; her sequestered inlets will become thriving industrial centers where the rumble of her thousand mills will mingle with the roar of many furnaces.
>
> Alaska is calling for people. Her outstretched arms are filled with generous offerings to those who would come and free her from the isolation she has suffered for unnumbered centuries.[75]

2

The Origins of the Matanuska Colony

In the summer of 1934 Alaskans heard once again that the territory was getting some attention outside and that the federal government might soon undertake some kind of project to develop Alaska. Lt. Col. H. H. Arnold led a squadron of army air corps bombers on a flight to Alaska; Delegate Anthony Dimond reminded Congress that Alaska lay on the short great circle air route to Asia and that some military spending in Alaska would be prudent; and Secretary of Commerce Daniel C. Roper returned to Washington from an Alaskan trip and spoke of the future of the territory in air transportation and predicted that some people with the necessary pioneer spirit would go there to find permanent homes.

At first the summer visit of Jacob Baker, assistant administrator of the FERA, received only routine attention, and in Juneau his trip was reported as an inspection of emergency public works projects and relief measures, an indication of the New Deal's lively interest in Alaskan welfare.[1] Ten days later Baker passed through Anchorage and went on to the Matanuska Valley, accompained by the governor's secretary and a group of Anchorage businessmen interested in promoting settlement in the valley. Although the highway to the Matanuska region was still incomplete, there were more than a hundred miles of passable roads in the valley. Baker and his party were able to inspect the area by car and, in a light plane, to see the scatter of homesteads in the still hardly broken timberland and bush. One of the men in the group was Arthur A. Shonbeck, an Anchorage businessman, a prominent member of the chamber of commerce, and chairman of the Territorial Democratic Central Committee. Shonbeck at that time owned a farm in the valley and a small herd of beef cattle from which he hoped soon to supply the local market.[2]

Baker returned to Anchorage enthusiastic and perhaps overpersuaded of the possibilities of agricultural settlement. He publicly guessed that in time the valley could support 2,500 settlers' families, and he thought that if a project for government-sponsored settlement were approved a start could be made with 500 families. In his remarks he commented on the plight of thousands of farmers in drought areas in the States. The *Anchorage Daily Times* took up the story eagerly, calling the plan—which was so far no more than an offhand idea—startling yet feasible, and said that there had never been a failure of Matanuska crops because of drought. The question whether the Alaskan market could absorb the increased farm production was dismissed. Perhaps there would be some Alaskan farm products for export. Wonderfully innocent about the facts of American agriculture, the editorial writer guessed that "Alaskan products may be needed to make up for the products lost to America from the vast areas in the States which are now practically put out of business." Two days later the newspaper reported that inquiries about the valley were pouring in to the territorial capital and to the Alaska Railroad, the chambers of commerce, and the newspapers. It argued that such a project for settlement would serve two good ends: it would open Alaska and it would offer relief to many drought sufferers. A few days later it quoted an editorial in a Hutchinson, Kansas, newspaper as evidence that the Midwest was interested in Alaskan colonization by drought victims.[3]

Baker, stopping in Juneau on his return trip to the States, conferred with Governor Troy and O. F. Ohlson, who was there en route to Anchorage from Washington. Ohlson promised to send Baker an outline of his ideas on colonization, but before it was sent, M. D. Snodgrass published in the Anchorage paper a long, signed article setting forth his own views of colonization planning.[4] He assumed that there was already an actual plan to settle "several thousand people from the drought stricken Middle West," and his suggestions for arranging the settlement anticipated a number of points that Ohlson made a few days later in the memorandum to Baker. He thought that tracts for the settlers should be limited to eighty acres in the Tanana Valley and forty in the Matanuska to encourage more intensive use, prevent land grabbing, and minimize the cost of road building. He suggested that unused farms in the Matanuska Valley might be bought and distributed to the colonists, for even though they were not currently being used as farms, and were perhaps not even occupied, many of them were desirable because they had some cleared land that could be used almost at once. He believed that a settler could become self-supporting in a short time on twenty cleared acres in the Matanuska Valley and forty in the Tanana, and he suggested a $250,000 revolving fund to aid settlers in land clearing and purchase of livestock.

Ohlson's letter to Baker included Snodgrass's suggestions, some of them discussed in greater detail.[5] He reviewed past settlement in Alaska and the efforts of the Alaska Railroad to bring settlers and estimated that Anchorage alone consumed annually $270,000 in agricultural goods that could be produced by local farmers. Like Snodgrass, and for the same reasons, he recommended the tracts of limited size in the two valleys, but he was somewhat more cautious in dealing with the number of settlers, estimating that in the Matanuska Valley there would be room for one hundred new settlers' families and in the Tanana Valley twenty or twenty-five. Later, as general growth took place, the number could be increased.

Later critics of the colony usually charged that the tracts had been far too small for commercial farming, that outsiders unacquainted with Alaskan conditions had done the planning, and that the plans resulted in the creation of a peasant-like subsistence economy rather than commercial agriculture.[6] The criticisms benefit by knowledge of what Alaska became during and after the war and overlook what Alaska was in 1935—a great area in which only a few scattered communities were available as markets for new agricultural settlement. Two hundred full-scale commercial farms were an impossibility in the Alaska of 1935, or in any Alaska foreseeable then. If the planning was done by outsiders, they followed the suggestions offered by men who were experienced in Alaska, and no Alaskan experts in land settlement or farming came forward in 1934 or 1935 with proposals for improving the plan. The only objections to the colony made at the beginning were from spokesmen for mining and fishing interests who feared that such settlement would lead to higher taxes by increasing the demand for schools and roads.

The critics' reference to a peasant or subsistence economy is intended to be damning; "peasant" suggests European or Asian conditions of poverty and plodding routine, not the idealized independent American farmer. But in the 1930s the ideal was seldom met. With an excess of population in agriculture, the escape from farm to city barred by heavy unemployment, and commercial farmers producing surpluses at ruinously low prices, a plan for general farming and a family living taken almost wholly from the land, a small sale to meet a few cash needs, and an agricultural community to provide necessary services and facilities seemed, lacking full recovery from the depression, sensible and obvious. The planners assumed that the colonists would depend little on cash, live simply and frugally, and find satisfaction in the careful development of their farms. They hoped also that the colonists would develop some of the attitudes toward rural life and work on the land found in such stable communities as those of the Amish, Mennonites, and others. To the extent that the planning did not put increased cash income before these other goals, the colony might be described as peasant-like. But the disappearing and grieved-for American "way-of-life" farming, to the extent that it had actually existed, was also peasant-like.[7]

The Division of Rural Rehabilitation of the FERA estimated that at the end of five years the colonists would have an annual net income per family of $500 from the sale of crops and livestock in addition to garden and dairy products used at home. It was calculated that from then on a representative colonist should be able to make payments on his indebtedness and have a small cash balance remaining. The colony was designed for families who had nothing to expect in their old homes but stagnation on a relief allowance of about $25 a month; it was intended to rehabilitate them and provide them with the bases for economic security and social independence.[8] In the light of the more than thirty years of claims about the agricultural potential of Alaska and the enthusiasm of boosters, the colony plans were remarkably sober.

Ohlson's letter to Baker conveyed his view of the kind of settlement that was possible and the kind of settlers needed. He assumed that there would be sustained hard work by muscle power aided little by heavy machinery, that there would be few comforts, and that the first aim was to win a simple subsistence. In his odd style, he described what might be done:

> [I]n case immediate action is deemed necessary to afford relief to farmers, with or without families, if they can arrive at Matanuska about October 1st, [they] can and without undue hardship locate upon the land and build log houses before colder weather sets in, and thus be in a position to start early next year cutting timber and clearing land. . . . Settlers arriving in the fall should have one cow and some chickens with them, and the reason for recommending only one cow is that they would have to buy fodder during winter months; those arriving in the spring should have two cows and some chickens with them.
>
> It has been ascertained through [a] reliable source that an active settler

can clear, cultivate and put under crop twenty acres during the first three years, which will make him self-supporting. Great care should be exercised and only the hardier type of settlers should be selected.[9]

Even in the Matanuska Valley, with a milder climate than the interior farther north, October might have seemed to the settlers a poor time for house building, but a small log house adequate for shelter could be put up by one man—more readily by a man with a son or two—in perhaps two weeks from timber standing on the land. Similarly, the clearing by hand could be done, but at the cost of great exertion. It was estimated that in the Matanuska area the timberland, not the areas of small growth and tangles of willows, had an average of three hundred trees per acre. Not many of the trees, except for the older cottonwoods, would be more than seven or eight inches in diameter at the butt. On such land, clearing twenty acres would have meant felling six thousand trees, two thousand a year or in that part of the year suitable and available for clearing. After felling, the trees would have to be limbed, cut into lengths of about sixteen feet, and skidded away; stumps would have to be pulled, brush cleared, roots grubbed out, moss stripped, and the ground broken, cultivated, and planted. Such labor could be performed by a man and his family, and it had been done by those of the older settlers who had completed the requirements for a homestead and had received patent. But in the summer of 1935, when the construction work at the colony was lagging, carpenters were hired at Fairbanks and Anchorage to work a 48-hour week at the colony for $200 a month and room and board. If the individual settler thought of his labor as having that value, then hand-clearing his land must have appeared impossibly difficult and expensive.

Earlier Alaskan homesteaders had been slow to meet the clearing and cultivation requirements and many of them had abandoned their entries because, at the time that they should have been busy clearing land and preparing it, they had been forced to take some paid employment in order to support their families. To meet that problem, Ohlson suggested in his letter to Baker that the $250,000 revolving fund be used, at least in part, to make successive advances of $35, $35, and $30 on each acre of land as the settler on the tract went through the three stages of removing trees, pulling stumps, and then breaking and cultivating the land. Thus living expenses would be provided for while the land was being improved. By Ohlson's plan for cash advances for each stage of land clearing, and at a rate of twenty acres in three years, family income would have been about $666 a year exclusive of what the land would produce for the family or for sale.

Discussion of the colony idea developed rapidly. Within a few days of his return to Washington, Baker wired Ohlson that plans for colonization had to wait until Harry Hopkins's return to Washington and that some program such as Ohlson had suggested was most likely. Ohlson worked to maintain interest in the plan by sending messages and copies of his memorandum to Baker, to Secretary of Commerce Roper, and to Secretary of the Interior Ickes, and the Anchorage newspaper ran the full correspondence between Ohlson, Baker, Ickes, and Roper. Keeping up with comments outside, the newspaper quoted the Princeton, Minnesota, *Union,* which deplored relief figures and the failure of relief recipients to contribute to their support by vacant-lot city gardening. The *Union* called for more self-reliance, greater pride in self-support, and more of the spirit of the pioneers.[10]

Assistant Secretary of the Interior Oscar L. Chapman contributed to the Alaskan excitement over possible colonization by saying that Alaska was underpopulated, that the administration had a plan to make the territories and island possessions more self-supporting and economically autonomous, and that there was under study a plan for moving to an Alaskan colony a number of Americans "imbued with the old pioneer spirit."[11] The town of Seward hoped for a colony on the Kenai Peninsula, but wherever in Westward Alaska the colony might be, Seward would be the first to benefit because of increased activity at the port and the Alaska Railroad terminal.[12] In Anchorage there were suggestions that fishing, mining, and lumbering also needed stimulation so that those industries would help build a market for the products of enlarged agriculture. The American Legion sponsored a railroad excursion to Matanuska, Delegate Dimond reported inquiries about a colony coming to his Washington office, and other inquiries were being directed to the Anchorage Chamber of Commerce, the local newspaper, the Alaska Railroad, and territorial officials.[13] Ross Sheely, the director of the extension service at the Alaska Agricultural College, offered his services to Ohlson and said that the college officials and the extension service were receiving many letters from potential colonists.[14] At about the same time Colonel Ohlson ordered a new printing of eight thousand copies of the railroad's settlement booklet, *Alaska, The Newest Homeland,* retaining half of them for distribution from the Anchorage office of the railroad.[15]

Some officials in Washington seemed too optimistic about the still unformed colonization plan. The Alaska Railroad agent in Chicago, Harold W. Snell, told Colonel Ohlson:

While in Washington and while with Mr. Gruening, we went together to call on Colonel Westbrook, who is connected with the FERC [*sic*]. Colonel Westbrook said that he had been instructed to take under consideration quite a formidable plan for Alaska and wanted to know what my reaction was.

I had pretty well in mind the facts which you had written to Mr. Baker on this subject . . . and voiced my sentiments as discouraging a large number of settlers at one time. They were talking in the thousands, and I told them they had better keep it in the hundreds and well down in that category.[16]

Perhaps because he feared runaway enthusiasm, Anthony Dimond warned that Alaska was no place for weaklings and that the settlers for the colony would have to be carefully chosen among people willing to work hard.[17] His warnings did not indicate disapproval of the project. On the contrary, he wanted it to succeed as a program for aiding Alaska, and from that point of view the colonists' needs were less important than their fitness as contributors to Alaska's development. Late in December, after conferring with Ernest Gruening, who, as director of the Division of Territories and Island Possessions, had for several months been familiar with the discussion of Alaskan colonization, Dimond announced that the settlement of about one hundred families would probably be made the next spring somewhere in the Matanuska region. Plans were not complete enough to give the exact location of the colony, and Dimond added that similar plans were being considered for the Fairbanks and Homer regions.[18] In spite of efforts to release accurate news of the planned colonization, some confusing rumors found their way into news reports. In Fairbanks, the center of a region almost wholly concerned with mining, the newspaper reported that three hundred families would be settled near various mining camps on land where they could grow some of their own food—and apparently spend the rest of their time mining. Later the newspaper reported that two thousand *families* were to be brought to Alaska.[19]

The Department of the Interior cooperated with the FERA in planning the colony, and in January 1935 Gruening invited Dimond to present his views to an interdepartmental committee. Dimond had already explained the advantages of the Matanuska area for climate, soils, railroad transportation, and a nearby market in Anchorage. He suggested a five-year delay in interest and principal payments after colonization, and at his invitation Arthur Shonbeck, the Anchorage businessman and owner of a Matanuska farm, came to Washington to lend his advice and help. Colonel Ohlson, in Washington on Alaska Railroad business, stayed on to help with the preparations, and early in March Don L. Irwin, the supervisor of the Matanuska experiment station, was called to Washington.[20] Years later Irwin believed that he would have been most usefully employed in selecting colonists suitable for Alaskan settlement, but instead he had been kept at the job of planning the initial procurement and movement of building materials, supplies, construction and farm equipment, and livestock.[21]

The Matanuska Colony was hardly more than established before confusion arose about its origins and intended purpose. In Alaska the colony was regarded as an inept federal attempt to compensate for past neglect and to stimulate Alaskan development, and the relief and rehabilitation of rural families from depressed areas elsewhere was looked upon as a complication grafted on the plan, a perversion of what was, or should have been, the real aim—making Alaska grow. Journalistic accounts and popular histories of Alaska treated the colony as an attempt to prove the practicality of agriculture in Alaska, to strengthen military defenses there, and to develop the territory and increase its population. The one detailed study of the colony, written from the viewpoint of a geographer and based on the assumption that bringing a greater population to Alaska and the North is a good thing, dismisses the question with the simple assertion that in the fall of 1934 President Roosevelt ordered that Alaska be added to the FERA program of state rural rehabilitation corporations.[22] Except for that reference, no discussion of the Matanuska Colony, outside of official correspondence, mentioned the several New Deal resettlement programs or hinted of any knowledge that many similar colonies had been established in the States. Nor was any attention given to the general agricultural depression of the 1930s, the surplus of agricultural population, the gluts of agricultural goods and the depressed prices, and the chronic rural poverty in several regions. Conditions outside Alaska were disposed of in a few words—"stricken agricultural areas" and refugees from the drought or the dust bowl. Such natural disasters were more understandable than prolonged rural stagnation and poverty; mention of the dust bowl did not undermine faith in the usefulness or wisdom of land settlement elsewhere, and the idea of a flight from drought areas to Alaska was consistent with boosting the advantages of the territory.

Twenty-five years after the establishment of the colony, Don L.

Irwin and G. W. Gasser, in 1935 the general director of the two agricultural experiment stations in Alaska, remembered the colony as originally a New Deal experiment ordered by Roosevelt partly for the purpose of strengthening Alaska militarily.[23] Ernest Gruening, in his *State of Alaska* (1954), attributed the origin of the colony to Roosevelt and ascribed to it three purposes: to rescue and give a new chance to people in "stricken agricultural areas," to stimulate the growth of population in Alaska, and to demonstrate Alaska's agricultural potential.[24] Later he recalled that the colony had been ordered by Roosevelt on 15 September 1934,[25] when in a discussion of the territories the president turned to Gruening and Oscar L. Chapman and said, "Alaska doesn't have enough people. We ought to do something to increase its population. I wish, next Spring, you would move 1,000 to 1,500 people from stricken agricultural areas into Alaska. That will help increase the population and also see what we can do to develop agriculture." Such a project would have fallen under the Division of Territories and Island Possessions in the Department of the Interior, but there were no funds available there. Gruening therefore turned to Hopkins, who had been present at the meeting, and asked whether he could supply the needed funds. Hopkins agreed provided he could manage the colony.

According to the FERA's own brief account of the origins of the project,[26] the relief agency had received private inquiries about settlement in Alaska as early as February 1934, and, after circulating a report among relief officials in the northwestern states, it had discovered some interest in Alaskan colonization. Therefore, Jacob Baker, an assistant administrator of the FERA, had been sent to Alaska in June, and he had reported favorably on Alaskan settlement. Lawrence Westbrook, who had become director of the FERA's Division of Rural Rehabilitation early in 1934, was interested in the problem of rescuing and resettling people stranded and stagnating in areas of sick mining and lumbering and inefficient subsistence farming.[27] Years later he recalled Jacob Baker's visit to Alaska as a vacation trip from which he had returned "full of enthusiasm for the beauty of the Territory and its possibilities as a 'new frontier.' "[28] Westbrook was impressed, requested information from the interior and agriculture departments, prepared a memorandum on a possible experimental colony for Harry Hopkins, and was later called to see Roosevelt. The president asked three questions—whether the territory could support a larger population, whether the proposed colony had any military importance,[29] and whether relief families would find the Alaskan winters endurable. Westbrook stated his conviction, based on still incomplete information, that Alaska could eventually support a larger population at a higher standard of living than all the Scandinavian countries combined. He thought that increased agricultural production in Alaska might play an important part in supplying the troops that could eventually be stationed there. As for the northern winters, he would select settlers from Michigan, Minnesota, and Wisconsin, where the people were inured to hardships and where temperatures fell below those in the Matanuska Valley.

Another explanation of the original plan for the colony attributed it to Westbrook's assistant, David Williams, who received inquiries from would-be pioneers, gathered information on Alaska, and took a proposal for an Alaskan colony to Roosevelt.[30] Another version was given by Anthony Dimond, who recalled that years earlier a Fairbanks mining engineer, John Ronan, had suggested to Franklin K. Lane that Alaska could be colonized by Scandinavians; however, World War I had interfered with the plan.[31] The idea of a colony was even traced to a simple proposal made by a William G. Hoffman, a male nurse and onetime dairy farmer in Washington, who wrote to Harry Hopkins to suggest the settlement of an Alaskan colony by Seventh Day Adventists.[32]

The accounts of the origin of the colony are not so contradictory that some must be entirely discarded, but they exaggerate the roles of a few men, and all them distort by simplifying or omitting the background—the back-to-the-land movement that was widely publicized during the early depression years, the realization of the chronic nature of much rural poverty, the existing New Deal resettlement and homestead programs, the thirty years of advertising Alaska's undeveloped potential for settlement, and, most important, the Alaska Railroad program for encouraging settlement, which was annually reported by the governor of Alaska and by the Department of the Interior. It would have been surprising had Alaska been overlooked as a possible site for resettlement. However, in Alaska a simple explanation for the establishment of the colony seemed satisfying. It was one of a number of good things coming to the territory through the federal government—defense bases, highways, air fields, radio beacons—and all of it would involve the spending of millions in federal funds. In addition, "The farm colonization plan, whether one believes in it from an economic standpoint, whether or not the market is available, will mean the bringing of hundreds of people, thus adding to the coastal passenger traffic and the import of heavy quantities of materials, stock, and the like for launching of the project."[33]

The Anchorage paper, even as it listed the federal projects planned for Alaska and praised Delegate Dimond for his encouragement of the colonization project, mentioning Finland as an example of northern development that should inspire Alaskans, warned that Alaska was determined to avoid being "over-run with incompetent and worse than useless misfits." Precautions should be taken to discourage too great an influx of job-seekers. "Prospectors and others able to finance and take care of themselves and such men as are actually needed as expansion justifies will be welcome, but Alaska is no place for a penniless and workless man." Ships were sailing from Seattle with big passenger lists, and many of the men were job-seekers almost without funds. The *Anchorage Daily Times* suggested that some agency should be created on the Pacific coast to bar from sailing to Alaska those who were unable to finance themselves.[34] At the same time, Governor John W. Troy was asked by the FERA to urge the territorial legislature then in session to assume some of the burden of relief for the unemployed. The FERA had made grants for work relief projects, but funds were low and further aid would depend on whether Alaska itself made some effort.[35]

There were some other disturbing developments. In November the farmers in the Fairbanks area had three hundred tons of unsold potatoes on hand, and the chamber of commerce urged local people to help their neighbors by using the potatoes.[36] The Matanuska Valley Farmers' Association resolved that someone in Anchorage should build cold and warm storage facilities so that the sale of farm products might be distributed more evenly and at prices that would appear reasonable to the farmers. In the past season their crops of hay, vegetables, potatoes, and berries had not sold well.[37] Other Alaskans doubted that the last frontier was attracting the right kind of interest. The state chamber of commerce met in Juneau and announced its opposition to the colonization project unless assurances were given that there would be no burden placed on Alaska. The chamber representative from Fairbanks, Andrew Nerland, was also chairman of the territorial legislature's House Committee on Education, Public Health, Quarantine, and Morals, and that committee introduced and the House passed a memorial to Anthony Dimond and Harold Ickes asking that no colonists be sent to Alaska unless ample funds were available for their support and for their return home in case of failure. The legislators also worried about school construction and maintenance costs and asked that there be no colonization if such a burden was expected to be shouldered by the territory. A similar memorial in the Senate requested that colonization be delayed until an investigation was made to determine its desirability and practicality.[38] The Anchorage newspaper, although it had called for the exclusion of "misfits" and moneyless job-seekers, felt that the attack on the plan for a colony in the Matanuska Valley was a blow at the interests of the Anchorage area. It argued that all necessary investigation had already been made and that the plan was practical and would no doubt receive ample federal support. It feared that protests of this kind would strangle growth at the start.[39]

In the latter part of 1934, early in the discussion of the colonization idea, as Alaskans began to count their possible blessings and as inquiries from potential colonists were arriving at Alaskan newspapers, chambers of commerce, and government offices, Colonel Ohlson of the Alaska Railroad received a series of letters and agricultural settlement plans from a would-be reorganizer of the American agriculture and rural life. The correspondence offers a fascinating glimpse of one of the things-that-did-not-happen and of a man who must have been prized in his own neighborhood as the eccentric violator of agrarian pieties.

In October 1934 Rudolph G. Ruste, introducing himself to Ohlson by letter as the principal of the high school at Verdon, South Dakota, said that he had been trying for months to interest Washington officials in his plan for the colonization of Alaska. The Information Division of the Department of Agriculture had referred him to Ohlson. He asked whether there was a fairly unbroken tract of public land near the railroad suitable for the mass production of hardy grains, grasses, and vegetables. If so

> then I should like to have opportunity to lay before those authorized to act on the matter a plan for colonization of that area with relief families from the United States, that is, from this part of the United States.
>
> I am an experienced grain and livestock farmer, experienced in this climate, which is as tough a climate as God allows. It may not get as cold as Alaska, but it has many other vile features that your climate may not have.

In his reply on November 5, Ohlson carefully misunderstood Ruste and gave the standard account of Alaska, the railbelt, the Matanuska Valley, the history of past settlement, the present opportunities, and the problems of farming in Alaska. He added that the FERA had a colonization plan under consideration and suggested that before Ruste committed himself to settlement he should come to Alaska and look over the country.

While awaiting Ohlson's reply, Ruste had been working on his plan and putting it in two-part form. His November 19 letter to Ohlson pleaded for some attention. "Will you not lend your influence? I know nothing about your administrative set-up there, but Ernest Gruening, Director of Island and Territorial Possession, [*sic*] Washington, D.C., has made inquiry regarding my plans, and a word from you might serve a good purpose there." He continued:

> Understand I am not the least interested in homesteading as was practiced here in the Dakotas. Standing here on this ground and viewing intimately the results I proclaim that the program [was] a dismal failure. Why repeat it in Alaska?

Taking Ohlson's figures for the current number of farms in the valley, Ruste pointed to the inefficiency, the duplication of effort, the waste involved in the separate ownership and intermittent use of machinery, the incredible appetites of all the horses owned separately by individual homesteaders, the scattered settlement, the social costs of the isolation, the absence of the conveniences of community life, and the lack of civilized amenities.

Ruste's plan was based on group settlement organized around a village of no more than one thousand people. Every branch of agriculture that the climate allowed would be undertaken, and in addition the village would provide all the retail trade, services, and occupations normally found in any community, but without inefficient duplication. He multiplied the examples of the inefficiency of individual farms, each widely separated from others and each forced to keep the full array of occasionally used tools and equipment. He listed the savings to be made in the reduction of fencing, the construction of fewer but better and larger farm buildings, the more effective use of breeding stock, the efficient division of labor. He wrote lovingly of the abundance of all good things to eat—"All the meats that could be consumed; not stringy flesh of cattle rescued from starvation, but such meat as kings eat." He listed the fields of activity in which the individual farmer had to engage—agronomy, animal husbandry, veterinary medicine, carpentry, mechanics, wholesale and retail trade, butchering, food processing, and financial management—and commented: "Is it any wonder if he fails in one or more of these fields? God doesn't make such men, at least not enough of them to put one on each 230 acres in South Dakota."

Ruste announced that his plan was designed to revolutionize the whole civilization. In time 75 percent of the people would live in such units as he described. His aim was to attain the world's highest standard of living by group effort and efficient production. He called the Subsistence Homesteads program a device condemning people to semi-pauperism through use of the inefficient methods of the feudal age. He aimed at "elimination of the farm population" and dreamed of farming made as efficient as the factory and of the transfer of the organization found in industry to a well-planned village. "The 'freedom' of farm life is either imaginary or insignificant, such as the right to empty slop in the front yard or to play a saxaphone at three o'clock in the morning."

Listing the variety and quality of the goods, services, and social gains that would be available, he mentioned an educational system through junior college, a nearly complete medical service, recreational facilities, musical clubs, sports, and dramatic societies. He added:

> The plan is avowedly culture centered. The ample leisure, the freedom from economic warfare, and the assurance of fundamental necessities of life should generate a culture equal to that of the Greek city states at their best. We should again see such interest in affairs of state, in drama, in literature, in physical culture, and in philosophy. In music and art, in excellence of speech, in tolerance, in beautiful family life, in everything that goes to make a broad, cultured life, the citizens of these units should be able to lead the world.

But Colonel Ohlson did not catch fire. On December 21 he acknowledged Ruste's letter and brusquely suggested that since Ruste had heard that Gruening was interested he should pursue that opening. He added that he would mention Ruste and his plan to Gruening when he got to Washington in January.[40]

Nothing more was heard of the Ruste plan, in Alaska or anywhere else, and the design of the Matanuska Valley included no Greek city-states.

3

The Source of the Colonists: The Great Lakes Cutover Region

For thirty years or more before the establishment of the Matanuska Colony, those who wrote about Alaska habitually made the expected comparisons with Scandinavia, Finland, and northern Russia, all to the advantage of Alaska. The colonists for the Matanuska project were chosen from the northern counties of Michigan, Minnesota, and Wisconsin partly because these regions had some climatic similarity to Alaska and partly because the people there were largely of that north European stock thought to have a special sturdiness and fondness for pioneering. One of the arguments made by promoters of the territory was that southeastern Alaska had winters as mild as those of Washington, D.C. or New York and that other regions were comparable with places in the northern tier of states. The zero isotherm for the winter months runs through south central Alaska, a little north of Anchorage, near the Matanuska Valley, then slants through British Columbia and Alberta into Minnesota and around the northern end of the Great Lakes.[1] It appeared therefore that agricultural settlement in that part of Alaska, or even farther north, was no less promising than settlement in northern Minnesota.

But a different conclusion could be drawn from the comparison. In 1935 the northern areas of Minnesota and the other two Great Lakes states were among the nation's seriously distressed rural areas, not in any important measure because of drought. In addition to the unemployment caused by the decline of lumbering, sawmilling, and mining, there was the problem of submarginal agriculture. Many of the rural people had been attempting to scratch out livings between tree stumps, on stony, infertile soil, and on wet, boggy land. The glaciated terrain, the shortness of the growing season, the character of the soils, the mucky, peaty bogs, and the pockets of unpredictable summer frosts all suggested some of the conditions that settlers might encounter in Alaska, and if the conditions made farming in Minnesota difficult, they could hardly be advantages in Alaska. Yet there was some difference. Marginally productive land and an inhospitable climate, where no better were close at hand and where almost all food was shipped from ports 1,500 miles away, might allow farmers to make a living.

Depending on the definition of the lake states cutover region, all or nearly all of the original Matanuska colonists were chosen from that area. According to one study, 47 of the 201 families were selected from counties outside but adjacent to the cutover,[2] but a somewhat more inclusive definiton of that region takes in 86 counties and would account for all the colonists.[3] The region was characterized by rural poverty, costly and inefficient services by local governments, stranded population, high relief rates, and ineffective farming on submarginal land. Like other such "rural problem areas"—the Appalachian–Ozark area, the several cotton areas, the short grass/winter wheat and short grass/spring wheat areas—the cutover region had already been the subject of several New Deal studies when the Matanuska Colony was established, and more followed later.[4] The circumstances of the stump farmers and of the rural forest- and mine-workers were like those of the colonists chosen for the Matanuska project, and the troubles of the region were only in part the result of the depression and were relieved very little by the partial economic recovery achieved during the New Deal. The isolation and poverty, the seasonal and uncertain employment, and the unrewarding agriculture were the products of the reckless exploitation of resources, free migration, unregulated settlement, and decades of frontier boosting and promotion.

After nearly two centuries in which the fur trade dominated the region, lead, iron, copper, and finally timber invited exploitation. Forests and mines made millionaires, but the boom passed and busy lumbering and mining centers became ghost towns. Early in the nineteenth century the mainstream of agricultural settlement passed by all but the southern edges of the lake states area. Lead mining in southern Wisconsin after 1823 and small-scale copper and iron mining in the Lake Superior ranges of the Michigan upper peninsula after 1844–45 brought added population, some farming, and a small lumbering industry to supply charcoal and mine timbers.[5] In the meantime, increasing agricultural settlement began to flow into the southern part of the lake region, to the mixed hardwood forest and prairie lands, the driftless area of southern Wisconsin, and the open prairie country of southwestern Minnesota. Even without official promotion activities, many of the settlers would have come, but in 1852 Wisconsin established an office of immigration and later maintained an agency in New York to meet immigrants and to inform them, through employees familiar with the several languages, of opportunities available in Wisconsin. Minnesota encouraged publicity in the press and in guide books and through campaigns of letter writing. The arguments intended to draw settlers to Minnesota would seem familiar to those who read the later writings of C. C. Georgeson on Alaska. It was said that the cold winters of the state were not at all objectionable because it was a dry cold; the high northern latitude meant longer hours of summer sunlight and thus more rapid plant growth and greater production; although rainfall was close to the minimum necessary for successful farming, its favorable distribution through the growing season assured good crops; and it was argued that crops yield most abundantly close to the limits of their range rather than in the center of the conditions seemingly most favorable to their growth.[6]

Yet the promotional activity could be justified as spreading the good news of real agricultural progress. In one representative county in southwestern Minnesota, for example, there were in 1870 only 143 farms, 535 inhabitants, and 782 improved acres, but by 1900 the population had increased to over 12,000, most of the land was in farms, and 92 percent of that was improved land. By 1920 the value of land and buildings had increased to $153 an acre, and with little more land available the growth of population had caused a slight decrease in the average size of farms in the county.[7]

As early as the 1850s the agricultural frontier had pushed to the edges of what later became the cutover region. In Trempealeau County, Wisconsin, on the edge of the "pineries," small lumbering and sawmilling supplemented the farming economy, and some farmers were able to add to their incomes by going into the lumbering areas for winter work.[8] But in the northern forests the plow did not quickly follow the ax. Moving westward from Maine and maritime Canada, lumbering penetrated the lake region in the 1860s and reached the bonanza level in Wisconsin in the 1870s and in Minnesota about a decade later. For the whole area the great lumbering period was from 1870 to 1920. By 1900 most of the pine was gone, and by 1920 most of the good hardwoods had been removed. Great tracts of timber were cut, but only the best logs were taken out, leaving behind a ruin of stumps, tops, and discarded smaller logs. Fires added to the devastation, sweeping across both virgin timberland and the slashed areas, and making poor land poorer by destroying the top layer of humus. In the cutover and burned-over tracts, brush and unmerchantable trees grew in the debris, and the brush and tangle and stumps were there for any possible settler to remove. The pine stumps, unlike hardwoods, remained unrotted for years and had to be pulled or blasted to clear the land for farming. By the turn of the century, lumbering was already in decline. The Great Lakes region produced 35 percent of the total United States lumber cut in 1890, 8 percent in 1920, and 4 percent in 1939.[9]

Cutover land was cheap because lumber companies were eager to dispose of it and thus escape the burden of taxation on land no longer useful to them. The old belief that any wooded land would grow crops after it was cleared drew some farm settlers who found a market in the small lumbering and sawmill towns. But as districts were cleared of commercial timber, lumberjacks and millmen moved on with the companies to new areas, the small communities declined and even disappeared, and the pioneer farmers were left with greatly reduced markets for their farm products and with some scavenger lumbering operations to help support them.[10] The old effort to attract settlement to the lake states continued, in competition with the appeal of the western plains country and western Canada, but after 1900 the promotion was intended to bring settlers to the cutover region rather than to the already settled southern areas. Land companies, banks, business organizations, local boosters, and agencies of the state and local governments joined in publicizing the new northern frontier.[11] By the 1920s several major railroads still had large tracts of land for sale in the cutover region, especially in Minnesota; lumber companies were selling land through subsidiaries or through agents or speculating dealers, and the three states maintained immigration offices and organizations for the disposal of state and school lands.[12]

Under such stimulation, settlement increased, and between 1910 and 1920 3.5 million acres were added to the farms in the region, but the rate of growth was not maintained and by 1920 only about one-third of the land in the region was in farms and less than half of that was improved.[13] Land companies were advertised as creating "made-to-order" farms and turning a wilderness of scrub timber and brush into a prosperous agricultural section.[14] The scale of operations was indicated in a study by the Department of Agriculture in 1925 based on surveys of 153 land companies, real-estate dealers, and company agents and the progress records of three thousand settlers.[15] The dealers in land maintained offices in the cutover region and in larger cities such as Chicago and Minneapolis, advertised in city and farm newspapers, arranged excursions for prospective buyers, and aimed their appeals at selected groups. Those companies with fairly good land to sell, usually in former hardwood belts, attempted to interest farmers or farmers' sons, men with some money to invest and with some knowledge of farming. Dealers with the least suitable land aimed at the foreign born (often former copper or iron miners with faint memories of past farming in Europe) or at the city dwellers of the "back-to-the-land type."[16] The larger dealers in land were settlement or colonizing agencies, offering planning and guidance, providing credit, arranging for seasonal employment, aiding or financing clearing, offering livestock on credit, operating model farms, and cooperating with local government in the planning or building of schools and roads.[17] Although many companies tried to conduct their businesses ethically and to restrain the enthusiasm of their salesmen, and although deliberate misrepresentation may have been rare, the companies were in the business of selling land, not enlightening the ill-informed or protecting the foolish. They took an optimistic view of the agricultural potential of the region and minimized the difficulties of land clearing, harsh climate, and short growing seasons. Some companies kept stands of hardwoods and let it be understood that the whole tract had been in such timber. One company for years ran an experimental farm and produced good potato crops without, however, letting it be known that manure had been applied in massive carload lots without regard for normal costs of cultivation.[18]

Although the states of the lake region did not themselves directly participate in promoting private land sales, agencies of the states published bulletins on the land available, soils, climate, and suitable crops. They did not issue warnings to guide settlers away from poor, sandy, stony stump-land or boggy areas.[19] At the end of World War I the Milwaukee Association of Commerce, veterans' organizations, and chambers of commerce promoted the idea of land settlement, and from 1921 to 1924 the Tri-State Development Congress brought together leaders and officials interested in publicizing settlement.[20] The University of Wisconsin was involved in the promotion of settlement through its experiment station, which established substations in the cutover after 1905, and through the activities of county agents, the demonstration of land-clearing methods, and the distribution of surplus military explosives for stump blasting. After 1907 the dean of the university's College of Agriculture, who had invested in northern land and in two colonizing companies as early as 1905, promoted cutover settlement, regarding it as a contribution to the nation's social stability.[21]

Under these conditions some settlers made progress. In 1925 a group of 162 settlers in Wisconsin and Minnesota who had been on their tracts nine to ten years had an average of 40 improved acres (19.2 cleared, 20.8 brushed), and total receipts from all sources—crops, livestock and livestock products, off-farm labor, and sale of timber products—of $755 a year. The value of their land, buildings, and equipment had increased over $3,000, or a gain of $345 a year. But these were settlers who had succeeded, who had stayed on their land and had kept some records, not those who had moved away after a period of unrewarding struggle.[22] One land company, by 1925 in operation for more than twenty years, had brought in many settlers, offered guidance and credit, and yet had a tract of nearly unbroken wilderness. Its show of supervision was part of the routine of attracting settlers, and its experimental farm was a showplace operated at high cost in fertilizer and labor. The company's profits came from forfeited down payments, the interest on purchase contracts, and the appreciation in land values caused by some land clearing and by what settlement persisted.[23]

Despite these settlement efforts, farming in the cutover region lagged in the 1920s, and later, as the early stages of the depression called attention to the concentrated rural poverty and high relief rates, it was clear that most of the region was unsuitable for agriculture and could best be used for reforestation, recreation, hunting, and fishing. The National Resources Board called the region and others like it the slums of the country and recommended the withdrawal of submarginal land from agriculture at the rate of five million acres a year for about fifteen years.[24]

The depression closed off much of the normal movement of population from country to town, and there was a widely publicized, unguided, and only roughly counted back-to-the-land movement. Those who fled the cities moved in with country relatives, rented or squatted on unused and usually hilly or scrubby farms, or, if they were unusually affluent for those times, bought farms of their own.[25] Because the movement occurred between census years, its volume was hard to measure. Later information made the peak in the farm population in 1933–35 appear largely the result of the reclassification of rural homes as farms and the damming of the normal flow of population toward the cities. Only in 1933 was there a net gain by migration, and also in that year 282,000 farms were added by reclassification.[26] Although the movement back to the farm was largely illusory, cheap or abandoned land did attract migrants, and in the so-called problem areas there was a larger than average swelling of the rural population and a larger reclassification as farms. As jobs in mining or lumbering disappeared, rural residences with a few cleared acres or garden patches were classified as farms, and their residents became farmers in the sense that they had no other jobs.[27] In the lake states cutover region the number of farms increased from 1930 to 1935 by 23.9 percent, second only to the gain of 32.2 percent in the Appalachian–Ozark region.[28]

The cheap land of the still sparsely settled cutover area seemed an obvious refuge from the city, and land agents and promoters publicized settlement as a practical method of escaping or ameliorating the effects of the depression. However, the results were not encouraging. One attempt to settle unemployed on vacant county land in Wisconsin in 1930–32 was a complete failure. Only 42 of 103 land buyers took any steps to improve their lands; 47 did nothing, and 14 allowed their land purchases to lapse at once.[29] The city man seeking a rural refuge needed funds to carry him through at least two years while he made his farm productive. Few men had such resources, and the others needed supplementary employment in sawmills and lumber camps and on the roads. The little work of that kind available in the early 1930s was jealously guarded by the older residents of the region, who regarded such jobs as their own by seniority.[30] In addition, the condition of agricultural markets did not allow much hope of a general turn to part-time farming. Nevertheless, it seemed that "there are some localities where development of part-time farming may be a means of aiding some workers who have had experience and prefer to live in the country."[31] A student of settlement programs, familiar with Canadian and American developments and with conditions in Minnesota, examined the notion that as many as twenty million Americans might be placed on the land to "restore the former balance" between urban and rural life and to relieve the effects of the depression.[32] Referring to Canadian experience, he showed how small a portion of even a rural population was prepared and qualified for such an enterprise, how limited were the suitable lands and localities, and how the already glutted agricultural markets would be further injured by added production or even by the reduction of sales caused by making thousands of families self-sufficient on their own land.[33]

In the cutover region, defined as the seventy-six northern counties of the three lake states, the return to the land, or the attempt to farm by those already on the land, did not relieve poverty, but rather increased the problems of the region, which included 42 percent of the land area of the three states and had 13.5 percent of the 1930 population, 17.6 percent of the farms, and 10.8 percent of the total value of farm products. The density of population was less than fifteen per square mile, including the clustered settlements around mines and lumbering centers. In many counties the farm population was less than five per square mile and less than ten in most, or under two families per section. Since many farmers were concentrated near village communities, the remaining population was scattered and isolated.[34] Of all families receiving relief or rehabilitation aid in rural depressed areas, those in the cutover showed the smallest proportion of family heads whose normal occupation was farming—32.9 percent.

The low percentage of farm laborers and tenants among those on relief—4.8 percent and 6.1 percent—was an indication of the agricultural poverty and stagnation of the region. In contrast, 22 percent of the relief clients were farm owners. The land was too poor and undeveloped and farming too near the subsistence level to support both owners and tenants or laborers.[35] From July 1933 through June 1934 an average of 11.6 percent of the population of the United States received relief, and if the four million men given work relief that winter by the Civil Works Administration (CWA) are included, the national rate was about 14.5 percent. The relief rates in the cutover region varied widely, but some of the county rates were among the highest in the nation even after allowing for population changes between 1930 and 1935. In the upper peninsula of Michigan, Keweenaw County in 1935 had 70 percent of its population on relief, the highest county rate in the nation.[36] Relief rates varied seasonally and with CWA activities; when CWA employment ended, the relief rate for the whole region rose above 25 percent for a time. In June 1935 18.4 percent of the cutover farmers were receiving either relief or rehabilitation aid, compared with the national rate of 8.8 percent.[37] At any one time the relief rolls did not show the full extent of the poverty. Families and individuals were seasonally dropped from relief, became rehabilitation clients of the RA, or were added to the WPA rolls, and between times they were briefly self-supporting through the sale of some farm products or temporary employment. At any time about 80 percent of the names added to direct- or work-relief rolls were those of persons previously on relief and returning to it.[38]

In the summer of 1935 the rural population of the cutover region receiving relief or rehabilitation included only 10.6 percent who had lived in their counties since birth, the lowest percentage found in any of the rural problem areas studied by the WPA, and over 14 percent had moved in since 1929.[39] In Sawyer County, Wisconsin, an extreme case, the immigration between early 1930 and the fall of 1933 was equal to 35 percent of the county's rural farm population of 1930, and over half the new residents were squatting on their tracts.[40] In a wider area in northern Wisconsin, 42 percent of 2,969 isolated settlers had been born in Wisconsin, 22 percent were foreign born, and 36 percent came from thirty-eight other states.[41] Three-quarters of the settlers were owner–operators of their land, 10 percent were renters, and 15 percent were squatters, most of them occupying land without the owner's knowledge or consent. Of the more than 2,200 owner–operators, only 1,233 had really begun to farm; the others had cleared so little land that their farms were simply places of residence. Almost three-quarters of those who had begun to farm had become farmers since World War I, or within fifteen to seventeen years of the time of the survey. The average cash income in 1933 was $312 per family, about half of which came from the farm and most of the remainder from CWA or Public Works Administration wages. More than a third of the group had paid no taxes for over two years, and 36 percent had been on relief for an average of more than six months.

In 1935 a study of about one-fourth of the families in the Forest County section of the federal land purchase project at Crandon, Wisconsin, showed that of 290 families, 105 were on farms with an average of nineteen acres of crops and six head of stock, including four cows; 139 were in open country but not farming, and 46 were in small villages.[42] Thirty of the families in the open country were squatting or occupying their places rent free. The farm families gained part of their income from odd jobs and wood cutting, and 40 percent of the nonfarm group gave forest or sawmill work as their normal occupations. Other common occupations were fire warden, watchman, truck driver, and railroad or highway worker. The value of all goods and services annually consumed by the farm families was $809, and by the nonfarm families $748, but the food and fuel used or sold from the land was worth only $302 annually for the farms and $161 for the unfarmed tracts. A few of the families showed small surpluses for the year, but most of them had deficits in unpaid loans, bills, and taxes, and 80 percent of all families received some aid from public funds at some time during the year.

Conditions elsewhere in the cutover region were about the same. In one northern Minnesota county, a sampling of seventeen farms in use from five to twenty-eight years showed an average of 117.6 acres per farm, but only 5.3 acres per farm were cultivated and 4.6 of the remaining 112.3 acres were potentially suitable for agriculture.[43] In the whole region it was common to find owners or operators of from 40 to 80 acres with only from 2 to 10 acres cleared. Settlers had depended on nonfarm jobs while they cleared land; when wages declined they needed even more time away from the farm, and the disappearance of all other employment turned many settlers into reluctant full-time farmers who found that formerly cleared acres had largely returned to brush.[44]

The experience of many families in the cutover region seemed to undermine the old faith in the occupation of a parcel of land as the guarantee of security. The poverty and the high relief rates seemed to demonstrate that the old pattern of individual settlement could no longer reliably provide tolerable standards of living. Crop failures and the low price levels of the depression period had some relevance to the problems of the region, but the trouble lay deeper. "The frontier philosophy which assumed that the individual, if given complete freedom, would pursue an economic course that was to the best interests of society, led to the present dilemma of stranded communities, bankrupt farmers, and widespread unemployment."[45]

Poverty and relief were not temporary, and partial recovery brought little change to the region. In October 1937, when economic conditions were comparatively good, the cutover counties of Michigan had over 38,000 cases of some form of relief or assistance by public works, or 16.5 percent of the 1930 population; in Minnesota over 79,000, or more than 22 percent, were receiving relief; and in Wisconsin cutover counties there were over 118,000 relief cases. In Florence County more than 70 percent of the population received relief at some time in 1937. The National Resources Committee reported: "Even with a Nation-wide improvement in economic conditions beyond anything ever experienced or expected, there would yet not be enough local private employment in this area to take care of all those wanting work."[46]

The decline in lumbering, sawmilling, woodworking, and mining had begun before the depression. By the early 1930s only about 15 percent of an area that had once been almost wholly forested remained in mature timber, and only a small part of that remainder was virgin growth. The reckless cutting continued. In Forest County, Wisconsin, for example, 62 percent of the timber that had been standing in 1927 was cut by 1936.[47] Although iron and copper production had remained high in the 1920s, employment in the mines had declined with electrification and mechanization. Michigan copper, which was produced from deep mines, never since 1916 at a cost less than 11.4 cents a pound, met increasing competition. Mines in Utah and Arizona produced copper more cheaply, and new African mines could deliver copper in London at five cents a pound.[48] The already reduced employment in mining declined further after 1929, as industry used less iron and copper during the depression.

Those who turned to farming as a substitute for other employment found the clearing of brush and stumps so laborious and the actual agricultural value of the land then cleared so low that they made little progress. After brush and stumps were removed, the soil beneath the forest litter was in many places stony. Heroic efforts might remove enough stone to make the soil tillable, but there still remained potholes and beds of peat and muck that resisted cultivation. The cost of land clearing in the cutover region, without removal of stones and boulders, was estimated at $50 an acre. In California and Washington some land cost as much as $200 an acre to clear, but it was then far more valuable.[49] In Brimson County, Minnesota, a settler on new, wild land of the less easily cleared kind, reckoning his labor at twenty cents an hour and that of a horse at ten cents an hour, might clear his land of stumps, brush, stones, and boulders at a cost of more than $150 an acre and then have a tract of expensive but agriculturally indifferent land. If the clearing were done by a public agency using hired labor at low wages, and if the work were spread over a five-year period to allow stumps to rot and grazing cattle to expose the roots, then the cost might be reduced to $30 an acre. But most settlers either could not afford to wait that long or made no progress at all in their clearing. "This consideration of the cash costs of clearing land leads to the conclusion that the successful development of a farm on wild, timbered land in northern Minnesota is dependent upon the willingness of the settler to put in a tremendous amount of work at a relatively low wage rate."[50]

Even before the depression, average incomes and levels of living in the northern section of the lake states were much lower than in the southern areas of the states. Among cutover farmers in Minnesota, the gross income in 1929, from all sources, including home consumption of food produced, was $1,107, while in the rest of the state it was $2,457.[51] The incomes of farmers declined from that point, especially the portion derived from off-farm lumbering or mining. In 1939, with farm prices improved over the depression low, the Department of Agriculture estimated that for the whole cutover region the income for each farm worker, after deducting costs, interest, and taxes, was $220 a year.[52]

The "plane of living" in the cutover region—the density of telephones, radios, and houses equipped with running water and electricity—when plotted on a map county by county, appeared quite high compared with the Appalachian–Ozark or old cotton areas.[53] However, the appearance was at least in part deceptive; in the cutover counties such conveniences were found mostly in the many small towns that had been lumbering or milling centers or in open-country resorts and hunting and fishing lodges. The farm and rural nonfarm people had few of them.[54] Generally they lived in isolation in houses that provided barely adequate shelter. They seldom enjoyed the benefits of plumbing and running water, rarely had electricity or telephones and radios, and were usually without adequate medical care. In the jargon of the sociologists who studied them, they had perhaps $10 to $18 a year per family for all "advancement items"—that is, all books, newspapers, magazines, church activities, charitable contributions[!], and organized recreation.[55]

In all three of the lake states, tax delinquency on land that had been cut over and had become valueless for timber was common before 1929 and after that became a major problem. By June 1934 more than two million acres had reverted to Michigan for unpaid taxes, and within another two years an equal amount had become subject to seizure. In one Wisconsin county the tax delinquency rate rose from 14 percent in 1927 to 46 percent in 1933.[56] By 1939 there were twenty million acres of county, state, and federal land in the three cutover states, land that had been acquired by local government units for unpaid taxes and land purchased by federal agencies.[57]

When most of the northern forests had still been uncut, the expectation that farm settlement would follow lumbering, as it had elsewhere, led to the organization of local governments normally found in established areas. But as settlement continued spotty and population remained sparse, the counties felt the strain of building and maintaining schools for isolated families, operating school buses over wide areas, and clearing snow and maintaining back country roads serving a few families that lived in part on wages from working on the roads they used. As delinquent taxes and reversion of the land to the state or county reduced local government income, the burden became heavier. During the back-to-the-land influx of the early depression, new schools had to be built or old ones re-opened for settlers' children. In poor counties the cost of local government was 5 to 7 percent, or even more, of the total assessed true value of real property, while in the better counties it was about 3 percent. In the more prosperous counties state aid to local government amounted to 10 percent of expenditures; in the poorer ones it was 25 to 40 percent.[58]

In one Wisconsin township the thirty-five settlers held property having a total value of less than $20,000 and paid 8 percent of the school taxes. The twenty-two families sending children to school paid a total of $175 in school taxes. Two families supplied eleven of the fifty-two children in school and received wages or relief from local and state funds. The head of one of these families was paid $450 a year for driving the school bus that took his own children to school. In another township one family was paid about $2,000 a year for maintaining a road that served mainly them, for driving a school bus chiefly for their own children, and for the wife's teaching a school attended mainly by her children.[59]

One partial solution to the problems of isolated settlement and the high costs of social services to local governments was to resettle in more favorable locations some of the families then on poor land in sparsely settled areas. A study made in northern Minnesota showed that the cost of such relocation would be offset in a few years by the savings resulting from consolidation of school districts, reduction of road maintenance, and lowered costs of local government.[60] But relocating a few hundred or a few thousand farmers on better land would solve nothing if at the same time the old policy of unrestricted settlement allowed and encouraged many others to take their places. The National Resources Board pointed out that in the year ending 30 June 1934 there had been 7,741 original homestead entries and that the rate was being maintained.[61] Except for a few entries in Minnesota, settlement on federal public land was not a problem in the lake states, and in any event the era of free settlement was closing even then with the passage of the Taylor Grazing Act and the executive orders of 1934 and 1935 withdrawing from entry, except in Alaska, all but odd parcels of the federal lands. However, closing the public lands to further entry would not correct or prevent misuse of or unwise settlement on land in private ownership.

The National Resources Board described the efforts of land promoters to create a land hunger among would-be settlers and to profit by it.

> Owners of idle lands are driven to make strenuous efforts to dispose of their holdings by the constantly increasing burden of carrying charges. Their efforts and those of professional land promoters have been powerfully

reinforced by State immigration bureaus, railroad companies, and local business interests which profit directly or indirectly from the sale and settlement of land. Local development associations, "booster" clubs, and banking and transportation interests very naturally have labored zealously to increase the population of their particular localities and thereby to enhance land values. As a result of these activities the landward movement of the past 20 years has been largely artificial, and frequently carried out without regard to the interests of the settlers themselves or to the national or local welfare.

To bring land use under some control and to reduce the probability of continued settlement on land that would not provide a living, Wisconsin in 1929 had already authorized its counties to zone rural areas to "regulate, restrict, and determine the areas within which agriculture, forestry, and recreation may be conducted." Within six years all the Wisconsin cutover counties had zoning ordinances and the other lake states followed, at first with less effective laws. The zoning was not retroactive, but a prohibited use could not be resumed after a lapse.[63] Attempting to correct some of the results of unwise past settlement, the lake states, with grants first from the FERA and then from the RA, helped some farmers in the cutover areas to become self-sufficient, if they were on adequate land, or to relocate on better land, if that was advisable.[64] In the Beltrami Island district of northern Minnesota, where 90 percent of the land had become tax delinquent by 1932, six and a half townships were organized as the Beltrami Island State Forest and the 310 families in the area were helped to resettle on better land, with the equipment, livestock, and credit necessary to establish themselves.[65] The state project was helped, with some bureaucratic snarls, by grants from the FERA to the Minnesota Rural Rehabilitation Corporation.

The misused land, rural poverty, and stagnation in the cutover region were only a part of a larger national problem. A study made in 1935 concluded that to achieve the best land use, five million people, 15 percent of the farm population, would have to be moved from inferior land and from problem areas and that such a shift of the least productive farmers entirely out of agriculture would have no appreciable effect on national agricultural production.[66] Rexford G. Tugwell, at the end of the first year of activities of the RA, reported that a study of 13,000 of 16,835 families in land acquisition areas showed 47 percent of them on relief and average gross family incomes for all of them in 1934 of $289. He estimated that there were an additional 600,000 to 650,000 families hopelessly struggling on poor land and further injuring the land by their efforts. Finally, two million young people who would ordinarily have moved to the cities had been held on the farms by depression conditions.[67]

Although, in the long run, hope for improvement in the condition of the rural poor lay in resumed movement to industry and to the towns and cities,[68] that escape was closed by continued mass unemployment. Although some farmers in poor areas, more often the foreign born than the American, succeeded after years of frugality and the hardest labor, many others on submarginal land were there because poor land had attracted poor settlers and because they had not managed to escape. Age, physical handicaps, training, and habit made them unlikely to break away from their rural homes even in good times and kept many of them during the depression in continuing need of public assistance.[69] For others, either rehabilitation grants or resettlement, individually or in agricultural communities, substituted for deferred industrial recovery.

Good farmers on poor land, inexpert farmers producing little, and rural workers taken to farming for lack of other employment might be helped toward more effective efforts where they were, or they could be resettled individually among other farms in established agricultural areas in so-called infiltration projects, or finally they might be resettled in new farm communities of several types. Whatever the method, if they produced more they would increase the gluts in the commercial agricultural markets; actual subsistence farming, if it were possible, meant a retreat from twentieth-century living standards, and a successful compromise between commercial and subsistence farming required the kind of supplementary employment that had already failed many rural settlers. At best it might be possible to do minimum damage to existing commercial agriculture and at the same time improve the condition of some rural families by helping them to live mostly from their land, to exchange services within their communities, and, with cash needs reduced, to produce only small quantities for sale. Such a program seemed to put the client farmers outside the existing economy, but they were already a surplus rural population only tenuously connected with the world of cash.

Of all the resettlement projects, the Matanuska Colony was most exciting to the press and to popular imagination. The location was remote, the colonists left familiar things far behind, and it was a return to an approximation of the frontier and to pioneer conditions. No farming that might be developed in the Alaskan colony could export and compete with outside agriculture; and if the colony reduced Alaskan food imports, the loss to American farmers would be a trifle. There was no well-established agriculture in Alaska that would be upset by the intrusion of new settlers. Few other places seemed to offer so assured a local market. Outside the native economy, 90 percent of the food requirements of the small population was imported, and although the colony could not be expected to sell its products much beyond the reach of the Alaska Railroad, even in that area there were about nine thousand potential customers for the 202 colonist families. The conditions that the colonists would find in the Matanuska Valley were not forbidding, despite popular notions about Alaska. The winters were long but much milder than those in interior Alaska, with an average mean temperature in January, the coldest month, of thirteen degrees above zero. The summers were even cooler and the frost-free growing season shorter than in most areas in the cutover region, but the long summer sunlight, with only a few hours of deep twilight each night through a third of the growing season, compensated for the coolness and the short season. Unlike the Tanana Valley, where permafrost was common in wide areas, or the Yukon Valley and northward, where it was universal, the Matanuska Valley had none, or perhaps a few insignificant pockets. The colonists were not coming to an entirely unsettled area, and the experiment station had been in operation there for nearly twenty years. If knowledge of Matanuska's soils, drainage, local variations in temperature and growing season, varieties of crops adaptable to the area, and markets available was less than minutely complete, it was at least as full as the knowledge of any other area in Alaska and was approached or matched only by agricultural knowledge of the Tanana Valley.[70]

The conditions of soil, climate, and land clearing found in the Matanuska Valley, if duplicated in an established farming region such as Iowa, would have marked the area submarginal for agriculture, and among the stranded stump farmers in the northern parts of the lake states there were conditions disturbingly like those in Alaska. But Alaska had no Iowa or Kansas close at hand, and imported farm products came a long way at high freight rates. Grains, grasses, and hardy vegetables could be grown, the land was cheap or free, outside incorporated towns or school districts there was no land tax, and timber for building or fuel was to be had for the labor of taking it.

As it seemed to Alaskans and others in 1935, the Matanuska Colony could contribute to progress in Alaska by creating a new community, by adding business for the Alaska Railroad, and by producing food locally and thus reducing the high cost of living. The colonists' residence and experience in the northern counties of the lake states were regarded as fitting them for Alaskan settlement. The habit of referring to them as "drought-stricken farmers" provided a simple explanation of their troubles and made unnecessary any disturbing examination of the pre-depression origins of the poverty and stagnation in the cutover region or the rather similar conditions the colonists would find in Alaska. Above all, reference to drought pushed aside any misgivings about the usefulness of agricultural settlement as the route to independence and security.

However, for the relief administrators who initiated the colony, the center of interest was not so much Alaska as the cutover region. There a few of the many who faced continued poverty as occasionally employed rural workers, as unsuccessful farmers on stump- and stone-dotted land, and, as relief clients, might be rescued from their circumstances and be given a new start in what seemed to be an exciting recovery of the American pioneer past.

4

The Selection and Arrival of the Colonists

Years after the establishment of the Matanuska Colony, when memory of the conditions in 1935 had blurred and when wartime boom and postwar military activities had transformed Alaska and swelled Anchorage to several times its former size, those who knew anything about the colony and remembered its early days grudgingly conceded that it had become at least a partial success and had floundered into a kind of stability. According to critics, the colony was hastily planned by men not familiar with Alaskan conditions; the tracts were too small to support commercial agriculture; it had not been foreseen that dairying would be the "climax" type of farming; land clearing had been too slow and full production had therefore been delayed; the cost of the colony far exceeded original estimates; there had not been a close preliminary study of local variations in climate, soils, and water supply; and there had been too much paternalism and supervision in the management of the colony. But above all, the colonists had been poorly selected. Supposedly the project had succeeded in spite of fumbling bureaucrats because the better few of the original colonists and the later replacement colonists who were "real farmers" had managed to establish themselves as commercial farmers.[1]

The rate of withdrawal from the project seemed to support the claim that the colonists had been unwisely or carelessly chosen. By 1948, 31 percent of the original members remained in the colony, and a few others had settled elsewhere in Alaska.[2] However, the colonists who withdrew were replaced by others; the farms were not abandoned, although their number was reduced by combination, and, in a somewhat unfair comparison, ordinary homesteading in Alaska outside the colony produced hardly more than one patent for each three original entries and many fewer farms than patented homesteads.[3] Outside Alaska, in some typical reclamation projects, where the prospect of rapid appreciation in land value drew many more applications than there were openings, about 35 percent of the settlers withdrew by the end of ten years.[4] Finally, it was not necessarily true that the colonists who left the project had failed. Like other Alaskans, who showed little fondness for agriculture, some of them found opportunity in mining, fishing, trade, or later in military construction.

Some information that might have been useful in planning the Matanuska Colony and in selecting the colonists became available only after 1935 in research reports by the WPA, the RA, the FSA, and other agencies. But in 1934 and 1935 the planners of the colony were aware of the problems and had for their guidance the record of settlement experience in federal reclamation projects, the subsistence homesteads already begun, the private settlement companies in the Northwest and elsewhere, and the other FERA projects then in progress. Col. Lawrence Westbrook and his assistant, David R. Williams, brought to the FERA's Division of Rural Rehabilitation their experience in Texas, and there was available some knowledge of both current and older European land-settlement programs.[5]

The evidence seemed to show that while certain traits of character or a real but hard-to-weigh desire to be on the land contributed something to individual success in settlement, considerable experience in farming and especially recent experience in good farming was most closely related to a settler's ability to establish himself and become self-supporting. But the resettlement program was not intended to invite disaster by increasing markedly the nation's supply of good farms and skilled farmers. Good farmers might be affected by drought, depressed farm prices, and general hard times, but usually they were on good land and their troubles were not likely to be corrected by resettlement. However much experienced commercial farmers might have been welcomed in Alaska, few of them would have had reason to move there; nor was the resettlement program intended for them.

Submarginal land had often attracted and kept submarginal farmers. The officials of resettlement agencies and those who studied the program believed that many such families, even though they were resettled, would be unable to farm effectively or to assume a sizable debt without close and prolonged supervision.[6] Colonel Westbrook referred to those who needed resettlement as generally neither successful commercial farmers nor persons who would readily be absorbed by modern industry.[7] Failure by reason of incompetence was not the criterion by which colonists were chosen for the Matanuska project, but the social workers who had to make the choice were bound to consider applicants on the basis of need and to eliminate those who were then self-supporting or who had some prospect of improvement where they were. In the first summer of the project, the agriculturist member of an inspecting group commented that most of the colonists had not been good farmers where they had been and that the change of location had not magically improved them. He thought that close supervision and instruction of the colonists would be needed for years.[8] After the colony had been in operation for five years, the general manager classified the colonists roughly as the industrious, the chiselers, and the indigents. Of the latter, he said:

If the indigents can be rehabilitated we are performing a genuine service to society. I am not sure it can be done with very many of them because it requires considerable ability and industry to make a farm pay anywhere. Some of our farmers could perform valuable services if the job consisted only of some simple manual operation under direction of a foreman, but to be left alone most of the time to plan and operate the numerous different kinds of tasks on a farm is expecting too much of them. What will become of such people? The simple manual labor jobs are becoming scarcer. There are few opportunities in mining, fishing, lumbering, etc. They might fit in on large farms where there is considerable division of labor, but it is hardly feasible to operate such large farms by the Government or by groups of farmers today. The problem bothers me a good deal, and the only thing I see to do at present is to be as helpful as possible in supervision and guidance (and often this help is resented), and to be firm in our insistence upon recognition of obligations.[9]

Although this harsh judgment was proved in part inaccurate by the readiness and ability of some of the "indigents" to profit by the wartime boom that soon followed, it is true that the background of many of the colonists was not promising. In the cutover region many of the settlers had become accustomed to living at a simple subsistence level, with few conveniences and a minimum need for cash. One community, perhaps an extreme example, in Lake County, Minnesota, had been settled in 1895 by a group of Finns who packed in their possessions. Some farming had developed with lumbering, but by 1934 the population had declined and stabilized at about 160, with an unusually large number of older persons; secondary roads had been abandoned, and four schools had been reduced to one with twenty-nine children. Under individual, corporate, and state ownership, the community had 235 tracts with a total of 24,320 acres, but only 3,966 acres were occupied in forty farms averaging 20 cleared acres each. But less than half the cleared area was in crops, and two-thirds of that was in hay. The community threshing machine and flour mill, once run cooperatively, were no longer in operation and all grain was fed to livestock. Many houses and farm buildings were made of logs, there was little running water or electricity, the two telephones were in the village stores, and 40 percent of the community area was tax delinquent. Those who had been able to find opportunity elsewhere had already left, and of those who remained few were adaptable either to urban surroundings or to commercial farming.[10]

With some minor variations, similar clusters of population could be found elsewhere in the cutover region and in other rural areas. Among the backwoods people there survived many of the qualities, both virtues and defects, commonly associated with the frontier and pioneers: self-sufficiency, but at a minimum level; a jack-of-all-trades adaptability, but with little merchantable specialization and little acquaintance with modern agricultural techniques; and independence and self-reliance, appearing often as stubbornness and resistance to guidance and supervision. In the lake states, the Ozarks, the Appalachians, and in rural areas elsewhere, many families supplemented subsistence farming with small game hunting, fishing, wood-cutting, odd jobs, and "making do" in lingering frontier style.[11] The "real farmers," who according to critics should have been chosen for the Matanuska project, were found only rarely in backwoods America. Journalists and others, influenced by received ideas about the pioneer past, regularly praised the pioneer character and found it little in evidence in the colony. However, what they saw among the colonists—the careless methods, the fondness for endlessly unresolved bickerings, the suspicion of expert advice or authority—perhaps resulted less from the disappearance of the frontier character than from its spotty persistence. FERA officials and others concerned with rural poverty and resettlement often made ceremonial references to the frontier and pioneers, but their problem was the reduction of relief rolls and the rehabilitation of rural families. The indefinite continuation of hundreds of thousands of such families on relief was intolerable, and it seemed to Harry Hopkins, for example, that people already on the land were more at home and were closer to self-support there than they would be in cities. With a little help, many of them could be made largely or entirely independent of public assistance.[12]

By March 1935 the preliminary plans for the colony were far enough advanced so that Don L. Irwin, superintendent of the Matanuska experiment station, was called to Washington to help in the final stages.

To his disappointment, he was assigned to planning for supplies and shipments rather than given authority to select the colonists, a job he would have preferred and believed he could have done well.[13] However, the selections were made by the emergency relief administrations in Michigan, Wisconsin, and Minnesota through their social workers, who were called to Washington in mid-March to meet with Lawrence Westbrook.[14] The basis for selection of the colonists was, first of all, need; those actually chosen were either already receiving relief or were eligible for it.[15] Because the selection was made in the cutover region, the colonists would supposedly be familiar with a climate and terrain approximately like those they would find in Alaska. All the colonists were to have some farming experience, occupational skills that would be useful in the community, and the hard-to-define pioneer spirit and desire to live on the land. They were to be between twenty-five and thirty-five years old (although there were some exceptions) and in good health, with families of average size, and they were to be generally of north European stock "because of its hardihood and pioneering abilities, proved and tested during colonization of the northwestern United States."[16]

Colonel Westbrook had suggested that in the FERA colonies the skills, trades, or occupations by which the colony members would supplement their farming should generally approximate those found in a standard small community.[17] For the Matanuska Colony, he suggested to the social workers that specialists with skills such as carpentry, blacksmithing, or machine work be chosen according to their willingness to do subsistence farming, since after the early period of settlement the specialty would require only a part of their time.[18]

The social workers for the relief administrations in the lake states drew up preliminary lists of potential colonists, examined their records, and asked the families whether they were interested in the colonization plan. They also interviewed the families and their neighbors to determine attitude, stability, initiative, intelligence, and relations with their community.[19] The applicants were asked to submit information on the ages, education, and religion of husband and wife, the number of children, present and past residence, farming experience and knowledge of special types of farming, other vocational experience, and the desire of both husband and wife to continue the rural and agricultural mode of life. The social workers completed forms asking about the family's past history, its relief record, relations with the community, assets, debts, adaptability, organizational memberships, religious activities, quality of family life, and evidence showing the degree of intelligence, possible personality problems, or oddities of temperament. One question asked of the social workers about the families indicates the faith of the FERA in the possibility of pinning down a certain elusive but desirable quality in colonists: "In your judgment does the husband represent an honest-to-God farmer, rugged pioneering type?"[20] This question was often left blank, and most of the time it was answered with an unsupported and unsatisfying "yes." Almost as difficult to weigh and highly regarded by officials was the applicant's desire to live in a rural community. Some information might be gathered from the application form, from the caseworker's interview, and from comments by neighbors, clergymen, merchants, bankers, community leaders, and extension agents.[21] However, since such a desire for rural community life was made to appear a virtue, it is doubtful that many of the applicants would have been harshly judged, by themselves or by others, as wanting that quality.

The colonists' actual backgrounds varied widely and often failed to meet the standards for selection.[22] Eighteen of them had no farming experience, and 27 others had five years' experience or less. Sixty-one of them were over the suggested age limit of thirty-five, and 12 were under twenty-five. The occupational list, with some colonists showing several trades, included bricklaying, carpentry, welding, truck driving, lumbering, sawmilling, blacksmithing, road work, and general mechanical work—103 occupations in all. An examination of the Alaska Rural Rehabilitation Corporation (ARRC) files on individual colonists, even twenty-five years after the start of the colony, when they were no longer complete, suggests how unreliable the information on colonists was. Farm experience expressed in years meant little, and other occupational listings were probably rather imaginative. The 181 colonists who reported their farm experience showed a total of more than 2,010 years on the farm, yet in the 34 most frequently reported of the 103 nonfarm occupations there were 232 listings. Much of the farm experience must have been limited to intermittent efforts to produce something on a few acres cleared in the brush. One colonist who later achieved the largest debt in the colony claimed eighteen years of farming experience; yet he was only thirty-five years old and had worked for years in or near Duluth as a truck driver, steamshovel firer, carpenter's helper, and cement worker. His years of farming appear to have been a boyhood spent on the farm, or perhaps simply in rural surroundings. A colonist's wife interviewed in the summer of 1961 denied that she and her husband had ever been on relief and claimed long experience in farming. However, in 1935 the caseworker reported that the couple had married in 1925, had bought a sixteen-acre farm and remained there while the husband worked occasionally in a gravel pit, had moved to Flint to work in the Buick automobile plant, and had returned to Minnesota in 1931, renting and operating several farms unsuccessfully between then and the spring of 1935. The family had been placed on the relief rolls, but the social worker reported that they had held off as long as the could and that their neighbors felt they deserved a chance for a new start. Similarly, ten teachers were reported among the colonists, but they were apparently colonists' wives who had at some time taught in rural schools despite the most limited qualifications. One wife, for example, had taught school for one year in 1923 and had then become a dressmaker in a small town.

In later years those who have written on the colony, men connected with its management, and the remaining colonists themselves have all generally agreed that some of the caseworkers selected men who were physically unfit or incompetent or chose others to get rid of supposed troublemakers or those longest on relief, and there has been agreement also that some of the colonists had no serious intention of developing a farm in Alaska but looked upon the project as an opportunity for an exciting break in their routines.[23] In part the agreement on the faults of selection may result from the automatic repetition of comments made in the first year or two of the colony. If many of the colonists selected were unlikely to contribute much to the progress of the colony, it is not necessarily true that the social workers were deliberately trying to rid themselves of problem cases. The purpose of the project was to rescue some families from continued relief, and the applicants themselves would naturally have presented their qualifications and experience in the most favorable way. Sympathy must often have caused friends and neighbors to speak well of the applicants, and the social workers had to weigh not only need, but the sincerity of the applicants' desire to be on the land and to participate in forming a rural community. And the selection of colonists had to be hurried unless the start of the colony was to be delayed and a year lost. Only a few days after the mid-March conference of state relief workers with Westbrook in Washington, Minnesota announced selection of its colonists, although notices were not sent until April 9.

The number of colonizing families was usually given in the press as 200, or nearly 1,000 people, though some exaggerated newspaper accounts reported 1,000 families.[24] But there were 201 families from the lake states—68 from Wisconsin, 66 from Minnesota, and 67 from Michigan—and two others were added, an Oklahoma family and a Minnesota man who had returned from Alaska with a still-pending Matanuska Valley homestead claim, which he relinquished in return for admission to the colony. Unlike the other colonists, he paid his own passage and shipped his own household goods to Alaska.[25] Still another man was added some weeks after the arrival of the colonists. He came to Alaska in February intending to homestead in the valley, only to find that in the preparations for the settlement project an executive order had closed the area to all forms of entry. After the colonists and construction workers arrived, he applied to the manger, Don L. Irwin, and was accepted and assigned a colony tract.[26] One other family among the lake states colonists had some connection with Alaska. The wife of a Wisconsin man had been born in Alaska and later inherited, with three brothers, her father's homestead in the valley. After an unsuccessful attempt to get a farm loan that would enable them to go to Alaska and develop the homestead, the family was instead enrolled for the colony.[27]

Before the colonists were chosen, President Roosevelt's Executive Order 6957 of 4 February 1935 closed to entry eleven townships in the Matanuska Valley. Of the 253,440 acres in the whole area, 241,332 were affected. The other 12,108 had passed to private title or were already under mineral or homestead entry.[28] The reserve ran from the Knik Arm of Cook Inlet north to the Talkeetna Mountains and from a line east of the Matanuska River to a point beyond the village of Wasilla in the west. Later an additional small area along Knik Arm was reserved as wild hay flats for the colony.[29] The reserved area was much larger than the colony needed, but there was an optimistic feeling that in time many additional settlers could be brought to the valley; visiting officials spoke easily of hundreds of additional families, three to four thousand more people who would before long settle there or in other Alaskan colonization projects.[30] In the next ten years the colony reserve was reduced by a series of executive orders, and some land was specially classified for disposal by the General Land Office, either by sale to the ARRC for the development or enlargment of colony tracts or by sale or lease to settlers certified by the ARRC as capable of developing the land (see chapter 6).

The whole valley, or that part reserved, was not an unbroken expanse of good agricultural land, and the word *valley* rather misleadingly suggests greater regularity than one would find there.[31] At the eastern end, at Matanuska Junction or Palmer, the mountains dominate three-quarters of the horizon, the Talkeetnas to the north and the Chugach on the east and south, rising so sharply just beyond the Matanuska River that their shadow affects the local climate, reducing the period of spring daylight and delaying plant growth. From near sea level at Knik Arm, the valley rises to the north in ridges and benches to almost 2,000 feet. In the west the elevation is about 200 feet, and in the east it varies from about 400 feet at the Matanuska River to 1,000 feet or more on some of the benches in the shadow of the Chugach.

The whole valley was once filled to a depth of several thousand feet by a great glacier, of which the Knik and Matanuska glaciers are the remnants. The terrain rises and falls and has hollows and ridges, rock outcroppings, and areas of exposed or thinly covered coarse gravel. Over the gravel is soil a few inches to three-feet thick, deposited by ice and water and still being augmented by wind-blown materials carried by the local Knik and Matanuska winds, which bring into the valley the silt and sand particles from the mountain ridges and the exposed gravel beds of the two braided rivers.

Although the average precipitation is only fifteen to sixteen inches a year, the low rate of evaporation and the distribution of the rainfall during the growing season make it adequate for agriculture. For an area with a rate of precipitation that would elsewhere classify it as sub-humid or semi-arid, the land is amazingly wet. Where the original vegetation is undisturbed, forest litter and a blanket of moss several feet thick retain moisture. Well-drained areas are usually marked by a cover of birch mixed with white spruce. Black spruce mark the poorly drained areas, and in the wettest spots there is no real forest cover but only the muskeg vegetation and dwarfed, sticklike trees. The climate results from the mixture of mild coastal influence with the harsher interior climate and from the low altitude, the northern latitude and the seasonal extremes in the hours of daylight, and the surrounding mountains and the local winds, themselves the result of the interacting influences of mountains, open valley, and water areas. In the limited area of the valley the weather is so variable that a number of distinct climates might be distinguished. In general, the valley winters are milder than the latitude alone would indicate, milder than those in some areas of the northern tier of states, but the springs and summers are much cooler than those in any other agricultural area in the United States.

The soils of the valley, which are equally variable, have been classified under twenty-two types, with sixteen additional sandy or stony variations and eight kinds of swampy or rough mountain land. Because of the climate and the hazard of wind erosion on cultivated land, none of the Matanuska soils has been considered Class I land (the best farmland), but four of five types of land that are fairly widely distributed in the valley are considered Class II, good agricultural land that can be cultivated with only moderate limitations in use.

The planning for the colony did not include scattering the settlers over a 250,000-acre reserve to reproduce the difficulties of isolated settlement found in the cutover region. Instead, the farms were to be concentrated near a center where community and social services, marketing, processing, distribution, and administration would be provided. In the spring of 1935, there were an estimated 117 families or single men living on homesteads in the valley, the survivors of nearly 600 original entries. Perhaps a quarter of them were doing some farming, but the total cultivated area was well under 1,000 acres, usually estimated at 650 to 850 acres. At least another 90 to 100 patented homesteads had been abandoned by their owners, and because there was neither a general land tax and tax deliquency nor any but very rare agricultural loans upon which foreclosure would result in resale, these tracts lay vacant and unused. In the years just before the colony was established, a number of patented homesteads had been offered for sale at $750 to $1,500 per quarter section, depending on the amount of land cleared and other improvements.[32]

No concentrated area for the colony could be selected without enclosing within it a number of patches of private holdings. Because it was important to have at least some land already cleared for the colonists when they arrived, and because cleared land was almost entirely under private ownership, Ross Sheely of the University of Alaska Extension Service was appointed to select and survey tracts for the colonists and to obtain options for the purchase of private holdings. He left Anchorage with the survey party on April 4, when the snow, which would have prevented any earlier work, was just beginning to leave the lowlands.[33] Although it had been hoped that all the private land within the colony area could be bought by the ARRC, not all the owners were willing to sell, and the corporation was able to buy only about 7,500 acres in 1935 and some smaller parcels in the following years so that by 1938 it had acquired 7,780 acres for $48,814, an average price of $6.27 per acre.[34] Some of the cleared area purchased was along the railroad spur at

Palmer and was used for the first main camp and for the development of the community center, and there too was the community garden. Except for that, the colonists had on their own tracts only about 175 acres cleared and ready for planting that first summer.

The selection and survey of 208 tracts were completed before the colonists arrived. Most of them, 144, were 40-acre tracts; the rest were enlarged to 80 acres or more because they included some poorer, untillable land.[35] Although it was said later that the land was hastily selected and that there was insufficient knowledge of its agricultural capacity, the soil and land capability study made in 1939–40 showed that for the whole colony only 720 acres then in use or being prepared for use should not be cultivated annually.[36]

A more serious problem, one that no one connected with planning or managing the colony apparently saw at the start, was the handling of colony tracts on land not purchased from private owners. Some of these tracts were on sections 16 and 36, reserved as school lands, and there was no way in which either the corporation or the colonists could obtain title until Congress later authorized territorial selection of substitute sections. The public land not in school sections also caused difficulties, since the ARRC could not grant title, and homestead entries by the colonists put them to some extent beyond control by the corporation.[37]

On 12 April 1935, late in the planning for the colony, the articles of incorporation of the ARRC were filed at Juneau, which was to be the corporation's principal office and place of business. Organized as a nonprofit, benevolent corporation with a life of fifty years, with nine shares of stock having no nominal or par value and held individually by the nine directors, the ARRC was intended to "rehabilitate individuals and families as self-sustaining human beings by enabling them to secure subsistence and gainful employment from the soil, from coordinated and affiliated industries and enterprises and otherwise, in accordance with economic and social standards of good citizenship."[38]

For its first six months, until its reorganization in October 1935 and the transfer of its headquarters from Juneau to Palmer,[39] the ARRC had little influence on the operation of the colony. Property was bought and contracts made in its name, but everyone exercising any degree of authority reported to the FERA's Division of Rural Rehabilitation in Washington, and the original funds for the colony were disbursed through the relief agencies of the colonists' home states or by the California Emergency Relief Administration, which handled purchases and shipment of supplies.

In the three lake states, each of the selected colonists was required to sign a "settlement agreement" with the newly organized ARRC.[40] In return for the opportunity to settle on tillable land in the valley, and "in order to obtain subsistence and gainful employment from the soil and coordinated enterprises, establish a home, and enjoy the benefits of the rural community now being formed there," the colonists agreed that (1) their predeparture purchases of necessary household goods, tools, and equipment would be charged to the accounts that they would eventually have to pay; (2) the relief administration would pay the cost of transporting the colonists' families and 2,000 pounds of household goods for each family; (3) at Palmer they would be housed in tents until the houses on the tracts were completed; (4) tracts of not less than forty acres would be available, at prices running upward from five dollars an acre for uncleared land to an unspecified price for improved land; (5) the terms were to be for thirty years, with the 3 percent interest rate to begin in 1938 and repayment in 1940; (6) the corporation would provide farm machinery, equipment, livestock, and supplies by sale, lease, rent, or use charge; (7) until the land supported them, the colonists could obtain from the corporation subsistence items at cost, charged to their accounts and to be paid later; (8) the corporation would provide educational, cultural, recreational, and health services as well as supervisory and consultation services; and (9) the colonists accepted the conditions and agreed to abide by the management's directives and to accept "supervision and control of crop production, processing, marketing, distribution, crop rotation, soil management, sanitation and other measures for the welfare of the community."

While the colonists and the land for the settlement were being selected, more than four hundred additional men were being recruited from Pacific Coast camps maintained by relief officials for transient workers. These men, usually called simply "transients" or "CCC men," were to precede the colonists to the valley, establish the main camp, set up the board-floored tents, and help to clear land and build houses and barns for the colonists.[41] The work of collecting supplies and equipment and preparing them for shipment, transporting the transient workers, and receiving the colonists and arranging for their departure created a flurry of activity on the West Coast. The Bureau of Indian Affairs vessel *North Star* and the army motorship transport *St. Mihiel* were chartered for the shipments, and on April 23 the *North Star* sailed from San Francisco with several assistants, a doctor and some nurses, a photographer, an architect, several construction supervisors, and 118 of the transient workers. It had on board tents, stoves, kitchen ranges, a thousand cots and mattresses, trucks, tractors, well-drilling equipment, and farm tools. At Ketchikan the vessel took aboard lumber and stopped again at Juneau for more. Although the second shipment of men and supplies eventually sailed from Seattle, San Francisco at first seemed to be monopolizing the work of supplying the colony, and Seattle businessmen complained bitterly.[42]

Before leaving home, the colonists disposed of inadequate or unsuitable clothing and furniture and were supplied with replacements by the state relief authorities.[43] Those from Minnesota gathered at St. Paul, where they heard a lecture on Alaska by a former member of the faculty of the University of Alaska. They traveled across the country in railroad day coaches, followed and interviewed by newspapermen, and were greeted in San Francisco with speeches and dinners. Before they sailed on May 1, they were given toys for the children, a motion picture projector and film to amuse them during the voyage, and a farewell concert by a hillbilly band.[44] Newspaper accounts described the excited children, tearful women, and grave men, all facing a great adventure, a little frightened but determined.[45]

At Seward the colonists were greeted by the townspeople, and the newspaper welcomed them to their new home in Alaska, "far from the vicissitudes of the make-believe, tinsel civilization Outside." The editorial promised that in Alaska only manhood and womanhood, not money, really counted.[46] Anchorage made May 10 a half-holiday for the town to turn out and welcome the first group of colonists. There were flags, bands, speeches, and reception committees and at the community hall a dinner of Matanuska products. The newspaper marked the occasion by printing Henley's "Invictus."[47] A special railroad train was arranged for the next day to take Anchorage people to see the colony, and on the same day the Minnesota colonists arrived at Palmer and found Irwin and more than four hundred transient workers already there and a tent city and its facilities ready for them.[48] Attempting to restrain the enthusiasm, Irwin told reporters that the life of the colony would not be easy; there would be years of toil ahead. He estimated that only about 15 percent of the land, roughly six acres on each forty-acre tract, would be cleared that summer and that it would take two or three years to clear the remainder. About the same period would be required to make the farms yield adequate livings.[49] In a few years, Irwin's sober estimate appeared far too optimistic.

The colonists from Michigan and Wisconsin traveled west about two weeks behind the Minnesotans, sailed from Seattle, and were welcomed at Seward. There were plans for another reception at Anchorage, although there was perhaps less spontaneous enthusiasm than there had been for the first group. The women and children remained behind at Seward while the men hurried through Anchorage and on to Palmer, where on May 23 the heads of families drew lots for their tracts.[50] For the next month exchanges of tracts were allowed so that old friends and neighbors could be near one another. By late June, ten camps were established: the original tent city at Palmer, where the community center was being developed, a camp for the transient workers, and eight camps for colonists, located reasonably close to the individual tracts.[51]

Because the work of building the community center and the colonists' houses was given priority, very little land was cleared that summer. Those tracts that were on old homesteads had some cleared land; there was more at the main camp, and some was rented from old settlers. By late June nearly four hundred acres had been planted, three hundred in grain for the livestock then being purchased through the state emergency relief administrations in Montana and Wyoming, the rest in potatoes and vegetables. A recreation and general-purpose building was ready for meetings and church services, and two portable sawmills were turning out daily four hundred three-quarter squared logs for construction of houses and barns. A camp council was created, in each of the colonists' camps, and each council sent two representatives to the weekly meetings of the colony council at Palmer.[52]

In the first weeks, interest in and enthusiasm about the colony continued, both in Alaska and outside. The Anchorage newspaper was cheered by the thought that the seven press associations and the newsreel men who had accompanied the transient workers and the colonists were turning out tens of thousands of words and countless pictures that reached millions—publicity for Alaska that was priceless, that would speed Alaska's growth and hasten the realization of Alaska's dreams.[53] A Scripps-Howard feature article described the transient workers as an advance army transforming the valley; the land was one of "threats and promises, a wilderness fast yielding to the axes, the tractors, the grit and determination of America's jobless come to make Alaska their homeland."[54] The *New York Times* had already seen in the planning of the colony evidence that some of the frontier remained and had rejoiced that the colonists and others who had volunteered to go had preferred to endure hardships rather than to continue on relief.[55] The *Fairbanks Daily News-Miner*, which normally limited its editorial page to appeals to buy from local merchants and to urging a welcome for the Dawson City curling team, took its first editorial notice of the colony by reprinting on May 27 the *New York Times* editorial of a month before. Like other newspapers, the *Times* repeated inaccurate information about the Matanuska region, mentioning, for example, the hazards of the bitter winters with temperatures of fifty degrees below zero.[56] At another time the paper's geography was confused: "At the edge of the colonization area, at Fairbanks, there is an experiment station of the Alaska Agricultural College. This will be a great help to these farmers in a strange land."[57]

Sometimes the colonization was explained simply by reference to the "rich" soil in the valley,[58] but often it was related to popular notions of the frontier safety valve that had disappeared:

> Many an observer had pointed out that past U.S. depressions were relieved by mass migrations to the frontier, that the present depression is uniquely acute because that safety valve is gone. But there is one last U.S. frontier: Alaska. A few hundred discouraged miners who have turned to farming produce only a small portion of Alaska's food. The rest, $6,000,000 worth a year, is imported. Meantime, U.S. farmers plow under their crops, kill livestock to prevent a surplus. Last January, FERA officials put these facts together, produced their most ambitious rural rehabilitation scheme to date.[59]

The first grumbling about the colony came not from the colonists, but from some Alaskans who were disturbed by the importation of transient labor, and from the transient workers themselves. The increase in federal spending was pleasing—besides the work on the colony itself, $446,000 for completion of the Anchorage–Matanuska road, the Knik River bridge, and the extension of roads in the valley—and it would provide jobs for local men,[60] but not all the changes in the region were encouraging. One old settler, Gerrit Snider of Wasilla, who had camped where Anchorage was later built, probably spoke for many others. Although he welcomed the colonists and wished them well, he complained that the summer jobs with the Alaska Railroad or the Alaska Road Commission, on which he and others had long depended, were now scarce and that the work for the colony that might replace such jobs was being done by cheap imported labor. To make matters worse, the transients were not even paid in full locally; most of their wages were held for them until their return outside. "We don't mind that soon our fishing and hunting days are over, but we sure object and no words are too strong for the taking away of our jobs and a general cut in wages by the importation of an army of cheap labor."[61]

A member of the territorial legislature, Alton Nordale, returning to Fairbanks by way of Matanuska from a trip outside, reported with pleasure that the colony was making publicity for the territory and that the transient workers were being held to their jobs in the valley and would not be allowed to leave and seek other employment in Alaska. In the fall, when the work at the colony would be suspended, the transients would be shipped back to the States, thus protecting the Alaska labor market. Nordale denied that there was discontent in the colony, but he conceded that a few transient workers were being shipped back to California because they were radicals and agitators.[62] At the time, thirty of the transient workers had quit their jobs and were in Anchorage awaiting transportation to the States. Some of them wanted to stay in Alaska and to find other work, but the mayor spoke for the city in announcing that they were not wanted there and in asking the colony officials for assurances that the workers would be moved along.[63]

Colonists spent their first weeks in the valley in floored tents, drew food and other supplies from the commissary on credit, and were employed by the corporation at construction and other labor at the rate of fifty cents an hour, which was usually applied to their subsistence accounts. A doctor and several nurses were ready to treat their illnesses, and a large tent had been set aside as a hospital. The valley was not a remote wilderness. The tent city at Palmer was on the Alaska Railroad branch line running to the coal fields, and Anchorage was less than fifty miles away. A daily round trip by railroad car, powered by a gasoline engine, had been added to the ordinary runs of the Alaska Railroad. There were more than one hundred miles of roads in the valley, and a beginning had been made in extending, linking, and improving the existing roads. The summer solstice was approaching when the sun would be below the horizon hardly more than four hours in twenty-four and there would be no real darkness.

The mosquito season had arrived, and the insects hovered in clouds where the air was still or where clearing had not removed the brush and the blanket of wet moss. Most days began with clear skies and then became overcast, clearing again in the late evening. The frequent light rains were typical of spring and early summer, amounting to little more than an inch of precipitation a month. In the late summer the rains would be heavier, but even a light rain, when added to the already moist soil churned by trucks and tractors, turned some areas into muddy bogs. The colonists faced no frontier dangers—subsistence and shelter were assured them—but hardly a month after the first of the colonists had arrived in the valley, before any appreciable progress had been made in developing their tracts or building their houses, the existence of the colony was threatened by protests that aroused attacks in Congress and brought a succession of investigators and special administrators to the troubled Matanuska project.

5

The Early Troubles

From the start some critics regarded the colony as a piece of foolishness. Former Congressman Cyrenus Cole of Iowa recalled his 1923 trip to Alaska and remembered that Harding's secretary of agriculture, Henry C. Wallace, had said, "Some time, now far away, when our lands have become exhausted, we may have to go up there to coax food from the soil, but I hope I will never have to go there to follow a plow with a mosquito net over my head." Cole charged that the United States was imitating Russia in sending victims of its professional dreamers to a "de luxe Siberia called Alaska," and predicted that the colonists there would die or fail.[1] Delegate Anthony Dimond replied angrily and at length to Cole's criticisms, supplying information on Alaska's soils, climate, crops, and resources, and remarking that in 1923 he had heard no comments of the kind Cole attributed to Secretary Wallace, but that on the contrary Wallace had been favorably impressed by the territory.[2] At about the same time Andrew Christensen, who, as head of the Department of the Interior's Land and Industrial Commission in Alaska during the building of the Alaska Railroad, had laid out the site of Anchorage, and who was now retired and living in Great Neck, New York, called Alaska the "spoiled child of Uncle Sam." He saw no basic industrial possibilities in Alaska other than fishing. Coal was plentiful but of poor quality and without a market; the gold and copper mines would in time be exhausted, and there were no other resources or possibilities that would justify development of the territory and the establishment of a large permanent population. "If you will investigate the facts, you will find that this action of the government in shipping these unfortunate people to the Territory of Alaska is not only an absolute waste of money but a great injustice to the poor people that they are shipping here." The Anchorage newspaper defended the colony plan against the "apostles of doom," who were "like a lot of flannel-mouthed critics of every progressive and sound policy,"[3] but within a few weeks the attacks were coming from the colonists themselves.

On June 19, Alaska newspapers reported that two colonists, Mrs. I. M. Sandvik and Patrick Hemmer, claiming to represent forty other families, had sent telegrams to Governor John W. Troy and President Roosevelt, complaining that houses and barns were not being built, wells dug, or roads constructed to the individual tracts. They claimed that there was a threatening epidemic and insufficient medical aid; further, no progress was being made toward building a school, and the commissary prices were too high. The telegrams were followed by a letter to Roosevelt elaborating the protests.[4] According to Hemmer and Mrs. Sandvik, promises made to the colonists were not being kept; for example, free labor was not being provided, and the transient workers were not cooperating with the colonists. Hemmer and Mrs. Sandvik demanded an investigation of the colony so that the colonists would work more effectively.[5]

At Palmer, Don L. Irwin, the manager of the colony, made little comment, but he minimized the importance of the discontent and pointed out that building was going on, that a large school would be built, and that the chief difficulty so far had been caused by a delay in shipping some building materials.[6] Governor Troy's office issued a statement that the territorial government and the ARRC were interested in the success of the colony but that neither had authority to deal with the complaints, and that the proper channel for protest was to the colony manager, Irwin, or through him to Colonel Westbrook and then to Harry Hopkins.[7] From Washington, Colonel Westbrook said that some difficulties had arisen because of the delay of one cargo of building materials, but that every effort was being made to speed construction. He thought the colonists were already better provided for than they had been at home.[8] In Michigan, a spokesman for the state emergency relief administration said there was little sympathy for those who were complaining, since they had gone into the project with eyes open, fully informed of the conditions they would meet. But the next day a resolution of the Michigan legislature called for the return of the colonists if their complaints proved well founded, and a few weeks later the governor of Michigan told the press that the Matanuska project had been a mistake and that northern Michigan had greater natural beauty and more natural advantages than Alaska.[9]

The protesting colonists sent wires also to the senators from the three lake states, and Senator Arthur Vandenberg, speaking also for Senators LaFollette and Shipstead, on June 21 asked the Senate to call on Harry Hopkins for an investigation and report on the colony.[10] Vandenberg added tales of Matanuska troubles gathered from the newspapers and placed in the record charges against the colony made in a telegram to Senator Couzzens by Hemmer and Mrs. Sandvik:

Six weeks passed; nothing done. No houses, wells, roads, inadequate machinery, tools. Government food undelivered; commissary prices exorbitant; educational facilities for season doubtful. Apparently men sent to pick political plums. Irwin and Washington officials O.K. Hands tied. Colonists cooperating. Request immediate investigation.[11]

Mrs. Fred Rotz, formerly of Plymouth, Michigan, whose letter to the *Detroit Times* was included in a feature article on June 18,[12] complained that colonists were paid only $.50 an hour while skilled workers other than the transients were paid $1.25 to $1.50; that an epidemic threatened and there was only one doctor; that there were inadequate medical supplies; that milk was so scarce that it was limited to children under six; that many expectant mothers wanted to go to Anchorage for prenatal care; that groceries were charged to the colonists instead of being free until they were self-sustaining; that the prices at the commissary were too high; and that there was bitter dissension among the colonists, partly because supplies intended for the Michigan and Wisconsin colonists had gone to the Minnesotans. She commented, rather oddly, that there were agitators who were trying to make things look worse than they were and added, "There are Communists even here."[13] She called for more than human aid, saying, "Pray for us, dear folks at home. We need the mighty hand of God in this undertaking, and the united prayer of people everywhere."

Senator Vandenberg mentioned the death of one colony child from measles and pneumonia, repeated the tales carried by the thirty-one transient workers leaving Alaska about the two hundred others who wanted to leave, and told the story of the women in the colony who had begged the transients for their identification tags so that they might disguise themselves as men and leave for the States.[14] Commenting on the settlement agreement that the colonists had signed, he found amazing the provisions for supervision over marketing, crop rotation, soil management, and other farming practices and the obligation of the ARRC to provide economic and social guidance as well as educational, cultural, recreational, and health services. "So . . . we have in net essence a complete commune under the American flag at Palmer, Alaska." It was bad enough that all this should be called for in the agreement, but the facilities promised in return for the surrender of all individual functions had not been provided. As a result, "these people are left stranded 5,000 miles from home in the face of threatening calamity." The isolation was more striking to the senator because he was under the impression that the colony was without roads and many miles from a railroad.[15] He predicted that unless something was done to return the colonists to civilization, there would be a major disaster.[16]

One article on the discontent in the colony perceptively attributed much of the bickering to the colonists' real fears about the future and mentioned, as one of many difficult tasks still to be done, the clearing of twelve acres for each colonist.[17] Through the rest of 1935 and later many colonists continued to claim that they had been promised free clearing of the twelve acres. Nothing in the settlement agreement indicated such a promise, and a footnote referred clearly to graduated prices for uncleared or improved land: "The Corporation is in a position to make available to the Colonists timbered land as low as five dollars an acre and other land at prices in proportion thereto depending upon the location and the extent to which the land has been cleared."[18] Nevertheless, the idea persisted, and in November, after the ARRC had been reorganized, the new manager, Ross Sheely, asked Lawrence Westbrook what should be done about the promise of twelve cleared acres. Westbrook denied that any promise of that kind had been made but gave Sheely authority to act on his own judgment, remembering the limits of the budget, and added that any officer of the colony who had made such a promise should be reprimanded.[19]

Early in the outbreak of colonist complaints, Eugene J. Carr, a representative of the Rural Rehabilitation Division of the FERA, was sent by air from Washington to Seattle and by ship to Alaska. Immediately on arriving at Palmer he discharged the commissary manager and announced that construction would be speeded and that there would be adequate shelter for families, livestock, and supplies before winter.[20] Carr described himself as a "trouble shooter" with authority to make decisions on the spot, but he denied that he was replacing Irwin as manager. However, more layers of authority were added. On June 28 Hopkins announced that a special inspection team, headed by S. R. Fuller, a New York industrialist, was about to depart for Alaska. In Seattle, Captain Charles E. Parsons, a naval supply officer, was making purchases for the colony, hiring additional laborers, and preparing to join the Fuller group.[21] By mid-July the management and staff of the colony had swollen far beyond the original size. Fuller, as special FERA representative, headed the list:

S. R. Fuller, Jr.	General administrator
Lt. Col. L. P. Hunt	Assistant general administrator
Lt. H. V. Martin	In charge of engineering and transport
Capt. Alan Perkins	In charge of construction
Don L. Irwin	Director of farming
Eugene J. Carr	Procurement and business administration
Leo B. Jacobs	Architect
Dr. C. Earl Albrecht	Medical director and colony physician
F. L. Biggs	Inspection engineer
F. L. Warden	Fire warden
Dr. Earl Osborne	Transients' physician

Fuller announced that he would return to the States at the end of the month, leaving Colonel Hunt as general administrator. However, there was supposedly no change in the basic organization of the colony; the ARRC was at the head of it, and Irwin was not only in charge of farming, but was the chief local officer of the ARRC.[22] In reality, the colony was directed through the rest of the summer and into the fall by the special representatives sent from Washington, and if Irwin was not stripped of his office and nominal authority, his real power was very much subdivided.

Early in the period of dissension in the colony rumors spread in Fairbanks and Anchorage that local men would be hired for construction work at the project, and in mid-July twenty-five carpenters were hired at Fairbanks and another hundred at Anchorage and elsewhere in Alaska. Except for the foremen and expert workers, the laborers at the colony were supposedly men who had been on relief. The local carpenters were classified as skilled workers and were paid board and $200 per month for a 48-hour work week. By the end of July an additional twenty-five carpenters had been hired at Fairbanks, the steamer *Yukon* was sailing from Seattle with another 150 workers, and a vessel was at Ketchikan taking on lumber for the colony.[23]

At that time and for some years after, it was a standard Alaskan comment that the chief trouble at the start of the colony had been the use of cheap outside labor and the failure to employ skilled and knowing Alaskans.[24] In the following winter, the Fairbanks newspaper, anticipating the annual spring revival of mining and the influx of job seekers, recalled the transient workers at the Matanuska Colony. It described them as worthless troublemakers and suggested that Alaska should follow the example of California and take measures to exclude penniless immigrants.[25] The objection to outside labor was extended to non-Alaskan management or supervision. In the summer of 1936 the general manager of the colony, a resident of Alaska long enough to be acceptable, was praised by the Fairbanks newspaper for again hiring Alaskan workers during the construction season, and his methods were contrasted with the cheechako management that, according to the *News-Miner*, had bungled the colony in 1935 and had made it a national joke.[26]

Only five days after the senate resolution of June 21 calling for a report on the Matanuska Colony, Harry Hopkins gave a reply based on the already available information coming to the FERA from the colony. He traced the planning of the colony, described the difficulties that had to be overcome, and conceded that because of adverse weather the building was about three weeks behind schedule. The colonists were living in tents with board floors and siding, with stoves, beds, chairs, and gasoline pressure lamps; their water had at first been supplied by railroad tank cars from Anchorage and now came from community wells; sanitation and toilet facilities were supervised by the camp doctor. Hopkins described the medical aid available to the colonists, the communication and transportation between the colony and Anchorage, the plain but wholesome food, the tracts on which the colonists would settle and have to clear largely for themselves, the modest debt that each colonist might expect and the terms for repayment, and the school and community buildings that would be provided. He said that the only direct complaint had been the one from Hemmer and Mrs. Sandvik. He could not promise that all construction would be completed on schedule, but he gave assurance that efforts were being made to hurry the building and that all colonists would be in habitable quarters before winter. Commenting on news reports, he said, "The great publicity which has been given to this undertaking has made news and headlines out of the very ordinary difficulties of construction and administration which would normally be expected in an enterprise of similar nature even if undertaken in a well-settled part of the United States." For example, the press repeated the charge made by Mrs. Rotz that there were 2,000 people ill in the colony, but the whole population of the project was 1,336—425 transient workers, 897 colonists and members of their families, and 14 in the administrative and supervisory staff—and only a few cases of measles and scarlatina had been reported.

Hopkins described the security and self-sufficiency the colonists could expect and contrasted this hope with their past condition:

This economic condition should be compared with the fact that if the families which have been moved to the Matanuska Valley had been left in the regions from which they have come, their sole outlook would have been to have received from emergency relief aid approximately $25 a month for each family. Because of the economic conditions in the areas from which they have come, there was no hope of economic recovery as compared to the opportunities which are now afforded to them by virtue of the Alaskan colonization project.[27]

A long, impassioned defense of the Matanuska Colony against the attacks of Vandenberg and others was made by Senator Homer T. Bone of Washington,[28] who contrasted the rich and fertile Matanuska Valley with the popular myth of Alaska's snow and ice, drew a picture of those hopelessly on relief in the colonists' home states, and described the millions of unemployed, "the tragic army of the jobless," from which had been taken one small group. In defending the project, Senator Bone gave a digest of the conventional view of the frontier as a safety valve and of the significance of its disappearance:

We took these people to Alaska in an effort to give them an opportunity to demonstrate whether or not Alaska will be our last frontier, the last social safety valve of this country. . . . There is not a thinker in this country who has presumed to write a book on social and economic conditions in recent years who has not expressed grave concern as to the future of this great Republic, because, forsooth, the frontier had disappeared, and there was no longer any outlet for the pent-up emotions of the people who were under the lash of economic adversity. So here was the opportunity, in a very tiny, infinitesimal way, to demonstrate whether or not America might say to [them], "Men and women of America, here is one, yet one, avenue of escape. We cannot say as Horace Greeley did, 'Go West,' but at least there is left to you the one hope, if it can be demonstrated to be justified, that you can go to Alaska and there find a haven of refuge.[29]

Senator Bone spoke of the Matanuska project as pioneering without the dangers of the raw, wild frontiers of the past, a revival of the past with inconveniences smoothed by modern science. He described the millions of the unemployed, the people in slums like rabbit warrens, living in horrifying conditions, children surrounded by filth and crime; but in contrast, "these people who go out into the great open spaces of Alaska can at least be men." Bone denied that there had been any attempt to mislead the colonists about conditions in the valley. He quoted FERA publicity releases and bulletins that referred to the temporary quarters in tents and the gasoline lamps, chemical toilets, and modest log or frame houses. One bulletin for FERA workers concluded:

This project has every indication of success, bringing to Alaska additional settlers, who are needed, and to these families an economic and social security. Care must be taken not to paint the picture to the families in colors that are too rosy. They should be informed as accurately as possible of existing conditions. Hardships will have to be faced, especially in the first couple of years, and many adjustments made.[30]

Not all the colonists were discontented. Several of them told reporters that in spite of some minor illnesses and confusion in the shipments of materials and equipment they liked Alaska and were determined to stay. Mrs. Lloyd Bell was fascinated by the brief twilights of the summer nights, the rapid growth of all vegetation, the wildflowers, and the development of the colony's community center. She thought that most of the colonists were pleased and contented and disappointed in those who had complained.[31] By late June, ten days after their protests, self-styled "colonists' representatives" seemed to have reconsidered. Patrick Hemmer said that he was tired of all the bickering and that he wanted to get on his forty acres and develop his farm. Mrs. Sandvik said, "I'm having the time of my life. I've never been in so much excitement before." When the rumor spread at Palmer that the colony would be abandoned and that the colonists would be returned to their old homes, newspapermen could find no enthusiasm for that proposal among the colonists.[32]

By the end of June, six colony families were ready to leave, having sold household goods to pay some of their bills. They were joined by three other families, and early in July the nine departed from Seward, leaving unpaid accounts for which they signed notes. By the end of October, after some additional families had departed, the notes amounted to $5,474.65. The colony management provided transportation for returning colonists as far as Seattle, but it had no arrangements for sending them on to their original homes.[33] For the first year or two most returning colonists went to Seattle, and many of them remained in the Pacific Northwest, frequently applying to the nearest relief authorities for aid. Others found their way back to the lake states, where for the first year they were treated as local residents by the relief officials. Later a number of the families who left the colony remained in Alaska, some moving to Anchorage or to other towns for employment, others taking up land elsewhere.[34]

As the first of the original colonists left, the colony management professed to be unconcerned and chose to regard them as unfit or maladjusted, and Eugene Carr, the special FERA representative, predicted that work would move more quickly because the dissatisfied ones were gone. Don L. Irwin pointedly announced that there were applications on file from 650 "real farmers" to replace the "deserters" or "misfits."[35] In mid-August Col. L. P. Hunt announced that about 15 percent of the colonists had gone and that perhaps a few more would leave, but that, on the whole, the departures were a good thing, since those that remained would be the best of the lot. The *New York Times* was tolerant of those who had quit the colony so soon, finding the explanation not in a lack of pioneer fiber but in exposure to such a temptation as earlier pioneers had not faced—the easy return to the States by government transport.[36]

Recalling the period of construction, some colonists in later years believed that one reason for discontent had been that the FERA's plans had prescribed one standard barn design and five house designs, that no variations had been allowed, and that qualified colonists had not been allowed to do their own house building.[37] However, colonists were employed in cutting and milling logs and in building houses, although not necessarily their own, and at least some modification of house plans had been allowed.[38] A more serious complaint was that the individual debts for houses and farm buildings were only approximately correct. House logs and imported construction materials were scattered about the colony and used, often wastefully, as needed and without accurate record. The colonists, transients, and skilled workers were shifted and mixed in the construction of houses and other buildings, and no one knew exactly what part of the cost of a colonist's house was offset by his own labor.[39] The confusion was, in effect, admitted when in the summer of 1936 the ARRC surveyed the individual colonists' tracts and attempted to arrive at an evaluation of houses and other buildings without relying on the fragmentary records.[40] Some colonists managed to do most of their own work and to keep their debts low. Joseph Puhl, who preferred fitted round logs to three-quarter squared logs, built his own house and barn with the help of neighbors, helped them in turn, and dug his own well. In the evaluation of tracts, Puhl's total debt for land, buildings, and improvements on 30 June 1936 was $2,437.[41]

A number of the colonists were less frugal. In the fall of 1935, the supposed commissary budget, not including credit purchases of tools, equipment, livestock, and livestock feed, was $45 per month per family, but many families exceeded the budget, and at least one colonist who was found charging groceries and selling them for cash was forced to withdraw from the colony.[42] One family of five had a total commissary bill from May to early October of $258, while a family of four had a bill of $267 for one month, and still another colonist abused the commissary manager for refusing to sell him a fifth new rifle on credit.[43] One colonist, who was already well on his way toward accumulating a startlingly large debt, by November felt able to offer $10 a week for a girl to do domestic work in his home.[44]

Colonel Hunt, about to leave the colony at the end of October, was cheerful about the project, saying that it would soon prove Alaska's capacity to support a population of three or four million and that there were three thousand families waiting to find places in the colony.[45] In Washington, Harry Hopkins said that the colony was all but established as a successful project and that direct FERA supervision was about to be withdrawn and replaced by full control by the ARRC.[46] On October 29 and 30, the ARRC board, with several newly appointed replacement members, met at Palmer, reorganized, and elected Colonel Otto F. Ohlson president and Luther C. Hess vice-president. It changed the corporation's place of business to Palmer and confirmed the already announced appointment of Ross Sheely as general manager and Don Irwin as assistant.[47] Sheely, the former director of the University of Alaska Extension Service, had selected and surveyed the colony tracts, bought a farm in the valley and settled there, and since July had been in charge of a part of the colony construction work. With the reorganization, the ARRC for the first time emerged from its shadowy existence and began active direction of the colony, although the management reported its activities in detail to Colonel Westbrook and the FERA in Washington.

By early September only 28 houses had been completed and were occupied; 140 houses, with most of their interiors still unfinished, were available by the end of October; in November all colonists were housed; and by the end of December, with 164 colonists remaining in the project, there was a surplus of 10 vacant houses.[48] At the end of the year other parts of the project were nearing completion. The warehouse trading post, and diesel-powered electric generating plant had been operating since summer. The school, gymnasium, dormitory, staff house, and hospital were nearly completed, and on the colonists' farms 149 successful wells had been drilled, 106 barns were finished, and a half dozen more were started. To speed the construction work, in response to colonists' complaints and the political and journalistic attacks on the colony, the original labor force of more than four hundred transient workers had been expanded to well over six hundred during the summer by the hiring of both outside and Alaskan workers. By late September the management began returning the transients to the States, although forty or fifty were kept through the winter as regular workers.[49] Even when winter limited outdoor construction, there were still, in addition to the managerial staff, 406 ARRC jobs, some of them filled part-time or full-time by colonists—nurses, clerks, stenographers, warehousemen, plumbers, steamfitters, electricians, mechanics, carpenters, truck drivers, welders, blacksmiths, janitors, and others.[50] Although the colony school was not ready as promptly as the colonists would have liked, temporary arrangements were made while it was being built. Some children attended the small schools at Matanuska and Wasilla, others went to school in three temporary buildings and several converted railroad cars, and six teachers traveled about the colony conducting home study classes.[51]

In the first months of the project, much of the help and guidance for the colonists came from outside the ARRC or the FERA staff. Before Ross Sheely became general manager, he helped the colonists with their gardens and cows, and Mrs. Lydia Fohn-Hansen, the home demonstration agent of the University of Alaska Extension Service, gave instruction in clothesmaking, handicrafts, and food processing and canning. The Alaska Game Commission ruled that the colonists could take salmon for their own use but not for sale, and that first summer over 3,500 cans of salmon were stored, along with the products of the community garden. The next summer, the Presbyterian minister, Bert J. Bingle, acted as volunteer conductor of salmon fishing trips, using ARRC equipment, and 6,500 salmon were taken at a cost of about four cents a fish.[52] Many of the colonists, and the transient workers as well, believing that they could take whatever big game they needed, armed themselves against moose, bear, and Dall sheep. After a series of messages between the office of the governor, the colony management, Harry Hopkins, Henry Wallace, and Lawrence Westbrook, the fish and game officials confirmed the ruling that the colonists would have to be in the territory for a year before they could hunt big game without paying the $50 nonresident fee and hiring a guide.[53] From the start, hunting and fishing were more attractive to some of the colonists than clearing timber and brush or farming, and as soon as it was possible several of them became commercial fishermen and gave only minimum attention to the development of their farms.[54]

In August 1935 the colony for the first time had a newspaper, a mimeographed weekly, usually of four pages, published by Jack Allman, war veteran, newspaperman, contributor to sporting magazines, and onetime Alaskan, who had returned to the territory by getting a job as a plumber with the construction workers.[55] No real newspaper could be supported while Palmer was a railroad siding, a post office, and the colony's tent city, but the management was pleased to have something more than the notices tacked to bulletin boards. It supplied Allman with a board-floored tent and the materials necessary for a mimeographed newspaper, and the *Matanuska Valley Pioneer* appeared August 22 with a box announcing "Published Every Thursday by ARRC at Palmer, Alaska, Jack Allman, Editor." The December 19 issue carried no ARRC tag, and in it Allman announced that without an ARRC subsidy he would have to charge for the paper— $2.50 for a year's subscription, five cents a copy in Palmer, and ten cents in Anchorage. However, the ARRC was still supplying Allman's quarters and subsistence in return for mimeographing work, and the management sometimes worried lest the connection should make it seem that Allman in his editorial comments spoke for the management.[56]

In the little newspaper can be found the notices marking the community's growth—the colony's first concert on September 3, the dance at the community hall with Father Sulzman playing the saxophone, the opening of a branch of Koslosky's department store of Anchorage, the establishment of a small library from contributions made by colonists and Anchorage people, the appearance of private enterprise with the opening of the Valley City Hotel—with hot water and steam heat. Advertisements in the August 29 issue showed some of the progress:

Taxi for Hire
John Howard . . . Tent No. 17
Opposite Hospital, Palmer
Any Place . . . Any Time
After Working Hours

Almer J. Peterson
Attorney at Law
Office at Palmer, Alaska
Log Cabin Beside Post Office

On October 17 Allman gave notice that the pioneer stage had passed and that civilization had come with the little back room at Koslosky's department store where one could find the first modern indoor plumbing in the valley.

Allman regularly defended the valley, the colony, and the colonists against politicians and journalists who used their brief visits to the valley as the basis for informing the outside world of the project's faults.[57]

When Mrs. Fred Rotz again wrote to the *Detroit Times,* describing supposed hardships in the colony and complaining that in return for loans the colonists lost their freedom, Allman replied by giving her neighbors' opinion that Mrs. Rotz's chief loss of freedom had been the management's refusal to send her son to a six-week radio technology course in Chicago.[58] Some colonists who had withdrawn and returned to their home states exploited the attention they received and justified their withdrawal by painting the blackest picture of the colony and its troubles. Allman countered their charges by describing their records in the colony and their current activities. One man who was telling his Minnesota neighbors that the colony venture had cost him over $1,000 had boasted before his departure of how he had taken advantage of the ARRC.[59] Another, who claimed to have been a colony sawmill foreman, had actually worked for ten days and was now back on relief and living in a house with his mother and ten other relatives.[60] A Minnesota man still in the colony was reported to be recruiting others to withdraw from the colony with him and return to Minnesota, saying that as a group they would find it easier to be readmitted to the relief rolls.[61] Another Minnesotan who had returned to St. Louis County had been arrested for nonsupport of his family.[62] In the meantime, some of the colonists who had withdrawn early had now reconsidered and were asking to be readmitted to the project.[63]

Even in the early months, some of the attacks on the colony came from within Alaska. The *Cordova Daily Times,* whose unfriendly editorials Allman tried to answer reasonably,[64] opposed the New Deal, deplored either direct relief or work relief, insisted that mining and fishing were the foundations of Alaska, denounced taxation of those industries, and lamented the waste of public funds in building roads such as those in the Matanuska Valley while mining companies were forced to build their own roads to bring in heavy equipment. The newspaper announced in September that the colony was a failure but that its obvious faults at least might discourage such paternalistic undertakings in the future. When the Kenai Peninsula would one day be colonized, it would be done by individualistic Alaskans. All history of past colonization showed that settlement required inspired spiritual leadership or leadership by experienced frontiersmen who knew the country. Once the settlers were on the land, it should be every man for himself. The editorial screeched into furious incoherence that no reasonable answer could affect:

Like other measures of relief the Matanuska Colony is the product of idealism steeped in the sordid slime of commercialism, where political favoritism and a desire to grab while the grabbing is good have taken all but a tithe of the billions appropriated in a worthy cause.

Unlike European fascism, ours has been accompanied by an idealism which loses its potency through the lack of a mailed fist. No safeguards were thrown around the idea which would prevent commercial looting. Thus instead of possessing the element of practicality, the eelemosenary [*sic*] scheme opened the way for profiteering on a scale similar to that of the World War.

This, if nothing else, has had a tendency to encourage a flabby mass to throw itself upon the burden of government and demand a share of the loot.[65]

Allman's newspaper had a circulation beyond the colony and even outside Alaska. References appearing occasionally in the paper indicated that it was sent to territorial and federal officials, to Lawrence Westbrook and other FERA administrators, and to some others, like Vilhjalmur Stefansson, interested in the North and Alaska. Then, near the end of his career in the valley, Allman nearly found his paper circulated in New York while the story of the colony was being presented for Broadway theater audiences. In his 13 August 1936 issue, Allman announced that by the end of the month the *Pioneer* would no longer be mimeographed but printed from a handset type on a small press. However, volume 1, number 1 of the printed *Pioneer* did not appear until October 26, and the later numbers followed irregularly. In the sixth and last printed issue, 19 December 1936, Allman explained that he was losing about fifty dollars an issue, that local subscriptions had fallen off with the end of the construction boom at Palmer, and that the half dozen local commerical enterprises were too few to provide advertising revenue. He thought that sometime later he might try again to run a newspaper for the colony, but early in 1937 he left the valley permanently.

While Allman was struggling with his newspaper, E. P. Conkle's play, *Two Hundred Were Chosen*, was being prepared for Broadway production. Lawrence Westbrook wired Ross Sheely:

A play entitled Two Hundred Were Chosen based on Matanuska project will be produced here commercially early in October. Have seen script and it is great boost for project and Alaska. In connection opening of this play we desire give exhibition of typical Matanuska agricultural and craft products together with diorama showing layout of colony houses, community facilities, etc. Request you assemble agricultural and other appropriate exhibits for shipment leaving Palmer not later than September twentieth.[66]

After additional telegrams were sent, vegetables, berries, canned goods, clothing, tents, tools, and samples of colonists' handicrafts were shipped, some of them, like the woodwork by Vernon Olmstead, price-tagged and intended to be sold or returned. Then Westbrook was struck with another idea. He asked Sheely to arrange with Allman for a special issue of the *Matanuska Valley Pioneer* to be distributed at the play. The shipments would be in lots of 5,000 to a possible total of 50,000.[67] Replying for Allman, Sheely explained that an issue that large would require more paper than could be obtained on short notice and more work than could be done on the small press. Nor could Allman hold the makeup for possible future shipments. Sheely suggested that Allman could supply stencils for the old mimeographed paper, and that they could be run off in New York at a two-cent royalty if the papers were sold and one cent if they were distributed free.[68] However, Westbrook abandoned the idea of a big supply of the papers and asked for only one hundred copies of the special printed edition for display.[69]

The play opened on November 20 at the Forty-eighth Street Theater and ran for thirty-five performances. The plot was obviously suggested by the early history of the colony, but actual events were modified or simplified, and the details of the setting were hastily and inaccurately sketched. According to the play, two hundred families were chosen from relief rolls, taken to the Matanuska Valley, and placed in a colony directed by army officers and tangled in bureaucratic confusion. Because their promised living quarters were not ready for them, the colonists built shacks which they were then ordered to pull down. They refused and went on a sitdown strike; at about the same time a fever epidemic broke out among the children. On the verge of disaster, the colonists achieved some cooperation and solidarity largely through the efforts of Jim Conwell, an idealistic young Alaskan engineer employed by the government for the project, and Jennie Walters, one of the women of the colony. In the play, crisis brings unity; in the actual colony there was no single crisis and no surge of dedication and community feeling. For Conwell, the question was whether the colonists would prove themselves worthy of Alaska:

This valley . . . those hills over there—Alaska! For years it's been lying here waiting for someone big enough to tame it—to lick its weather and tap its resources. This country means something to me. It's what I care about, and this little batch of farmers don't mean that beside it. They don't matter. They're not big enough to matter . . . I'm not worrying about Alaska, being any good. I'm wondering whether they're good enough for it! They've got the idea that because they were chosen to come up here they're God's elect! Well, that's not true. Most of 'em were chosen because they were God's worst off and no one knew what the hell to do with them![70]

In the final issue of his newspaper on 19 December 1936, Allman said that he had tried to tell the story of the colony as accurately as possible and to correct such distortions as those spread by Pledge Brown, an itinerant newspaperman who used his brief acquaintance with southeastern Alaska to lend authority to the tales and feature stories he peddled outside. Even before Allman's article appeared, Brown's gross inaccuracies and his shaky claims to Alaskan experience had been described by Delegate Anthony Dimond and the *Ketchikan Chronicle,* the newspaper for which Brown falsely claimed he had been a reporter.[71] By his own account, Brown knew Alaska from Ketchikan to Nome and Point Barrow and knew the terrible odds facing the colonists. There had never been any agriculture in Alaska. The experiment stations had tried and failed for thirty-five years to produce crops. There was no top soil; those who intended to farm in the valley would have to clear brush and moss to get at a layer of sandy gravel, then dig through that to find the soil in which they would have to plant. The terrible cold, the isolation, the endless winter darkness would make life unbearable for the settlers. It would be unsafe for them to venture from their cabins at night, for huge packs of fifty to one hundred wolves roamed the country and, when they were hungry, even invaded the large coastal towns. Medical service was inadequate; there were none of the comforts and only the scant necessities of civilized life. Some things could be grown—potatoes and strawberries, for example—but in the long sunlight of the brief summer they grew unhealthily large and were mushy, watery, and unfit to eat.

Pledge Brown, as he was described in the *Ketchikan Chronicle* and by Delegate Dimond, was an occasional newspaperman who had left a trail of bad debts and bad checks throughout the States. He had been in Alaska for a few months in the winter of 1934–35, but he had never traveled beyond southeastern Alaska and had never worked for the *Ketchikan Chronicle.* Dimond found Brown's ignorance of Alaska's climate, vegetation, wildlife, soil, and living conditions complete. For example, Dimond had never seen, nor had he heard authentic reports of, more than five wolves in a pack. There was a bounty of twenty dollars on wolves, but no wolf had been taken in the Matanuska Valley in the past five years. However, Brown's version of Alaska spread because it fitted many popular notions. The arctic climate and permafrost found farther north in Alaska were described as characteristic of the Matanuska Valley and were given as reasons for the inevitable failure of the colony.[72] The *Literary Digest* oddly combined routine information from the administrators of the colony with the kind of nonsense spread by Brown. The magazine reported the number of houses, barns, and wells completed and then repeated Brown's tale of digging through gravel to find tillable soil. It mentioned the wolf packs, but improved on Brown's story by raising the upper limit to two hundred.[73] Other misinformation about Alaska and the colony persisted, although most of it could not be attributed to Brown. Congressman Roy O. Woodruff exaggerated the isolation of the colony and thought it was on or near the Arctic Circle. Congressman Dewey Short, perhaps intending humor, listed as chief products of the colony region reindeer, Eskimos, icebergs, and polar bears.[74]

In popular articles on Alaska and the colony, however factually detailed, a certain distortion of emphasis or heightening of effect seemed necessary. Hard work, mortagages, and routine chores were too commonplace. One popular article used as central figures a colonist, his wife, and their small child. They are young, clear-eyed, innocent pioneers making a new home in a land that should support a population of 18,000,000 rather than 65,000. They are the future. Peter and his wife are refugees from the dust bowl—a more widely understood explanation of a farmer's troubles than a reference to his original home in the cutover region would have been. Peter, who has perhaps studied how such things are done in the movies, squats, picks up a handful of earth, crumbles it, and says, "This is good dirt, mister." Later, Peter handles more dirt:

> Mayta, his wife, came near and stared with us at the fisted earth. She was tall and slim and young, and their baby was in a sling upon her back. "I seen two farms blow away from me in the States," said Peter. "This one ain't goin' to blow away."[75]

Elsewhere the colony was discussed in gloomy tones because the individualistic farmers, busy planning their futures, little realized the degree of control the government would exercise. The plan for cooperative marketing was enough to label the colony "Uncle Sam's first collective farm." The colonists would occupy for years the "front row of test tubes in the sanctums of psychologists, economists, and students of political science."[76] The nature of the early discontent was misrepresented. "Rare were the day when a Red-tinctured round robin or petition of protest didn't go in to Irwin or Carr." Telegrams were "raining" on Washington, and the misfits, the weaklings, and the "bred-in-the-bone malcontents" had to be sent home. The quite ordinary habits of automatic complaint, of being restless and suspicious of any authority or direction, and of finding joy in haggling and controversy were thus attributed to Reds, never otherwise identified, and to misfits. Those who remained would have the pride of having proved themselves. From them would spring a "new and vigorous strain," and descendants of the Matanuska Valley pioneers might one day boast of their ancestry as others have boasted of their Pilgrim fathers.[77]

Prominent Alaskans, whatever their private doubts of the colony's practicality may have been, publicly defended it for its symbolic value as a modern version of frontier development or for its increase in federal aid to Alaska. Luther C. Hess, after his nomination to the reorganized ARRC board and his election as vice-president, told Governor Troy that he had been far from enthusiastic when the plans for a colony had first been made public and that he retained some doubts,[78] but once involved he and the other members of the board were genuinely interested in making the colony succeed. Some men who shied at the thought of government planning or any active role for the federal government in economic matters at the same time approved of the colony for Alaska's sake. E. A. Rasmuson, a Skagway banker, said:

> Though I don't approve of our government establishing anybody in business anywhere with taxpayers' money, still the Matanuska project will help Alaska and prove a blessing to those lucky enough to get in on it. . . . The project will succeed in spite of governmental blunders unless the colonists themselves fail to live up to Alaska expectations.[79]

Among ordinary Alaskans and the neighbors in the Matanuska Valley the reaction to the colony was mixed but not unfriendly. The position of the so-called old settlers in the valley, those who had settled and homesteaded there before the founding of the colony, was improved by the building of the roads, the hospital, school, and community facilities. In addition in the fall of 1935 the ARRC decided that old settlers would be allowed to borrow ARRC funds for improving and stocking their farms.[80] Only a few years after colonization some of the valley people grew nostalgic for the lost simplicity, the neighborly bustle of social gatherings, the unspoiled natural beauty they had known in the past. Some old settlers spoke in mixed scorn and envy of the colonists' fine houses and furniture and thought the valley was becoming too crowded.[81] The wife of one old settler could not suppress a feeling of superiority toward the colonists. They had tractors for clearing the land and pulling stumps, fine equipment, a community hall, help in building their fine houses, and curtains for the windows; but they were soft, they had not known real struggle, and they had lost their independence and had debts that would take thirty years to pay.[82] Perhaps the most representative reaction to the colony among old-time Alaskans was that of Gerrit Snider, who sympathized with the colonists and offered his help when some of them turned briefly and unsuccessfully to fur farming,[83] but who also resented the construction jobs that went to outsiders and regretted the passing of the old ways and the probable end of the hunting and fishing life in the valley.

6

Managing the Colony

While the planning for the Matanuska Colony was in its final stages, the FERA was within a few months of being replaced by the Works Progress Administration (WPA), established on 6 May 1935 by Executive Order 7034 under the Emergency Relief Appropriation Act of 1935. By the end of the year the last FERA relief grants to the states were being allotted, and under subsequent relief appropriation acts Congress authorized Harry Hopkins, as administrator first of the FERA and then of the successor WPA, to liquidate the FERA.[1] In the meantime, on 30 April 1935 Roosevelt created the Resettlement Administration by executive order and at the same time transferred to it the FERA land acquisition and retirement program. On May 15 the Division of Subsistence Homesteads went to the RA, on June 1 the Land Policy Section of the Agricultural Adjustment Administration was transferred, and on June 30 the RA got the Rural Rehabilitation Division of the FERA, with the state corporations and the resettlement communities.[2] However, Hopkins and Westbrook retained four of the largest of the twenty-nine FERA community projects that had been started or were being planned (Dyess Colony, Arkansas; Pine Mountain Valley, Georgia; Cherry Lake Farms, Florida; and the Matanuska Colony). These four continued first as FERA and then as WPA undertakings. Eventually, in 1939, the first three were transferred to the Farm Security Administration (FSA), but the Matanuska Colony was turned over to the Department of the Interior in September 1938.[3]

Through the last months of 1935, Westbrook and the management of the colony expected the transfer of the project to the RA, but in January Westbrook told Sheely there would be no change.[4] For the next year and a half grants to the colony, reduced in size, continued to come from remaining FERA funds, although the administration of the colony was answerable to the WPA. No sharp distinction seems to have been made between the two federal agencies, and the colony was referred to either as an FERA or a WPA project.[5] By June 1937 the FERA funds for the colony were exhausted, but Westbrook assured the management that additional funds would be available to keep the project on its feet until it became self-supporting.[6]

Secretary of the Interior Ickes, who believed that Hopkins was eager to get rid of the Matanuska project, visited the valley during his Alaska trip in the summer of 1938, inspected the colony, and noted that before he would accept the colony it would have to be in tidy condition and that a final grant of at least $350,000 should come from Hopkins to help the colony through the next few years.[7] In his few pages of impressions of the colony, he repeated the old saw about the superiority of settlers of north European stock, attributed the quite small but close-set trees to the great fertility of the soil, thought the whole project was splendidly equipped, and pronounced the barns bigger than needed on forty-acre tracts. Then and later the barns were generally thought too small, and when Ickes was gently told that they had been built for future expansion of dairying, he triumphantly replied that with more cows there would be less hay to store in barns.[8]

In September the announcement of the transfer of the colony to the Interior Department from the WPA, with a final grant of $350,000,[9] re-aroused newspaper interest in the project. One paper called it "our glacialized New Jerusalem" and suggested that Ickes might as well provide blankets, salt pork, and reservations for descendants of pioneers and "dole farmers" as for Indians. The *Philadelphia Bulletin* announced that "The Pioneer Spirit Still Lives" on the ground that there were still about 170 colonists at Matanuska and 1,500 applications on file. The *Reno Gazette* described the colony as a failure from the start, disapproved by those who had to pay for it, by those who had to live in it, and by those who stayed because they could not get away.[10]

Like other rural and community projects and the RA, the Matanuska Colony was attacked by critics as being far too costly to build and to operate.[11] In April 1936 Congressman Roy O. Woodruff of Michigan announced that the government had already spent about $18,000 per family and that the colonists had assumed mortgages averaging about $6,000.[12] At the end of May, Senator Vandenberg again attacked the colony, saying that by the end of December 1935 the estimated expenditures totaling $2,325,000 were already more than double Hopkins's original estimate and that at least another $100,000 would be needed for the project.[13] However, by the time the last federal funds had been granted to the colony, Vandenberg's own figure was more than doubled. The FERA gave its total expenditures for the colony as

$4,732,499,[14] but if money advanced to the California Emergency Relief Administration and other federal grants for road and bridge building in the valley and completion of the highway from Anchorage were included, the total would be $5,400,000.[15] Even that figure was sometimes arbitrarily raised in press accounts, although there were no additional funds granted to the colony.[16] Giving the cost of colonization for each family dramatized the spending on the project. Early in 1939 a magazine article gave an estimate, based on all costs and the number of colonists then remaining in the project, of $34,000 for each family, an often repeated figure that gained an almost official standing and was found useful in editorials deploring the folly or wickedness of such projects.[17] "In all fairness, it is probable that even the most ardent advocates of the venture didn't envision Communism as a by-product and certainly they believed that rehabilitation could be done for less than $34,000 a family to date."[18]

The colony was embarrassingly expensive, although the tone of critics indicated that the cost was not the reason for attack but a happily discovered weapon. Most of the New Deal resettlement and community-building projects far exceeded their originally planned cost. A study of ninety-nine projects (not including the Matanuska Colony) undertaken by the Division of Subsistence Homesteads, the FERA, and the RA, showed an average family unit cost of $9,691.[19] These projects varied from cottages on one- or two-acre garden plots to suburban communities, cooperative farm villages, and clusters of individually operated farms. A half dozen projects, all of them subsistence homesteads, cost less than $3,000 per family, but for eight projects the unit cost was from $14,000 to slightly more than $16,000. By any reckoning, the Matanuska project had the highest unit cost of all. Elsewhere, planning and administration, unexpected delays, the limited success of light industry and farming in the communities, and the necessity of providing social and community services all added to the cost. In the Matanuska Colony the scramble of activity after the early and well-publicized colonists' protests increased the confusion, the wages paid additional labor were higher than those outside, and almost all materials and equipment needed for building and operating the colony or individual farms were expensively freighted from outside. These freight rates, optimistically viewed as a tariff wall protecting the Alaskan farmer, raised his cost of living and of developing a farm.

But above all, the Matanuska project had to create an agricultural community where there had been no more than a scattering of half-developed homesteads, and, unlike other projects, the colony had to provide almost every facility or service that a new community would need. There was no existing system of storing, processing, and marketing the products of the new farms, and the project built and equipped a general store or trading post, warehouses, shops, garage, community hall, dormitory, offices, staff houses, power plant, cannery, creamery, hatchery, hospital, and school. In less than five years the community facilities were turned over to the cooperative association, and the school, which had cost over $100,000 to build, was transferred to the territorial department of education for one dollar. The establishment of the colony made Palmer attractive to noncolonists and to small businesses, which began moving to the community almost at once, buying or leasing sites from the ARRC. In the chorus of hostile press comment, there were few mentions of this community building, although one magazine did point out that the approximately $4 million that the colonists would never repay was about the paper value of an American country town of similar size.[20]

The cost of establishing a colony farm is more realistically indicated by the colonists' debts of all kinds than by total ARRC expenditures. By the spring of 1937, because the debts were admittedly too large ever to be repaid out of the production of small farms the ARRC prepared to reduce individual debts to manageable size. Since few colonists had then made even token payments, and since most of them were still dependent on ARRC credit, an individual colonist's debt for land, house, barn, well, land clearing, livestock, feed, seed, tools, and family subsistence approximated the cost of developing his farm. One colonist, in April 1937, had a debt of almost $16,000; there were a few with debts from $12,000 to $14,000, and some whose debts were under $6,000, but the average total debt for the 164 farmers still in the colony was $9,694.50.[21] The colony farms were not yet fully developed; much land was still to be cleared, livestock and equipment had to be added, and those who chose to develop dairy farms had to improve their barns and enlarge their herds. The contrast between the smallest and largest debts sometimes indicated extremes of frugality or improvidence, but it also indicated differences between those planning for heavily equipped and stocked farms and others who aimed at small operations, perhaps truck gardening. Before the colony, settlers in the valley and elsewhere in Alaska had homesteaded and farmed with little cash investment and much labor, but their farms remained small while they worked for wages, their houses were often one-room log cabins, and their efforts developed no agricultural region or community. If the debts of the Matanuska colonists were high, the near absence of farm debt in an earlier period was not a sign of agricultural health but rather an indication both of the scarcity of agricultural credit and of the lack of farm values to secure loans. In 1920, by the most inclusive definition, there were 364 farms in Alaska, including fur farms and some cattle and sheep ranches. Only 19 were operated by tenants or managers, and of the 345 owner-operated farms, 251 were free of mortgages, 83 made no report, 11 reported mortgages, and the 7 whose debt was known had a total value of $63,000 and a total debt of $7,500 at an average interest of 9.3 percent.[22]

A few years after the war, when price increases had raised farm-making costs, the estimated investment in cash and family labor necessary for establishing a fifteen-cow dairy farm on a quarter section in the Matanuska Valley was $46,400.[23] Although the farms and the periods are not comparable, the postwar estimate made obvious what had already been true in the 1930s—that a family farm and independence could not be established in Alaska with no more than free or cheap land, a few tools, and hard work. Twenty-five years after the start of the colony an agricultural economist observed:

> The only agriculture of any scale or indication of permanence has developed in the Matanuska Valley. This probably developed largely because it came about as part of a total program. . . . In this plan it was not taken for granted that the farmers' produce would store, process, transport itself automatically to market as would appear to be true of the settlement attempts by individuals.[24]

After the first confused and troubled summer of the colony, when Irwin's authority as manager was replaced by or at least diluted with that of the special representative from the FERA in Washington, and after the reorganization of the ARRC, with Ross Sheely as general manager and Irwin as assistant, the changes in management came less rapidly. In the spring of 1936 Irwin announced that he would leave the project on June 1 to return to his old position at the experiment station.[25] Leo B. Jacobs, who had come to the colony as its architect, succeeded him as assistant manager and then became general manager in the summer of 1937 when Ross Sheely resigned to give full attention to his own valley farm.[26] When the colony was transferred from the WPA to the Department of the Interior in September 1938, Jacobs resigned in order to stay with the WPA, and Sheely returned as manager.[27] When he left the managership in January 1940, he was followed by Herbert C. Hanson, formerly director of the agricultural experiment station at Fargo, North Dakota, who remained until 1945. By the last year or two of Hanson's management, the ARRC was becoming less involved in the social and community affairs of the colony, less concerned with supervision of the activities of the colony families, and more simply an agency handling old and new farm mortgages and advancing funds for land clearing and farm improvements.[28] Ten years after the founding of the colony, Don Irwin returned for another two years as general manager, followed by C. W. Peters, formerly a specialist on farm cooperatives with the FSA and the Farm Home Administration (FHA), and then, into the 1960s, by James J. Hurley, an agricultural economist.

Except for Leo Jacobs, all the managers were professionally interested in agricultural technology and successful farm management. In a farming community in Iowa or Kansas they would have been most at ease with the substantial commercial farmers; lacking such a group in the valley, they tried to direct the Matanuska colonists toward a combination of thrifty living from the land and efficient commercial agriculture. They were practical, matter-of-fact men who would have been intensely uncomfortable had they been required to talk about the spiritual values of rural life or the aesthetic standards to be applied in planning a rural community. They looked upon the development of a farmers' cooperative in the colony as a useful, common-sense step in solving the problems of processing, transporting, and marketing the community's products. The frequent press attacks on the colony that pointed to the cooperative and the compulsory membership in the marketing association as evidence of radicalism must have puzzled and angered them.

Leo Jacobs, unlike the other managers, regularly referred to the colony as only one of the administration's cooperative rural communities. He spoke of President Roosevelt's desire to bring the advantages of the town to the country and to make rural life as desirable as city life. In the colony, that meant establishing a sound economy and planning construction that would be both economical and aesthetically satisfying, encouraging the development of handicrafts and small home and community industries, instructing the colonists in living well from their own farms by producing and preserving most of the food they needed, and developing the kind of education and culture, and the arts, crafts, music, and dances that would make the community sufficiently interesting, beautiful, and picturesque "to hold the children of the colonists so that they will not want to leave it."[29] In the summer of 1938, reporting to the board of the ARRC the activities of the past year, Jacobs described the founding of the Matanuska Colony as the direct result of "economic oppression" and with good will and wobbly history compared it with the earliest American colonies, finding similarities in their origins, sources of support, objectives, cooperative character, and guidance by chartered companies. Although there was then in Palmer little evidence of government but for the presence of a United States marshal and the quasi-governmental activities of the ARRC, and although the colonists' civic organization was limited to speech-making and protests, Jacobs found in that organization also a parallel with colonial American history and took satisfaction in the colonists' frequently demonstrated capacity for complaint:

> The internal government of our own Project is similar to that of the early American colonies in that our Civic Association and Colony Council correspond to their town meetings and we find our own, as well as the early colonists, as they become more settled and sure of their continued residence in the community, assuming a larger voice in the affairs of the community by passing laws to regulate their own behaviour and pointing out the unjustness of some of the acts of the company with the demand that they be corrected.[30]

Interested though they were in the practical and technical aspects of farming, the other managers were also compelled by their positions to give attention to a bewildering variety of problems that had little or no connection with agriculture, wrestling with family budgets, petty quarrels, marital difficulties, health, the education of the colony's children, and almost every problem that might arise in a small community. In addition, the managers had the burden of supplying information to the many journalists who wanted to do articles on the colony, answering and soothing politicians, and sending information to those in the States who thought they were interested in settling in the valley or elsewhere in Alaska.[31]

The difficulties and complaints of one colonist indicate how the managers must have been harassed by the problems of the many. George Connors, formerly of Douglas County, Wisconsin, had well trouble on Tract 132. On most colony tracts there was little trouble in getting water, but the water table was irregular, and of 220 wells drilled by 1 April 1937, 54 had to be abandoned.[32] The average well depth was under 90 feet, but on some tracts good water was obtainable at 20 or 30 feet, on others at two or three hundred. Connors had 9 wells drilled on his tract, to a total depth of 1,888 feet. Some wells were dry, others produced water and then failed, still others yielded water that was not potable. One of Connors's wells froze in spite of repeated warnings from Sheely that he should install a well cover and sawdust insulation. After exceeding his furniture allowance, Connors demanded a radio from the trading post manager, and, when refused, threatened to take one from another colonist's house. In 1936 he complained to Westbrook that colonists' wages were too low, seed too expensive, land costly to clear, his wells unproductive, and the ARRC inattentive to his troubles. After leaving the colony early in 1937 and becoming established on the relief rolls in Washington, Connors again wrote to Westbrook on 7 May 1937, claiming wages for the work he had done to develop Tract 132, which had in the meantime been abandoned by the ARRC management. He wrote also to Eleanor Roosevelt, saying that he had done his part, that the ARRC had failed him, that he was in dire need, and that something should be done to secure what he was owed. Like other such complaints, this one was referred through Westbrook to the colony general manager. It rested there until December 1937, when Jacobs received from the relief authorities of King County, Washington, an inquiry about George Connors and his claim that he was unable to collect from the ARRC for his property in the Matanuska Colony.[33]

The ARRC general managers did what they could to inform themselves about farmers' cooperatives and the management of rural settlement projects and attempted also to arouse a sense of community among the colonists and to encourage them to live from the land and to develop their farms effectively. Sheely drew up plans for five types of farm development, all intended to provide most of a family's subsistence and a small but adequate income from sales, and he and Irwin corresponded with cooperatives in the United States and with cooperative managers and public officials in New Zealand. Sheely obtained from the WPA Information Service such films as *Hands, Work Pays America, Man Against River,* and *America's Modern Pioneers,* and Jacobs, who was also manager of the not yet fully developed cooperative association, wrote to the WPA, the Department of Agriculture, and the National Cooperative Council for films and publications to inform the colonists about such associations and to instill in them a "spirit of cooperation."[34]

Later, Herbert C. Hanson carried on an extensive correspondence with persons and organizations offering some guidance in the problems of developing a rural community. He exchanged letters with James G.

Maddox of the FSA and obtained FSA family budgets, farm plans, and reports on rural planning and social relationships in new rural communities. Searching for useful information, he asked state experiment stations for publications on animal husbandry, the formula for an improved whitewash, or the design for a better poultry building, and asked organizations such as the Refugee Economic Corporation, the International Relief Organization, and the New World Resettlement Fund for comments on their methods of helping new colonists with their farming and handicraft work.[35] Shortly after he became manager, he wrote and issued 250 copies of a pamphlet, "Does Agriculture in Norway Point the Way for Alaska?"[36] The writing was inspired by what Hanson had seen of the colony in his three months as manager, and the description of Norwegian diligence and frugality, the intensive farming, the well-built and comfortable houses, and the Norwegian family's attachment to the land and the farm was intended to stimulate the Matanuska colonists to greater efforts.

Of the four men who were managers of the colony in its first ten years, before it became an established farming community, and excluding the special representatives from Washington, Irwin was the most popular. In the first summer, after the complaints began and the FERA sent additional representatives, Irwin had the advantage of being present, sympathetic, and not really responsible for the colony's troubles. Later, as assistant manager, he could persuade, coax, and jolly colonists into good humor while bearing no blame for general colony policy, which was the affair of the ARRC and the general manager. By the time he became general manager again in 1945, when the troubles of the colony had largely passed, he appeared to be an old friend mingling familiarly with the valley people, reporting the activities of the community, tending to ARRC mortgages and loans, but not interfering. Some of his popularity may have resulted from his unwillingness to exercise the degree of direction and control that others thought necessary and that had to be imposed later. For example, in the summer of 1935 the colonists were apparently free to make almost unlimited purchases on credit at the commissary, and when they began to crossbreed their dairy cows with locally owned bulls, against the advice of the agricultural expert with the S. R. Fuller group, Irwin felt that he had no authority to interfere.[37]

Next to Irwin, Leo Jacobs appears to have been the most popular manager. He was earnest, devoted to his job, convinced of the national importance of projects like the Matanuska, and willing to explain the colony policy to the colonists carefully and repeatedly. Ross Sheely, on the other hand, with an expert knowledge of agriculture and himself a successful farmer, was far less popular. He was thought brusque, heavy-handed, unsympathetic to the colonists; in his second period as manager he was charged with being secretly an enemy of the colony, interested in undermining it because he was the biggest producer of agricultural goods with which the production of the colony would compete, and able to develop his own farm successfully because he was subsidized by his monthly salary of $500 from the ARRC.

Sheely's successor, Herbert C. Hanson, was even less popular. He began with a handicap, since payments on the colonists' real estate debts as well as those on seed, chattel, and other loans were coming due for the first time. His doctoral degree was no advantage in dealing with some of the colonists who were habitually discontented, and he did little to conceal his reaction to the endless bickering that passed for public discussion in colony meetings. He saw the colony in a larger setting, as a detail of the problems arising from the revolutionary increase in agricultural productivity, the redundancy of much of the rural population, and the lack of opportunity in industry for the surplus population on the farms. He recorded his belief that many of the colonists were simply incompetent to manage their affairs efficiently and that they were representative of a group ill-fitted either for a hustling urban industrial society or for commercial agriculture.

Behind the managers was the corporation itself, the source of funds and authority, resented and distrusted by the colonists in the manner of farmers of the past who had damned bankers, trusts, and railroads. Considering themselves grateful and loyal supporters of the New Deal, many of the colonists seemed often to think of the ARRC and its officers and directors as enemies of the whole colony project. (For the colonists' opposition to the ARRC and the management, see chapter 8, especially on the so-called Ice Worms). The nine men of the ARRC board were bankers, lawyers, businessmen, professional agriculturists, conservative by habit and temperament, yet placed in charge of a project often described in the anti-New Deal press as radical, socialistic, collectivist. Ironically, in trying to establish such a project in the manner planned by the FERA, the directors were accused by many of the colonists of being interested only in extending their own power and of being opposed to the basic concept of such a colony. The board, as it was reorganized in the fall of 1935 and as it remained until one death and two resignations altered it in 1939, consisted of Ernest Gruening, director of the Division of Territories and Island Possessions; Governor John W. Troy; Otto F. Ohlson, general manager of the Alaska Railroad; Luther C. Hess, Fairbanks lawyer, banker, investor in gold mines, who had come north in the stampede of 1898; Ross Sheely; William J. Bouwens, a colonist; A. H. McDonald, an official of the Alaska Steamship Company who had also come to Alaska by way of the Klondike in 1898; and P. C. McMullen and E. R. Tarwater, businessmen of Anchorage.

Although they attended several board meetings when their other duties allowed, neither Governor Troy in Juneau nor Gruening in Washington could be full-time directors. The most active and influential board members were Ohlson, Sheely, and Hess. Sheely had the experience of two periods as general manager and as an agricultural extension agent and farmer; Hess had no special knowledge of farming, but he was an old Alaskan and well known in the territory, and he took an active interest in the colony and in its financial affairs. However, it was Col. Otto F. Ohlson, manager of the railroad and president of the ARRC board, who was chief policy-shaper for the colony and frequently the target when colonists or others attacked the corporation. Already fifty-eight years old when he became the general manager of the Alaska Railroad in 1928, he served far beyond the standard retirement age of sixty-two. His direction of the railroad demanded a continuous balancing of Alaskan complaints and cries for better service against congressional penny-pinching, and probably no one at that time had greater combined knowledge of Alaskan conditions and the federal machinery in Washington. He was energetic, opinionated, quick-tempered, and little troubled by self-doubt, and he averted disaster for the Alaska Railroad and carried it through the 1930s. He remained general manager of the railroad and president of the board of the ARRC until 1945, through the period of the colony's development and through the great changes brought by World War II.[38]

The Alaska Railroad, from its completion until World War II, normally operated at a loss, and the management was caught between congressional demands for economy and Alaskan charges that the railroad was not fulfilling its purpose of stimulating settlement and development, that the freight rates choked growth, and that the failure to construct feeder roads blocked the exploitation of resources. Alaskans were further aroused when, following a recommendation of the Senate's Howell Committee, freight and passenger rates were raised in 1931 and, by authorization of Congress, the secretary of the interior in 1932 placed a nine dollar per ton toll on freight trucked on the Richardson Highway.[39] When Ohlson curtailed railroad operations during a maritime strike in 1936, the Anchorage Democratic Club demanded that Secretary Ickes remove him, and Delegate Anthony Dimond charged him with operating the railroad to squeeze out a profit regardless of Alaska's welfare.[40] In spite of his colonizing activity before 1935 and his part in bringing about the establishment of the Matanuska project, Ohlson was sometime accused of privately opposing the settlement of Alaska and of following policies as manager of the railroad and as president of the ARRC board of directors that would vindicate his belief in the eventual failure of the colony.[41]

In the first months after it assumed control of the colony, the reorganized ARRC had to deal with the problem of replacing the colonists who had left the project. The departures continued irregularly until at the end of the first year of the colony sixty families had gone; nineteen more left in the second year and sixteen in the third.[42] Had there been no replacements, the colony would have shrunk almost to disappearance and houses and barns would have stood empty. However, despite jibes in the press, the first withdrawals at least helped the colony management by reducing the time and the amount of construction necessary before it could announce that all the colonists were adequately housed and livestock sheltered. In the first months only the total withdrawals were reported; later, the managers' reports mentioned withdrawing colonists by name, sometimes with the supposed reason for withdrawal. Departures for poor health, injury, or once the death of a child in a fire were listed without further comment, and the remarks that a colonist was "undesirable" or "not fitted for pioneer conditions" are not very enlightening. Under Leo Jacobs, who of all managers most emphasized the social and cooperative goals of the colony, there was a note of stern disapproval of colonists who were "uncooperative" and had been unable to adjust to life in a close-knit rural community. By 1939 and 1940 the adjustment of the individual colonists' debts and the provisions of the realty purchase contract were the issues between colonists and management. Those who left or were expected to leave were described as unreliable, shiftless, careless about the debt on their farms, and they were contrasted with the industrious, diligent, reliable colonists who remained. One reason for departure, mentioned only once—the inability to adjust to a farmer's seasonally fluctuating income after habitually working for weekly wages[43]—probably applied to many others who left the colony, for it was repeatedly noted and deplored by the management that colonists eagerly sought any employment for wages while they neglected the development of their farms.

After early 1936, there were often fourteen or fifteen more houses and tracts available than colonists to fill them. By May, ten new colonists had been added from applicants already in Alaska. Some of them had apparently come to Alaska intending to homestead and had found the realities of a wilderness cabin less attractive than they had expected; others had past farming experience and saw in the colony an opportunity to return to agriculture. In mid-May, with Ernest Gruening for the first time present at a board meeting, Sheely reported that fifteen more vacancies could be filled, and the board voted to have Washington fill six of them and to retain nine to be appointed by the general manager and the board.[44] L. C. Hess thought that clearing and construction in the coming summer would allow the colony to return to its originally planned 200 colonists, but at no time after that did the colony population rise above 170 families, except as new arrivals briefly overlapped departures.

According to the common view, the original colonists, culled from relief rolls, were not real farmers and not seriously interested in becoming members of a farming community; they were not adaptable and not made of pioneer stuff.[45] The replacements for those who left the colony were chosen partly from people who were already in Alaska and were known to the management or were available for interview. When the first openings were offered to replacements, one tract was taken by the son of colonist Paul Onkka and two others by Charles E. Bisson and John Bourdon, both of whom had been in Alaska for several years. Bisson had once farmed in Idaho, and Bourdon and his wife had attempted to develop a wilderness farm in eastern Oregon.[46] Those who applied while they were still in the States were sometimes visited and interviewed by WPA officials and were required to submit forms giving farm experience, the record of other employment, a family history, and a list of references.[47] The replacements were required to have at least enough funds to get them from their home to Alaska, and to that extent need was no longer the test for admission to the colony. However, the new colonists took over tracts under the same conditions of credit and aid offered the original ones. The newcomers could be considered replacements only to about 1938. Then, and more clearly after a few years, new arrivals were judged good risks simply if they were competent farmers and financially responsible, and the ARRC's dealings with them were progressively less personal and supervisory and more obviously those of a land managing and money lending agency. In the summer of 1938 the general manager of the ARRC was authorized to fill vacant tracts by leasing them to qualified applicants who could renew the lease for another year, and after that sign a purchase contract, with payments under the lease applied to the price of the farm.[48] By the mid-war years a farm of 80 ot 160 acres could be leased from the ARRC for $25 to $35 a month; if the farm were bought at the end of the year, two-fifths of the lease payments were applied to the down payment. Such a farm, with 20 to 40 acres cleared, a barn, and a five- to seven-room house cost $4,500 to $6,000 with a 20 percent down payment. The interest rate was still 3 percent, far below the rate a farmer could get elsewhere in Alaska, but the payments were scheduled for ten to fifteen years rather than the thirty years allowed the early colonists.[49] In addition, by the mid-1940s an increasing portion of the new arrivals in the valley was negotiating farm purchases directly with the current occupants.

ARRC officials were eager to get good farmers as recruits for the colony, but they were compelled to accept those who were willing to come to Alaska and who had the money for the trip and for beginning their farming. Good farmers in the States were accustomed to large-scale machine operations, wary of land and settlement promotion schemes, and doubtful about the opportunities or markets for agriculture in Alaska, as the ARRC management learned in trying to find experienced farmers for the colony through several landholding insurance companies.[50]

After the first five or six years, and as the ARRC terms for new farmers were altered, the original distinctive character of the colony faded. The original colonists and the early replacements continued to give the community much of its color, but the corporation dealt with new arrivals as farmers, and relief and rehabilitation were rarely mentioned. No one talked, as Leo Jacobs had, of an experiment in establishing a cooperative rural community in which the modern conveniences of the city would be so joined with the joys of rural living and with so distinctive a community culture that the project would, with others like it, serve as a model and inspiration for redirecting American life. The term "colonist" no longer indicated a wardlike dependence on the corporation but became a convenient way of identifying the early arrivals. More and more the ARRC managers spoke of the men with whom they dealt simply as "farmers."

Those who believe that the replacement colonists were better farmers or generally more successful point to the more careful selection and to their lower rate of withdrawal from the colony. In 1948 an estimated 31 percent of all original colonists remained, while 43 percent of the replacements were still there.[51] Because such comments are made on the assumption that from the start the aim of the colony was to find settlers to develop Alaska, they overlook the original objectives of relief and rehabilitation, the primary consideration given to an applicant's need, and the stagnation of the region from which colonists were taken. The replacement colonists who came in the late 1930s and early 1940s took up tracts that were already well advanced toward being real farms. They entered an established community with an expanding available market, and by that time the boom in military construction in the Anchorage area was providing off-farm work at good wages.

Measuring success or failure by the rate at which either original colonists or replacements remained in the colony does not take into account the fact that for many colonists success meant an opportunity to get out of farming. Like the cities in the States, the smaller cities of Alaska drew recruits from the rural population. Even the colonists who were regarded as misfits by the management often failed only in being less than wholly devoted to cultivating the land. One colonist who was indifferent to farming had succeeded well enough in commercial fishing to keep a hired hand to operate his farm. Another lamented his poverty and the deprivation suffered by his children, but he was a skilled mechanic employed by the Fairbanks Exploration Company in the mines and had installed a generator to electrify his farm before the other colonists had such improvements.[52] A replacement colonist from Arkansas withdrew from the colony after a year and moved to Wasilla to teach in the territorial school. After three years in the colony, one of the original colonists moved to Anchorage, where he had already begun to develop his own carpentry and construction business. Still another, convinced that his farm debt was too high, moved to Anchorage, acquired several parcels of land, profited by the rise in land prices during the war boom, and in later years spent his summers at his home on the Kenai Peninsula and wintered in Florida. One family of three withdrew from the colony, bought a house in Anchorage, and found three civilian jobs at Fort Richardson at several times the family income that the farm could conceivably promise. Even those who remained in the colony frequently had as the chief source of income some nonfarm employment—mining, construction, trucking, and the like.[53] One of the most successful colonists was from the start a man of many occupations to whom farming was of only incidental interest. Walter Huntley was appointed U.S. Commissioner for Palmer in 1935, and he was among those who were fairly regularly employed by the ARRC, enjoying an advantage over others without that cash income. He became president of the board of directors of the cooperative association, was selected as an outstanding colonist in 1938 and appeared in New York on a national radio broadcast, served in the territorial legislature in 1945 and 1946, incorporated with others to build and operate a hotel at Palmer, and operated a garage and service station and an automobile and trailer sales agency.[54]

By the 1950s, increasing age would account for much of the reduction in the number of original colonists, but a survey made for the Colony Day of 1953 showed 130 original colonist husbands and wives (some by then widowed) still in the valley. They listed themselves as housewife, farmer, laborer, carpenter, retail clerk, store manager, cafe operator, contractor, trucker, bartender, telephone operator, among other occupations.[55] There were 25 farmers, and if 25 of the 47 housewives were married to those farmers, then 40 out of 65 successful colonist families had found occupations other than farming even though they continued to live in a farming area.

While the colony management struggled with the problems of finance and of maintaining a suitable number of colonists in the project, it was faced also with confusion in the control of public land in the project reserve. Apparently no one connected with planning the colony had anticipated such a difficulty. In the planning stage, Executive Order 6957, 4 February 1935, closed to entry the public land in eleven townships; after the arrival of the staff, construction workers, and most of the colonists, Executive Order 7047 of May 20 opened the area to settlement, and several later orders reserved for the colony some wild hay land along Knik Arm.

These orders did not solve the colony's land problem. The ARRC did not hold title to the public land in the colony area, and it appeared that with the withdrawal of the closure order anyone, colonist or not, could make homestead or other entry. Further, the original 208 tracts had been selected and surveyed largely on purchased land, but some of them were on public land, including parts of sections 16 and 36 in several townships, sections which had been reserved since 1915 for the support of the schools of the territory. The corporation would eventually be able to convey to successful colonists the land that it held, but it could not control public land within the reserve unless it first acquired title. By the spring of 1936, the ARRC was concerned about the land problem and expected congressional action to give the corporation title.[56] Sheely and the board of the ARRC were disturbed by the possibility that colonists might gain patent to the land by virtue of improvements on it that had been made at ARRC expense, and Sheely wired Westbrook, requesting that a proposed order allowing colonist homestead entry not be issued. Westbrook assured Sheely that there was nothing for the ARRC to fear in such homesteading. The FERA's legal staff had found precedents for a homesteader's mortgaging improvements on his claim or even his interest in the land itself, and, since the colonists had signed the project settlement agreement acknowledging an obligation to repay the cost of developing their tracts, the corporation would have a hold on the improvements on such homesteaded tracts and the land itself should the colonists fail to make proper payments.[57]

By Executive Order 7416, 17 July 1936, the orders of February and May 1935 were revoked or modified to reclose most of the colony reserve and to permit homestead entry in parts of ten sections of two townships where colonists were already located. In spite of Westbrook's assurances and explanations by the FERA's counsel, H. M. Colvin, the colony management remained uneasy, but in August thirty-two colonists made homestead entries on their tracts after signing contracts acknowledging the ARRC's claim to buildings and improvements on the land.[58]

Difficulties did arise from the homesteading policy. The corporation could protect its claims, although at some cost in wrangling and legal services, but the aim of developing a farming community was threatened by the fact that a colonist could obtain patent to his tract, using improvements made by the ARRC, and let the land lie idle while using the farm as a rural residence and supporting himself by nonfarm work.[59] When an ARRC debt statement was sent to J. R. Sieber, a colonist on homesteaded land, it was returned marked "Address Unknown—Gone Outside." Sieber had already satisfied the residence requirement on his land, and his patent was pending.[60]

The colony tracts on school lands, sections 16 and 36, were still a problem. Charles G. Elliott joined the colony in 1935 and settled on Tract 200, a school-land tract. In 1937 he refused to sign both a statement of his adjusted colony debt and a realty purchase contract, and although he declared his withdrawal from the colony, he refused to leave the tract. The ARRC after nearly a year of fretting about this "noncolonist" squatting on land improved by the corporation, but to which neither it nor the squatter had legal claim, finally obtained from the territory a ten-year lease on the quarter section where Elliott's 80-acre tract was located, served an eviction notice, and had another colonist ready to occupy the tract, assume the debt, and make a homestead entry that would become valid if congressional action released that and other school lands from reservation.[61]

Finally, more than five years after colonization, Congress provided that sections 16 and 36 of townships 17 and 18, ranges one and two east, Seward meridian, should be released from reservation as Alaska territorial school lands and that the territory should select in lieu of those lands an equal area of vacant, nonmineral, surveyed, and unreserved public land. By the same act, the secretary of the interior was authorized to sell at not less than $1.25 an acre the land in released school sections and other public land in the colony area.[62] In 1946 the ARRC bought slightly more than five thousand acres of the land, taking parcels scattered in the settled colony area to have land available for the expansion of some farms and to gain control of onetime school land or other public land within the settlement.[63] Beginning in 1943, the Department of the Interior offered the public land in the colony reserve for sale to settlers approved by the ARRC as persons who intended to farm and were capable of developing farms. Such land, uncleared and unimproved, cost $1.25 to $5.00 an acre.[64] There remained a few colony tracts for which homestead entries had been made on school lands, even though there had been no legal basis for such entry. That was corrected in 1942 when Congress validated those entries, if regulations were met, and authorized the territory to make selections of other land.[65]

From the spring of 1945, by a series of land orders,[66] the remaining public land suitable for agriculture in the original colony reserve of eleven townships was gradually opened to settlers who would not be colonists and who would have little connection with the ARRC except as possible borrowers or renters of ARRC land-clearing equipment. By the middle or late 1950s, new farmers, or those who were expanding, could buy land from precolony settlers, from colonists, from ARRC holdings of colony land or unoccupied colony farms, or from the land office if they had ARRC recommendation. If none of these methods was attractive, the settler could homestead a quarter section or obtain a small tract of five acres.[67] In the onetime reserve there was enough land to enlarge colony farms and to double or treble the number of all farms in the valley. A network of surfaced or graveled roads connected most points in the valley, and few new farms would need to be more than ten miles from the railroad. The cooperative association provided marketing facilities, the market had grown with the increase in both military and civilian population, the discomforts and inconveniences of the earlier period were past, and much of the valley had the appearance of a stable farming area.

Yet the critics of federal land policy and of the colony did not believe that enough progress had been made. According to them, agricultural development in Alaska generally had been hampered by the restrictions of the land laws and by its confinement to the "inadequate" homestead quarter section; in the colony the 40-acre tracts had been far too small, the colonists had been guided toward a peasant-like, semisubsistence farming rather than toward real commercial agriculture, the little farms were huddled too tightly to allow expansion—much closer together than the farms in the states from which the colonists had come—and the planners and managers of the colony had not made provision for the dairying that became the leading type of agriculture in the area.[68]

However, in 1935 and for some years after, there was little evidence that land restrictions had limited agricultural growth or that colony planning and management had been seriously out of touch with Alaskan realities, except, perhaps, in at first relying too heavily on the colonists' devotion to farming and rural life. In the 1930s very few Alaskan farms were fully enough developed to make the 160-acre homestead cramping, the average small colony tract was little more than half cleared even in 1941, and the tracts had been rather closely grouped in part to avoid the social costs and the costs of public services found in areas of isolated settlement in the northern lake states. In trying to develop the colony, the managers had to compete with attractions that lured the colonists from agriculture. Like other Americans, the colonists made their ceremonial bows to farming, but they no longer looked upon the family farm as the ideal of security and independence. However fond they were of rural residences, they found employment for cash almost irresistible, and the wartime boom that brightened the colony's prospects by enlarging the market for its products also provided well-paid jobs that made farming less attractive.

7

Paternalism and Pioneers

In the press and among politicians and boosters of the Alaskan frontier it was a commonplace that the Matanuska project had been too costly, that essential pioneer qualities had been lacking among the colonists or had been stifled and weakened by paternalistic coddling. With no sense of contradiction, it was also said that frontier independence and individualism had been offended and made rebellious by bureaucratic controls, by the plans and regulations, and by the steps in building the colony that had been taken for the colonists rather than through them. Yet it was also claimed that much that should have been accomplished early for the welfare of the colony remained undone when the colonists arrived—land clearing, construction of the community center, much of the work of house building, detailed soil analyses of each tract, weather studies and analyses of local variations, a water reconnaissance for each tract, studies of timber and grazing resources and of markets for the colony's products, an examination of employment opportunities and labor conditions, a farm management plan, and an investigation of past occupation of the region by Indians and the Russians and of settlement in such areas as the Peace River country of Canada.[1]

In reality, the information necessary for successful settlement and farming in the valley was available; the planners had the advice of men familiar with Alaska; the settlement was in one of the two or three areas best suited by climate, soils, and markets for agricultural development, and, since the object was to remove some stranded rural families from relief and to rehabilitate them, the original preparations were rather modest. The new pioneers were expected to do some pioneering.

The news stories and editorials about new pioneers taming the Alaskan wilderness, proving the persistence of pioneer virtues and demonstrating that a twentieth-century frontier offered opportunity, could be written almost without thought by a quick skimming of the stereotyped ideas ready at hand to a newspaperman. But there was a widespread popular interest in the back-to-the-land movement and a sentimental attachment to the idea of a common frontier past, which Americans could now watch as it was relived. When the bickering among the colonists and their complaints about conditions were made public, the spectator's pleasure in the re-creation of the frontier experience was destroyed, and the reaction was as marked as the original enthusiasm. The modern pioneers demanded all conveniences at once, expected security and help, and wanted more tractors and few axes.

Even twenty-five years or more after the settling of the colony, it is difficult not to feel some of the disappointment in the project. The colonists seemed to find little difficulty in throwing off the discipline and habit of work; most of them showed distressing willingness to accept more aid, and in their social gatherings and in the meetings of their community organization they haggled over the distribution of benefits and kept fresh the complaints that no concessions by the management could ever quite silence. However, the troubles in the colony cannot be explained simply as a result of flawed planning, ineffective management, or weaknesses in the character of the colonists. Rather, the too enthusiastic publicity at first given the colony made it vulnerable to later adverse reports and to political attacks after a few colonists complained and were at once given nationwide attention. The management could bravely survive the first withdrawals of colonist families, describing them as the unfit, the troublemakers, but as the cost of the colony was increased by the efforts to hurry construction, it became obvious that the investment had to be protected. To allow the project to collapse was politically unthinkable. With about 170 houses built and the community center developed, the colony had to be kept going in some way with a reasonable number of colonists, old or new. Thus, almost from the beginning, aid was granted beyond the original plans for the project, while many of the colonists bitterly complained that conditions in the colony did not measure up to what had been promised them.

If the colony was to succeed, it had to be by agriculture, and even in the long run wage or salaried employment in the community would depend on an agricultural base. Land had to be cleared and made ready for cultivation, but that was slow work, and in the first summer and later many colonists complained that the management had failed to fulfill a promise to provide each of them with twelve cleared acres. At the time the FERA and the colony management gave no credit to the supposed promise, and in the first winter Ross Sheely tried to push the colonists in the work of preliminary clearing and improvement of their tracts. In January 1936 he announced that each colonist would be required to have at least ten acres slashed by the first of May to be ready for mechanized stump pulling and clearing. He also issued an order that all colonists were to clean the areas around their houses within a few days, although he knew that his efforts might lose the project some of its members. Neither order was effective, for no real coercion could be applied.[2] At the same time, the system of family credit allowances was altered to simplify bookkeeping and to facilitate direct transactions among colonists by the introduction of brass and aluminum tokens called bingles. The bingles could supposedly be used only by colonists at the trading post, but within a few days a Palmer taxi driver was offering to accept them.[3]

It was expected that while book credit or bingles supported them, and while their debts rose, the colonists would do the slashing—cutting the brush, felling and limbing trees, windrowing the debris—preliminary to stumping, breaking, and plowing. But the work did not proceed as quickly as it should have. In the spring the manager reported that completed land clearing averaged about 25 or 30 acres a week for the whole colony, and in June the total cleared area, in addition to the ARRC's 175 acres in and around the community center and the small clearings that had been on privately owned land at the start of the project, was about 225 acres. More land was cleared that summer, too late for that year's crops, and by the end of September 635 acres had been cleared since the start of the colony. However, much of that land was apparently not fully ready for cultivation. A 1940 survey of all clearing and improvement programs showed only 275 acres made ready for cultivation by January 1937.[4]

Some livestock had been brought to the colony in the first summer, and more dairy cattle, horses, sheep, and chickens were distributed among the colonists in 1936. But much of the stock feed had to be imported; the families used most of their own milk and eggs and had little left for sale. In the late summer and fall of 1936 some colonists were reported "on their own" or "off the bingle system." They had notified the corporation that they would no longer draw the monthly family allowance in bingles and would pay cash at the trading post. However, although they may have been independent for their daily subsistence, they still had ARRC credit for seed, livestock, feed, and equipment, and their day-to-day independence resulted largely from cash employment, not income from farming.[5] The employment of colonists by the ARRC caused endless difficulties. Those who were not given work charged that the employees were the beneficiaries of the corporation's favoritism, and the jobholders usually made little progress in clearing and developing their tracts. The crawling progress of the clearing program troubled the management, and there were repeated warnings to the colonists that in time they would have to depend on the land for their support.

The hard work of slashing and clearing could be done much more rapidly than the colonists did it, and it could produce some gain from the wood used as fuel or sold for firewood or mine timbers. In the fall and winter season, noncolonists clearing for themselves or under contract to others spent forty-eight man-hours per acre on lightly timbered and brush land to fell trees, limb them, and stack the brush. On more heavily timbered land ninety-six hours were spent in the same operations and in burning the brush and cutting the logs into sixteen-foot lengths. In addition, five days, or forty man-hours, and one day with a tractor were required to remove the logs from one acre. If cut for firewood, that amounted to about twenty-eight cords.[6] In 1936 and 1937, as clearing dragged along, the value of the wood products should have encouraged the colonists to make greater efforts. In 1937 they sold mine props worth a total of $7,000 and an undetermined quantity of firewood. By 1941 the new population in booming Anchorage was living mostly in hurriedly built little houses, and the price of firewood was $20 or more a cord. Even at a much lower price, the cordwood from a well-timbered acre should have paid the cost of clearing—the colonist's wages at the going rate and the rent for a tractor—and each cleared acre added to the value of the tract.

By the end of 1936 progress under the bingle system was obviously too slow. Leo Jacobs, the assistant manager, issued a bulletin to the colonists contrasting stagnation at Matanuska with the progress made at the FERA Dyess Colony in Arkansas.[7] Anton Anderson, the ARRC man in charge of clearing, had already suggested to Sheely a plan for making advances to colonists based on family size and the work done in slashing, burning, windrowing, fencing, plowing, and general development. The so-called work credit program was intended to provide the colonists with subsistence incomes while speeding progress toward self-support through agriculture. The plan was a more elaborate version of the proposals made in 1934 by M. D. Snodgrass and O. F. Ohlson for a revolving fund from which settlers would be given payments at each of three stages of farm development, thus making reliance on nonfarm work for support unnecessary. Under Anderson's plan, as under the older one, each payment to a colonist would be charged against his farm; the value of his tract, or his real estate debt, would be increased as he received payments, and in thirty years the whole debt would be paid.[8]

However, the work credit program and its later variations did not work as smoothly as had been expected, and repayment of the advances to colonists eventually disappeared in a general debt reduction. By January 1937 Sheely had the ARRC board's approval, and he informed Westbrook of the plan and of the end of the system of subsidy by bingles.[9] The colony was divided into districts, and Anderson's men assessed the improvements already made on each tract and estimated the work still to be done and the payments that would be made. The plan began by stages in late January and early February, but by April it was clear that many of the colonists had seen in the new arrangement an opportunity for businesslike enterprise. Rather than working themselves, they hired others or contracted with noncolonists and pocketed the difference between that cost and the allowance under the work credit system—although some of them had complained that the allowance was too small.[10] In the first full month of the plan, $12,996.50 was paid for clearing alone. Some of it went to colonists who did clearing for others in the colony, but $5,362.01, about 40 percent of the payments, went out of the project to noncolonists hired to do clearing.[11] Sheely addressed a letter to each colonist urging compliance with the intention of the program, and early in June it was announced that no more advances would be made for payment of outside help.[12] However, the drain continued; by August the program was costing more than $20,000 a month, about 41 percent of the payments were going to outside labor, and, because no limit had been set, some families at times received surprisingly large cash incomes. In June one family got $442.60 from the work credit plan, $110 in ARRC wages, and $52 from the sale of cream and eggs, a total of $604.60. Another got $718.89—$389 from work credit and $329.89 from wages and sale of milk and produce. Five other families received more than $500 a month and fifteen drew from $200 to $300. Some of the income was from the sale of milk, cream, and eggs from cattle and poultry they fed on ARRC credit, and a large but undetermined part of their bonanza incomes went to pay for the labor they hired to do their work. There was little evidence that the families receiving the highest incomes were approaching self-sufficiency from their farms.[13]

By mid-October the old system was discontinued and a "security and development" program was begun. Payment for most work other than land clearing was eliminated, the amount of clearing on each tract necessary to bring it to fifteen tillable acres was estimated, and a limit, varying with family size, was placed on monthly payments. A surplus of work in one month was credited toward full payment in months when the normal work could not be done.[14] The payment for slashing was about the same as under the old system, from $30 to $50 an acre depending on the operations performed.

When the last work under the old system was finished on 9 October 1937, the colony had 1,742 acres ready for cultivation and another 973 slashed and ready for stumping. About 940 acres of tillable land had been added under the system and 801 acres slashed. The average colony farm had 10 acres ready for cultivation and another 6 acres partly cleared. For that work of clearing and for other improvements, the ARRC had paid out in about eight months slightly more than $170,000.[15]

In spite of all that was done to make farm development attractive, most colonists steadily yearned for any regular cash employment in preference to farming or paid land clearing. As the ARRC reduced its force of outside workers, and as colonists and their wives edged into full- or part-time work in the community center, the management recognized that the employed colonists did little to develop their farms and aroused the envy of those who had not found jobs. However, the job-hungry colonists had an ally in Colonel Westbrook, who was perhaps influenced by the well-publicized trip to Washington by the most heavily indebted colonist, who claimed that the ARRC mistreated him and refused to hire him for work in the power plant despite his qualifications. (On that colonist, Charles E. Ruddell, see chapter 8.) Westbrook instructed the colony management to train colonists for all the jobs of the community center and to hire them as rapidly as possible in place of noncolonist workers. Sheely, Ohlson, and the board members resisted, believing that such a policy would substitute the half-trained for the skilled, turn many colonists from farming, and cause dissension. The only virtue of the policy was that it would provide work relief in place of some of the other aids to the colonists and would thus spread ARRC funds over a longer period. The ARRC board first voted to reject Westbrook's instructions, then yielded[16] and, as it reduced its total work force, hired a larger proportion of colonists and their families. Old settlers in the valley, who had already been declared eligible for ARRC loans, now asked for jobs also. In the spring of 1937 an old settler and ARRC borrower representing the local grange appeared before the ARRC board of directors to urge that the settlers be considered for jobs on an equal basis with colonists.[17] By 1 January 1938 the ARRC had seventy-five employees, fifty-five of them colonists or members of their families, and about twenty other colonists were regularly employed away from their farms.[18] Seasonally the ARRC added tractor and bulldozer operators for land clearing, and more than 70 percent of those jobs and the regular ones were held by colonists and old settlers and their families.

Leo Jacobs managed to be cheerful about what he could not avoid and reported to the ARRC board of directors that the employment of colonists was beneficial in teaching them new skills, increasing their security, and enabling them to meet their obligations, but he added that repeated warnings were necessary to keep the colonists from abandoning farming entirely and that land clearing and farm development were lagging.[19] The corporation gained no popularity by the policy; only if it could have hired everyone would the grumbling have ceased. The management was accused of favoritism, and the colonists who were not employed regarded the ARRC workers as toadies of the ARRC. After late 1939, as the corporation by stages turned the facilities of the community center over to the cooperative association, its own staff shrank to a few clerical workers and the manager, and the Matanuska Valley Farmers Cooperating Association took on the thankless task of keeping job-hungry colonists happy by fitting them into the trading post, garage, power plant, creamery, hatchery, and elsewhere.

In the meantime the ARRC's expenses continued, the development of farming was frustratingly slow, and land clearing almost halted. Colonists cleared little more than the security and development program subsidized or even limited their efforts in order to save uncleared land for the higher rates they expected. In October 1938, with the harvest over and winter not yet limiting outdoor activity, only 12.12 acres were cleared—8.5 by the ARRC's bulldozers and 3.62 acres by more than 150 colonists on more than 150 farms.[20]

The colonists were living rather well; many of them made the planners' ideal of frugality and careful husbandry seem remote. Paying no rent, no interest, and nothing on the principal of their debts and with their milk and eggs, vegetables, and potatoes available from their farms for a little effort, they were accumulating debts beyond those for real estate and chattels at a rate of $2,500 to $3,000 a year. Some debt was for items such as livestock feed; however, that was balanced by dairy products, poultry, and eggs consumed or sold. If sold, the proceeds could be applied to the feed debt. Some colonists pocketed the money from sales and went on charging feed. Disregarding the real estate and chattel debt, the small incomes from sale of timber products, and the consumption of food from their own production, they were spending in credit purchases and from wages and farm development subsidies several times the average American farm family income and more than that of the average nonfarm family.[21]

Although they were generally living more comfortably than they had been before joining the project, many of the colonists were discontented; they grumbled that they were mistreated by the ARRC and the colony management, that certain vaguely specified promises had not been kept, and that they were hampered by restrictions and red tape.[22] All this was perhaps related to their nagging awareness of the burden of debt, but the Matanuska colonists were like project members elsewhere. A study of subsistence homesteads after seven or eight years concluded that improvement in the homesteaders' level of living failed to quiet discontent because a corresponding rise in the standard of living—that is, their expectations—left the gap between actuality and desires unchanged. In these other settlements, indebtedness seemed little related to discontent; the claims of mistreatment and broken promises were sometimes evidence of real clashes and grievances, but they seemed also the result of the settlers' attempts to find a convenient person on whom to throw responsibility for difficulties that were of the settlers' own making or were beyond human control—the weather, perhaps.[23]

But unlike some other sources of complaint, debt was real and definite. The average had quickly risen above the modest $3,500 often mentioned at the start of the colony; the individual debts were used by newspapermen and politicians in attacking the colony, and it had been clear for some time that the debts were larger than a colony farm could repay—even if the colonists finally did make their farms fully productive. In addition, the large debts contracted in the early months were at least in part attributable to haste, fumbling, ineffectively employed labor, and confusion in record-keeping.

In April 1937 an ARRC survey showed the combined debts of the 164 families in the colony to be $1,589,899.06 as of January 31, a family average of $9,694.50.(The debt survey is included in appendix 1.) At a special meeting the ARRC board voted to lower the debts by eliminating some items and reducing other charges.[24] Dental, medical, and hospital charges, well drilling costs over $25, livestock feed up to $250, the cost of the first purchases of clothing, and the subsistence and clothing bills that were within the recommended family budgets between 1 June 1935 and 31 January 1937 were all canceled. The cost of building materials for houses and farm buildings was reduced by $500, allowances were made for work done by colonists on their own houses and land, and, after these reductions, debts were to be further reduced to bring them to an $8,000 maximum. By this system the total colonist debt would have been lowered by more than $500,000 and the average individual debt reduced by more than $3,000. However, the reduction was not made at once, and nearly a year later the debts were cut even more sharply under an altered plan.

The debt reduction hung fire from spring until mid-November 1937, while H. M. Colvin, special counsel for the WPA, was in the colony studying the related problems of colonists' debts, their estimated ability to pay, their cooperative association, and their arrangements for self-government. The last two matters seemed least troublesome and were dealt with first. From the period of planning, there had been references to a cooperative system for the colony, but there had been little that could be cooperatively managed. A consumers' cooperative was meaningless as long as the colonists drew subsistence goods from the commissary on credit or made purchases with bingles issued to them and charged to their accounts, and no marketing cooperative was necessary until there was something to sell. In the first summer the colonists produced little, even for their own use, and in 1936 there was no great change. Some colonists individually marketed milk, eggs, poultry, and vegetables even though there was an informally organized marketing association supposedly ready to sell the colonists' goods. In October 1936 the Matanuska Valley Farmers [*sic*] Cooperative Association (MVFCA) filed its articles of incorporation, and the following May the articles and bylaws were amended and the name changed to the Matanuska Valley Farmers Cooperating Association to comply with territorial law limiting "cooperative" to marketing associations only.[25]

By Colvin's arrangements, a profit-sharing system was begun, including colonists and old settlers who signed a marketing agreement and subscribed to one share of stock at five dollars. However, there would be small profits to share; most sales to consumers were still on credit and added to their accumulating debt. By another agreement, the MVFCA, which owned nothing and did not have the storage, processing, and marketing facilities necessary for it to perform its functions for its members, was to be managed by the ARRC, which did own those facilities.[26]

In the same period the colony's system of self-government was revived and reorganized. The original colony council and the system of representatives from ten camps had withered as the colonists scattered to their separate tracts. Early in 1937 the council was restored to life, new members were elected in May, and on 8 November 1937 the Matanuska Valley Civic Association (MVCA) adopted the constitution drawn up by Colvin.[27] Although the meeting was called a constitutional convention, it simply ratified a constitution that closely followed those used in several other colonies. Colvin spoke of the civic association as the colony's means of self-government and its instrument of communication with the management. He praised the sincerity and dedication of the members of the council and was in turn applauded, thanked, and invited to remain in the colony. Whether the MVCA could be effective was doubtful. It owned no property, it could not tax or spend, and it was without means of enforcing its will, if that will could be determined. All property, and the power it conferred, was in the hands of the ARRC; the federal and territorial governments were represented by a marshal, a commissioner, and the teachers and employees of several bureaus. Palmer had no official independent existence; it had not been incorporated, and no independent school district had been organized. The association would be limited to voicing grievances against the ARRC and to passing resolutions for changes in policy, an increase in the rate of payment for slashing, for example, without regard for the obligations or financial position of the corporation.

However, federal officials apparently felt that the association and its council would be useful in moderating outside criticism and could be manipulated for public relations.[28] In September 1937 the council sent a long telegram to President Roosevelt inviting him to extend his western tour to the valley to see what was being accomplished and thus to be reaffirmed in his faith in Alaska, the colony, and the colonists. The telegram was released to the press, and Colvin sent a copy to Westbrook, with this note:

> This is in answer to criticisms that the Colonists are failures. *I was glad to help the Council in the wording of the wire.* . . . The invitation definitely records the attitude and spirit of the Colonists, as it has been carried by the Associated Press and, to some extent, will offset the unfounded criticisms that appeared in the September 13 issue of *Time* and that appeared in other publications.[29]

While he was busy with the still rudimentary cooperative and civic association, Colvin was considering also the level of colonists' debts, their eventual ability to pay, and the proposed reduction. The high debt level raised the question of what costs had been anticipated at the start and what promises or "inducements" had been made by the state relief workers who had recruited for the colony. In June, Colvin informed Westbrook that there was a basis for the colonists' charges of promises made and unkept.[30] His evidence was a memorandum from FERA to the Division of Social Services of the Minnesota Emergency Relief Administration in which the discussions of the Matanuska Project at the 13 March 1935 conference of social workers in Washington were used to describe the colony, to give an estimate of the cost to each colonist, to list the costs of the whole undertaking, and to show the total cost of the colony, including the community facilities. (See appendix 1 for Colvin's letter to Westbrook and the memorandum as he copied it.)

The confusion and inconsistencies in the memorandum suggest that although it came from one person it had been hastily pulled together from several sources and then sent without being checked for accuracy. The two promises supposedly made and not kept were that the cost to the colonists would be low, "not over $3,500.00 and, undoubtedly, considerably less," and that each colonist would have twelve acres of land cleared for him free of charge. Colvin told Colonel Westbrook that the same memorandum had been sent to social workers in Michigan and Wisconsin and that colonists from all three states had agreed, when he questioned them, that low cost and free clearing had been promised. Yet, when Ross Sheely, shortly after he became manager, had asked Colonel Westbrook what should be done about the supposedly promised clearing of twelve acres, Westbrook had denied almost angrily that the FERA had made such a promise, but he added that if any officer of the ARRC had done so it should be carried out and the officer appropriately disciplined.[31]

Nowhere in the memorandum was there a reference to "free" clearing, although the analysis of costs is headed, "Estimated Cost Under Plan of Using 400 Transients as Work Relief Project, Clearing 12 Acres The First Year, The Balance to Be Cleared by the Home Unit Owners at Rate of Five Acres per Year." Elsewhere, obscure, imprecise language, typographical errors, and mistakes in arithmetic gave plentiful opportunities for misunderstanding, and, as the contents of the memorandum was received by the colonists from the social workers, there probably were a distortion and an unwarranted emphasis on the low cost and cleared land. However, the cost obviously depended on the effectiveness of colonist and transient labor. The plan optimistically overestimated the speed of construction and clearing, minimized the difficulty of establishing two hundred farms, and assumed hard work, frugality, and, by the second year, self-support for the colonists from their land, at least for food. The cleared land seemed "free" because it was balanced by cheap transient labor and colonist labor paid only in subsistence:

The first year's subsistence is to be taken care of by the Corporation as the individuals are working for them. As individuals they are getting a certain amount of land cleared and buildings constructed. All the property is listed under RRC until the loan is entirely liquidated. The second year enough food should be raised to make them self-supporting and after the fourth year the individuals begin paying on their property.

The great difference between the very modest individual debts mentioned in advance and the much heavier debts two years later could be attributed in part to unrealistic and hazy planning, uncertain management, and the inefficiency of the transient labor. But it was also in part the result of a sharp change in the colonists' habits of consumption and the consistent reluctance of a majority of them to lift an ax or shovel without first being assured that their labor would be rewarded in cash rather than in the long-run improvement of their farms.

If the colonists' debts were to be lowered, some justification had to be found, and it was useful to mention the inducements of low cost and free clearing, especially since the lack of cleared land in the first year had delayed self-support. The level of debt had become impossible; an arbitrary partial cancellation would be criticized as another example of character-destroying pampering, but no colony farm could support a debt of $12,000,[32] and even at a lower debt level self-support by farming was years ahead for most colonists. It was politically unthinkable to abandon the colony and yet impossible to continue indefinitely with the colonists discontented, their debts large and growing, and their claims to their farms undefined. The colonists had to be satisfied and their status made clear.

A special committee—Colvin, Jacobs, and Sheely—calculated that an average colonist giving normal management to a typical colony farm could carry and eventually liquidate a debt of $5,000. In the fall and winter of 1937–38, the committee began with the debt reduction already authorized by the ARRC, reviewed accounts, made further reductions, and then applied a further blanket reduction of 20 percent to reduce all debts to approximately the $5,000 average. By the spring of 1938 all colonists but three who soon left had signed a "Satisfaction Agreement."[33]

In computing individual indebtedness, the twelve acres supposedly to be cleared free became fifteen, probably because windrows and stump piles would reduce fifteen acres to a tillable twelve. The contract of sale for each farm showed fifteen acres cleared, whether or not that had already been done. Nowhere was it explicitly stated that the clearing was to be free of charge, but that was the effect. The cost of final tractor clearing, charged against the farm, was put at $36 an acre, but that was more than offset by the allowance in the debt reduction for colonists' labor already performed and by continuing payments under several development programs for preliminary clearing work. The ARRC was obligated to use its tractors to bring each farm to the fifteen-acre level—Leo Jacobs estimated that tractor work would have to be done on 1,100 acres[34]—and each colonist would be paid for slashing at a rate higher than the charge for tractors.

There was some grumbling about the debt reduction because it seemed to reward the spendthrifts and to give less to those who had never enjoyed the pleasures of easy spending. A colonist with a total debt of $12,000 or more would have it reduced to near the $5,000 level. At the same time a thrifty colonist with a realty debt of $5,310.31 for forty acres with fifteen cleared, a house, well house, barn, two poultry houses, brooder house, and root cellar, had it reduced by about $1,600 to $3,700. His debt for subsistence, seed, equipment, and feed was also scaled down, but the total reduction was proportionately far less than that of his free-spending neighbor.[35]

However, the greatest cause of dissatisfaction among the colonists was the realty contract.[36] While the debts were being adjusted, H. M. Colvin prepared a conditional land sales contract and a chattel mortgage form to secure the newly computed indebtedness. (The realty sales contract is given in appendix 2.) Although Colvin produced the contract, his unacknowledged joint authors were the many anonymous designers of the goals of rural resettlement, rehabilitation, and community building. The agreement was unlike anything the colonists had been prepared by experience to understand and unlike any contract a lawyer would ordinarily encounter.[37]

The unconventional preamble to the contract set forth the social goals of the colony—the rehabilitation of "worthy and well qualified persons and their families" in a "cooperative rural community"—and made membership in the MVFCA a condition of membership in the colony. The body of the contract unobjectionably gave the usual property description, the conditions for payment, and provisions for adequate care, payment of taxes, and maintenance of insurance. However, it then repeated the provision for MVFCA membership and required that the colonist use his tract as his family's farm and home, follow good farm management practices under the direction and guidance of the corporation, and not establish any mercantile or other business enterprise on the tract. Describing the "public trust and purpose" for which federal funds had been spent and which was a condition impressed upon the land and running with it in the hands of all future holders, the contract gave the ARRC first option to buy a colony farm if it were being offered to a purchaser the corporation did not approve and the power to evict a colonist for violation of the contract.

There was some advantage to the colonist in the provision for an impartial board of appraisers should the ARRC exercise its option to buy and should the corporation and the colonist fail to agree on a fair value. If the colonist were evicted for violation of the contract, the ARRC was required to pay to him within sixty days whatever payment would be required in exercise of its option to buy. On the other hand, the contract extracted the colonist's promise that he would not acquire the property for resale or speculation and that he and his family would live harmoniously with other members of the community and with the cooperative and the corporation. How that harmony was to be measured was not said. To carry out its duty of supervision, the corporation was to have the right of entry to the property for inspection. Most objectionable of all, the final section of the contract provided that after payment had been completed the corporation should give the colonist a deed reciting Section VII of the contract, which described the public trust and purpose impressed upon and running with the land and improvements, and which provided for reversion of title to the corporation if at any time the public trust and purpose were violated.

As the colonists saw it then, or as it might appear to a lawyer or an outsider, the contract seemed to make the colonist, his family, and his heirs wards of the corporation. Presented as it was three years after the beginning of the project, the colonists, many of them entering middle age, had little choice but reluctantly to accept it or to depart from the colony for an uncertain new start elsewhere. The slovenly errors in details of composition (e.g., *altar* for alter; *personality* for personalty) would not inspire confidence; its language did not follow usages conventional among lawyers and raised questions of intentions and effect; and it was pointlessly verbose.

In defense of the contract, it might be said that it was well intended.

Its peculiarities were largely the result of an attempt to insert sermons on rural social reform in an approximation of the form and language of a legal document. Even those who drew up the contract probably recognized that some parts of it were admonitions rather than clear provisions reliably enforceable in the courts. No colonist was pushed from the colony for simple failure to live harmoniously in the cooperative rural community. The first of those evicted had refused either to sign the contract or to join the cooperative, and the others were in default on their debts and unwilling to make token payments or to give assurances of future cooperation.

New Dealers who were connected with land and resource management or rural resettlement often deplored the old pattern of undirected and individualistic land settlement that had benefited speculators and promoters, and they saw no reason to repeat the mistakes that had led to misused land, stagnating farm areas, and rural poverty.[38] Before the New Deal, at the end of World War I, some advocates of soldier colonization had recommended leasehold rather than fee simple ownership, and reports on land use and settlement in the 1930s suggested that government agencies might wisely retain title to the land, normally leasing it to the settlers and allowing outright sale only to those who had demonstrated their ability.[39] The people who were to be resettled were not usually good farmers caught in the depression and struggling against poor land and lack of opportunity; many of them lacked skill, knowledge, and managerial ability. It had long been assumed that most Americans shared a kind of instinctive pioneering and farm-making ability and that once helped to settle on his own land a man might be trusted to make his way by his own energy and initiative. Actual settlement had not supported the belief, and experience in government-sponsored land settlement in Europe and the British dominions had shown the need for careful selection of settlers according to demonstrated farming ability or for special training courses and prolonged guidance.[40]

In spite of Leo Jacobs's defense of the realty contract and his argument for its advantages,[41] the Matanuska colonists remained unconvinced. Their own experience before colonization had not shaken their faith in individualistic land settlement and control, and nothing in their comments and discussions indicated awareness of the often unfortunate results of such settlement in the past. Supervision seemed to meddle and to interfere with the individual's absolute right to do as he pleased with his own property. Twenty-five years later the realty contract was remembered with resentment by colonists who remained in the region, and one of them called it an attempt to mortgage the soul of the colonist and those of his family as well.[42] In practice, the colony management could exert only occasional and mild supervision, as when colonists who needed additional seed loans in 1940 were required to sign a farm management plan agreement and to keep a farm record and budget.[43] Such occasions were rare; the usual guidance amounted to appeals and urgings, and the colonists felt only enough of the restraining authority to make them restless and to add enthusiasm to their protest meetings.

The civic association listened to the outcries against the contract and accepted from several district councils resolutions to modify or set aside some of its provisions, especially that one making permanent the "public trust and purpose" impressed on the land. One resolution would have placed all farm supervision in the hands of democratically elected representatives of the colony, who would be authorized to hire expert assistance. The decisions of the colony representatives and their advisers would be binding on the ARRC, which would, it seemed, also have to pay the experts, since the civic association certainly could not. Other resolutions declared that the contract had been forced on the colonists by "coercion, threats, promises, and other illegal means," that it should be considered void whenever it violated the colonists' constitutional rights, and that it should never be allowed to stand between the colonist and his "duty to himself, his family and God."[44]

The Land Use Planning Committee (LUPC), including representatives of the colonists, the cooperative, the ARRC, the Soil Conservation Service, and the Extension Service, was formed in July 1940 to study market conditions, soil variations, crop rotation, erosion control, and improved methods of land clearing, but the extension agent and the colony manager agreed that a "radical element" among the colonists regularly diverted discussion to complaints about the realty contract.[45] A subcommittee of the LUPC asked the ARRC for concessions in debt payment for those colonists who were making progress in the development of their farms and proposed that the restricted deed be replaced by an ordinary warranty deed allowing the ARRC to buy any colony tract at the best price offered by another buyer.[46] Colonel Ohlson forwarded the proposal to Rupert Emerson, the new director of the Division of Territories and Island Possessions, with his recommendation that restrictions in the realty contract and in future deeds be retained. However, to soften the colonists' objections, he suggested that the price charged the MVFCA for properties acquired from the ARRC, already only half the appraised value, be reduced from $278,000 to $200,000. Ohlson's recommendation was approved, the charge to the MVFCA was reduced, and the restrictions in the contract were retained.[47]

In the spring of 1938, when the debt revision was barely completed and some realty contracts were still unsigned, the ARRC contracted with some of the colonists to clear land beyond the fifteen acres up to thirty at a charge of $72 an acre, which would be added to the colonists' debts while the corporation paid them $40 an acre for the slashing.[48] In August, when Colonel Westbrook ordered the ARRC to budget for clearing a total of thirty-five acres on each tract, free of charge, the corporation directors balked. If the clearing were free, the cost to the ARRC would be no less, but there would be smaller debt repayment providing income for future ARRC operations. In addition, under the realty contract, the corporation was obligated to pay a withdrawing colonist his equity in the farm, and the directors feared that by making improvements through free clearing it would be increasing the claims that might eventually be made against it. Finally, not all forty-acre tracts had thirty-five tillable acres, and the requirements for control of wind and water erosion would limit clearing to about thirty acres.[49]

A little more than a month after Westbrook's order, the colony was transferred to the Department of the Interior, and no more was heard about free clearing. Under the thirty-acre program begun in November 1938, the charges and payments to the colonists were as they had been planned in the spring. Under the old clearing program in 1937, the total of all payments for hand operations in clearing had been as high as $65 an acre; under the new one the maximum was $40, a rate that was intended to end the colonists' practice of hiring outside labor to do their slashing.[50] The management continued to complain that not enough land had been cleared to make the colonists self-supporting or to make the operation of the community processing and marketing facilities efficient and economical. The colonists looked upon the $40 rate simply as an unsatisfactory wage, and by late 1939 clearing had almost halted while they awaited a rumored increase in the rate.[51] In January, after Ross Sheely left the general manager's position, deploring the "relief" payments that had always burdened the colony, the cooperative called on the ARRC and the new manager, Herbert C. Hanson, to raise the slashing rate and thus strengthen the colony by making the clearing program a success. The new manager rejected the proposal because the funds were not available.[52]

The refusal came as the ARRC was transferring ownership of its property in the community center to the cooperative. Since its organization, the MVFCA had been intended eventually to acquire the facilities, but until then the ARRC provided management and an operating staff and turned over to the cooperative the supervision but not the ownership of the profitable enterprises, while retaining the necessary but money-losing activities. From one-half the profits of the trading post and the garage, the MVFCA paid savings dividends to its members; from the other half it built a fund intended to allow the association to buy the properties in three years or whenever it had accumulated enough for a down payment.[53] In 1938 the ARRC and Westbrook agreed that the price eventually charged the cooperative for the community center should be based on the probable return from the properties and the association's ability to pay rather than on the actual cost of land, buildings, and equipment.[54] In the winter of 1939–40, the MVFCA, which had by then acquired its own manager and staff, although it was still dependent on the ARRC for funds, applied for an operating loan of $300,000 from the FSA and arranged to acquire the community center properties from the ARRC, with no down payment and giving the ARRC a second mortgage in order that it could offer the properties as security for the FSA loan. Control of the property was transferred in mid-January, the FSA loan was made in March, and only later, with the approval of the secretary of the interior, was the selling price set at $280,327.07, or one-half the appraised value.[55] Minor adjustments reduced the price to $278,000, and in 1941, on Colonel Ohlson's suggestion, it was further reduced to $200,000.

In spite of what seemed generous terms, the relations between the cooperative and the ARRC were usually strained. The MVFCA had acquired the community facilities, including land-clearing equipment, at a reduced price and with no down payment, but at the same time it wanted the ARRC to increase the slashing payments and to go on clearing land, paying the cooperative for the use of tractors. The ARRC finally agreed to go on clearing, meeting its expenses and paying for the use of equipment out of the cooperative's payment for stock inventories, a payment made possible by the FSA loan.[56] The hostility between the cooperative and the ARRC was increased by the FSA's appointment of Hanson rather than a special manager to administer the $300,000 loan. To the colonists and the MVFCA board, the necessity of obtaining Hanson's approval and countersignature on all checks drawn on the loan was a constant irritant, and Hanson was upset by the cooperative's failure to make required reports to the FSA promptly and correctly.[57]

Although the press often represented the cooperative as having been forced on the individualistic colonists by New Deal planners and the bureaucratic ARRC, only a few colonists were wholly opposed to membership in a cooperative. Within a short time after it was created, they had begun to look upon it as the organization through which they could resist the corporation, and twenty-five years later the original colonists who remained declared themselves always supporters of the cooperative and remembered their experience with cooperatives in their home states before coming to Alaska. They did not think of the MVFCA as an organization forced on them by the ARRC, but instead, and somewhat inaccurately, as an association the colonists themselves had created despite the ARRC's grudging outward agreement and concealed but real hostility.[58]

Before the colonists arrived, the settlers in the valley had lacked storage, processing, and marketing facilities; when these were supplied, first by the ARRC and then by the cooperative financed by the ARRC, it became possible for old settlers as well as colonists to dispose of their products without the wasteful, inefficient duplication of effort of a competitive search by many small producers for buyers in the limited market of the Anchorage area. While the cooperative was in its early stages, before reorganization, some colonists dodged the marketing agreement, and Leo Jacobs, then both assistant general manager and manager of the cooperative, warned of the effort-wasting peddling and the price cutting that would result from such evasion of the cooperative's rules.[59]

Nowhere within reach of the colony were there any large wholesale buyers of farm products. Without the cooperative, the 135 to 150 colonists and the several dozen old settlers and other farmers would have been small hucksters making the rounds of consumers and small retail stores in Fairbanks and Anchorage. In the second half of 1939 the colonists' sales averaged less than $150 each, and after more land was cleared, at the peak of the wartime boom in 1943, the MVFCA paid colonists and other farmers $302,781 for their products.[60] By 1947, there were only 100 farmers in the whole valley who sold over $500 in farm goods that year, and 74 of them were among the 152 farmers selling through the MVFCA.[61]

The press attacks on the colony cooperative were based on the comments of disgruntled colonists, on inaccurate notions about Alaskan conditions, and on social and economic views that automatically rejected "New Deal planning" and the colony cooperative along with it. Newspaper readers outside were told that the colonists had accepted the cooperative only reluctantly and that they wanted to run it themselves rather than have it mismanaged by bureaucrats.[62] Or they read that the cooperative was a part of a "planned new social order" that was unwanted by the colonists, who wished only to farm and to buy and sell as they pleased.[63] When 160 editors and publishers of the National Editorial Association visited Anchorage and the Matanuska Colony in June 1939, they praised the scenery and the colonists, marveled at the crops growing in the north, and spoke of their open-mindedness and objectivity and of their efforts to check their information during the four-hour visit to the colony. However, they could not approve of the colony's cooperative; they found it "un-American . . . more Russian than Russia." *The Anchorage Daily Times* commented:

It is hoped by Alaskans that the editors will make special efforts to point out in their stories that this feature [the cooperative] was promulgated from Washington, D.C., and not here in Alaska. Remote control has been a continuous source of trouble since the colony was started four years ago, and it appears that it will continue without surcease for years to come.

However, it should also be noted that this cooperative feature was not handed to the colonists as a surprise after they arrived in Alaska. The original agreement, signed in the States before they were enrolled as colonists, showed clearly that the cooperative feature would be enforced at Matanuska.[64]

Although Colvin's official connection with the colony had ended with its transfer to the Department of the Interior the preceding fall, he responded to the attacks on the cooperative and wrote to the ARRC's attorney, L. V. Ray, enclosing bulletins on farm cooperatives and their organization in government settlement projects. He called special attention to the Capper–Volstead or Agricultural Marketing Act of 1922, passed in a Republican administration, and added,

I am writing you this letter and presenting to you this information for the reason that I have understood that attempts have been made in Alaska to make it appear as though the cooperating association at Palmer is something peculiar or unique. It has been said often that it is socialistic or communistic. All these reports are untrue.[65]

The cooperative association survived and grew despite the attacks and by the end of the war was operating a large general store, a dairy with a branch at Anchorage, a garage, a warehouse, a slaughterhouse, a cold storage plant for meat and vegetables, and other facilities. After the war it marketed more than two-thirds of the valley's milk production and the bulk of other farm products, and in 1954 it opened a branch plant at Fairbanks.[66]

By the summer of 1939 agriculture had not yet made the colonists self-supporting or capable of meeting their debt payments. Under the realty contract, payments would begin in the fall of 1940, with over $24,000 due from all the colonists, but earlier, in 1939, the colonists collectively owed payments of $94,000, or $600 each, on chattel mortgages, seed loans, and short-term notes. By the most liberal estimate, the typical colonist would have less than $200 available for the coming year after paying current debts and making a small allowance for farm operating costs. Some colonists who had contracted large debts to improve barns, add equipment, and build dairy herds had good prospects, but they were not yet able to make full payments. The ARRC board and Sheely agreed that partial payments should be accepted from farmers making real progress,[67] and again in the following spring further seed loans were made if the farmers agreed to keep management and budget records for the ARRC's inspection.[68] In mid-1940, anticipating the first realty payment and the regular or overdue payments on other loans, the ARRC board authorized the general manager to adjust payments or postpone them for diligent farmers who were developing their farms.[69] After satisfactory arrangements had been made with some colonists and others had finally responded to repeated notices to discuss their situations with the manager,[70] the ARRC brought eviction proceedings against six colonists who refused either to make payments or to discuss their debts with the management. One of the six, who was employed at the new air base in Anchorage, vacated his tract; the other cases were heard in the court at Anchorage through late 1941 and early 1942 and were decided in favor of the ARRC. (See chapter 8 for an account of the proceedings.) After that success, the manager sent additional notices to forty-nine other delinquent colonists, and finally notes to quit their tracts were sent to twelve of them.[71]

A calculation of the colonists' ability to pay based on farm income alone was unrealistic, but so was the claim of some colonists that they were destitute and unable to make even token payments. Most of them had supplementary incomes from employment by the ARRC, the cooperative, the Alaska Railroad, or the road commission. They had had the opportunity under the several development programs to earn perhaps $2,000 over several years by slashing uncleared land and doing other improvement work; after the first year or two they should have produced all their own potatoes, vegetables, poultry, eggs, and milk; there was no property tax, and until the first realty payment in November 1940, their housing was in effect rent-free. Increased military activity and construction began to have some effect in 1939 and by 1940 the wartime boom had begun. While twenty colonists were employed full-time by the cooperative and several part-time, fifty-eight others were employed in the summer and fall of 1940 in army construction near Anchorage at average wages of $250 to $350 a month. By the end of the year a majority of these construction workers had earned over $1,000, some of them nearly $2,000, and their combined incomes from construction amounted to $65,000.[72]

Increasingly colonists leased their land to others to farm, used their farm homes as residences for their families, and moved to construction sites. Some families abandoned their farms without notifying the corporation, removed equipment, left houses and barns unattended, and turned stock loose in the woods. Vacant farm buildings were rented to the army as warehouses, and, because colonist labor was scarce, forty air corps enlisted men in September 1941 helped in the harvest of potatoes and carrots for a quarter share of the crop, which was turned over to their messes to release ration allowances to their welfare and recreation funds.[73]

The war and the boom, the departure of old colonists and the admission of new farmers to colony tracts, and the performance by the MVFCA of many functions that had once been the responsibility of the ARRC all changed the nature of the colony. The ARRC was a landlord and creditor, but it was no longer preoccupied with rehabilitation of the rural poor. H. C. Hanson continued to worry about the careless farm management he saw and to preach the gospel of diligence and thrift, but the ARRC's and his own hold on the colonists had been weakened. By 1942 inquirers about settlement in the Matanuska Valley were sent a standard form supplying technical details about farming and financing settlement through the ARRC. The corporation worked to stimulate Alaskan growth through farm settlement, but the new farmers were not "colonists" in the old sense and helping them to settle had become a routine business of selling or renting farms.[74] In 1945 a publicity release commented on the changes in the colony:

> Since 1942 all remaining aspects of the colonization period have disappeared. Many of the social and economic conditions in the Valley today trace their

origin to the colonization program, but no control of the social or economic conditions or the farming development is any longer exercised by the colonization program or the corporation management.[75]

One of the signs of change in the colony was the quiet elimination of the restrictions in the realty purchase contract and the deeds to colony farms. The colony managers and the ARRC board had resisted proposals for changes in the contract and deeds, and when one colonist in 1941 offered to pay his realty debt in full if he were given an unrestricted deed, the corporation refused.[76] The end of the restrictions a few years later was brought about not only by the altered position of the ARRC, but by congressional and Farm Bureau Federation attacks on the FSA, the last of the settlement and rehabilitation agencies. Only a small part of the FSA's funds went to resettlement projects, but critics treated the projects as though they were the whole of the FSA program and likened their cooperative organizations to Russian kolkhozy. By 1943 the FSA was weakened, and in 1946 it died and was replaced by the Farmers' Home Administration, an agency occupied largely with making farm loans, chiefly to veterans.[77] The FSA's nonfarm housing projects, mainly former subsistence homestead communities, were taken over by the Federal Public Housing Authority (FPHA), created 24 February 1942 by Executive Order 9070. When, in 1944, the FPHA suggested to the homestead associations that restrictions be placed in their deeds to give the corporations options to buy individual homesteads and to prevent commercial undertakings and inharmonious architectural changes, Congress reacted by prohibiting any restrictions in FPHA deeds.[78]

Neither of these developments—the attack on the FSA or the limitations on the FPHA—directly affected the Department of the Interior or the Matanuska Colony, but the mood of the mid-1930s had clearly passed and Congress was opposed to any planning that would alter the familiar pattern of fee simple ownership. Without publicity, the first deed to a colony farm, given 1 May 1944,[79] contained none of the restrictions to which the colonists had once objected. The new realty contract adopted at about the same time made no reference to a "public trust and purpose," mentioned nothing of rehabilitation in a cooperative rural community, made no requirement for membership in the cooperative association, and set no conditions for the deed ultimately to be given.

By the late war years the original aims of the colony no longer affected its operation, and in time the colonists and Alaskans generally forgot that there had been some purpose in addition to populating and developing Alaska. The colony was remembered as a project at first botched by bureaucratic planners and then rescued by the best of the original colonists, by additional colonists who were real farmers, and by pioneer-spirited men who knew Alaskan conditions. The painfully slow growth of the colony might have suggested how little would have been done without the years of financial aid and supervision, but instead the ARRC, like the FSA, was found guilty both of treating its clients badly and of doing too much for them.[80]

8

The Press, a Hero of Self-Help, and Some Rebels

Perhaps the earliest and most important failure of the Matanuska Colony was that it did not for long remain a dramatic and satisfying demonstration of a recovered pioneer past. When the colony was new it was pleasant to think that once it had been possible to escape towns and panics and to start fresh, but the journalistic accounts of the colony before long spoiled the pleasure of vicarious pioneering. Even while the colonists were arriving in the valley, settling temporarily in the tent city, drawing lots for their tracts, and becoming accustomed to the long northern summer days and the mosquitoes, the journalists who reported the color and excitement seemed to feel a growing disappointment. Their references to the quick railroad trip to the coast, the easy voyage to Alaska, the tools and machinery ready to ease and speed the colonist's labor, and the commissary to supply subsistence and comforts on easy credit, hinted some regret that there were no covered wagons and no need to rely on ax and rifle. There were no real dangers or privations and no crises except in the relations between the colonists and the management of the project.

The press's treatment of the colony was affected not only by the disappointment of the reporters, who shared the myths and clichés of the frontier with their readers, but by an increasing general anti-New Deal slant in the press in the middle and late 1930s. Alaskans had regarded the colony as important for the publicity that might further the development of the territory, and the officials of the several federal agencies concerned with the colony and the board of management of the ARRC looked upon publicity for the colony as normal and desirable.[1] From Washington and Palmer a stream of news releases supplied the press associations with a rather accurate factual account of the day-to-day developments in the colony, and countless hours were spent answering the inquiries of journalists, politicians, busybodies, and the curious. The news itself, accurate in detail but selected to emphasize the hundreds of applicants on the colony's waiting list, the amount of land being cleared and the first crops being harvested, and the formation of a colony council, was so heavily seasoned with determined official optimism that the management was regularly burdened with the difficult task of explaining the contrast between the cheery press items and the inching progress of the colony.[2]

The increasingly unfriendly attitude toward the colony was not found in straight news stories from official sources but in magazine and newspaper feature articles, straining for color and written in the language of frontierism, and in editorials that showed a growing willingness to use the colony to embarrass the Roosevelt administration.[3] Charges such as the one that colonists complained that they were not furnished electric refrigerators and washing machines free of charge were inaccurate and unfair—there was at that time, after all, no electric power system outside the community center—but they reflected the political slant of the press and the general disappointment in the colonists' failure to measure up to the standards of pioneering the press itself had set for them. Some colonists were given attention in the press for their steady habits, frugality, and dedication to hard work,[4] and had all the others been of their character and had the settlement developed as a community of modest log-house farms scattered around a quiet village, with contented families living thriftily from the products of their land and selling a little milk and a few eggs and chickens to meet their small debts, the unexciting outcome would have satisfied the planners' vision of rustic peace and security and the colony would soon have disappeared from news columns and editorials.

But in the long run the colony developed otherwise, and in the meantime the management, eager to show that there were capable and industrious farmers among the colonists, called newspapermen's attention to Walter Pippel. Neither an ineffectual farmer requiring careful guidance toward decent self-support, nor a man who would settle for rural contentment, Pippel became the most widely publicized colonist and probably the one American farmer most often mentioned in news stories and editorials.[5] Yet the hero of the press was not what the colony planners had expected, and a cooperative rural community could hardly have survived the presence of many such dedicated and energetic pursuers of individual success.

After the drawing for colony tracts, Pippel traded the farm he had drawn for one that had been laid out on privately owned land and included about six cleared acres. While most of the other colonists could produce only a few potatoes and vegetables in the community garden, Pippel set busily to work, built starting beds for tender vegetables, and managed in the first short season to produce some vegetables for the Anchorage market. By the next summer he had a small second-hand truck and sold his produce in Anchorage and to the Alaska Steamship Company and even undertook marketing trips as far as Fairbanks. Within two years of the settlement of the colony Pippel was being publicized as the project's outstanding farmer, and at the end of another year he was at war with the ARRC and was being treated in the anti-New Deal press as a successful but lonely individualist struggling against bureaucratic regimentation.

For the first two years of the colony, while the cooperative had little to market and had been limited to serving consumers, Pippel had been a member of its board of directors. However, he was not among the officers of the reorganized cooperative, and in the spring of 1938, after adjustment of the colonists' debts, he refused to sign either the new realty purchase contract or the agreement to market through the cooperative. Those provisions of the contract intended to preserve the colony as a "cooperative rural community" appeared to him as a threat to his freedom to do as he pleased with his farm, and he regarded the restrictions included in the deed that he would eventually get as conveying less than clear title. Convinced that his success was explained entirely by his initiative and hard work, both in developing his truck farm and in offering his produce attractively in the market, he looked upon cooperative marketing as a forced sharing of the fruits of his enterprise with the indolent and incompetent.

In the articles and editorials paying tribute to Pippel's undeniable ability, little attention was given to the benefits he shared with other colonists.[6] Besides the school, the roads, and the community services, there was the advantage of liberal credit. By the summer of 1937, Pippel's real estate, chattel, and other debts amounted to about $9,500. Through the fall of the year and into 1938, the program of debt adjustment reduced his debt by more than $4,000 and then by another 20 percent to bring it below the $5,000 level that was considered within the ability of the colonists to repay.[7] The most important distortion of the Pippel story was the implication that what he had done the other colonists could also do. His truck gardening required concentrated labor for a small area and, if the produce could be sold, returned a higher value per acre than any other variety of farming. According to a study by an agricultural extension agent in the valley, truck gardening would produce a profit of slightly more than $500 an acre in addition to a small allowance for the farmer's labor, and a special crop such as radishes would return $2,325.50 an acre. However, one acre of radishes would supply the whole Alaska market.[8] Pippel's advantage of an early start would have disappeared if all the colonists, or even a dozen or two, had turned to truck gardening and had thus reduced the opportunities for each to the peddling of a few bunches of onions or heads of lettuce.

In spite of the ARRC's difficulties in dealing with Pippel, the manager and the board of directors—a professional agriculturist and solid businessmen—seemed privately to admire him. Even in the midst of their battle they were willing to use his success by estimating his two-year gross income at $11,000 and implying that other colonists, if they were diligent, might hope for equal prosperity.[9] Further, their sympathy probably gained Pippel a more generous settlement than another colonist would have received. After months of Pippel's refusal to sign the realty contract and the marketing agreement, the ARRC was granted an injunction restraining him from marketing his produce except through the cooperative, and finally at the beginning of August 1939 Pippel withdrew from the colony, turning over the farm to the ARRC and receiving $6,800 for the improvements he had made and for the crop then in the ground.[10] Interviewed along the way on his trip back to Minnesota, Pippel said that he intended to return to Alaska and predicted that the colony would last only as long as the federal subsidy continued. He blamed the troubles of the project on the fumbling paternalism of the management and the unwillingness of most of the colonists to work as hard as he had.[11] After one season of farming in Minnesota, Pippel returned to Alaska early in 1941, leased twenty-five cleared acres near Anchorage, bought additional land, and prepared to resume farming.[12] Although he again prospered and by 1945 added retail pork products and bulk sale of fertilizers to his vegetable farming,[13] he was no longer of interest to the press after he became simply another farmer.

Pippel's greatest usefulness to the anti-New Deal press came during the period he remained in the colony and stoutly resisted the management. Two magazine articles, widely reprinted or quoted and used by editorial writers, offered Pippel as a stalwart and lonely champion of individualism and self-help surrounded by shirkers and incompetents ever clamoring for more aid. In the earlier of the articles, in the *Nation's Business*,[14] the ARRC management was accused of using the colonists' debt reduction program to force acceptance of the realty contract and the cooperative, and Pippel was represented as proudly refusing the reduction. The comments ascribed to him—that Americans wanted only to work for themselves, without interference, that America had not been built by such coddling of the unfit, and that in only one country, not the United States, were such equalitarian principles followed—were quoted in feature articles and editorials.[15]

An even more violent attack followed a month later, when, in the *American Mercury*, a Ted Leitzell, who said he had come to Alaska to see what had happened to the New Deal experiment of transplanting Americans to a sub-Arctic wilderness, reported that "collectivism, following the Soviet pattern with the utmost fidelity, has come to the Matanuska Valley."[16] Only one man, Walter Pippel, was a good farmer and had prospered, and because he had resisted the ARRC he was an outcast. The others, the "relief-demoralized derelicts," had surrendered to the "collectivist experiment." "Save only castor oil, concentration camps, and firing squads, the settlers have been subjected to almost every form of coercion invented by European dictators." But the coercion, it seemed, was the lure offered by the ARRC—jobs, credit, and other help for those who were quietly cooperative. And Leitzell thought that from the start most of the colonists had been lazy misfits quite ready to be corrupted and coerced by charity.

In spite of the extravagance of Leitzell's language and his guiding assumption that such a project, if undertaken at all, should have been limited to the businesslike extension of credit to good risks in farming, he did touch sensitive points. Credit had been almost unlimited; some colonists' debts were startlingly high, but the sum of individual debts was far short of the total amount spent on the colony; the cost per family, if all expenditures were divided by the number of farms then occupied, was about $34,000; the system of debt reduction had favored those who had used their credit most liberally; and the colonists' general complaint against the ARRC was that it refused or was unable to fill the whole gap between their actual and desired standards of living.

The attitude toward the ARRC perhaps explains the surprising absence in the colony of any marked reaction to the Leitzell article. If the colonists did not see the *American Mercury*, they were able to read the article when it was reprinted serially and somewhat abridged in the weekly newspaper issued by the MVFCA.[17] There were no accompanying editorial comments, no replies by spokesmen for the ARRC, and no letters to the editor. Many of the colonists and most of the board members and officers of the MVFCA were hostile to the ARRC, and though they were themselves harshly treated in the article and though their reason for opposing the ARRC was not that it had pampered them but that it had done too little, they were apparently pleased to accept any ally in the attack on the colony management. Some months later Carl Rasmussen, an anti-ARRC member of the cooperative's board of directors, in a long letter to the *American Mercury*[18] ostensibly intended to clarify questions raised by the Leitzell article, gave no attention to its criticisms of the colonists. Blandly ignoring the nature of Leitzell's attack and assuming no disagreement about the desirability of establishing the colony as a cooperative community, he saddled all the difficulties of the colony on the management and attributed to it an excess of the individualism and prudent business spirit that Leitzell had found entirely lacking.

Walter Pippel's hard work, good luck, and prickly independence brought the colony unfavorable publicity, but the management avoided probably even worse attention in the press by surrendering to an agile and enterprising opportunist, Charles E. Ruddell.[19] The social worker who interviewed him for the Matanuska project checked the form to indicate that he was an "honest-to-God farmer of the pioneering type." Living then on the edge of Duluth on a small lot with his wife, six children, a cow, twelve chickens, a few tools, and the minimum of clothing and furniture, Ruddell listed eighteen years of farming experience even though he was only thrity-five, had served in World War I, and had worked for years as a truck driver, carpenter's helper, and cement worker. A house in Duluth that Ruddell had bought earlier was rented to a tenant, with the rent going to the mortgagee; he had borrowed the maximum on his veteran's bonus, and the family had been receiving an average of $38 a month in relief payments.

Re-outfitted with clothing and household goods, the Ruddell family arrived in the colony and at once showed a startling change in its living standards. The costly illness of one son required medical attention in Anchorage and bone surgery in Seattle, but that debt was eventually canceled. From May to October 1935 the Ruddell family increased its debt by nearly $600 a month and thereafter by more than $400 a month. By 31 January 1937, after twenty months in the colony, Ruddell's debt to the ARRC, in addition to that for the house and the land, was $9,339.15. After trying fur farming and sheep raising, and after the neglected mink and sheep had died or had been lost or strayed, Ruddell acquired a few cows and entered the dairy business at a time when no territorial regulations hampered his direct sale to consumers. Doing little to clear the land for the cultivation of either subsistence or forage crops, he fed the cattle in part on summer grass and mostly on commercial feed bought on credit from the ARRC. As early as November 1935, with his wife doing laundry for the construction workers employed by the colony, Ruddell felt prosperous enough to offer ten dollars a week for a girl to do part-time domestic work.[20]

Throughout the protracted haggling with the ARRC management, Ruddell refused to assign any of the proceeds of his milk sales for payment of the feed bill or to return his cows to the ARRC for redistribution to colonists who had enough cleared land to feed them. Finally on 27 January 1937 Ross Sheely, the general manager, after informing Colonel Westbrook and O. F. Ohlson and getting their approval, ended Ruddell's credit and began eviction proceedings. However, Ruddell, with a conspiratorial flourish, left the valley hidden in an Alaska Railroad caboose and sailed for Seattle under an assumed name. Pausing there on his way to Washington, D.C., he told the press that he represented over a hundred colonists who were, like him, shocked at the mismanagement and expense of the colony. He, for example, in only eighteen months of occupying a five-acre farm (i.e., five cleared acres) owed the government $12,300 although he had originally been promised that in five years his debt would be $3,200.[21]

Sheely warned Delegate Anthony Dimond of Ruddell's approach. Dimond agreed that Ruddell was a problem, but he thought that members of Congress would not be sympathetic, although they might be shocked to learn of the scale of Ruddell's spending and the credit advanced to him.[22] Sheely also gave Colonel Westbrook advance notice that Ruddell was a persuasive talker and sent accounts of his slovenly farming, his refusal to pay for cattle feed, his neglect of land clearing, and the reports of his sending cash, bonds, and money orders outside for deposit. The ARRC would have taken action against Ruddell earlier but for fear of unfavorable publicity during the political campaign of the preceding fall.

Ruddell was persuasive. He saw Westbrook, Harry Hopkins, and several representatives and senators, and by February 23 Westbrook was telling Sheely that Ruddell really wanted only the success of the colony. Between late February and April 1, Sheely repeatedly protested concessions to Ruddell, although he yielded to the WPA's legal counsel and withdrew the eviction order. Westbrook, while assuring Sheely that all decisions were, of course, in his hands, and obviously wishing that Ruddell would somehow disappear, wired and wrote that Ruddell was sincere in his desire to cooperate, that he wanted to help Sheely, and that after Ruddell's return Sheely would no doubt find it to his advantage to work with him for the colony's welfare. By the end of March Ruddell was back in the valley. Sheely resisted a little longer, but the ARRC directors, although sympathetic, finally yielded and Ruddell was reinstated on April 26. In the press Ruddell was presented as a popular hero among the colonists, and he was photographed with a group of men clearing some of his land, supposedly a gesture of gratitude for his representation of their complaints against the ARRC.[23] In reality, Ruddell was using payments under the colony's new work-credit plan to hire men for the improvement work expected of him.

By November 1937 Ruddell was again restless. His obligations were now something in excess of the $15,926.48 total of real estate, chattel, and other debts of the preceding January. Determined to leave the colony permanently, he demanded transportation for his family back to Minnesota. The ARRC compromised by paying their fare to Seattle, although it saved appearances by having Ruddell supposedly earn the transportation costs by doing odd jobs for the management. Like the other colonists, Ruddell had his debt reduced in the fall and winter of 1937–38, and in mid-December he obligingly signed a statement that although the ARRC had invited him to remain, he wanted to leave the colony for what he grandly described as "business reasons." After relinquishing his real estate and chattels to the ARRC in satisfaction of his debts, Ruddell left late in January.[24] However, the ARRC had not heard the last of him. In Seattle, he represented himself as destitute and still owing the ARRC over $10,000. He applied for and was refused transportation back to Duluth, but the King County, Washington, relief office and the local FSA office gave emergency relief grants until it was discovered that Ruddell had quietly bought for cash a small house and five acres of land.[25]

In the final echo of the case, Congressman Albert J. Engel, who had apparently read about Ruddell, anxiously inquired about him and about the colonists from his own state of Michigan. Leo Jacobs, then general manager, assured the congressman that the colonists were being well treated. He described the system of debt adjustment, quoted Ruddell's departing statement, said that Ruddell had reportedly located near Seattle, and discreetly said nothing about the dealings with the Washington relief authorities.[26]

If Walter Pippel was a hero of industry and self-help and Ruddell a talented dissembler and opportunist, Elmer J. LeDuc, one of the early replacement colonists, was a dedicated agitator and pamphleteer.[27] In the summer of 1936 LeDuc was thirty-seven years old. Born in Minnesota, he was a war veteran, had two years of high school education, and had worked as a laborer, as a printer and linotype operator on small newspapers, on a WPA project, and, most recently, as an employee of the Forest Service in the Absaroka National Forest in Montana, where he had built a cabin for his family and used some land for gardening. When he heard that the Matanuska Colony would accept new recruits who could transport themselves to Alaska, he wrote to Milton S. Eisenhower, director of information for the Department of Agriculture, proudly describing his family's pioneer willingness to settle in Alaska after experiencing the isolation of their forest home.[28]

Like other prospective new colonists at the time, the LeDuc family was visited by Stuart C. Campbell, who had been at the colony in 1935 as a member of the administrative group headed by Col. Leroy Hunt and who later served as assistant to H. M. Colvin during the period of debt adjustment and reorganization of the cooperative. Besides filling in the prescribed form, Campbell wrote a 2,500-word report in which he gave a most enthusiastic recommendation of LeDuc and his family. It was true that LeDuc had little farming background—his mention of five years of farm labor was no doubt an exaggeration of some occasional contact with farm work—but there were many other factors to be considered. LeDuc himself was intelligent, energetic, and adaptable. He had acquired a variety of skills in which he had no training—masonry, carpentry, and log work, for example—and the family lived well and in ideal harmony on limited resources. Campbell believed that the LeDucs would be a real asset to the Matanuska community.

In October 1936 LeDuc was approved for admission to the colony and signed an agreement for new replacement colonists by which it was understood that he would cooperate under the ARRC's supervision, but would be required to pay his own transportation to the colony and his return from it, if he should leave. The LeDuc assets were $200 in savings, a light truck worth $600, the cabin, on leased forest land, worth $500, and furniture worth $50. LeDuc sent his family ahead, sold the cabin and furniture, drove to Seattle, and sailed for Alaska at steerage fare. In the colony, he received Tract 67, and by January 1938 his total debt for the farm, chattels, seed, tools, and subsistence items was $7,443.53. The debt adjustment program reduced the debt first to $4,874.81 and then another 20 percent to $3,899.85. In effect, he and his family lived for the time without payment of rent; like other colonists, he was paid for land clearing and other improvement work on his tract, and the product of his land was his for sale or subsistence.

Yet without contradicting by his behavior Campbell's high estimate of his abilities and independence, LeDuc within two years became a problem for the colony management. By September 1938 he was delinquent in payments on his non-real-estate debt, his farming was not successful, and he soon became a determined, energetic, and most articulate enemy of the ARRC. He disposed of his poultry flock and, disregarding the advice of the management, attempted the farming least profitable for a given acreage, the production of hay and grain for sale rather than for feeding his own stock. Although he worked occasionally for the ARRC and the cooperative, he found additional employment at the camp of the Civilian Conservation Corps and, without informing the management, freed himself for that wage earning by leasing part of his land to be farmed by others.

LeDuc's career as propagandist for the rebellious colonists began with a long letter published in the colony newspaper early in 1939 in which, in the most general language and without citing any specific faults of the management, he denounced the ARRC and said:

We are sick and tired of promises, we want reality. For many of us this venture is our last opportunity to provide security for our children and ourselves. Are we going to give up without a struggle? Are we going to capitulate and permit the complete wreckage of our hopes? Can we afford to sacrifice so much? What are we going to do? . . . Are we whipped? Hell, no, we are just beginning to fight![29]

A little later LeDuc's letters to politicians brought an inquiry from Senator Burton K. Wheeler of Montana to Ernest Gruening, the director of the Division of Territories and Island Possessions. In reply to the senator's quotation of LeDuc's complaint about discrimination and favoritism, Gruening informed him of LeDuc's cash income of approximately $1,000 in 1938 and the first quarter of 1939, his rent-free occupation of the farm, the opportunities for production of his own food crops and other produce for sale. He concluded:

Discrimination against them [the LeDucs] cannot be sustained. Neither can it be said that the management in this instance has failed in any way to cooperate. On the other hand, if they have not benefitted from the relief given them and the opportunities afforded them, it seems that much of the responsibility is their own.[30]

In his agitation against the ARRC, LeDuc joined a group of dissident colonists that appeared about the beginning of 1939, calling themselves either the Matanuska Valley Protective Association or more popularly, recalling tall tales told to Alaska tourists, the Ice Worms.[31] The loose, semisecret organization had a half dozen very active members and a somewhat shifting group of about twenty others who were usually identified as Ice Worms but who did not themselves attempt to shape opinion or arouse the colony. In addition, other colonists at times sympathized with the Ice Worms, if only because they stood opposed to the power and authority of the ARRC.[32] The Ice Worms' discontent, like LeDuc's, was unspecified, broad, unfocused—except that the ARRC was the source of credit, supervision, and nagging guidance. In a midwestern farming community in a bad year, resentments would have been scattered to include the local bankers and lawyers, the railroad, the dealers in farm supplies, the representatives of several levels of government, and the solidly prosperous members of the community. In the Matanuska Colony the ARRC stood in place of all these. The resentments were too scattered to be put clearly or openly, but if a colonist worried about his present short-term debts or the land payments that would begin in 1940, if the reward for his efforts seemed always in the future while he had little present cash in his pocket, if he was envious of the salaried affluence of the ARRC management or the regular ARRC jobs held by some colonists, or if he felt painfully cramped in the range of decision open to him, he located the source of his discontent in the corporation and identified his interests with the cooperative, which he wished to make the community defense against the colony administration. The Ice Worm group, from early 1939 to its gradual disappearance after 1942, seemed to be the voice of the more resentful and rebellious colonists and the champion of the cooperative.

A prominent Ice Worm rebel was Carl Rasmussen, a replacement colonist. In the spring of 1939 he and his wife Lulu, the proprietor of a beauty shop in Palmer, wrote to Senator Sheridan Downey of California[33] complaining that the colony was being mismanaged, that the ARRC was benefiting from public money advanced to it, that a few favored colonists got cash jobs with the ARRC while others got nothing, and that for a year and a half he had slaved to support himself and his wife by land clearing and by the products of his farm. Nothing was said about the reduction of his total debt, the further credit extended to him, his own occasional employment by the ARRC, or Mrs. Rasmussen's beauty shop. Rasmussen was forty-nine when he came to the colony from California in the summer of 1937. He had had farming and other employment experience in Kansas, Colorado, Montana, Oregon, and California, but farming in the colony did not seem to go well for him, and by the fall of 1938 he was one of the discontented group. In January he was elected to the board of directors of the cooperative and at the same time became one of the most active members of the Ice Worms.

In February 1939 the Ice Worms organized several mass meetings, demanded an increase in land-clearing payments from the corporation, condemned the ARRC's management of the colony, described the colonists as destitute and in urgent need of relief from the territory, and prepared a resolution calling on the territorial legislature to petition Congress for an investigation of the colony.[34] Although in a general meeting on February 22 the colonists failed to support the Ice Worms' resolution, it had already been sent to the legislature, which addressed to Congress a memorial asking for such an investigation.[35] However, no more was heard from either the legislature or Congress, and a non-colonist and very active sympathizer with the Ice Worms, a teacher in the Palmer High School, was summarily dismissed by the school board at the suggestion of the commissioner of education.[36] LeDuc, Rasmussen, and the other Ice Worms continued their activities, circulating anti-ARRC petitions, demanding further reduction or cancellation of colonists' debts, and attempting by threats to force colonist employees of the ARRC to leave their jobs.[37] The letters by LeDuc and Rasmussen to Senators Wheeler and Downey and Rasmussen's long letter to the *American Mercury* were a part of the effort to discredit the management of the colony and to carry the attack beyond Alaska.

In the late summer or early fall of 1939 a mimeographed, undated, and irregularly published news sheet or pamphlet began to appear in the colony,[38] each issue headed by the notice:

Prepared by
E. J. LeDuc
for the
Order of Ice Worms

An organization of Matanuska Valley farmers who believe that Democracy is worthy of their defense, and that it has ever been the kernel of America's creed that a man shall and must provide for himself and for his own.

In the Ice Worm sheet LeDuc regularly repeated the demand for a congressional investigation of the ARRC and charged that O. F.

Ohlson mismanaged the Alaska Railroad as well as the colony. He called Herbert C. Hanson, by then general manager of the ARRC, Judas Iscariot and Benedict Arnold, headlined an article "Totalitarianism in Matanuska," and wrote of the "fascist policies of the Alaska Rural Rehabilitation Corporation." In an issue that appeared about December 1939 LeDuc described the ARRC as a fund-consuming machine:

> Let the colonists suffer and die, but the machine must be satisfied! . . . While the machine's hunger is being sated, little children must exist on half rations—pinched, tired faces showing the inroads of malnutrition. They must face bravely the penetrating cold that numbs their frail bodies through the fragile covering of threadbare coats and summer underwear.

A June 1940 issue carried a crude cartoon showing a poultry brooder, labeled "ARRC," decorated with swastikas, and newly hatched chickens marked *Illness, Poverty, Greed,* and *Strife.* In several issues of the spring and summer of 1941 the ARRC and the colony's general managers were charged with deliberately working for the collapse of the cooperative. The end of payments for land clearing was interpreted as a scheme to limit the agricultural development of the colony, and, because military activity in Alaska was increasing, the ARRC was denounced for sabotaging the food production necessary for defense.

Behind the wild charges made against the ARRC were the debts the colonists owed and either the simple desire to evade them or the persistent anxiety they caused. In April 1940 Carl Rasmussen addressed an obviously insincere letter to the new general manager, Herbert C. Hanson, asking for a statement of his total indebtedness and inquiring with mock obsequiousness, "I would also like to know if my farming operations of last year were satisfactory to the officers of the corporation, and if not, would like to know what I can do to regain my good standing."[39] Because realty payments were coming due for the first time, and because Rasmussen in three years had paid little or nothing on chattel mortgages, seed loans, and the like, his total payments due in the fall of that year amounted to $1,114.32.[40] Unless he had accumulated some reserve in the preceding two or three years, that was obviously more than he could pay out of one year's faming, and there was reason for worry. Other colonists were in about the same position. However, as the time for payment approached and notices were sent to colonists asking that they come to the ARRC to discuss arrangements, the manager indicated a willingness to accept some token payment.[41]

Those colonists who refused to make even a token payment or to discuss their debts were encouraged by a valley lawyer, Almer Peterson, who had been elected to the legislature early in November after a campaign calling for the cancellation of all colonists' debts. Early in December he urged the colonists to ignore any threat of eviction and to prove whether they were American citizens or peons. Hanson replied that many of the colonists had additional nonfarm incomes and were buying luxuries and living quite well.[42]

After making no payment and ignoring the first of three or four letters from Hanson, Elmer J. LeDuc in February 1941 replied at length but insisted on discussing only the affairs of the whole colony, not his debts. "During the last four years I have spent hundreds of hours in the offices of the ARRC in sincere efforts to work out a definite understanding between us, but to no avail." He charged Hanson with being belligerent and despotic and announced that he had turned over his case to his attorney, Almer Peterson.[43]

As payments on the realty contracts came due, a syndicated newspaper article represented the colonists as victims of a program to consolidate the colony's farms and to increase production to meet the needs of the growing military forces in the territory. Supposedly the ARRC, after consultation with military commanders, planned to give more land to successful farmers and to evict the others. "The edict, if enforced, threatens to make homeless refugees of the colonists in the snow-covered, sub-zero valley and jeopardize the colony's future."[44] However, a special Ice Worm sheet, an open letter distributed in the valley on 15 February 1941, the day of the annual stockholders' meeting of the MVFCA, offered a different view. After customary attacks on the ARRC, its management, and Colonel Ohlson, and after boasting that the colonists had survived five years of coercion, intimidation, and corruption, and had been subjected to hunger, illness, and illegal contracts, the newsletter claimed that the ARRC was attempting to interfere with the colonists' attempts to earn a decent living:

> Yes, many of us have gone to work at the Anchorage air base—the first opportunity we have had in five years to make a decent living. Now we are threatened that unless we pay over a part of our earnings, we will be deprived of our well improved farms. . . . Our original agreements called for *payments to be made from the soil*—which we have done, insofar as possible.[45]

Thus it seemed to some colonists that their ability to pay should be judged by their farming alone and that their increasing income from employment that kept them away from their farms had no bearing on their debts to the ARRC. However, after making further attempts to reach an understanding with the delinquent colonists, the ARRC filed complaints against six of them, including Rasmussen and LeDuc. One of the six withdrew from the colony and the case was dropped. The other five were heard in late 1941 and early 1942. In all the cases, judgments and orders for foreclosure were entered against the colonists,[46] but Rasmussen, LeDuc, and one other managed to arrive at an agreement with the ARRC to keep their farms. Notices were sent to forty-nine other delinquent colonists, some of whom made further payments or received extensions; orders to vacate tracts were sent to twelve colonists. The anti-ARRC agitation almost disappeared, and LeDuc issued no more handbills. In spite of his plea of poverty, he fiinshed paying for his farm in December 1946 and received his deed in January, with none of the restrictions mentioned in the contract. Through 1946 eight colonists finished payments on their realty contracts and were given deeds, several others purchased additional land, and at the end of the year 105 colony farms remained under purchase contract.[47]

Although the outcome of his own and the other foreclosure proceedings cramped his leadership of colonist discontent, Carl Rasmussen remained an opponent of the ARRC. In January 1942 he was replaced on the board of directors of the MVFCA, but in November of that year the cooperative's newspaper, *The Valley Settler,* needed an editor, and Rasmussen took the job. In addition, during the war years various jobs took Rasmussen back and forth to Anchorage while his wife continued to operate her Palmer beauty shop. In June 1946 he bought a colony tract for cash, and in 1952 he received a deed for his original colony farm.[48] In 1949 and 1950 he was manager of the MVFCA and again for a short period in 1951. He made clear his continuing enmity toward the ARRC in a brief history of the cooperative that he wrote for a short-lived local magazine. The tone was matter-of-fact, but he said: "The ARRC built the co-op plant, ran it for several years at a loss, and when the funds were nearly gone, appointed a hand-picked Board, set up the administrative machinery to run it, saddled it with a heavy indebtedness, extracted the price of purchase, and then slipped out from under a white elephant."[49]

His article did not mention that the value of the properties had been more than halved, that there had been no down payment, and that the ARRC had taken a second mortagage to make possible an operating loan from the FSA. Rasmussen shortly thereafter retired to California, but the relations between the cooperative and the ARRC remained cool. Years later, at the end of 1964, when the cooperative paid the last of its indebtedness, the announcement made by a member of the board, an original colonist, exaggerated the price paid for the community facilities by making the FSA operating loan appear a part of the price charged by the ARRC and attributed the success of the cooperative wholly to the hard work and determination of the colonists and not at all to the early colony management.[50]

From the beginning, the troubles of the colony, and especially of the ARRC, were multiplied by the fact that the project, for the very reason of its location, attracted the attention of journalists and politicians outside as well as in Alaska. In the press, the colonists, at first modern pioneers, became relief-demoralized incompetents and malcontents. Yet when they clashed with the ARRC they became rebels against New Deal regimentation and bureaucracy. Although the colonists were regarded as not "real" farmers at all, the ARRC staff members were often thought to be impractical theorists given to a "scientific hot-house" approach to farming.[51] When the colony received by error Russian winter wheat seed instead of the spring wheat that had been ordered and the mistake was not discovered until after planting, newspapers seized the occasion to comment on the colonists' having to "goose-step to the orders of New Dealers who don't know the difference between spring and winter wheat."[52] Normally the colony management was charged with extravagance, but reports of tightening credit brought some expression of satisfaction mixed with warnings of the hardships the colonists would face.[53] Editorial writers regularly proceeded confidently on little or mistaken information. When the coming transfer of the ARRC property to the cooperative was announced, it was treated as a transfer to the settlers individually and as the reorganization of the colony as a community of individual agricultural enterprisers.[54] A newspaper that had condemned the New Deal management of the colony now rejoiced, on wholly mistaken grounds, that the project was now sound and sane, working out in the "self-reliant American manner," reasserting "rugged individualism," and discarding every New Deal theory and practice.[55] When an early snow in October 1939 caught some crops unharvested, a rash of editorials commented on the incompetence of both colonists and management, on the calls that would soon be heard for further government aid, and on the softness of the Matanuska settlers compared with those in the Middle West a century before.[56] An imaginative newspaperman sent out a press association story from Palmer about colonists who had used sled dogs and snowshoes to salvage what cabbages and root crops they could.[57] Conceivably, the trick may have been tried lightly, in sport or for publicity, but its absurdity would have been clear to anyone who knew the region or dog sleds or who questioned the necessity of snowshoes in nine inches of snow. Nevertheless, the incident was used for solemn editorials on the self-reliant few, the foolishness of the New Deal experiment, and the inadequate guidance provided by New Deal farm experts and college professors.[58] Under the heading "In Soviet Alaska," the *Chicago Tribune* used the occasion of the snow and the threatened crop loss to retell Walter Pippel's success and to repeat tales of colonists' extravagance and foolishness. It referred to the pattern of the colony's organization as communism and spoke of "Commissars" in Washington and the "Santa Claus Soviet."[59]

If the press was often confused, frequently hostile, and occasionally friendly but for the wrong reasons, the colonists were at least equally confused. Because the ARRC was near and combined authority, credit, and a persistent shepherding, many of the colonists made it their chief enemy. The officers of the corporation, practical and successful men, found themselves caught between the Pippels, Ruddells, Ice Worms and the press, which described them as visionary New Deal experimenters. While attempting to carry out the original aims of the colony, they were attacked by many colonists as betrayers of the purpose of the project and enemies of the New Deal.

9

Promoting the Last Frontier: The Closed Safety Valve

In the 1930s and after, when a continuous frontier line in the continental United States had long since disappeared, and when federal land policy had turned from easy disposal to retention and careful management, Alaskans were still awaiting the frontier boom that would bring settlers, a growing population, and rising cities. In Alaska, where the withdrawal of the public domain from entry did not apply, homesteading, and with it general settlement and development, continued at a trickle of forty or fifty patents a year, fewer than in some western states where only scattered remnants of the public lands remained open to entry.[1] To Alaskans the problem was not to avoid repetition of the mistakes of past unregulated pioneering, but to encourage somehow another, later rush of settlement and the "opening" of the country. The existence of a great area of unoccupied land was considered so attractive to settlers, such a vacuum into which pioneers should irresistibly be drawn, that only bureaucratic confusion and the federal policy of "locking up" Alaska's resources could explain the failure of a wave of twentieth-century settlement to appear.

Many Alaskans found the Matanuska Colony less interesting in itself than as an indication of a change in federal policy toward Alaska and as a sign that outside there was a growing interest in the territory. For several years there were rumors that the Matanuska colonists were only the vanguard of many more who would be brought to the valley or that other colonies would be established elsewhere, and in 1937 the governor called for additional settlements modeled on the Matanuska project.[2]

Later the enthusiasm for the colony faded, and Alaskans repeated many of the criticisms found in the outside press, with the additional complaint that the project had been planned by outsiders, not Alaskans, and that it burdened the territory with the need to provide schools, school buses, and teachers. Further, if the roads built in the valley had been constructed elsewhere they would have opened new mining areas and brought increased prosperity.[3] However, there was no loss of faith in the possibility of settlement itself, and a wave of pioneer homesteaders was eagerly awaited. Each cluster of homesteads appeared to be part of a swelling tide of settlement. Three homesteading families in the Tanana Valley were called "the first of the new migratory movement from the states to Alaska," and a few others on the Kenai Peninsula were reported as the first of five hundred new homesteading families that could be expected there that summer.[4] In the fall of 1936 it was reported that about twenty-five miles out of Fairbanks, along the Alaska Railroad, 30,000 acres of "rich farm land" was being divided into homesteads and that 5,000 families were ready to come north to Alaska.[5] The division into homesteads meant only that the land office was surveying the area, and more than twenty years later there were no homesteads being operated as farms there. A durable rumor, first heard long before the establishment of the Matanuska Colony, was that the Mormons intended large-scale colonization in Alaska. In the autumn of 1938 Mormon officials in Utah were supposedly planning to send 800 to 1,000 families to the Fairbanks region, and the next summer two officials of the church visited the Matanuska project.[6] They were escorted by the local director of agricultural extension work for the University of Alaska, himself a Mormon, who later told the manager of the colony that he could not recommend Mormon settlement because of the low morale and dissension among the present colonists.[7] The rumor of Mormon settlement faded after the announcement by the ARRC in November 1939 that it would fill five to ten of the colony's twenty-one vacancies with Mormons.[8] But not even those few appeared.

At the beginning of 1938, when the Matanuska Colony was no longer exciting news, it appeared to promoters of Alaskan development that the federal government was taking a new step toward opening the territory. In the summer of 1937 Congress had called on the president to have the appropriate agencies prepare a report on a comprehensive plan for the development of Alaskan resources and the expansion of commerce between the territory and the States. The work was given to the National Resources Committee, which submitted its report by the end of the year.[9] The advance notices of the commuttee's report, *Alaska—Its Resources and Development*, were greeted enthusiastically in Alaska as evidence of a new interest among federal officials, and Alaskans were urged to support the men who were trying to do something for the territory. However, when the report itself and its recommendations on policy were actually seen, the enthusiasm turned to bitter condemnation, and the National Resources Committee became, in Alaskan eyes, another federal agency dedicated to delaying the territory's growth and frustrating the settlement of the last frontier.

The bulk of the report, the staff studies of Alaskan forests, minerals, water resources, transportation, agricultural land, wildlife, industry, and trade, aroused little controversy. The much briefer historical study of federal policy in Alaska and recommendations for the future[10] aroused the indignant outcries of Alaskan politicians and promoters. The deepest wound to Alaskan orthodoxy was the committee's fundamental conclusion, repeated in several versions: "An appraisal of national interests indicates that there is no clear need to speed up the development of Alaska." The committee denied that Alaska was needed as an outlet for American population or to satisfy land hunger of the American people and questioned the suitability of much of northern Alaska for white settlement, suggesting that most of that region be reserved primarily for native use. They discarded the notion of Alaska as a "vast storehouse" of natural resources and suggested that the national economy had no immediate or urgent need for Alaskan minerals or other resources, leaving open the question of the importance of some resources for military or strategic reasons. Further, the committee struck another blow by examining the parallels customarily drawn between Alaska and Scandinavia, Finland, and northern Russia and finding them superficial and misleading. The expectation that Alaska would one day have a population comparable to that of Scandinavia was based on a failure to see the economic, social, and political differences that made European experiences inapplicable as a guide for Alaskan development. The committee acknowledged that Alaska's soil and climate allowed agriculture in the sense of the production of crops, but no expansion of agriculture in Alaska was required by the national interest, and farming, the chief basis of past pioneer settlement elsewhere, would not support Alaskan development and population growth. Few potential immigrants to the territory would willingly follow the old pattern of laborious mastering of the land, subsistence farming, and a generation-long struggle for simple security and comfort. Rather, some agriculture would develop in a few areas where local markets created by mining, lumbering, or other enterprises made some commercial farming possible.

Admitting that Alaskans regarded federal policy as a locking-up of resources and a brake on the development of the territory, the committee considered the possible alternatives: either the elimination of all restraints and the encouragement of the quickest exploitation of all resources or a policy intended to develop an independent and balanced economy. From the first there might be expected a boom, profits for some users of resources, concentration of ownership, the export of profits, and then declining population, ghost towns, and the burden of maintaining the government and social services established during the boom. Of the alternative—the balanced, independent economy—the committee said, "Whether this Alaska is possible is by no means certain." Such a development would require heavy and systematic federal investigation; the cost would be enormous and the outcome uncertain. In the long run, that kind of Alaska would probably never emerge, "for the Territory is subject to as many and perhaps more handicaps than [*sic*] have been involved in the settlement of other pioneer regions." Believing that some middle course between these extremes could be found, the committee recommended studies of Alaska's resources, the speeding of land surveys and mapping, geological studies, measures to improve the federal management of resources, studies of industrial use and markets for Alaskan products, aid to transportation, especially in regions already having some concentrated population and industry, and efforts to increase the recreational use of Alaska's natural attractions.

The one section of the report that irritated Alaskans more than any other was the one-page appendix added by Robert Marshall of the U.S. Forest Service, who had visited Alaska several times and had taken a year's leave of absence to live in the village of Wiseman on the upper Koyukuk. His affection for the mixed population of aging white bachelor miners, Indians, and Eskimos, and for the life in that little spot of settlement in the unpeopled emptiness made him the enemy of all plans for forced progress.[11] He suggested that the greatest value of northern Alaska was in its frontier quality and proposed that the unspoiled wilderness be preserved both for the population there and for those Americans outside who might manage to visit such a frontier as had disappeared elsewhere. He recommended that the whole of Alaska north of the Yukon, except for an area around Nome, be preserved as a frontier, where the federal government would build no roads and allow no leasing for industry.

Everything that the prophets of Alaskan settlement and growth had always claimed was contradicted in the report—there was no national need for Alaskan development, no pressure of population, no land hunger, no urgent need for Alaskan minerals, no important reason to expect any great change in policy. Alaskan resentment was sharpened by the ancient grudge against the federal bureaus that had a part in managing Alaskan resources, and especially against the Department of the Interior. That summer, Harold L. Ickes, secretary of the interior and chairman of the National Resources Committee, made a tour of Alaska and was greeted at each stop by delegations of businessmen and promoters with proposals for federal projects to help the local economy.[12] The trip coincided with the closing of the Kennecott copper mines and the resulting loss of employment and creation of several ghost towns. The incident dramatized the National Resources Committee's view that simple exploitation would not build a permanent population, and Ickes commented on the sickness of the mining economy. Although he treated the delegations of businessmen rather brusquely and told Alaskan audiences what he thought would be good for them, the press accounts and editorials on his visit were at least polite as long as he was in Alaska. After his departure and his announcement that he favored an increase in the gold mining tax to 8 percent of production, the restraint disappeared. Ickes, the Interior Department, and the National Resources Committee all became objects of Alaskans' attacks.[13]

A subcommittee of the Alaska Planning Council undertook to answer the National Resources Committee. Its report, *Land Use in Alaska,* issued in October 1938, firmly asserted what the national committee had denied—that Alaskan development was a real possibility and that the national interest required it. Surveys of resources, road building, aids to mining and other industries, regional studies, and stimulation of settlement were all demanded. The recommendations of group settlement seemed unusual for such a committee, but the term was used to mean consolidated land settlement in compact areas. Because settlers expected government services, civilized conditions, and the conveniences of modern living, the report suggested that in selected areas roads, schools, and other facilities be built in advance of settlement, a system that would encourage consolidation and avoid the expense of supplying the services to widely scattered, isolated settlers. The committee did not, however, discuss the financing of that ambitious program. Later, when the Alaska Planning Council issued its reply to the National Resources Committee, rejecting all its assumptions and calling for immediate measures for the development of the territory, the council was editorially praised and *Alaska—Its Resources and Development* was described as a crackpot production by Washington officials, not informed Alaskans.[14]

However, the demands for the development of Alaska did not indicate that settlement and increasing population were desired under all circumstances. Although they were always upset by suggestions that a large part of Alaska should remain a wilderness, Alaskan boosters, newspapers, and chambers of commerce were annually disturbed by the northward migration each spring of so-called penniless jobseekers.[15] Alaska was no place for the penniless, the misfits, the unemployed; only the skilled and experienced and those with funds to invest could hope to succeed on the last frontier. It was even suggested that too rosy a picture of the Alaskan frontier had been painted and that Alaska might well follow the example of California and other western states and bar "penniless drifters" from entering the territory.[16]

The alarm about casual drifters was unimportant in comparison with another source of anxiety—the threat of refugee settlement. The world depression, the reduction of international migration, the continuing belief that the vacant places of the earth could or should offer havens and opportunity for the homeless, the belief that general poverty in some countries was caused by overpopulation, and, most important, the increasingly severe anti-Semitic policy in Germany, combined to arouse a remarkable surge of interest in migration and settlement.[17] There were warnings, as there had been for years, that the unsettled places in the world offered little hope for pioneering immigrants.[18] If climate, soil, or undeveloped transportation did not stand in the way, then political, social, and economic barriers limited settlement to a few highly capitalized business ventures or the efforts of those already accustomed to or ready to accept a bare subsistence standard of living. But despite the warnings, the empty spaces of the world seemed to offer hope; if individual immigrants or families could not succeed, perhaps larger groups aided by sponsoring organizations could settle successfully in frontier regions. Early in 1938 a conference sponsored by the International Labor Office examined the problem of international migration for land settlement and reported on conditions in ten countries having a supply of potential emigrants and eight countries that might provide areas for settlement.[19]

The increasingly open and violent Nazi anti-Semitism in the spring and summer of 1938 led to the Evian Conference, which fruitlessly attempted a solution through intergovernmental agreements on migration. The United States was no more ready than other countries to receive refugees. While there was still a chance to save many European Jews, the American government hesitated; when general war made the escape of more than a few Jews unlikely, American policy became bolder.[20]

To Alaskans, reading in their newspapers the brief items of international news, living in a manner not greatly changed since the early gold stampedes, and always aware of the distance between them and the densely populated parts of the world—that is, the "outside"—political oppression and refugee settlement were unreal. But the rest of the world was suddenly brought much closer when in the autumn of 1938 a group of men in Denver, Colorado, formed a corporation for colonizing Alaska with European refugees and unemployed Americans.[21] The group used the arguments that had been made standard by Alaskan boosters—Alaska's great size, its sparse population, the wealth of resources awaiting use, and the potential for development on the pattern of Scandinavia.

Alaskan newspapers, businessmen, and promoters were horrified at the idea. The admission of refugees and the unemployed would turn Alaska into a swarming beehive, but no good would come of it. Alaska needed more people, but only those selected for their pioneering qualities, their fortitude, and their adaptability to frontier conditions. The Matanuska Colony was put to use in arguing against such settlement. "The Matanuska Colony, gradually evolving into a success, is a striking example of the fact that Alaska, with all her rich lands and abundant other resources, is no place for the unfit or those unwilling to work."[22]

In mid-November, Congressman Charles A. Buckley of New York, in an open letter to President Roosevelt, supported the idea of refugee settlement, called Alaska ideal for the purpose, and offered to sponsor a bill to exempt Alaska from the restrictions of the immigration laws in order to advance the refugee plan. There was no immediate response by Congress, but the Fairbanks newspaper polled local citizens—businessmen, members of the chamber of commerce, past or current members of the legislature, a member of the board of regents of the university—and published the views of fifteen of them under the heading, "German Jews Unsuited for Alaska Settlers Is Prevailing View Here."[23] Two of the fifteen were willing to have refugees admitted; one dodged and suggested that the Alaska Planning Council should settle the matter; two or three were chiefly concerned about practical plans. The others spoke of making Alaska a "dumping ground," compared the proposal with past suggestions for a penal colony in Alaska, questioned whether the refugees would have the required hardiness, pioneer spirit, and qualities found among settlers of the "sturdy Scandinavian type," or said that Alaska had problems enough in caring for "refugees from jobs" without bringing in destitute aliens.

Among outside newspapers there was greater awareness of the intolerable conditions in Germany, and some gave cautious support to the idea of refugee settlement. The *Seattle Times*, however, duplicated the Alaskan attitude and used the Matanuska Colony as a warning against such a plan.[24] Secretary Ickes carefully distinguished between actual recommendation of Jewish refugee settlement and approval of the idea for humanitarian reasons, but he believed that the United States and Alaska had ample room to receive newcomers and he offered the Matanuska Colony, despite the high initial costs caused by expensive land clearing, as evidence of the practicality of such settlement. But Ickes's support was in itself a guarantee of stiffened Alaskan opposition. The acting governor, E. W. Griffin, replied to Ickes and said that only self-reliant settlers with capital would be welcome in Alaska. The Fairbanks paper surveyed opinion in other Alaskan cities and found almost unamimous rejection of the refugee plan. Denying that anti-Semitism was the cause of the opposition, the newspaper added, "Let others settle the Jewish problem, but as for Alaska, open the way for her to march on toward statehood with people schooled in American traditions and such as she can assimilate and with whom she can build from the ground up with security and solidarity."[25]

The excitement died, and even a resolution by Andrew J. May, chairman of the House Military Affairs Committee, to admit to Alaska refugees equal in number to all unused national quotas aroused only a languid response.[26] Then on 14 August 1939 Secretary Ickes released to the press a plan for settling Alaska with refugees and unemployed Americans. The published plan, *The Problem of Alaskan Development*, usually called the Slattery Plan, after its author, Harry A. Slattery, aroused almost unanimous Alaskan opposition and increased Alaska's normal suspicion of the Department of the Interior and other agencies.[27] The reaction might have been even stronger had any Alaskan newspaper discovered and reported Slattery's long career as a conservationist, his connection with Secretary Franklin K. Lane's plan for the settlement of World War I veterans, his former position as executive secretary and then counsel for the National Conservation Association, and his years of close association with Gifford Pinchot, whose name Alaskans had connected for thirty years, for reasons almost forgotten, with a conservation policy aimed at "locking up" Alaska's resources.[28] The *Anchorage Daily Times* summarized the report and published it in ten installments beginning August 29; other newspapers editorialized; chambers of commerce studied and denounced it; and every rumored development in the refugee settlement plan was quickly reported.[29] Surprisingly, however, one incident went unnoticed in the press. Just after the release of the Slattery report, the Matanuska Valley and the colony were visited by Ethel J. Lindgren, surveying the settlement possibilities in Alaska as the representative of a Netherlands group sponsoring settlement.[30]

The Slattery report delicately circled the sensitive issue of refugee settlement and nearly buried it in a discussion of the general problem of Alaskan development, a discussion that duplicated much of *Alaska—Its Resources and Development*.[31] However, the conclusions were different. Since individual settlers faced isolation, high living costs, high freight rates, and lack of markets, and since unplanned settlement had not produced a growing Alaska, what was needed was planned and coordinated settlement by groups sharing background and interests and having the proper distribution of necessary skills. The report offered two examples of successful planned settlement in Alaska: the Tsimshian Indian community of Metlakatla, which had moved to Annette Island from British Columbia in 1887, and the Matanuska Colony. The view of the colony given in the Slattery report was far rosier than the conditions of 1939 or early 1940 warranted. There was no mention of the dissension in the colony, the problem of debt collection still to be faced, or the fact that after nearly five years agriculture was still far short of supporting the colony.

Taking up the idea of the Denver group, the Slattery report suggested the formation of "public purpose corporations" resembling the chartered companies that had engaged in colonizing three hundred years before. The corporations, operating under the regulations of the Department of the Interior, would work for settlement rather than for profit and would engage in general agriculture, in activities necessary for community self-sufficiency, and in new industrial developments not competitive with established Alaskan industries. Some of the new developments might be in fisheries other than salmon, fish processing and fish byproducts, wood-working, and various handicrafts. The settlers would be selected among unemployed Americans and European refugees according to skill and experience. Some modifications of the immigration laws would be required to admit the refugees to Alaska but not to the rest of the United States until they qualified under the quota.

A week after the first appearance of the Slattery report, the Department of the Interior announced that more than five hundred inquiries had been received, about half of them from abroad, and from both private persons and business firms.[32] By February 1940 Ickes was able to say that of 238 newspapers outside Alaska that had commented editorially on the plan, 85 percent had approved and 7 percent had been noncommittal.[33] Most of the comments in the outside press made some reference to the Matanuska Colony, but there was no agreement on the degree of success or failure of the colony or what it signified.[34] Even more common were references to the frontier. Alaska was *another* or *new* or *last* frontier, beckoning those with the pioneer spirit and offering haven to refugees or to the American unemployed and victims of drought and farm depression.

Some outside newspapers doubted that the settlement plan would actually benefit the unemployed and the refugees. One paper called the proposal a "cruel act of kindness" because such settlement, if actually undertaken, would result only in harsh struggle and ultimate failure for most of the settlers and cruel disappointment for many thousands of potential refugees.[35] Nevertheless, the press widely supported the idea, and in Alaska there was an uneasy realization that the boosters' claims about resources and opportunities, broadcast for so long, had succeeded too well and had been taken up by the advocates of the Slattery Plan.[36]

Probably unknown to most Alaskans, and ironically because he was himself Jewish, Robert Marshall, whose brief contribution to *Alaska—Its Resources and Development* had so infuriated boosters, joined the opponents of the Slattery Plan, although his views were published after his sudden death in late November.[37] He believed the plan was based on a wholly unrealistic estimate of Alaska's capacity to absorb and support a significant number of new settlers. Further, the proposal overlooked the social and economic problems chronic in the United States. By turning attention to Alaskan settlement, it dodged the questions of why unemployment continued, factories were only partially used, and plentiful resources went without a market. A brief answer to Marshall's article by Robert Morss Lovett[38] exemplified the extreme optimism of some of the plan's supporters. He guessed that "in a rather short period" a million or more settlers could be brought to Alaska and that the increase of population would in itself provide a foundation for economic development. Lovett gave no answer to Marshall's most damaging comment—that the Slattery Plan passed over the fact of continued economic stagnation in the forty-eight states. If land and resources in Alaska promised opportunity, they why the persistent unemployment and the unused resources in the States?

Through late 1939 and early 1940 the chambers of commerce of the larger Alaskan towns publicized their opposition to the Slattery Plan and exchanged angry words with members of the Department of the Interior.[39] Delegate Anthony Dimond conducted a skillful campaign against the settlement proposal, expressing sympathy for the "savagely persecuted" people who were the intended settlers, but denying that such settlement was practical. At the same time he maintained the claim that the development of Alaska and its bountiful resources awaited only the lifting of federal restraints. All that was needed was a highway to Alaska and a federal road-building program within the territory; then five thousand new settlers would take up land along the roads each year. Dimond argued that Alaska had to rely on federal grants for such projects because 99 percent of the territory remained federal land. Turn that public domain over to the territory and Alaska would ask no more. Race prejudice had no part in the Alaskan opposition to the Slattery Plan. There was less of that in Alaska than elsewhere. Yet it was true that first thought should be given to the hundreds of thousands of American citizens, victims of the dust bowl or of prolonged unemployment, sturdy, industrious people with Yankee ingenuity, who would make admirable settlers and would be welcome in Alaska—if they were properly financed and engaged in enterprises not competitive with established Alaskan businesses.[40]

The anxiety in Alaska was increased by the introduction in the House and Senate of identical bills supported by the Interior Department for carrying out the Slattery Plan of colonization and settlement.[41] The hearings on the so-called King–Havenner bill gave a wide variety of witnesses opportunity to voice their views.[42] Vilhjalmur Stefansson, who said that the army had requested reports from him on Alaskan conditions related to defense and who believed that settlement of Alaska would make it more secure militarily, reaffirmed his faith in the hospitality of the Arctic and once again listed the similarities between Alaska and Scandinavia. Clarence E. Pickett, of the American Friends Service Committee and once assistant to M. L. Wilson in the Division of Subsistence Homesteads, assured the senators that the admission of refugee aliens would not deprive Americans of jobs but would create additional employment.[43] Alvin Johnson, director of the New School for Social Research in New York and long interested in land settlement planning, was involved also in establishing refugee European scholars in America.[44] He believed that Europeans could establish the kind of handicraft industries and specialized farming neglected by Americans and that they would benefit by their group spirit and cooperation, which he thought had been lacking in the Matanuska Colony.[45] Dr. Frank Bohn identified himself as a student of land settlement, a former associate of Richard T. Ely, and a representative before the committee of a group of business and professional men and women, philanthropists, artists, religious leaders, and others supporting the King–Havenner bill. In supporting refugee settlement in Alaska, he used arguments usually used by racists, eugenicists, and celebrators of unspoiled and virtuous American rural life—all of them normally advocates of immigration restrictions. He believed that the drift to the cities and the failure to establish a stable and secure rural population threatened the United States with slow degeneration and spiritual decay. Such a project as the settlement of the great frontier in Alaska by a combination of American settlers and the selected best of the European immigrants would revitalize the country and serve as a model for the kind of land settlement necessary to restore the "blood" of the people, which had been deteriorating for generations.[46]

Joseph O. Hefter testified that he was packed and ready to settle in Alaska and that he represented a group of carefully selected and trained men who were also ready to go. Although his New York residence on West Forty-sixth Street lacked the desirable rural quality, he claimed to have had training as a farmer and that his group was then operating two farms near New York. He and his associates had been delayed in executing their plans for Alaskan settlement by their discovery that the land laws made no provision for contiguous tracts suitable for group settlement on a cooperative basis.[47] Some months later Hefter was reported to be heading the "Great West Colonization Company" and enlisting "tough young Jews" for colonization on the Kenai Peninsula, and the recruits for frontier settlement had added military drill to their training.[48]

The Alaskan opponents of the bill, who sent their statements through Delegate Dimond, included all but one or two of the chambers of commerce, the Alaska Miners' Association, and the Pioneers of Alaska. Mayor Don Carlos Brownell of Seward, claiming to speak for himself and the city council as well as for the settlers on the Kenai Peninsula, presented a long list of grievances and demanded a congressional investigation of the Alaska Railroad, Col. Otto F. Ohlson, the Matanuska Colony, and the operation and rates of the Alaska Steamship Company. Brownell said that he and the Seward City Council would support the settlement measure only if the control of all projects were turned over to the territorial legislature.

Both in Alaska and outside, the opposition to the Slattery Plan and to later proposals for refugee settlement had a solid foundation of practical objections, but there was also a broad streak of anti-alienism and anti-Semitism running through it. Delegate Dimond and Alaska newspapers denied that anti-Semitism was at the root of Alaskan opposition,[49] and it is probably true that in Alaskan communities there was little evidence of racial or religious intolerance. In scores of articles and editorials the words Jew or Jewish were used no more than a half dozen times, but the clumsy circumlocutions—"members of a single racial and religious group" or "almost wholly urban and commercialized members of a single religious faith"—indicated an intense awareness that most of the refugees were Jews. In dealing with the Slattery Plan, Alaskans seemed at times almost forced into adopting anti-Semitism as a strategy because the practical objections to the refugee settlement plan could not be fully discussed without violating the faith in the promise of the frontier and contradicting the glowing claims of Alaskan boosters. The Alaska Planning Council's report on the Slattery Plan, for example, presented a very strong case against the idea. Pointing out the shakiness of the parallel between seventeenth-century chartered colonizing companies and any that would be established in Alaska, showing that nothing in the plan would alter the federal title to or regulation of most Alaskan resources and that the Slattery Plan would introduce nothing new to Alaska except refugees, the council turned to an examination of Alaskan resources and industries. One after another was shown already to be operating close to the limit of good conservation practice, the small markets available limited expansion, or the employment that might be added by the fuller development of a given industry was small. However, that part of the report, or any other argument too much in violation of the frontier booster spirit, received little attention. The question was turned from whether Alaska was good enough for refugee settlers to whether the settlers were good enough for Alaska. The planning council asked whether Alaska could "absorb unscathed several thousand aliens, of one racial type, of wholly alien racial and religious character, people who have not and for the most part are without knowledge or conception of our ideals, traditions, history and political faiths."[50]

There was some further excuse for the Alaskan attitude. The provisions for refugee settlement were included in the Slattery report and in the King–Havenner bill with such a laboriously achieved offhand air that opposition seemed almost expected and invited. In addition, very little that appeared in the Alaskan press would have made Nazism and the plight of the refugee real to Alaskans. Editorials, news stories, and the comments of businessmen and politicians showed interests that rarely ventured beyond the territory, that centered on the gossip and trade in the small towns, the level of gold production, the size and value of the salmon catch, the high freight rates, and the continuing wicked neglect of Alaska by the federal government.

Early in the discussion of the Slattery Plan, the Fairbanks neswpaper on October 3 cried, "Keep Alaska American," and the president of the Anchorage Chamber of Commerce felt that the Jewish refugees would not be readily assimilated; their past record was against them: "Without casting any reflections on that race in our country which are of the same faith religiously as the refugees which the colonization plan is meant to embrace, we can safely say without fear of contradiction, that those refugees have proven their non-assimilability which has resulted in the disaster which has overtaken them."[51]

John B. Trevor, of the American Coalition of Patriotic Societies, suspicious of all immigration, opposed the Slattery Plan because it would admit people he described as "fifth columnists." He too found that German Jewish refugees had only themselves to blame. They were people who "have become unpopular in the land of their origin because of their beliefs in the Marxian philosophy. I believe the original Nazi movement in Germany was due to a revulsion of feeling by the majority of the German people that certain minorities were really acting as a fifth column under the influence of Moscow."[52] Colonel John Thomas Taylor of the American Legion recommended that all immigration be closed for at least fifteen years, and he predicted that if the proposed Alaska development bill were passed, Alaska would become an alien colony that the United States would have to defend. He asked, "Would we be willing to go to war in behalf of a few thousand aliens who lack the courage and patriotism to stay at home and fight their own battles?"[53]

Although the chairman of the subcommittee, Senator William H. King, showed no sympathy for the open or veiled anti-Semitism of some of the witnesses, Senator Robert R. Reynolds of North Carolina, playing the role of preserver of the frontier for America's own poor and unemployed, harassed witnesses who favored the bill, used Joseph Hefter's testimony as an opening for ponderously sly anti-Semitic remarks, and read into the *Congressional Record* messages and editorials unfriendly both to the Slattery Plan and to refugees.[54]

No vote or sampling of opinion was taken in Alaska to show the degree of opposition to alien settlement, although some estimate could be made from the reaction of the press, chambers of commerce, and some prominent Alaskans. If there was opposition to the admission of German Jewish refugees, American job-seekers and refugees from the dust bowl were equally unwelcome, and outside Alaska opinion surveys taken just before the release of the Slattery report showed a majority of Americans opposed to the admission of refugees from Nazism and a larger majority opposed to any liberalizing of the immigration quotas for that purpose.[55]

The death of the Alaska settlement bill did not calm Alaskans' fears.[56] At the end of the Russo–Finnish War Maury Maverick of San Antonio suggested that Finns would make splendid settlers for Alaska, but those who had argued that urban Jews would not be adaptable to America's last frontier were no more enthusiastic about Finns.[57] Secretary Ickes's attempt to keep alive the idea of refugee settlement, with the proportion of immigrants reduced from 50 to 25 percent, aroused the Alaska legislature to memorialize President Roosevelt for Ickes's resignation.[58] Another bill for quota modification and refugee settlement introduced by Congressman Samuel Dickstein of New York[59] aroused renewed indignation. The newspaper in the territorial capital called the bill a plan to admit to Alaska those who had failed in the defense of their own countries against totalitarianism, and it predicted that such refugees would fail in Alaska, would be unable to return home, would be ineligible to enter the continental states in less than five years, and would become a "dissatisfied, disillusioned, hungry mob, on which the termites of anarchy and revolution will thrive."[60]

In October 1939 President Roosevelt had predicted that at the end of the war it would be necessary to find places in the unsettled parts of the world for from ten to twenty million refugees from devastated Europe.[61] Such prophecies and estimates of the size of postwar migration were repeated in spite of warnings that the comparatively unpopulated places of the world would neither attract nor be capable of supporting large numbers of Europeans, that the cost of establishing settlers would be prohibitive, and that no settlement plans would alter a worldwide tendency to move in the direction already taken by developed societies with concentrated urban populations, established industry, and efficient commercial agriculture employing a shrinking portion of the whole population.[62] And in fact, despite continued discussion and the work, during and after the war, of committees studying the prospects of refugee land settlement,[63] few of those who left Europe in the 1930s and 1940s found land and refuge in the world's unsettled areas. About three-quarters of the refugee immigrants who entered the United States from 1933 to 1945 settled in or near the large cities in the eight most populous states.[64] The few refugees who found their way to Alaska were generally moving on after original immigration to one of the forty-eight states, and they sought urban employment rather than land for settlement and agricultural or rural work. In Canada, except for two small farm colonies established on the eve of the war, most immigration flowed toward the already well-settled areas, and in the postwar period less than one-tenth of one percent of the immigrants to Canada settled in the Yukon or Northwest territories or even in more fully developed Alberta.[65] Finland, with which Alaska had been so often compared, had 477,000 of its own refugees to care for in 1940 and 1945. Despite the scarcity of good land and the dense population in southern Finland, it was there, rather than on northern, forested, marshy farms, that most of the refugees chose to settle. The northern part of the country, comparable with Alaska, was left with less than 5 percent of the land cultivated.[66]

Yet the myth of open spaces and the back-to-the-land faith were not easily dispelled. It was easy and useful for politicians and journalists to suggest land settlement as a remedy for a variety of social and economic ills, and through the fading New Deal and into the war years the sentimental agrarians, the romantic rebels against urban life, and the believers in the superior character and morality of the rural population maintained their interest in the land and in semisubsistence farming.[67] However, something more than romantic nostalgia was at times involved. M. L. Wilson, former director of the Division of Subsistence Homesteads and later undersecretary of agriculture, felt a strong attachment to rural life, but in addition he had by 1939 decided that both rural poverty and industrial unemployment were chronic in the existing economy. It seemed to him that until some way could be found to provide jobs, there was at least some hope in community building and land settlement for small farming and decentralized small industry. Such a program might allow some to escape reliance on either large-scale industry or commercial agriculture, and there would be the additional gain of recovering some of the pleasures of rural life.[68] He recognized that the solution for the problems of unemployment and a surplus population in agriculture would in the long run have to be found in renewed industrial activity. "But however that may be true for the more distant future, it has in most cases no practical present application, because it would depend, if effected in a short time, upon drastic reforms that the temper of the people is not ready to admit. And before such a solution can be effected, most of us now living will be dead." He suggested that for the surplus agricultural population, living beside rather than in the existing economy, without cultural amenities, "subsistence or peasant-type farming constitutes a pronounced improvement in physical living standards, and provides also the physical basis on which cultural improvements can rest."[69]

With less explicit gloom and without fundamental criticism of the existing economic system, the press often reflected a similar attitude. Raising no doubts about the value of farming as a way of life, treating farmers with proper deference, and praising the rugged simplicity of rural life, anti-New Deal newspapers could attack fumbling in the farm and resettlement programs and then, as if coming upon a new idea, suggest land settlement as a palliative for unemployment and relief.[70] The various proposals for refugee settlement reminded some editors of the attractions of unpeopled spaces and prompted them to suggest that the example of refugee settlement might reawaken the American pioneering impulse or that Alaska should be first of all a refuge for unemployed Americans.[71]

In thoughtful contrast to such easy playing with the frontier and pioneer themes, and making a reference to the leading frontier historian not found in hundreds of editorials and articles published elsewhere, *Commonweal* examined the Alaskan frontier and found it no safety valve, no escape from the reality of the depression.[72] The editorial called Alaska as truly a frontier as any Turner had mentioned, "but people in this country, however oppressed in their jobs and however meager the prospects for public relief, do not look as a hope, for land where they can live off themselves." Nor had they in the past. Nineteenth-century pioneers eventually had a surplus to sell, but what would Alaskan pioneers produce in order to buy the products of American industry and agriculture? And far from needing Alaska for its production, the United States still had areas in which production could be greatly increased and was not because no market existed. "Far from furnishing a radical solution to economic problems, the present frontier gives us a particularly sharp angle from which to observe the spectacle of want in the midst of plenty. . . . " Nevertheless, the editorial suggested that not enough study had been given to the Matanuska Colony, that land in Alaska or the sparsely settled states, while not entirely free, offered some opportunity for "relatively pioneer' activity, and that Alaska could be made a homeland for some of the world's refugees.

Goodwill, enthusiasm, and the need to find the striking approach that would make an article marketable led some writers into surprisine foolishness. Early in 1941, while there were still about eight million unemployed, Richard Neuberger suggested that the western states of the mountain region, the Great Basin, and the Pacific Northwest still contained a tremendous area whose "inexhaustibility," as he oddly put it, had been underestimated.[73] Millions of acres of land there could be reclaimed and made available for European refugees and unemployed Americans from the cities. The Pacific Northwest alone offered room for 2.5 million additional families, and no problem of increased farm surpluses would arise because the new settlers would concentrate on specialty crops rather than overproduced staples and would consume most of their own production. During the war Neuberger's articles in popular magazines publicized Alaska, the building of the Alaska Highway, and the predicted settlement of the territory by new pioneers,[74] and after the war he argued that Alaska's land, resources, and still unfilled space could easily accommodate five million more people.[75] He thought that his recommendation for the settlement of 500,000 European refugees in Alaska was conservative, especially since the settlement would not come all at once, but at a rate of about 25,000 a year. As if to correct the bad aim of bigots who opposed the admission of refugees, he pointed out that the potential immigrants were not in the main Jewish but Catholic.

Wartime production and the demand for military and industrial manpower finally brought a dramatic reduction of unemployment and a prosperity unimaginable a few years before, but depression had come to seem almost normal and there was an uneasy feeling that the benefits of the war would disappear with peace. It was sometimes suggested that after the war a federal program of settlement on small plots might be resumed, not as a complete answer to the problem of relief and unemployment, but as a supplement for low incomes, and industrial workers were sometimes advised to take advantage of prosperity to acquire rural homes and small tracts of land as insurance against a return of hard times.[76] There was, in addition, the prospect of millions of returning veterans who would be, it was supposed, restless, impatient with routine, and adventurously willing to seek new opportunities, perhaps in Alaska.

The widespread fear of postwar depression lingered, but, with only a little faltering, wartime prosperity was extended through the years of the cold war. Alaska was transformed—not because it became a haven for land-hungry pioneers, depression victims, refugees, or adventurous veterans, but because of an increase in federal spending, largely for military construction. In the new Alaska, as in the States, if it was not quite assumed that the military spending could go on forever, few cared to think about its reduction; and in new circumstances the old formulas of the frontier, land settlement, and pioneering were repeated by those who felt keenly the obligations of others to preserve the American pioneer tradition and by new Alaskans, largely wage earners or salaried workers, who brought the standards and tastes of urban America with them.

10

Promoting the Last Frontier: Military Alaska

In his authoritative study of the origins and the present development of the Alaskan economy, George W. Rogers makes a useful distinction between three successive but overlapping and interrelated Alaskas: *native* Alaska, an aboriginal subsistence economy based on hunting and fishing; *colonial* Alaska, an economy based on commercial exploitation of resources—mainly fur, fish, and gold—largely for the profit of outside investors; and *military* Alaska, the Alaska since World War II, with a population trebled, urbanized, and economically dependent directly or indirectly on federal spending and military construction.[1]

In the three or four years preceding World War II, while Alaska's territorial delegate was urging Congress to build air fields and other military defenses in the territory, the total military force in Alaska was about four hundred men, many of them assigned to operate the Alaska Communication System.[2] By the latter part of 1939 there were over five hundred soldiers and sailors in Alaska and in 1940 an average of one thousand. The force rapidly increased—8,000 in 1941, 60,000 in 1942, and in the peak year, 1943, there was an average of 152,000.[3] After the war had started in Europe, Alaskan newspapers single-mindedly considered what might be the effect of the war on the territory. The Fairbanks newspaper called gold the sinews of war, suggesting that the president might raise the price of gold to encourage its production, and it echoed the Alaska Miners' Association in recommending that the territorial government nurse the war boom by a policy of the closest frugality and by avoiding any increase in taxes.[4] Newspapers outside noted that defense spending and the construction of air and naval bases were bringing a surge of prosperity to the territory,[5] but it was an Alaska newspaper that most accurately described the new development: Alaska had a major new industry—defense. In the spring of 1941, the Juneau *Daily Alaska Empire,* in its annual "progress edition," commented that the past year had been different from any other in Alaska's history. The territory had not simply made progress; it had taken a great leap ahead.

For the first time we do not speak resoundingly of Alaska's greatest industry, fishing, and second greatest, mining. In 1940 first place has been taken over by a development which we could not foresee even a year ago. National defense is today—perhaps only briefly, but nevertheless undeniably—Alaska's greatest industry. . . . More men are working on Army bases at Anchorage, Fairbanks, Annette Island and Yakutat and on Navy bases at Sitka, Kodiak, Dutch Harbor and Kiska than ever worked in the Territory at this season of the year. More millions are being spent for national defense installations in Alaska this year than were ever spent in a single year in the canning of salmon or mining of gold. The defense program is a great boon to the Territory and one which will leave its mark for all time to come.

But within a few years this great industry, which has meant and will mean so much to the development of Alaska, may have vanished. Then we will fall back again upon fishing, mining, the trapping and farming of furs and other civilian pursuits which have made Alaska the rich, the great, country it is.[6]

The new industry did not vanish but continued and increased. By the late 1950s the injection of federal money into the Alaskan economy through defense spending had continued so long that to many Alaskans its reduction was unthinkable, and it seemed that the future could be built on perpetual defense. In 1957 the Fairbanks newspaper happily accepted the assurance of a military spokesman that military construction was already being planned as far ahead as the 1961 season and that the region, as an important defense center, would not falter in prosperity and growth. The editorial, as though peevishly rejecting unspoken doubts, asked, "What is wrong with being a defense center?" and assured readers that defense was as sound an economic base as Chicago's position as a transportation center or Seattle's Boeing plant and the Bremerton Navy Yard. "Fairbanks is a center of defense activity in a Territory that is one of the most strategic areas on earth. Our economy is based on as solid a foundation as can be found in this uncertain age.[7]

During the war, when military Alaska was in the making, the future had not been seen in quite that way. The strategic importance of Alaska and the rapid increase of military strength there, the Japanese occupation of Attu and Kiska in the summer of 1942 and the recovery of the islands the next year, the several hundred thousand men who saw Alaska as servicemen or construction workers, the rapid construction of the highway through Canada, and the ferrying of aircraft to Russia by way of Fairbanks and Nome, all brought unprecedented attention and one of the periodic rediscoveries of Alaska made by journalists and politicians.[8] The attention itself and the more widespread knowledge of the territory suggested that after the war there could well be the long-awaited boom of rapid settlement, investment, growing industry, and agriculture. American and Canadian cooperation in building the highway and the Canol pipeline and in constructing and operating a chain of airfields indicated that the cooperation might be extended to a study of the postwar development of the whole region—Alaska, the northern parts of Alberta and British Columbia, and the Yukon and Northwest territories. The Joint Economic Committees of the United States and Canada created the North Pacific Planning Project, publicly announced in January 1943, and assigned the American section of the study to Region Ten of the National Resources Planning Board, which had already begun a number of investigations of the Alaskan economy and had issued a report on Alaska's postwar development.[9] The studies of Alaska's population, employment, living conditions, resources, and economy were issued in fifteen preliminary mimeographed reports, but, unlike the Canadian project, they were never brought together and published as a unified survey.[10] The project was undertaken on the assumption that military attention to the region would be followed by accelerated postwar development and by a rapid increase in population. It was expected that, besides Americans or Canadians, many European refugees would come to the northern region if American and Canadian immigration policies were adjusted to allow their entry. The advance planning for settlement was regarded as an opportunity to demonstrate what could be done for settlement in other sparsely populated areas.[11]

There was enough official and other publicity about Alaska to have created the expected influx of population. In the summer of 1944 Roosevelt inspected naval installations in the Aleutians, and there and at the Bremerton Navy Yard in Washington, after returning from Alaska, he predicted that many veterans who had no strong ties elsewhere would want to go to Alaska and pioneer as their ancestors had. He spoke of the nearly untouched natural wealth of the territory and repeated the usual comparisons with Scandinavia.[12]

Governor Gruening urged "Go North, Young Man," and expected that veterans would want to try the new frontier. "They've been places and seen things. The home town will seem too small, too set in its ways. They'll want more freedom, greater opportunities to make careers for themselves."[13] Even those who doubted the forecasts of a great movement of population to Alaska accepted the idea that ten or fifteen thousand settlers a year could be accommodated and that a million or more Americans had the kind of pioneer urge that would make Alaska appealing to them.[14]

In the expectation that after the war many veterans would want to settle on the land, the Department of Agriculture in 1945 published a soberly realistic survey of opportunities in agriculture in which the discussion of farming in Alaska was especially full of warnings.[15] The Interior Department had already published in 1944 a compact guide for servicemen interested in settling in Alaska[16] and the next year issued a new information bulletin on the territory. Although it was supposed to clear away misconceptions, the warnings about the difficulties faced by settlers sounded very much like invitations to adventure, and Secretary Ickes, in a forword, spoke of "our last big land frontier" and described Alaska as a "land almost without people—half a million square miles of unbelievably rich country inhabited by fewer persons than live in Little Rock, Arkansas."[17] Early in 1946 he again raised the issue of refugee settlement in Alaska, but his language was that of the Alaska booster. He cried, "Let's open up Alaska!" and referred to the past exploitation of resources, the drain of wealth to outside absentee owners, the opportunity awaiting "hardy adventurous Americans who have the spirit of the pioneer." He mentioned the love of comforts and luxuries that spoiled most Americans for pioneering, and he believed that the many Europeans eager to settle in Alaska, if accompanied by enough people from the States to preserve the American character of the territory, would soon build a great self-sustaining economic empire, supply the resources needed to replace those used in war, make Alaska a crossroad in the coming transpolar airways, give the United States the "firmly populated" northern territory it needed, and contribute, in an unspecified manner, to national defense.[18]

That renewed call for settlement of refugees, coming just before Ickes resigned on 15 February 1946, did nothing to reduce the normal Alaskan hostility toward the Department of the Interior or to soothe the attitude toward Ickes. A year before both houses of the Alaska legislature had memorialized the president and Congress for the investigation of Ickes's policies in Alaska and for his removal, on the grounds that he hampered Alaskan growth and that his several proposed Indian reservations in southeast Alaska would have included choice timberland and fishing areas.[19] When Ickes did resign, Alaska's delegate called it a blessing and said that Ickes was "very much despised by the people of Alaska."[20]

Yet the flurry of Alaskan development activities that began even before the war ended was largely the work of the Interior Department and Ickes. The Division of Territories and Island Possessions helped in drafting the Alaska statehood bill introduced in 1945, and, following Roosevelt's 1944 speech on postwar Alaskan pioneer settlement and his call for a program of development, the Interior Department presented an ambitious plan for comprehensive studies of Alaskan resources and encouragement of settlement.[21] In appearances at committee hearings and in letters to committee members, Ickes urged the subcommittee on appropriations for the Department of the Interior to inspect Alaska and observe the need for federal aid in development of the territory.[22] Although two successive budget proposals for the Interior Department in Alaska were rejected, the subcommittee did visit Alaska in the summer of 1945 and reported favorably on enlarging federal activity there.[23] The next year the appropriations for Interior Department activities in Alaska in fiscal 1947 were greatly increased, to a total of about $10 million; in addition to the direct grants for the rehabilitation of the Alaska Railroad, up to $15 million in transfer of supplies and equipment from other federal agencies to the railroad was authorized, and the War Department announced that in addition to its other activities in Alaska, it would spend $24 million for construction at Fort Richardson near Anchorage and Ladd Air Force Base at Fairbanks.[24]

Studies, projects, and reports followed in clusters. The Department of the Interior created an Interagency Committee on Group Settlement and cooperated with the Department of Agriculture in studying and promoting settlement. Members of the Interior Department in the program were convinced that increased land settlement in Alaska would depend largely on planned group settlement projects and they regarded the Matanuska Colony as a useful lesson for planners.[25] Among the early products of this interest in settlement were reports on farming opportunities in the Anchorage region and on areas of Alaska suitable for group settlement. The latter report concluded that the number of Alaskan farms, other than fur farms, and the number of cultivated acres could be more than doubled in the near future by the establishment of 640 new farms in six or seven areas, but it warned that success depended on careful planning and proper location for good soils and access to local markets.[26]

The settlement committee sponsored a bill, H. R. 5880, to aid Alaskan settlement by the selection of suitable areas, systematic survey and classification, subdivision and disposal of the land in suitable units, extension of aid to settlers, and establishment of group or project settlements. Although the bill was not acted upon, in 1948 and 1949 five areas totaling more than 300,000 acres were withdrawn from entry for classification and planned settlement.[27] Some Alaskans, as champions of pioneer individualism, protested such planning and land withdrawals and suspected that the Interior Department was again scheming to settle refugees.[28] The protests were unnecessary, for almost at once the withdrawals began to be revoked by stages. Some sections were clearly not agricultural; in others good land was so broken by private title, entry, reservation, or lease that no pattern of settlement could be drawn; elsewhere parcels of useful land were separated by swamp and muskeg. The two withdrawals in the Fairbanks region were entirely revoked largely because of the permafrost in the area and the resulting heaving that made continued machine cultivation impractical.[29]

While land was being considered for settlement, a "task group" of eight technical specialists of the Department of Agriculture, assisted by federal and territorial employees in Alaska, studied the existing Alaskan agriculture and the bases for its possible future growth and then deflated past optimism about Alaska's great agricultural potential. The group found that anywhere in Alaska the cost of developing a farm was high, land clearing was slow and costly, only the local Alaskan market was available, and isolation and expensive transportation raised the price not only of farm products but also of what the farmer had to buy for his own consumption and the operation of this farm. The task group reduced the old estimates of more than forty million acres of land for cultivation and more than twenty million acres for pasture, and commented, "Perhaps a rather large total area could be farmed if the United States were to become desperate for land. The task group estimates that there probably is not more than a million acres of suitable farm land, although much more might be developed if the local need for agricultural products should become more critical." A summary of conditions in different areas of Alaska showed a great variation in the kind of local problems, but everywhere there were some difficulties—permafrost, muskeg, short growing seasons, thin soils, unproductive podzols, better soils made droughty by underlying gravel and cobbles, low soil temperatures, shallow root growth, and cool summers that prevented the ripening of small grains. In addition, unless settlers avoided inferior land and followed necessary special practices, a high rate of failure, land abandonment, and social cost would be inevitable.[30]

The report of the task group was followed by several studies of the economic aspects of agriculture in Alaska[31] and dozens of technical papers and reports, such as those of the experiment station on soils, climate, erosion, land clearing, crops, cultivation, food processing, and the like. The agricultural experts were generally interested in their technical specialties, not in publicizing Alaska or promoting settlement,[32] and those who turned their attention to past American settlement recognized that changes in the American society and economy since the nineteenth-century settlement of the West had something to do with the failure of any large movement of population to Alaska.[33]

The passing of pioneer settlement was sometimes sentimentally regretted, but there was some awareness that continued settlement in the old pattern, individualistic and isolated, brought with it a heavy burden of social costs, although the emphasis was on the plight of the isolated families rather than on the costs of bringing them schools and roads.[34]

In contrast, there was little restraint in the promotional activities of the territorial government and of booster groups. The Alaska Development Board, created early in 1945, was impatient with Alaska's slow growth and commented that Alaska had been "planned and studied to death" and that the territory needed "less planning and more action, less talk and more work." Nevertheless, the board itself was limited to publicity, exhortation, and optimistic forecasts. It sponsored bulletins on settlement and agriculture, livestock raising, trade and industry, and opportunities in recreational and tourist activities.[35] The most extreme example of promotion running counter to the actual direction of economic development was the bulletin on opportunities in fur farming.[36] In 1939 there had been 164 fur farms, most of them raising silver or blue foxes, on 1,042,253 acres of land, including whole islands leased from the Interior Department for the purpose; by 1949 changes in fashion and high costs in Alaska had reduced the number to nine fur farms on 345 acres,[37] and a few years later there were none. The bulletins prepared by G. W. Gasser, commissioner of the territorial Department of Agriculture, were informative and in no way minimized the problems connected with farm development in Alaska, but their publication and distribution were pointless unless intended to encourage settlement.[38] Within a year of the original issue of these circulars, the Alaska Development Board had distributed about ten thousand copies.[39]

In postwar Alaskan boosting there were no more dedicated believers in pioneer land settlement and no more consistent users of the special language of frontierism than those who nostalgically recalled a pioneer past reconstructed from romantic fiction and moving pictures and those whose occupations kept them close to office and business, from which vantage point it was clear that the nation urgently needed to keep alive the pioneer tradition and to encourage the settlement of unfilled spaces. That attitude could be found among the witnesses who appeared before a congressional committee to support the Lemke bill, the Alaska Veterans' Homesteading Act of 1947. Congressman William Lemke himself supplied much of the pioneer fervor and the vocabulary of frontierism as he pressed and pushed reluctant witnesses toward the position he wanted them to take. One witness in favor of the proposed legislation, Ray H. Brannaman, Senior Vice Commander in Chief, Veterans of Foreign Wars, was sure that veterans would not be concerned with cash incomes but would value the food, shelter, and clothing they could win from their own land. "I believe, on the whole," he said, "that the opening of this Territory for the men who have known rough warfare and living will be an important step in the economic development of this vast empire. Certainly the requirements of our national security demand that Alaska be inhabited by as many sturdy Americans as possible."[40] He added his tribute to the earlier generation of settlers who had won the West, and he was complimented by a member of the committee for his use of "western language."

The bill would have offered veterans Alaskan homesteads of from 320 to 1,920 acres, with selections open in the Tongass and Chugach national forests, with military service applied to reduce the residence requirement to one year, and the cultivation requirement eliminated and replaced by a provision that the veteran gain a part of the income necessary for his support from any combination of farming, grazing, lumbering, hunting, fishing, trapping, or fur raising. Almost all the witnesses who had any knowledge of those activities in Alaska or any professional familiarity with Alaskan agriculture or lumbering strongly opposed the bill. Even those who ordinarily complained bitterly of federal control of Alaskan resources pointed out that, for every one of the activities mentioned in the bill, land was available under existing laws and regulations, and that the proposal was an invitation to veterans to speculate in timberlands, that the forest homesteads would be cut over because they could not be lumbered on a sustained yield basis, and that the promise of a wood pulp industry in southeast Alaska would be killed.[41] Don L. Irwin, then with the agricultural experiment station at Palmer, opposed the Lemke bill, calling it an inducement to speculation. He then tallied the areas of agricultural, grazing, and timberlands available, and, assuming that the size of most of the multipurpose homesteads would be midway between the limits set in the Lemke bill, or about 1,120 acres, he calculated that such settlement would add *too little* to Alaska's population, no more than 75,000 to 100,000 additional people.[42] Congressman Lemke, who regarded the Matanuska Colony as a fumbling and expensive attempt at settlement, was willing to grant to veterans timber homesteads worth about $40,000 each and to encourage the hopeless attempt to make farms by destroying the dense but narrow band of rainforest lining the twisting shoreline of the islands and mainland in southeastern Alaska.[43]

Although the Lemke bill died in the Senate, special advantages were extended to veterans in ordinary homesteading. The advantages offered the veterans of World War I were given to those of World War II and Korea. Military service could be applied to reduce the homesteading residence requirement to one year, and allowable absence from the homestead could reduce that year to seven months.[44] By careful timing to avoid the crop season, a veteran could escape the requirement that he clear and cultivate a portion of his land. If the timing failed, the cultivation requirement was so interpreted that the homesteader could plant a grass crop with no intention of actually harvesting it.

A large part of postwar homesteading in Alaska was done by men in the military services, many of whom were veterans in the sense that at some time they had received a discharge, perhaps between enlistments. Other men in military service found homesteading attractive because base housing was never sufficient to accommodate all married servicemen and because the rent for barely adequate housing in town was high. A soldier or airman could live off the military reservation and draw a rental allowance, select a homestead site, hire a bulldozer to clear a few acres, buy a surplus military building and move it to his claim, and thus satisfy the requirements for a patent. Another inducement was that there was no general property tax in Alaska except for the years 1949–53, and property outside incorporated towns and school districts was entirely free of taxes. After patenting his claim, the soldier–homesteader could leave Alaska for his next military assignment, knowing that his homestead would not be seized for delinquent taxes and that the growth of towns near the military bases would probably raise the value of his land in a few years.

In postwar Alaska the promotion of development and settlement merged with the campaign for statehood. After Delegate James Wickersham's introduction of an Alaska statehood bill in 1916, the admission of Alaska was only occasionally mentioned until Delegate Anthony Diamond in 1943 and Delegate E. L. Bartlett in 1945 introduced later statehood bills. Following a petition to Congress by the territorial legislature, a referendum on statehood in 1946 gave approval by a vote of 9,630 to 6,822.[45]

The advocates of statehood justified it as the normal outcome of the territory's growth during the war, as a measure related to national defense, and as an essential step in the economic development of Alaska. The publisher of the *Anchorage Daily Times* worried about Soviet designs on Alaska and argued that eighty years of failure to settle and populate Alaska made the American hold on the territory feeble, while, in contrast, the colonization of Siberia was being hurried—especially in the regions nearest Alaska.[46] The publisher's wife believed that one reason for the lag in development was that Alaskans could not feel the loyalty and pride that would come with possession and control of resources. "It is glaringly evident that the cause of our sparse population does not lie in Alaska. We cannot expect to have a more stable population until we have something more than a slippery lease under our feet."[47]

Many themes were repeated and combined: statehood for Alaska would bring development; a larger population would contribute to military defense; thousands of Americans longed to come to Alaska and to settle there; and the growth of the Alaskan frontier would stimulate the whole American economy. An airline official estimated that there was opportunity for private investment of $5 billion in Alaska and explained rather murkily that such opportunity was important for American business and industry "to extend the optimum point of the economic curve beyond its normal maturity date, that date which we are fast approaching within the United States, if new frontiers are not immediately developed." He also thought that "a million American citizens residing in Alaska, and supporting themselves from the bounties of Alaska, is a more adequate defensive bastion against any aggressor than the greatest military fortification ever developed by man."[58] An American Legion official spoke of many thousands of veterans waiting to come to Alaska, and the wartime organizer of the Alaska Scouts predicted that if Alaska were "opened," a million people, many of them veterans, would come to the territory and by their presence end any worry about military security. When he thought of what the pioneer spirit, if freed of bureaucratic restraints, could do in Alaska, he choked:

They want to come and find their home in a new land. . . . That old pioneer spirit that you looked for yourself to defend is among us now. Down in the old country it needs just a little fanning and the flame will grow to a big blaze and people will come and occupy the land, and I think the one thing we need is to look to ourselves, the old pioneer spirit that built America, that built the West, and will build the great frontier here, one-fifth the size of all the United States, and we can't run our government and we are stymied here.[48]

Groups attentive to local interests joined in promoting the frontier and pressing for statehood. By 1947 the boosters of the Matanuska Valley and the little town of Palmer were calling for the establishment of the future state capital at Palmer. One of the old settlers, John Bugge, offered to donate land for the location of the capital, and similar offers were later made by M. D. Snodgrass and others.[49] Early in 1949, while a constitutional convention in advance of a statehood enabling act was being discussed, the Palmer Chamber of Commerce extended an invitation to the legislature to hold the convention at Palmer, and the boosting continued for several years, as the chamber of commerce posted the town with signs proclaiming, "Palmer, Future Capital of Alaska."[50]

The ambition of the town contrasted oddly with the failure of local people to assume the responsibility for local affairs. There was no longer a colony in any real sense: the ARRC had become primarily a credit agency, the town of Palmer was not a "community center" but simply the settlement in a farming area, and the town had no government. In 1947, when the manager of the Alaska Railroad gave a fire station and equipment to the town, there was no government or group of citizens to accept the gift or maintain the equipment. Finally the volunteer fire company arranged for storage, maintenance, and insurance of the property.[51] All essential government services were supplied in some form at federal or territorial expense by the Territorial Department of Education, the United States marshal, the Territorial Highway Patrol, and the Alaska Road Commission. Then, in 1949, the legislature for the first time provided for a general territorial property tax. It was repealed in 1953, but in those four years local incorporation and taxation appeared more attractive, for if no local school district were organized, taxes would go directly to the territorial treasury. An independent school district was approved by the voters in 1949, becoming effective on July 1, and two years later, 1 May 1951, Palmer became an incorporated town.[52]

The enthusiasm of promotion often overrode experience. Despite his long service at the experiment station and his career as old settler, farmer, and railroad colonizing agent, M. D. Snodgrass, then a member of the legislature, joined in the cry for statehood as a cure for stagnation and predicted that if homesteading regulations were liberalized, if grazing and crop land were sold from the public domain at $1.25 an acre, and if grazing leases were made generously, then within five years many thousands of young settlers would flock to Alaska, increased farming would lower living costs, and Alaska's other industries would revive.[53] The agricultural agent at Homer, an instructor for veterans in agricultural training, deplored the pessimism of those who doubted the future of agriculture there. He believed that the Kenai Peninsula would become a great crop-producing area and would contribute to American security by supporting the "ever-enlarging military establishment being built on this first line of defense.[54]

As land at the western end of the Matanuska reserve and then the reserved strips along more than three hundred miles of the Alaska Highway were opened to homesteading, boosters awaited a great influx of settlers,[55] but the prospect that cheered them threatened disorder in existing agriculture, markets, and employment. Inflated forecasts of the number of arrivals by air and highway in the 1948 travel season, and the belief that a large portion of the people who arrived planned to stay and homestead, troubled the established farmers and businessmen in the valley, and in the spring there were reports of many Alaska-bound travelers through Canada, ill-informed, poorly equipped, and full of unrealistic expectations. The general manager of the ARRC, C. W. Peters, urged Anchorage businessmen to cooperate with Matanuska farmers, who found existing markets uncertain and who faced competition from new homesteaders. The new homesteaders, unable to finance themselves, needing off-farm employment for subsistence and farm development, and slow to reach the level of commercial farming, would, as soon as they became real producers, make the problem of insufficient markets even more acute.[56]

However, such misgivings were usually limited to the few Alaskans who had firsthand knowledge of the difficulties of settling and farming. The leaders in the drive for statehood and development seldom entertained such doubts:

For 83 years Alaska has been deprived of development under the territorial system. It has been demonstrated that the territory will never enjoy its share of the nation's growth and prosperity under its present position outside the family.

Statehood is the only key that has been found to unlock the wealth of Alaska and permit the development which would support a population of millions. Only through statehood can the federally-imposed vacuum in the northland be filled.[57]

As if sensitive to charges of neglect, federal officials sometimes wrote articles in the official version of the booster spirit.[58] Official boosterism was pressed to its limit in a long report by the Bureau of Reclamation on the possibilities of developing Alaskan water resources for power and other purposes.[59] The authors of the report, looking upon all hydroelectric, drainage, and irrigation projects with favor, were not concerned primarily with technical problems but with finding in the existing Alaskan economy or the hoped-for future Alaska the justification for such a program. Repeating glowing prophecies in the language of promoters, the report took lightly the past studies that advised caution, and assumed that the American economy needed Alaska for expansion and for its resources and that the American people needed it for land and homes.[60] It waved aside the National Resources Committee report, *Alaska—Its Resources and Development*, repeated the old comparison with Scandinavia, and predicted a future Alaskan population of five to ten million people requiring the cultivation of ten to twenty million acres of land to produce those crops suitable to the Alaska climate. Thus the estimate of only one million tillable acres made by the agricultural reconnaissance task force in 1947 seemed too low, and the report accepted an estimate by the territorial commissioner of agriculture, who put the tillable area at seventeen million acres and who believed that further surveys would reveal more.[61]

For good measure the report added 200,000 square miles of land suitable for reindeer grazing and capable of supporting four million animals, which would produce one million hides and 150 million pounds of meat annually. The herds that had once been estimated at over 700,000 animals had declined to fewer than 40,000 through overgrazing and destruction of the winter range, parasitic infestation, predation by wolves, failure to maintain close herding, and mixture with migrating caribou herds. The basic trouble had been the difficulty of fitting the nomadic life of effective reindeer herding into the hunting and fishing economy and sedentary life of the Eskimos. Ignoring this, accepting old overestimates of the capacity of the range, and forgetting that since 1937 white herders had been excluded in favor of native ownership, the report suggested that many veterans, always assumed to be yearning for outdoor life and adventure, would find opportunity in the enterprise. If the Alaska tundra and taiga would support the four million animals, and if a conservative estimate were made of the number of herders required to maintain close herding and move the animals between summer and winter ranges, then there would be an opportunity for 40,000 veterans to undertake the harshest kind of life and win precarious subsistence.[62]

The report dealt imaginatively with the relationship between agriculture and military defense during the war. Supposedly, as men and equipment were rushed to Alaska after Pearl Harbor, "Matanuska farmers, by almost superhuman efforts, were able to supply much of the necessary food supply in those critical days, thus freeing additional shipping space for defense materials."[63] In reality, actual production remained small despite official appeals for greater farm production, the classification of agriculture as an essential industry to which manpower would be directed, the offer of special food production loans by the FSA, the complaints of the ARRC management that farms were being neglected or abandoned if favor of employment in military construction, and the effect of land clearing and farm development begun before the war.[64] In Alaska in 1943, with a civilian population of 81,000 and the military population at its peak of about 152,000, the imports of food products for civilians alone had a value of nearly $26 million, or nearly $321 per capita.[65] In the same year, the MVFCA, which handled about 90 percent of all commercial agricultural sales for the valley, paid colonists and other farmers $302,781 for their products.[66] If 10 percent is added for sales outside the cooperative, and if all the farm products went to the military, then in 1943 the Matanuska farmers supplied the defense force in Alaska at the rate of approximately $2.24 per soldier, per year. Army purchasers required large quantities, graded quality, and reliable delivery. After the war, when local purchasing policy became more favorable, the actual deliveries on contracts in the valley for potatoes and vegetables averaged only 62 percent.[67] On the other hand, farmers were made cautious by unpredictable changes in the market. Early in 1946, with the war ended, farmers in the valley were at a loss to know what cash crops to plant. Many of them had assigned potatoes to the ARRC for debt payments and would be delinquent if the potatoes were not sold. Yet 1,600 tons of them were still in storage, with no market in sight, and some were eventually shipped to Canada on the chance that they could be sold for seed.[68]

In submitting the report on water resources in Alaska, the commissioner of the Bureau of Reclamation made the familar reference to the military significance of Alaska:

> It is interesting to note that the military authorities feel that the military works being constructed in Alaska, however modern they may be, are not sufficient to provide local security or protection to the United States. Alaska must have more people, more railroads, more farms, more industries.[69]

But from the days when it had been suggested that the establishment of the Matanuska Colony was militarily important,[70] it had never been explained how accelerated settlement would contribute to defense or what military role the settlers would play. However, populated or not, Alaska and the Candian North took on added importance with advances in long-range aviation. The Arctic and sub-Arctic region, crossed by the intercontinental great circle route for propeller-driven aircraft and later for jets and missiles, the region in which aircraft and missile early warning and communication systems were installed, became accessible in a few hours of flight, rather than by the long, hazardous, and costly surface travel that had been necessary a few years before.

In 1945, early in the new airborne penetration of the Arctic, the Arctic Institute of North America was organized to encourage and sponsor scientific research in the North, a new frontier challenging science to provide a basis "for the orderly development of a new land."[71] In its journal, *Arctic,* the institute published articles of technical and general interest; in its first ten years it sponsored approximately 160 research projects, and it prepared for publication by the Department of Defense a massive ten-volume bibliography of more than 62,000 entries on subjects related to the Arctic.[72] The difficulties encountered by the military services in keeping men and machines operating in extreme cold and in living, traveling, and building in the Arctic in any season, led to a variety of research projects undertaken by military organizations or by civilian researchers under contract.[73] By 1960 the army was spending about $50 million a year on basic scientific research in the Arctic, apart from programs of applied research and development.[74]

Out of the military activity and construction, federal spending, and subsidized research projects, a new kind of frontier developed—a cold-war, jet-and-missile-age version of the promoters' frontier. Alaska was the Gibraltar of the North, key to the defense of the whole polar and Arctic region, which was in the space age what the Mediterranean had been in the past.[75] The development of the whole American Arctic and sub-Arctic region was represented as lagging far behind Soviet achievements. With sufficient interest and scientific effort, the race for control of the polar region might yet be won:

However, unless we surrender, permanently and soon, the view that there is some quite fundamental difference between the Arctic and areas farther south, we shall not colonize any appreciable part of it in the lifetime of those here today—and our descendants may watch "The Northward Course of Empire," in Asia, spilling over the pole to become a southward one in North America![76]

Stimulated by research opportunities, sometimes subsidized by defense agencies, a number of geographers contributed to the promotion of the new military frontier in the North. Disregarding the continued worldwide urban drift of population, some writers referred to a movement of population to Alaska as already in progress and needing only encouragement and helpful planning.[77] Spokesmen for the new or last frontier altered the supposed relationship between people and free land or resources. If people no longer needed, or did not know they needed, the frontier, the frontier needed people and in time would get them. Thus it was possible to assert with assurance, as a matter of common agreement, what was not at all agreed upon: "Few people would doubt that northern North America needs more people. Nor is there much question that the region can support and will have a greater population in the near future."[78]

To less optimistic observers, the northward flow of population seemed choked off or feebly trickling. In language that had often been used in connection with Alaska, a group of American geographers produced for the Office of the Chief of Naval Operations a study of the whole of northern Canada. In discussing the Arctic and sub-Arctic region, the contributors lamented the sparsity of population and the decline of Dawson and Whitehorse since the slackening of the gold-mining boom and, for Whitehorse, the end of wartime activity.[79] In tone and content the study suggested that the contributors had contrived to miss the cautionary studies of Alaska and the historical and economic studies of the Candian frontier and of fringe pioneer settlement:

Yukon Territory, like other northern portions of North America, suffers from the lack of any comprehensive plan for its development. Capable of providing homes for millions of people, it is now inhabited by a mere handful, too few adequately to provide for its primary needs. The greater part of Norway and Sweden and all of Finland lie in the same latitude as Yukon Territory; they provide homes for ten million people, and yet their natural resources cannot compare with those in Yukon Territory. It is obvious that the methods of settling and developing the western portions of the United States and Canada will not suffice for the opening up of the North, and some plan more in keeping with the requirements of the situation must be devised.[80]

The interest in northern development turned research to old and presumably permanent settlements that might be used as models.[81] The Office of Naval Research sponsored an ambitious investigation of settlements in Scandinavia, Finland, Iceland, and Canada. For three years investigators from the United States, Canada, Norway, Sweden, and Finland examined old and new settlement and mile by mile plotted farm after farm on special maps "to determine what settlement experience in Norden [Scandinavia and Finland] . . . may be used in planning for present and additional settlement in northern North America."[82] Such projects stimulated graduate students in geography to undertake studies of northern Canada and Alaska.[83] A dissertation on Fairbanks examined climate, soil, terrain, urban development, transportation, and "amenties," and traced the development of mining and farming and the more recent military activity, without, however giving attention to the stagnation of farming and the sharp decline in mining. In presenting the study as a guide for planning future settlement the writer gave no hint of what settlement other than military might be expected or of who would plan and for what motive.

For some years during and just after the war, veterans had been expected to lead the way to Alaska because they were thought especially susceptible to the challenge of the modern frontier, but even they needed encouragement. Federal measures to liberalize credit and encourage housing construction and to aid in the building of various useful public works were justified because, "to develop this vast territory, a vast influx of people is needed," and such aids would "foster settlement and increase the permanent residents of Alaska."[84] By the late 1950s the view had changed somewhat. Alaska would be populated not only by the pull of the frontier but by the push from the outside. The pressure of population, the need for space, the increasing world demand for food, would bring thousands and then millions to tame the wilderness and develop industry and agriculture. That Alaska's population would swell with the overflow from the ever more crowded forty-eight states, and that the growth of the population would itself create the necessary economy, seemed a proposition so obvious to observation and common sense that it was usually offered as an axiom.[85] The actual increase in population in the older states and the expected increase in Alaska were useful in pressing for large projects such as the paving of the Canadian portion of the Alaska Highway or the construction of a huge hydroelectric dam on the Yukon, or in opposing another "lock up of Alaksa's resources" such as the creation of a great Arctic wildlife range.[86]

The popular attempts to guess Alaska's future population were hardly more varied than the estimates by federal and state agencies, economists, and business consultants.[87] All the estimates assumed continued migration to Alaska and an increase higher than the natural rate, and the highest, by the Bureau of Land Management, predicted a population of 1.5 million in 1980 and 5 million in the year 2012 (the 150th anniversary of the Homestead Act). One of the lowest estimates—a population of 393,000 by 1980—was based on an attempt to relate population growth to possible employment. The report by the Battelle Memorial Institute, a firm of consultants retained by the Alaska International Rail and Highway Commission, mentioned the possibility that federal and military spending in Alaska might be reduced and indicated the difficulties that had slowed agricultural development.[88] Yet it assumed that the level of federal spending would be maintained, that agriculture would be expanded eightfold in twenty years,[89] and that there would be expansion also in oil, gas, forest products, minerals, and metal processing. But all of that would add less than half of the increase of population to 393,000 by 1980. The rest, 87,600, would be added by tourism—if an already planned south-eastern ferry system were completed, if about $24 million were spent for highways, and if there were an "effective" promotion campaign. The authors of the report admitted that its view of the future was speculative and that statistical information of tourism was "limited, vague, and frequently unreliable." Nevertheless, they defended the value of the forecast: "Although the process of developing reasonable or plausible projections to 1980 was largely based on intuitive judgments, the final result is considered to be conservative and attainable."[90]

Military Alaska had grown from a population of 128,643 in 1950 to 226,127 in 1960. No vision of continued growth was possible unless continued military and other federal expenditures were assumed. If some uncertainty remained, the burden of economic prophecy could be simplified by entrusting the future, in familiar ceremonial language, to the pioneer spirit: "The indomitable and venturesome spirit of the Area's optimistic, industrious, pioneering populace will help greatly in ultimately hurdling obstacles lying in the way of full realization of the Area's promising economic potentials."[91]

11

The Frontier and Actuality: The New State

During the final campaign for statehood and upon Alaska's admission as the forty-ninth state, newspaper articles and editorials repeated the familiar themes of the wilderness, vast spaces, still unexploited resources, the promise of the future, and the cheerful hardiness of the twentieth-century pioneers.[1] Forty or fifty years of boosting and of popular writings had identified the *real* Alaska with mining towns, prospectors, trappers, sled dogs, wintry isolation, and uncounted wealth in fish and game. Journalists mentioned military bases, radar sites, and a largely urbanized population, but they more often used what they found ready-made, the stereotypes familiar to their readers. The real, essential Alaska was whatever it was that made it different from urban America. The old, wilderness Alaska that caught the imagination still did exist; some Alaskans lived and worked in a manner easily romanticized and falsified by misplaced emphasis. But the life of towns and apartments and employment in stores, banks, and offices, too commonplace to be Alaskan, received only passing attention.

The changes in the size and composition of the population and the decline or near disappearance of some of the older industries based on natural resources marked the difference between the old Alaska, which lingered through the 1930s, and postwar Alaska.[2] The Alaskan population of 59,278 in 1930 was smaller than that of 1910 or 1920, but with the rise in the price of gold to $35 an ounce, the publicity given the establishment of the Matanuska Colony, and the beginning of defense preparations, the population rose in the late 1930s and even more markedly in the following periods of war or prolonged military preparations. From 1950 to 1960 the population increased nearly 76 percent, from 128,643 to 226,127, while the simple extractive economy that had once supported most of a much smaller population shrank until it employed only 3 percent of the 1960 work force, except during the short salmon fishing and canning season. Copper mining, which had been worth about $200 million in less than thirty years, had already all but disappeared with the closing of the Kennecott mines in 1938; gold mining, pinched by rising costs and fixed price, declined from its peak of $23.9 million average annual production in the late 1930s to $3.9 million in 1961, with further reductions scheduled as the chief mining company planned the closing of remaining dredges in the Fairbanks and Nome districts. The salmon industry fell from an average annual pack of 6.9 million cases in the mid-1930s to an average of 2.5 million in the late 1950s and a low of 1.8 million in 1959, and although efforts to restore the salmon and to develop other fisheries gave promise of some improvement, there was little prospect that fishing would ever support more than a small part of the enlarged Alaskan population. Similarly, trapping wild furs supplemented the native economy and supported some white trappers or provided incidental income for others,[3] but changing fashions and rising costs caused the disappearance of fur farms. In 1939 there had been 164 fur farms with about 34,000 silver and blue foxes and mink; in 1960 not one fur farm was reported operating regularly in Alaska.[4]

Some of the declining industries were being replaced by others based on different resources. In southeastern Alaska the wood pulp industry, beginning with a mill opened at Ketchikan in 1954 and another at Sitka in 1959, by 1960 employed nearly 2,700 men at the seasonal peak; oil or natural gas exploration and production, the latter mostly on the Kenai Peninsula and in the Cook Inlet region, employed nearly 500 men by 1960, and the industry was expanding with the construction of a pipeline and refinery and paying in leases and royalties an important part of the public revenue of the state.[5]

However, the chief props of the Alaskan economy continued to be military and civilian government employment and the stream of federal money supporting military defense projects, public works, and the activities of the many federal agencies operating in Alaska. In 1960 the 32,692 men in the military service in Alaska amounted to one-third of all employed workers in the state. With their wives and children, they accounted for 20 to 25 percent of the population of the state. Employment by state and local governments accounted for about 7 percent of the work force, comparable with the rest of the United States, but federal military and civilian employment was 48.7 percent compared with a national rate of 6.8 percent.[6] The modest pay scales in lower military and civil service ranks and the sending of many military pay allotments to other states gave federal employees in Alaska a somewhat smaller share of total income (39 percent) than of jobs, but the rate was higher than that of any other state, exceeding even the 32 percent in the District of Columbia.[7] In addition, much military or government work, such as operating the DEW (Distant Early Warning) line, the White Alice communications system, and the BMEWS (Ballistic Missile Early Warning System) was done under civilian contract. As direct expenditures for large defense construction projects declined from the peak of $175 million in 1951, other public works increased. By the late 1950s, construction, 80 percent of it military or public works, provided 12.5 percent of Alaskan incomes, compared with the national average of 5 percent.[8] Finally, much of Alaska's wholesale and retail trade, transportation, and service industries depended on government purchases or on sales to military personnel and their families.[9]

Economic and military changes affected also the composition of the population and the ratio between the sexes. In 1910 only 1,288 of the whole population of 39,025 had been born in Alaska, and about half the foreign born were from Scandinavia, Finland, or Canada. By 1950 the foreign-born whites numbered less than 7 percent of the nonaboriginal population of 94,780, which included 13,295 Alaska-born whites.[10] The number of males per one hundred females declined from 259 in 1900 to 132 in 1960, and if the white population alone were considered the decline was from 852 to 138.[11] Despite the apparently increased stability of population, Alaskans continued to be largely newcomers: in the whole 1960 population over the age of five years, more than 40 percent had been living in another state in 1955, and the recent arrivals, unlike earlier immigrants, appeared to include a large number originally from the South and Southwest who had been brought to Alaska by military service or construction work and by the possibility of combining seasonal employment with homesteading or residence on a rural tract.[12]

The concentrated areas of population growth left much of Alaska still almost untouched wilderness. In 1960 the population density for the whole state was .4 persons per square mile, and great areas were crossed by air traffic but otherwise seldom penetrated and almost unpopulated. Far beyond the railroad and the highways, scattered villages in the bush were linked with each other and to the outside by air routes and winter sled trails or by river travel in summer. Alaska's population was concentrated in three areas: in the towns of the long-settled and comparatively stabilized southeast region; in south central Alaska, in Anchorage and the nearby military bases and civilian communities; and in a similar but smaller cluster around Fairbanks in the interior.

The 1960 census report of an urban population of 85,767, or 37.9 percent, understates the actual degree of urbanization. Minor changes in definition or in methods of reporting, to include in the Anchorage and Fairbanks urban population the immediately adjacent settlements and the nearby military bases, would realistically have classified nearly half the Alaskan population as urban.[13]

The publicity connected with statehood and a widespread belief in an Alaskan bonanza of jobs and high wages[14] helped restore the flow of migrating civilians—job-seekers, speculators, would-be homesteaders, rebels against urban life, the ill-informed, and those vaguely seeking a new start in a frontier conceived in television images. The post-World War II population gain by migration had reached an estimated maximum of 16,200 for the year 1952, but with the end of the Korean War, the completion of the largest construction projects, and the reduction of military forces from about 50,000 to 35,000, there had been a corresponding net emigration of civilians from 1954 through 1958.[15] In 1959 and 1960 there was again a gain by civilian immigration, in part attributable to the building of the BMEW station, but perhaps even more to the publicity of statehood. In the ten years after World War II the original homestead entries on more than 350,000 acres exceeded the prewar rate, but that homesteading seemed incidental to employment in construction, and after the passage of the required residence period only about one-third of the entries were patented.[16] Suddenly in 1959 and 1960, although the net population gain by migration was only 2,000 and 1,600, homesteading increased sharply to about four times the rate for the preceding ten years. Original entries were made on 130,967 acres in fiscal 1959 and in the following year there were 1,046 entries on 142,568 acres.[17]

The new homesteading rush was marked by a well-publicized and naïve attempt to reenact pioneer settlement—the incident of the so-called Fifty-niners[18]—organized in the Detroit area and inspired by a romantic desire to escape to the simplicity of the wilderness, by a remarkable ignorance of Alaskan conditions, and by the nationwide attention they received before they started and as they moved toward Alaska accompanied by two Detroit newspapermen and a photographer from *Life* magazine. In January an officer of the group appeared at Anchorage, inspected possible settlement areas on the Kenai Peninsula, interviewed the state commissioner of agriculture and the manager of the ARRC, and spoke of the fifty settlers who would soon come as the advance party for hundreds of others.

In the following weeks the Fifty-niners interested Congressman William S. Broomfield of Michigan in their undertaking and through him applied to officials in the Interior and Agriculture departments for the following special concessions: (1) the reservation of a block of 35,000 acres on Kenai Peninsula, where they hoped to settle; (2) designation of a part of the block as a townsite; (3) release to them of federal surplus food supplies; (4) donations of bulldozers, hospital and fire-fighting equipment, and other machinery; (5) modification of existing homesteading regulations so that they could meet settlement and cultivation requirements as a group rather than on individual 160-acre-tracts; and relaxation of the game laws so that they could live off the land. Although the concessions were not granted, Congressman Broomfield continued his efforts on behalf of the Fifty-niners even after they had arrived in Anchorage—supposedly the vanguard of a group of six hundred, according to exaggerated accounts in the news releases. The Anchorage newspaper urged every possible aid for the settlers and called for a federal program of road building and public improvements in the settlement areas "so that the latter half of the twentieth century will bring the reenactment of the drama that marked the latter half of the nineteenth, and the United States will reap the benefits by being bigger and stronger."[19]

On March 5, the Fifty-niners left Detroit—not fifty families, but thirty-eight people, including ten married couples, fourteen children, three bachelors, and one unmarried woman. They were tile-layers, pipe-fitters, workers in automobile parts factories, salesmen, and the leader was the former director of a dance studio. Perhaps prompted by reporters, they said they hoped in Alaska to get away from "the rat race." In preparation, many of the men had already grown beards. Traveling in convoy, they crawled at the pace of the twenty-three-year-old moving van that carried many of their heavy supplies. The van collapsed and had to be replaced and there were other mechanical troubles and delays, but the thirty-eight Fifty-niners were increased to forty-two by the recruitment of two Alaska-bound couples along the way. After twenty-three days of travel, more than twice as long as the journey should have taken, the caravan arrived at Palmer and was met and entertained by Don Irwin and old colonists and settlers. The next day the group arrived in Anchorage, where the public celebration, dinners, speeches, and the townspeople's generous interest and offers of help recalled the reception of the Matanuska colonists in 1935.[20]

The Fifty-niners as a group disintegrated in less than the time it had taken them to travel to Alaska. Two days after arriving in Anchorage, the leader resigned because of his wife's illness.[21] In another week most of the group members had stored their heavy equipment in borrowed sheds and were scattered at several places on the Kenai Peninsula helplessly awaiting the spring breakup and the melting of the heavy, rotting snow that prevented them from leaving the roads to look for homesteads.[22] In another ten days most of them straggled back to Anchorage, where four men had remained to study maps and records of the Bureau of Land Management. After an inspection trip northward, they recommended settlement on the west bank of the Susitna River, across from the little village of Talkeetna, about one hundred miles north of Anchorage by the Alaska Railroad.[23] Here there was little to hinder settlement. There were a few homesteads, some land had been leased for grazing but was unused, and there had been some prospecting and mining. But no highways connected Talkeetna's population of less than one hundred with the outside world. No bridge crossed the Susitna. In winter the frozen river could be crossed by vehicles; in summer by small boat or light aircraft, neither means capable of moving settlers' motor vehicles, house trailers, or household goods. Beyond the river there were no roads, only a tractor trail leading about thirty miles into the bush. However, the Fifty-niners believed the climate there would be better than on the Kenai Peninsula, and there undoubtedly was ample space for the large group of settlers they expected to follow them later that spring.[24]

Late in April, the Fifty-niners moved their possessions by Alaska Railroad to Talkeetna, unloaded, and faced the task, impossible without help, of crossing the river. The rotting ice would no longer bear the weight of trucks or trailers. Several Talkeetna men who had heavy tractors and winches helped them build log skids for the house trailers and other heavy equipment and pulled and winched the loads across the river ice. By April 24 most of the crossing was done, but leads opened in the ice and the rest of the goods had to wait in Talkeetna until the next winter. On the far side of the river fifteen people with three house trailers, two light trucks, one jeep, a light tractor, and some food supplies waited for the remaining slush to melt and then for drying ground so that they could move on the tractor trail to find homestead sites.[25] Of the other Fifty-niners, a few remained on the Kenai Peninsula looking for homesteads or jobs; the bachelors and the unmarried woman were reported looking for work in Anchorage, and others dropped out of sight.[26]

While the Fifty-niners were traveling and seeking their homestead sites, newspapers used the conventional language to speak of modern pioneers headed northward as earlier Americans had pushed West. Alaska's two senators and one representative praised the spirit of the new settlers and spoke of the countless inquiries they had received from others interested in Alaskan homesteading, although they dutifully added cautions about the difficulties to be faced.[27] *Life*, whose photographer supplied the pictures of the caravan, retold the story of the winning of the West and editorially counted the blessings of the frontier—the strength of a hybrid people, the boundless energy and optimism, the conviction that all barriers were made to be conquered. "As long as this spirit lives, the frontier will never die. Already some 'Fifty-niners' are prodding into the Alaskan spaces. But even when all new land is gone, the pioneer spirit will continue to uphold what the new land offered: freedom, equality, justice and the dignity of man."[28]

In Alaska the *Anchorage Daily Times*, from the center of the region in which most new settlement was expected, predicted more benefits to Alaska from people settling on the land than from all "boomers and apartment dwellers." "It is grand that Alaska is attractive and has the land for new settlers. It is equally grand that modern-day Americans have the physical, mental, and spiritual courage to undertake the hard life of opening the frontier." The pioneering would not be easy, and the Fifty-niners were to be praised for their courage in undertaking a migration to the wilderness in which the weak would be screened out. "Those who lack vision, imagination, courage, and ambition are eliminated in this screening. Weaklings rarely survive it." After the group reached Anchorage, the newspaper found a special significance in the arrival. A new chapter in American history was being written:

> The great Christian civilization is reaching a new apex in its constant march to the north. . . . The pioneer spirit of 100 years ago has been rekindled. Americans are once more on the march. Last century, the spirit prompted waves of pioneers to move westward across the Appalachians, the central and western plains and the Rocky Mountains to the Pacific Coast. Today the same spirit has initiated another great migration. This time it is northward to Alaska, the newest state of the union.
>
> Hundreds of persons have already arrived in quest of a new life. Indications are that thousands more are coming. They are attracted by the prospect of free land, the same lure that inspired their forefathers to pull up stakes and move westward.[29]

Other hopeful settlers did follow the first group of Fifty-niners to Alaska: three families from northern New York, one three-generation family of twenty-six people from Michigan, an Iowa man traveling on foot and pushing a golf cart,[30] and others whose migration went unnoticed by the press. The main body of Michigan Fifty-niners, once estimated at six hundred, numbered only nineteen families or seventy-six persons when in June they finally left for Alaska.[31] Given less newspaper attention than the first group of Fifty-niners, they scattered through the region at the west end of the Matanuska Valley and toward the Susitna River, or moved to Anchorage to look for work, or returned discouraged to Michigan.[32]

The Fifty-niners who had settled across the Susitna lived in their trailers and tents, struggled through the mud to select homestead sites, cut small clearings, began putting up log cabins and wanigans, and planted potato and vegetable gardens on land cleared by an earlier settler. Some of the men found occasional employment in the fall and winter, and by the following spring, after several withdrawals and the birth of a child in one family, there were thirteen left. A magazine account of their homesteading related success simply to sufficient pioneer sturdiness.[33] Two and a half years later the group had been joined by several bachelors and numbered seventeen. Feeling comfortably assured of their success, they spoke to a reporter of mistakes in the original planning, their struggle to make homes in the bush, and, as it seemed to them, the homesteads and security won by their unaided efforts.[34]

However, their security and homesteads were uncertain victories. The land would supply them with vegetables and potatoes; the grain and hay from the cleared acres would feed a few cows, and the bush and the river would supply them with moose, caribou, and fish. But no products of their farming could be moved to market except in tiny quantities across the river to the scattering of people along the railroad, most of whom had their own truck gardens. Some part-time trapping might add a little cash income, but full-time trapping would require movement far into the bush for months at a time. For all Alaska, trapping could not be significantly increased; its yield could only be spread thinner. Had they depended solely on their homesteads and on fish and game, the Fifty-niners would have gained the barest subsistence from which they would have been compelled to trim almost every need requiring cash. However, one couple operated a small grocery store at Talkeetna, and other men found employment off their homesteads, largely work on the still unconnected highway being pushed through the Susitna Valley and along the line of the Alaska Railroad.[35] Such highway construction provided the summer jobs that made it possible for much of Alaska's isolated village and bush population to live through the rest of the year. Desirable in themselves, added highways were especially attractive as job-making projects because the federal share of the cost was about 94.6 percent.[36]

If the Fifty-niners' success was not the kind usually associated with homesteading, few others made any more rapid progress in turning the Alaskan wilderness into farms. Had the approximately 2,000 homestead entries of 1959 and 1960 on 272,000 acres been cleared and cultivated at the rate of one-sixteenth in the second year and one-eighth in the third and succeeding years, then 34,000 acres should have been added to Alaska's cropland in those two years alone. However, if the pattern of the past was repeated, only about one-third of all original entries would continue successfully to patent,[37] and many patented homesteads would became rural residences only or would be abandoned. A homesteader, even while he was fulfilling the residence and cultivation requirements, was unlikely to add much to the total area of cropland since "cultivation" was interpreted to allow casual plowing and the planting of a forage crop that the homesteader had no intention of harvesting.[38] By 1963, in the whole state 10,680 acres were planted in crops, an increase of 1 percent over 1962; 9,815 acres were harvested, and there was in addition a harvest of 8,700 acres of seeded or native grasses for a total of 19,380 acres that could be called cultivated agricultural land.[39] Agricultural statistics in Alaska have been notoriously unreliable,[40] but it appeared that in spite of land clearing averaging about 2,000 acres a year, the area of actual cultivation had increased slowly through the 1950s and little more in the early 1960s when the effects of increased homesteading should have been seen.[41] Like the cultivated area, the value of agricultural production increased slowly and gave little support for the belief in the state's "tremendous agricultural potential." By including the value of products consumed by farm families and by double-counting the value of farm-produced livestock feed and the products of the livestock, the total value of Alaskan farm production in 1960 was put at $5.4 million, but the value of actual commercial production was only 3.8 million.[42] To reach that level there had been nearly sixty years of homesteading in Alaska, 3,277 patented homesteads, and 375,000 acres patented.[43] Yet at the end of 1959 there were only 175 full-time farmers in Alaska, 328 part-time farmers, another 125 settlers likely to become full- or part-time farmers in five or ten years, and 1,170 homesteads then occupied and in the process of developing toward patent.[44]

Except for reindeer herding in western Alaska and on Nunivak Island, by law confined to natives and regulated by the Bureau of Indian Affairs, and beef and sheep raising, mostly by a few ranchers using leased public land for grazing on Kodiak and Chirikof islands and on part of the Aleutians, Alaskan agriculture was clustered in a few limited areas: the scattered parts of the southeastern panhandle of Alaska where climate and terrain were favorable, the Kenai Peninsula, the Anchorage area, the Tanana Valley around Fairbanks, and the Matanuska Valley.[45] In the Fairbanks region, where there had been some farming from early in the century, the number of farmers in 1959 was about the same as it had been in the early 1920s, although the cropped area had trebled to about 3,000 acres. Although there were 260 current homesteaders and for miles around Fairbanks most accessible land that was not under mineral claims or in military reservations had passed to private title by homesteading, one large dairy farm, several smaller ones, and some potato farms accounted for most of the farm production. In spite of the six hundred or more homesteads that had been patented in the area,[46] a visitor accustomed to the appearance of farming areas in the forty-eight states would have found the Tanana Valley no more than touched by agriculture.

In southeastern Alaska—the old, long-established Alaska—there were fifteen full-time and thirty part-time farmers. Few areas suitable for agriculture could be found in the strip of islands, channels, mountains, and rain forests. With their market confined to the nearest towns in the region, those who hoped to farm in southeastern Alaska were limited in their choice of land, especially since most of the area lay in the Tongass National Forest. However, the Forest Homestead Act of 1906, until its repeal in 1962, allowed the secretary of agriculture to declare areas within the national forest agricultural in character and to relinquish them to the Department of the Interior for the purpose of homesteading.[47] By 1948 in the southeastern region, there had been 466 such forest homestead applications in the Tongass Forest, but 250 were rejected before they were released for homesteading. Of the 216 open for filing, 26 were revoked after further examination, and the remaining 190 were entered, some several times, two of them by five successive homesteaders. Patents had been given on 102 of them, with the others in various stages short of patent, but 69 of the 102 patented homesteads had been abandoned.[48] In 1959, the other 33 patented homesteads were presumably among the 45 full- and part-time farms, and an additional 40 homestead entries were then current.

The west side of the Kenai Peninsula, which had been publicized for forty or fifty years as a promising area for future agricultural growth, in 1959 had 295 active homesteaders but only 10 full-time and 30 part-time farmers and 5 percent of the state's agricultural production. A few homestead entries had been made before 1920, but the two or three hundred people in the area had depended on some fishing, local salmon canneries, and a succession of small and eventually fading enterprises in gold and coal mining and fur farming.[49] In the late 1930s interest in the area was increased by the publicity given the Matanuska Colony and by the frequent suggestions that a similar colony be established on the peninsula. Again, after World War II, increased homesteading was probably caused by the proposals for government-sponsored group settlement and by the homesteading advantages enjoyed by veterans. In anticipation of the group-settlement plan, several areas on the peninsula were withdrawn from entry, but when Congress failed to pass enabling legislation, and before the revocation of the withdrawals, soil surveys were used to lay out in four localities 178 desirable homesteads, which were then opened to entry, with veterans given first preference. By 1955 there were 851 homesteads on the west side of the peninsula, 458 of them patented, containing 109,629 acres. However, many tracts had been entered several times, some four or five times, and one tract had had nine successive entries. The average number of entries for all 851 homestead tracts was 1.8 per tract, or more than 1,500 original homestead entries in the region. Nevertheless, 59 percent of the land was unoccupied and abandoned, 31 percent was used solely for rural residences, and only 10 percent was occupied by persons who were farming or planning to farm. The 17 full-time and 21 part-time farms contained 5,682 acres, but all cropland and newly cleared land amounted to 1,585 acres and only 460 acres were actually cropped in 1955. The persistence of settlement despite the scanty farm production and the lack of any other solid economic base was a triumph of endurance and patched-together family economies. No important industries or centers of population provided employment. On the east side of the peninsula, far from main homesteading areas, the port town of Seward was shrinking to fewer than 2,000 people. Homesteaders nevertheless in 1955 drew 86 percent of their incomes from nonfarm sources: for some years after the war, payments to about half the homesteaders by the Veterans Administration for their on-the-farm training, then seasonal or full-time employment in construction, local canneries, fishing, and highway maintenance by the Alaska Road Commission. In addition, there were incomes from other real estate, pensions, self-employment, and small businesses. Most of the families stretched their cash incomes by using their own vegetables, wild berries, and wood for fuel, and by hunting and fishing. Moose meat was worth $32,889 to the 84 families that reported, or nearly $400 per family and about one-tenth of average total family income, and many others who used moose meat failed to report. For the average homesteader all income in cash or goods failed to meet total expenses, and the difference, about $100 a year per family was drawn from savings or borrowed. By these expedients homesteaders and farmers clung to their holdings and even made some gains. Reported farm sales for the whole area were $91,535 in 1955. By 1959 there were only ten full-time and thirty part-time farmers, but sales more than doubled to $186,192. However, $106,097 of that was in egg production by a few poultry farmers supplying the Anchorage market, and of 2,060 acres of cropland over a thousand were idle and 715 out of the 968 cropped acres were in grass.[50]

In contrast to the scatter of small farms and the barely perceptible agriculture in other areas, the Matanuska Valley had the appearance and atmosphere of a farming area, although the cropland and production of the valley could have been equaled in the corner of one county in a midwestern state. By 1949 the valley had 69 percent of Alaska's cropped acreage, more than two-thirds of its milk production, more than half its potato crop, and half its poultry and egg production. Ten years later there were 105 full-time and 120 part-time farmers and 250 homesteaders in the valley. Just under 60 percent of all Alaskan farm production was in the valley, and if the area were defined to include the farmers closer to Anchorage, it would account for 70 percent or more of Alaskan production.[51] In 1948, 63 original colonist families remained in the valley, 6 without the original family heads; 35 of them were living on their colony tracts, but only 12 families were deriving all or most of their incomes from farming.[52] By 1961 age, retirement, and death had thinned the colonist group. Members of 60 colonist families were still in Alaska, 50 were in the general valley area, 5 or 6 were farming full-time, and a few farmed part-time or gardened on small plots they had retained after retirement.[53] The movement out of farming was not limited to the colonists or especially notable among them. The 255 part- and full-time farmers and the 40,000 acres in farms were what was left after more than forty years of settlement—the 117 homesteading families or single settlers in the valley just before colonization, the 202 colonists, the 100 or more replacements in the colony by the early war years, the

ARRC-approved purchasers of land in the Matanuska Reserve after the war, and the several hundred final homestead entries in the late 1940s and through the 1950s. If all had stayed, there would have been 700 or 800 operating farms in the valley by 1960.

In the constant movement of settlers in and out of the valley and in the rapid change of ownership of even well-developed farms—among one hundred full-time farmers there were twenty-five transfers of ownership in the three years from 1951 through 1953[54]—there appeared always to be new recruits for farming. In farm sales in the late 1950s uncleared land on unimproved tracts sold for $100 an acre or more, and well-developed farms brought, exclusive of stock and equipment, as high as $65,000 with cleared areas at $250 and $300 an acre.[55] With the transfer of ownership there was a consolidation and enlargement of farms, and the old colony tracts of from forty to eighty acres almost disappeared. As early as 1939 or 1940, while it still exercised close control over the colony, the ARRC had begun to combine tracts as some became vacant, and later the farmers themselves purchased neighboring tracts or bought additional land from the ARRC reserve. By 1960 the valley farms averaged 226 acres.[56] A study of fifteen well-established dairy farms in the valley showed an average investment of $66,303, an owner's equity of 58 percent, and a net cash income of $7,523.[57] Such farms were among the few most highly developed in Alaska, and even by the agricultural standards of the other forty-eight states they were substantial, qualifying at the lower end of the best and most productive tenth of all farms.[58] However, adjusting the Matanuska dairy farmer's income by a conservative 20 to 25 percent to allow for the high Alaska price level at which he had to buy all goods and services would make his income about $5,600 to $6,000, well below those from comparably developed dairy farms in eastern Wisconsin, for example.[59]

The twenty-five years of development in the valley, with all its uncertainties, built the only Alaskan community based on agriculture. In 1930 there had been no town of Palmer, and in the whole region from the Matanuska River to the Susitna and north to the village of Talkeetna and beyond, well over 20,000 square miles, there were 876 people. With the coming of the Matanuska settlement project, the district population grew to 2,390 in 1939 and Palmer and the community center across the railroad tracks together had a population of 244. By 1950 Palmer's population was 890; in 1961 it reached 1,181, and the whole district had a population of 5,188. By Alaskan standards of community growth, Palmer had become a town of considerable importance.[60] In 1958 the assessed valuation of real and personal property in the town was $6.4 million, and the valuation in the school district, an area larger than the town itself, was $14.4 million.[61] The Matanuska Valley Farmers Cooperating Association, with 125 employees and branches in Anchorage, Fairbanks, and Kodiak,[62] marketed most of the valley's potatoes, milk, and vegetables and sold general merchandise, agricultural supplies, machinery, and equipment. Palmer and most of the farms in the valley were served by the Matanuska Electric Association, the first Rural Electrification Administration (REA) cooperative organized in Alaska, and where once, at the start of the colony, there had been a single telephone linking the colonists to Anchorage, the Matanuska Telephone Association reached nearly one thousand subscribers. Other cooperatives operated the community hospital, crop improvement and artificial breeding associations, a recreation camp and a fair, and Palmer and Wasilla had granges, 4-H clubs, and other farm organizations.[63]

Although Palmer was Alaska's nearest approach to a farming community, farming there and elsewhere in Alaska was delicately sensitive to the rate of federal spending and the amount of military or other construction. Dairy farmers in 1958 circulated a petition for the suspension of homesteading until the market for fresh milk should improve, producers of potatoes and other crops felt similarly pinched, and the total Alaska net income from farming (gross income by sale or use, less farm production expenses) was about $2 million, or less than .5 percent of all personal income in the state.[64] Even the official buoyancy of salaried agriculturists at times sagged. The long series of bulletins begun in 1902 by C. C. Georgeson to advise pioneer settlers in Alaska was continued with a 1958 edition that seemed more a warning than an invitation.[65] Although it called Alaskan agriculture a growing industry, the bulletin gloomily warned of the uncertainties of the market, the high cost of land clearing, the heavy investment in labor and cash needed to make a farm, the tightness of credit, and the inadequacy of the 160-acre homestead. A few years later the Department of the Interior published a thorough and useful guide for prospective settlers that minimized none of the difficulties of agricultural settlement and warned off the romantic searchers for wilderness simplicity and those who had no stomach for heavy work, hardship, and isolation.[66]

If, despite the warnings, farming or the chance to acquire a quarter section of the wilderness continued to draw some settlers to Alaska, the end of the old pattern of homesteading federal land was in sight after

Alaska became a state. Under the Statehood Act of 7 July 1958 the new state was authorized to acquire within twenty-five years 103,350,000 acres, or slightly more than one-fourth the area of the whole state, from the vacant, unappropriated, and unreserved federal lands.[67] Since the act barred the state land selection in the great area north and west of the Porcupine and Yukon rivers, on the west coast, or on the western end of the Alaska Peninsula or the Aleutian Islands, all of which was held for possible defense withdrawals by presidential order,[68] the state's selections would be concentrated near population centers or where settlement might sometime be expected. In the first few years after Alaska's admission to the Union, the Division of Lands began selecting the areas along highways and rivers, the land under oil and gas leases, and the most promising mineral and agricultural land.[69] In twenty-five years, on the completion of the program of land acquisition, there would remain about 260 million acres of federal land, of which approximately 92 million acres would be in national defense, forest, wildlife, mineral, or other reserves. The remaining 168 million acres would almost all be inaccessible, much of it in tundra or mountainous regions.[70]

To replace dwindling opportunities for homesteading, to gain revenue from the disposal of state land, and to avoid any appearance of continuing the supposed federal "lock up" of land and resources, the first state legislature created the Division of Lands in the Department of Natural Resources and authorized it to sell agricultural land at public auction or, failing sale by auction, at the minimum appraised price.[71] The division limited buyers to 640 acres, four times the size of the old "inadequate" quarter section, but allowed both husband and wife to buy, required a 10 percent down payment, gave credit for ten years at 5 percent, and provided that the buyer could pay most of the balance of the debt by claiming credit for such specific development work as clearing, cultivating, fencing, and construction.[72] Most of the tracts offered for sale were 80 to 320 acres, valued as high as $60 an acre. By the end of 1963, the Division of Lands had sold sixty-three such homesteads. Two sales had been canceled, fifty-three were being paid for in cash, and eight were being paid partly in credits for buildings or construction of access roads.[73]

Although by the 1950s few agricultural experts or economists any longer expected marked growth in Alaskan farming or land settlement, men in public life knew that farming and settlement, like mining and fishing, were relics of the old Alaska and were to be treated with prudence and ceremony. When George W. Rogers, an economist long familiar with Alaska and a consultant to the Alaska State Division of Planning, was quoted by a newspaper in Washington, D.C., on the difficulties facing Alaskan farmers and the economic waste involved in attempting to develop farming, he was answered indignantly by the director of the Division of Agriculture, and one member of the legislature demanded that the governor discharge Rogers because "we need realistic economists in the State Division of Planning—those who will advise how to do it better instead of crying it can't be done."[74]

Nor did public officials or the press find it wise to comment on the social cost of continued settlement. In the older Alaska the settlers in remote areas, largely bachelors who mixed homesteading and some truck gardening with mining or trapping, had expected, and perhaps wanted, very little development of roads, schools, and school-bus systems. For children beyond the small settlements where there were schools, the territory and later the state provided correspondence courses. But in the new Alaska many settlers were convinced that by homesteading in remote areas they were engaged in the praiseworthy task of opening the frontier. They complained bitterly if roads and schools did not follow them promptly into the bush, or they petitioned the governor, the legislature, and the school districts to keep pioneer access roads open through the winter and to operate school buses over long routes for a few children.[75] In the region northwest of the Matanuska Colony area, homesteaders in the late 1950s and early 1960s awaited prosperity from increasing tourism or oil exploration. A few of them seriously intended to develop full-time farms and had the necessary experience, equipment, and suitable land, but, even so, self-supporting agriculture for them lay years ahead. Others had arrived in Alaska bearded, long-haired, dressed in television-inspired frontier style, believing that a garden patch and ten acres of potatoes would support a family and that any homesteader could shoot a moose according to need, without regard to season or limit.[76] Depending on construction, railroad, or highway work in the brief summer season, they were certain that settlement itself would soon create a thriving economy in the region. Whether patented or not, their homesteads were free of any property tax, state funds were allotted for local public works projects at the village of Willow, and, until a local school could be built, four buses traveled more than sixty miles twice a day to take settlers' children to the school at Wasilla, a school operated entirely by the state in an unincorporated town and school district where villagers paid no property tax.[77]

Yet there was little protest, and continued homesteading, which helped to preserve some flavor of the past, was always treated with ceremonial respect in the press. Even to urban Alaskans, vicarious homesteaders and wilderness dwellers, a growing city such as Anchorage, with its surrounding communities and military bases, all together having about one-third of Alaska's population, was not the *real* Alaska. In the bush one found the increasingly rare *typical* Alaskan.[78] Those who had energetically promoted Alaskan development and the growth of Anchorage into a "Fifth Avenue on the tundra," and who had fretted at any delay in Alaskan growth, then nostalgically recalled the old ways and regretted their passing. One long-time publicist of Alaskan growth recommended to new Alaskan readers the published reminiscences of an old Alaskan:

> Mr. Snider has portrayed an Alaskan way of life which is no more, and it brings a tug at the heartstrings to read of the days when men's closeness to nature brought out the best in them. So-called civilization is extinguishing those sparks of courage, adventure, and selflessness which characterized the early settlers. I recommend this book to Alaska's newcomers to challenge their recognition of the unique qualities which Alaska has to offer in building a way of life satisfactory to the inner soul.[79]

Newcomers often joined old Alaskans in sighing for the past. In the towns, as log houses and wood-burning stoves were replaced by steel and concrete buildings and fuel oil, the preserved remnants of the commercially valuable frontier were mixed with incongruous importations, and dog sleds, river boats, and other once necessary equipment were kept for sport and for their power to evoke real or fanciful recollections of the past. Beyond the towns and away from the few highways, the tremendous area of the bush remained almost unchanged. But even there the old ways were affected by the new. Helicopters delivered men and equipment for oil exploration; plastic-wrapped bread, baked in Fairbanks of flour milled perhaps in Minneapolis from Kansas wheat, was delivered in airplanes to Indian and Eskimo villages far to the north and piled for sale beside raw furs on trading post counters; and in Fort Yukon a river freighter between trips on the Porcupine brought ready-cooked and frozen foil-wrapped dinners. Some men still lived in the bush by hunting, trapping, and mining, appearing in a village now and then to buy a few of their supplies. Others ingeniously combined the activities of trader, guide, postmaster, bush pilot, freighter, and commercial fisherman.

Those who lived in approximately frontier style were generally not impatient promoters of the last frontier. Both the sentimental farewells to pioneer days and the urgent demands for growth and development issued from offices in the towns. In the Matanuska Valley, the remaining original colonists, living neither in the Alaskan urban pattern nor in the isolation of the bush, were generally settled and content, neither boosters nor mourners of the past. None of them regretted the move to Alaska, nearly all felt that their standards of living had in the long run been improved, and, but for a lingering memory of conflict with the ARRC, the old troubles of the colony were forgotten.

The ceremonial frontier vocabulary continued to be expected on public occasions. Nearly thirty years after his service as physician in the Matanuska Colony, a professor at an eastern medical school repeated the familiar catalogue of Alaska's natural wealth and urged the members of a university graduating class—educated as accountants, teachers, engineers—to be inspired by Alaska's vastness, to be taught by Alaska's mountains, and to be made strong and courageous by the wilderness.[80]

But it seemed clear that although the frontier beyond the Alaskan towns exerted a sentimental attraction, it offered only what Rexford G. Tugwell had seen in the subsistence homesteads of the 1930s—"small eddies of retreat for exceptional persons."[81]

12

Conclusion

In 1914, when American pioneer settlement was still a recent experience, well within the memories of middle-aged men, Frederick Jackson Turner made one brief reference to American wheat farmers invading the Canandian West and to Alaska beckoning with its resources.[1] Although he did not write on western Canada and Alaska, Turner kept notes and gathered clippings and articles on farmers migrating to Canada, land speculations, promotion of boom towns, Alaskan resources, and early twentieth-century controversies over conservation.[2] In his collection is a 1911 article by the Canadian-born writer Arthur Stringer celebrating progress in the Canadian West and the growth yet to come—the railroads being built to develop the vast area, the promise everywhere, north to the Peace River country, the Mackenzie, even to the Arctic Ocean.

> The one thing that all this great treasure land lacks is labor. All it needs is men and women, stout-hearted men and deep-bosomed women, millions and millions of them, to follow the ever creeping threads of steel . . . to make their homes where a new century has so amazingly thrown open what is destined to be a new empire.[3]

Twenty-five years later, Stringer, by then an established novelist and Hollywood script writer, was disappointed in the Matanuska Colony. He wrote of misfits, weaklings, and malcontents, but he thought that those colonists who persisted would establish a "new and vigorous strain of pioneers."[4]

When Turner mentioned Alaska and western Canada, agricultural settlement was still a believable form of opportunity. Some flavor of the frontier lingered in many parts of rural America, and farm life was more self-sufficient than could be imagined a few decades later. In the early period of the Matanuska Colony, when Stringer wrote, examples of pioneer settlement in Canada, in regions comparable with Alaska, seemed models of what might be hoped for in the territory. From the late 1890s to 1914, about one million Americans had entered western Canada, drawn by the advertisement of settlement opportunities or pushed by the shrinking supply of good, cheap agricultural land in the western states.[5] Most settlers remained within reach of the railroads and as quickly as they could became commercial wheat producers, but some, Canadians, Americans, and others, pushed to the fringes of settlement and beyond, to areas that could be reached only after weeks of difficult wagon travel. As early as 1907 there were some Americans in the Peace River district, where there were no roads, no schools, no medical service, and where mail to and from Edmonton took two months.[6] Except for broken patches of prairie, the land was in brush and timber and required heavy labor with axes and stump pullers to be prepared for cultivation. The rainfall was barely adequate, the growing season was short, there were pockets of local frost at almost any time in the year, and there were no markets. Yet even before the railroad in 1916 reached the town of Peace River on the edge of the district, there was a rush of optimistic settlers; the population of the area rose from less than 2,000 in 1911 and less than 20,000 in 1921 to 50,000 in 1931, the year after the railroad finally reached Dawson Creek.[7]

Despite the decline of American immigration after 1914, the effects of the war, and the postwar depression, settlement continued in the 1920s and early 1930s, notably in the northern fringe areas of the prairie provinces, aided by British and Canadian arrangements for assisted settlement by veterans, and by encouragement of European immigration and land settlement. Declining prices distressed the highly specialized wheat farmers, but in fringe areas, especially among European immigrant settlers, more general farming, production and storage for family consumption, the use of available natural products—fish, game, berries, and wood for fuel—and the thrifty reduction of cash needs, allowed many families to weather the depression.[8]

In the United States there was still some successful homesteading in the 1930s; in backwater areas of older settlements a combination of small farming or gardening, occasional cash employment, hunting and fishing, woodcutting, and barter and exchange of services provided more comfortable livings than small cash incomes would indicate; and in a few closely knit rural communities customary frugality, intensive farming, and mutual help created a solid prosperity in startling contrast to the general agricultural depression elsewhere.[9]

However, the examples of continued pioneer settlement were misleading. On closer examination, the million Americans who migrated to western Canada shrink to one-fifth that number in permanent settlement; an increasing portion of American settlers moved to the eastern provinces and to occupations other than farming, and at no time in the early years of the century did the number of final patents on Canadian homestead land exceed one-third the number of entries.[10] Whatever was accomplished to win pioneer self-sufficiency on the fringes of settlement, population remained thickly concentrated in the southern areas of the prairie provinces, and the prosperity and development of the region depended on the production of wheat for the world market.[11]

In both Canada and the United States, stability and permanence of settlement, the habit of community cooperation, and success in resisting the effects of depression were found most marked in settlements united by religious or ethnic ties.[12] In backwoods America, where an approximation of the frontier style persisted, the modern pioneers lived beside rather than in the American economy, and their necessary skills and versatility and ability to do without many of the goods and services obtainable for cash were fast disappearing.

In contrast to American dedication to individualism in land settlement and farming, those parts of the world outside North America that in the twentieth century had space for added settlement looked for group colonization by men who were experienced or trained in the most modern agricultural methods, who were well financed or subsidized and willing to work cooperatively. Even in the late nineteenth century persecuted Jews from Eastern Europe found refuge in South America, especially Argentina, where agricultural colonies were formed under the sponsorship of the Jewish Colonizing Association and the Baron Maurice de Hirsch.[13] After World War I, and especially in the period of Nazi persecutions, the colonization continued, settling mostly German Jews until World War II stopped migration. In such colonization projects there was financial aid for travel and settlement and provision for supervision and community social services and for occupational training or apprenticeship. By the 1960s some of the Argentine colonies had been in existence for well over a half century, second and third generation colonists had taken on the "gaucho culture," and Argentina had a Jewish population of half a million, including current or past colonists and persons in many other occupations.[14]

Between 1947 and 1952 the International Refugee Organization helped resettle one million European refugees, most of them overseas.

From 1952 to 1972 the Intergovernmental Committee for European Migration (ICEM) aided the resettlement of just under two million persons, about half of them classified as refugees. Latin America received over 300,000 European immigrants, many of them professionally or technically trained in specialties requested by the host countries. Among the newcomers were skilled farmers, including settlers in cooperative colonies. Their own production raised agricultural standards, and in addition, under ICEM sponsorship, some of them provided instruction in agricultural schools for neighboring farmers. The ICEM refers to its work as a contribution or investment of human capital for economic and social development, particularly in Latin America.[15]

Those countries receiving farmer–immigrants hoped to gain not only by improvement in the standards of agriculture and by more varied and intensive production, but also by offsetting the mass movement of rural people to the cities. The migrating European farmers, typically members of families that had farmed for many generations, found that as urbanization ate up the countryside, agricultural opportunity was increasingly cramped. An ICEM agricultural consultant, discussing planned, directed, cooperative immigrant land settlement, wrote:

> Tens of thousands of landless farmers and their sons are ready and willing to uproot themselves from their ancestral homes and settle in new lands, rather than give up the farming way of life. It is indeed remarkable how . . . these men, whose families have been wedded to agriculture for generations, have refused new opportunities in towns and factories created by the present industrial boom in Europe. The availability of these settlers for any land settlement scheme is the foremost guarantee of success.[16]

Such steadfast devotion to agriculture was rarely found in Alaska. Until the late 1930s, land settlement there on a modest scale still seemed possible, but even during the depression the goal of simple subsistence and family security was changing, becoming less attractive, and poverty meant the lack of urban conveniences and standards of consumption. Skilled, established farmers could not be selected for the Matanuska Colony; they had no reason to move to Alaska, and the project was not designed for them. Many of the colonists actually selected had much of the pioneer jack-of-all-trades versatility, and if selection could have been made to include in addition some peasant attachment to the land and belief in the virtue of work, some of the community feeling found among the Mormons, Amish, and Mennonites, and perhaps some of the romantic rejection of the city and of the lures of a commercial civilization, then the career of the colony might have been smoother. Most of the colonists were probably not good enough farmers to proceed on their own; yet they were familiar enough with farming to resent guidance. They were largely rural residents and relief clients, but they came from an area with a fairly high level of living, and they expected cars, radios, telephones, decent roads, schools, and buses. They were accused by journalists and others of lacking pioneer qualities—that is, virtues. But they displayed other traits that may also have been characteristic of some pioneers—restlessness, impatience with careful routine, suspicion of authority, garrulity in discussing local civic affairs, a fondness for open country life, and a very moderate taste for farm drudgery.[17]

The troubles of the colony were much like those reported in other resettlement projects. Although they enjoyed a rise in their levels of living after admission to the projects, and higher levels than their non-project neighbors, and although they showed a degree of participation in community affairs that pleased reporting sociologists, the members of such resettlement communities were chronically uneasy and indefinably discontented, bickered among themselves and with the management, complained of mistreatment, and withdrew from the communities for reasons that could not be clearly stated.[18] The Dyess Colony, Arkansas, was originally planned for 750 family units, but that was reduced to 500 before occupancy. Between March 1936 and March 1938 252 families left the project because of "bad health," "general dissatisfaction," "failure to cooperate," and "outside attractions."[19] At the Casa Grande project in Arizona, a cooperative farm community, the settlers, many of whom had formerly been squatting in abandoned shacks or sleeping in fields in makeshift tents, had better houses and higher wages than the local standard and, in addition, growing equities in the successful group-operated farm. Yet they quarreled, accused the management of incompetence, wrote letters of complaint that, by their tone, might have come from the Matanuska Colony, and hastily liquidated the project when FSA management was withdrawn, losing the greater part of their equities and returning to agricultural labor or other uncertain employment.[20]

The Matanuska Colony faced hazards not met in other resettlement projects. For the first five or six years its affairs were conducted in a glare of publicity that neither the management nor the colonists could ignore; the colonists were led to think of themselves as truly pioneers, and onlookers were disappointed to find that they were not. After the war boom and postwar military construction had transformed Alaska and had removed whatever remained of the possibility of pioneer settlement—or had made such settlement a by-product of continued government expenditures—the boosters' references to the frontier, the pioneer spirit, the wilderness ready to be conquered and to yield its riches, became even more regular and insistent and provided a vocabulary without which Alaska could not be discussed at all.

Local pride, a belief that growth and size mean progress, and an awareness of the gains to be made from rising property values and increased retail trade explain the boosting activities, but in addition promoters, journalists, and politicians swayed to their own incantations. As promoters of the Great Lakes cutover region had once cheerfully observed the exhaustion of free land in the West and had prepared to receive swarms of land-hungry settlers, promoters of Alaska were encouraged by the growing population of the older states and made ready to receive the overflow. In the meantime they eagerly awaited the urban and industrial development that Americans outside sometimes nostalgically regretted and hoped to escape in Alaska.

The promoters' view was a method for misunderstanding both Alaska and America. In the 1930s the idea that some Americans could escape the depression by turning to Alaska's space, land, and resources diverted attention from the reality of unused resources in the States. In the postwar period continued frontierism was a means of blinking away complex economic and social problems that could not be escaped in the wilderness. For all but an eccentric or unusual few, pioneer settlement meant not opportunity but poverty. The disappointing experience with settlement and the Matanuska Colony would seem to have been enough to end the thoughtless encouragement of would-be pioneers, but the publicity given the Fifty-niners showed the frontier theme still familiar, still available for journalistic exploitation, and perhaps more appealing as the reality became more remote.

Epilogue

By the early 1970s Alaska had nearly fifteen years of experience in statehood, its population had grown to more than 300,000, and its resources, particularly oil, seemed about to be exploited.[1] Through every channel of communication, more insistently than ever, the promotional and ceremonial phrases were repeated—Alaska, the Great Land, the last frontier, the frontier state; Alaska facing the challenge of the future; Alaska's hardy pioneer people. Yet Alaskans were more than ever concentrated in or near a few cities; the six largest of these clusters accounted for more than two-thirds of the state's population, and in those places people lived as they might in a midwestern city, escaping to woods, mountains, rivers, and seacoasts on weekends and vacations. Even the Alaskan natives had become more urban, at least in the sense that almost half of them lived in or within reach of a dozen larger villages or towns,[2] some of the communities supported by the fishing industry, but all of them centers for schools, medical services, and welfare payments. In the "real Alaska," the bush, there were some natives, a few aging trappers and small miners, visiting guides and big-game hunters, wandering research scientists, and oil exploration crews.

Alaskan agriculture was hardly more visible than it had been twenty years earlier, and, with a larger population in the state, the farms provided a smaller, a minute, proportion of total food needs. Without having passed through the expected stage of pioneer expansion, Alaskan agriculture had apparently entered a period in which the number of farms and farmers remained static or declined and any increase in production came from a few large, highly capitalized enterprises. Statistics for total land in Alaskan farms have always included large leases of public lands, and the effect has been misleading because such land has been only partially used in grazing beef cattle and sheep. The total livestock of all kinds has been about 25,000 head, but the total acreage in farms has fluctuated widely as new leases have been made and old ones lapsed—1.8 million acres in 1940, .4 million in 1950, .9 million in 1959, 2 million in 1964, and 1.6 million in 1969.[3] Better indicators of the condition of agriculture are the number of farms and the acres of harvested cropland, including hay. In 1940 there were 623 farms and

11,000 acres; 367 farms and 14,500 acres in 1959; 382 farms and 16,500 acres in 1964. By 1969 there were 332 farms with 13,000 acres harvested, and only 148 of those farms produced $2,500 or more for sale annually; 184 produced less than $2,500, and 40 less than $1,000.[4] Since the 1970 census showed 1.4 percent of the Alaskan population, or about 4,230 persons, as farm residents,[5] about two-thirds of that number must have called their rural places farms in spite of insignificant production, too small to be counted among those 332 farms.

As elsewhere in America, rural life in Alaska had become for many persons a hobby and a part-time release from the routine of urban employment. By the early 1970s there were over 3,000 horses in the state, more than the number of dairy cattle.[6] A few were used as pack animals by guides and outfitters, fewer still as farm animals; most were kept for recreational use in the same way that Alaskans kept private airplanes, boats, snow vehicles, and sled dogs. An air freight service advertised quick and comfortable transportation of horses from Seattle to Alaska, and a large portion of pasture land, harvested hay, and imported feed was needed to support these animals.

Palmer, the center of the Matanuska farming area, declined 5 percent in population between 1960 and 1970 and took on an appearance of slow decay.[7] The cooperative general store was closed, the offices of the farmers' cooperative and the dairy were moved to Anchorage, and the sales through the cooperative declined. Outside the town, land once farmed was subdivided as recreational sites or as rural residences for retired persons or those who would commute to their jobs in Anchorage.

In 1969 the value of all Alaskan agricultural products sold was $3.6 million, compared with $3.8 million in 1964 and $3.2 million in 1959.[8] By 1971 the total market value of that year's production was $3.9 million, but inflation since 1959 would cancel the apparent gain. The larger total value was in part attributable to the organization of several large-scale farming enterprises. In the upper Tanana Valley a corporate farm holding 7,000 owned or leased acres was planning full production of barley and hogs by 1975. Its production accounted for most of the rise in harvested cropland to nearly 18,000 acres for the whole state in 1971.[9] The backers of the farm included men with professional, business, and political connections and sources of credit not available to ordinary farmers. Of the 1972 incentive payments to small grain producers, totaling $24,776.84, almost 90 percent went to farmers in that Tanana area, and most of that to the one large enterprise.[10] Only one-quarter of the family farmers in Alaska managed to do without off-farm employment; 60 percent of them worked off their farms for wages for one hundred or more days a year.[11]

In spite of the slow pace of Alaskan agricultural development and the slim chance of success in farming, official publications encouraged would-be farmers. The director of the Institute of Agricultural Sciences, formerly the agricultural experiment station at Fairbanks, addressed an editorial to those who hoped to farm in Alaska:

> The great American dream! To be independent. To be completely self reliant and, if possible, self sufficient. Not necessarily to be rich, but to be one's own boss and beholden to no one. This is what brought our forefathers to this continent in the first place. This is the rainbow that led them over the Alleghenies, across the plains, and through the mountain passes to California and Oregon. This is the magnet that still draws people to Alaska.[12]

His description of the efforts and sacrifices necessary was a challenge and an invitation rather than a warning, and he concluded by exclaiming:

> Can they succeed? Of course they can! People like them have been succeeding for 350 years. That's how America was settled. . . . and as we have already explained many times on these pages, Alaska shows great agricultural promise. The land will not fail them. Their ultimate success depends largely on their judgment, managerial skills, and farming abilities, just as it would anywhere else. We think their prospects look pretty good!

The director of the institute, before taking that position, had himself tried since the 1950s to develop a farm while employed as a civilian biologist on a local military base. When the editorial appeared, farming was some years behind him. The dairy herd was gone, most of the three hundred acres was grown up in willows, a pasture had not been grazed or mowed in years, and the assessed value of the land and buildings of the farm was lower than that of an operating farm half its size.

Those who wished to answer the challenge and try farming in Alaska would have to do it without homesteading federal public land. By 1967, the state, choosing carefully, had selected only about one-fourth of the 103.5 million acres to which it was entitled under the statehood act. Because state selections and mineral or other claims had already aroused native opposition, Secretary of the Interior Stewart Udall in November 1966 suspended mineral leasing on lands where there were native claims of occupancy or use. By the summer of 1967 that administrative suspension had been extended to cover most forms of entry on public lands, a condition referred to in Alaska as the "land freeze," and in January 1969 just before leaving office, Udall issued an order suspending all forms of land entry or disposal, including state selection, for a period of two years, to be followed by a period of ninety days in which state selection would have priority over private claims.[13] In the same period came the oil discoveries on the North Slope near Prudhoe Bay in 1968, the state sale of oil leases for over $900 million in 1969, and then the impatient and finally frantic demands of Alaskans for removal of any barrier to the construction of a great eight-hundred-mile oil pipeline.

Because there was a delay in the settlement of native claims, several subsequent land orders extended the land freeze.[14] In the meantime, the Bureau of Indian Affairs urged natives to make individual allotment claims wherever they had trapped, fished, hunted, or otherwise used the land. When the Alaska Native Claims Settlement Act[15] was passed in December 1971 it provided for the creation over a number of years of an "Alaska Native Fund" of just under $1 billion, the organization of Native Regional Corporations, Village Corporations, and special native groups of twenty-five persons or less, the transfer of 40 million acres of land with both surface and subsurface rights to these organizations and to those natives who applied individually for 160-acre residence sites. The native land selections could be made in large areas around 206 listed villages where public land was withdrawn for that purpose, or native corporations could select part of their lands elsewhere, including some selection in national parks, wildlife refuges, and other reserves. The act also provided for the secretary of the interior to withdraw up to 80 million acres of public land for inclusion in the system of national parks, forests, wildlife refuges, and wilderness and scenic rivers areas.

With the system for satisfying the native claims established, a land order on 9 March 1972[16] gave the state of Alaska three months of preferential right of selection in areas not reserved or withdrawn. Then, beginning 19 June 1972 what remained of unreserved public land would again be open to private entry. A Bureau of Land Management map issued in September 1972 showed the situation—multicolored patches indicating thirteen categories of land, including state selections patented, pending, or tentative, various earlier federal reservations, areas withdrawn for native selection, areas awaiting classification, a utility or oil pipeline corridor, and others. Here and there, in roadless, remote mountainous areas, spots of yellow showed unreserved federal public land on which private entries for homesteads or homesites could be made. There was still magic in the idea of acquiring 160 acres by homesteading. At the Fairbanks office of the Bureau of Land Management, for example, there was a daily stream of those who examined maps and asked for help in finding a spot to homestead. None wished to hear warnings of the difficulties, few would make the attempt, and fewer had any real intention of living from the land in remote areas unsuited for agriculture. They were aware that the scarcity of privately held land, the increase in population, the state's cautious land-disposal policy, and the years of the federal land freeze had raised the price of land tremendously. A potential homesteader could dream of some stroke of luck that would bring settlement and development to his remote area and turn a quarter section into a fortune.

Others had been lucky. For the whole state, including mountains, tundra, muskeg, as well as more habitable places, there were just under two square miles per person, but those areas within reach of population centers were, by Alaskan standards, crowded. For miles around Fairbanks a reasonably accessible and attractive rural residential site could rarely be found for less than $2,000 an acre. At the western end of the Matanuska farming region, sixty or seventy miles from Anchorage, residence sites were sometimes offered for as little as $500 an acre, but farther still, in less settled and therefore more attractive areas where city residents might build cabins for summer use and for hunting and fishing, prices were higher. More than a hundred miles from Anchorage and an additional ten miles into the woods by a deadend dirt road barely passable for most of the year because of snow or mud, a small general store and gasoline station had been built by 1971, in the expectation that the state would improve the road for more settlers and for tourist travel. On a small creek nearby, cabin sites were being offered at $1,800 an acre.

In that region the so-called Fifty-niners had settled, but in the early 1970s there was still little evidence of their homesteading except for mailboxes along the highway and glimpses of clearings, small cabins, and metal-sheathed trailer houses. The highway linking Anchorage and Fairbanks by a shorter route paralleling the railroad and making Mount McKinley Park more accessible was under construction for more than ten years. One family of Fifty-niners had prospered by operating a combined store, cafe, and motel, first for the construction crews and then for tourists who drove as far as the road allowed. Another of the Fifty-niners maintained his homestead while for years steadily employed in highway construction. When the road became more than a dirt track and ballast was needed, his homestead was found to be underlaid with gravel from the old course of the Susitna River, and payment for the truckloads of stone carried to the highway gave him additional income. In the spring of 1971 he vacationed in Europe.

The new highway, bringing Anchorage and Fairbanks closer by nearly 150 miles, was open for the 1972 tourist season. At Mount McKinley National Park it was necessary to reserve campsites and tour the park by bus rather than by private car. In other places, cars, trailers, and truck campers crowded whatever roads and campgrounds could be found. Many young people, usually expensively equipped and dressed in carefully rough, frontier style, summered in the woods not too far from town, using, when they could, unoccupied cabins and abandoned mining camps.

Notices in Alaskan newspapers of the death or retirement of old settlers, miners, and trappers marked the passing of the old ways. One man who had trapped the middle Porcupine since 1910 and whose solitary cabin appears on standard maps as one of the few inhabited places on the river, died at ninety in Fairbanks in 1972 after having visited that far "outside" only two or three times in sixty years.[17] Tracked snow machines made it possible for trappers to cover in a day as many miles of trapline as had once required a week or more by dog team, and some men could trap for sport while living close to town and their regular employments. The thousands of snow machines also made it possible for some to harass and run down animals, rob traplines,[18] and leave their marks everywhere on the winter snow.

Yet a fifteen-minute flight by small aircraft from Alaskan cities took one over seemingly untouched country. In the long daylight of summer, over hundreds of miles the faint mark of a trail might here and there be seen, and in winter darkness a single light below might be the only sign of man in an hour. But there was change. Thousands of flying hours were spent in the fall of 1972 in the unsuccessful search for the lost airplane carrying Congressmen Hale Boggs of Louisiana and Nick Begich of Alaska. Others more fortunate were rescued in remote areas—a member of the University of Alaska faculty, for example[19]—with no great trouble and by use of emergency equipment and procedures that had not been available twenty or thirty years before.

Alaska had become for many residents and visitors an escape, a romantic adventure, a way of acting out a fantasy of frontier independence and individualism—playing at chain-sawing firewood and subsisting on moose or caribou meat and fish, and sometimes vacationing at the far end of costly jet air travel. The play has sometimes been fatal. In the early fall of 1972 the search for a lost student from California was abandoned. He had started alone on foot from the Indian community of Arctic Village in the Brooks Range to Barter Island on the north coast.[20] Food caches had been delivered by air in advance along his route, but he deviated from his course or did not find them. Earlier that year, in February, the young wife of a thirty-year-old "trapper," originally from Alabama, died on the trail when her snow machine failed on her return from a visit to Stevens Village on the Yukon. Some seventy- and eighty-year-old men deal with such emergencies routinely each winter, but she left her heavy parka with the machine in –40 degree weather, left behind gasoline with which she could have started a fire in seconds, took only one or two matches, discarded her snowshoes along the trail, and died of fatigue and exposure a mile or two short of the cabin. The widowed young trapper, leaving his infant son temporarily with friends in Fairbanks to return to the Yukon cabin, said that only there could he support himself and provide for his child, although trapping would not explain air travel and air supply, snow machines, generator, and two-way radio.[21]

Pulled equally by the desire for the development of resources that will bring booming prosperity[22] and by an attachment to the idea of the frontier, Alaskans display on their car bumpers such stickers (tags) as "Sierra Go Home," "We Don't Give a Damn How They Do It Outside," and "Let the Bastards Freeze to Death in the Dark." They sign a supposedly serious petition originated by a sometime miner and real estate developer calling for peaceful separation from the United States and a new nation of Alaska, and they display signs and tags reading "Independence Now."[23]

As what was called "way-of-life" farming was disappearing in the 1930s, so the frontier as a way of life had all but vanished in Alaska by the 1970s. Still, the frontier atmosphere was to be preserved. Saddles, branding irons, and ropes ornament clubs and bars in Cheyenne, and in Alaska the frontier is neither yeoman self-sufficiency nor the trapper's or prospector's isolated life, but gold pans, snowshoes, traps, and dogsleds collected for the entertainment of tourists.

Appendix 1

Excerpt from a letter to Col. Lawrence Westbrook, Assistant Administrator, Works Progress Administration, from H. M. Colvin, 18 June 1937, and supporting material on "inducements" made to the colonists:

Dear Colonel:

Within are two enclosures, Exhibit A and Exhibit B.

Exhibit A: This is material which, according to our information from the State Board of Control of Minnesota, was shown to each colonist who left that State for Alaska. These data were carefully read over to him and gone over with him before he signed up, and therefore became a part of the inducement for him to come. The figures of Exhibit A came from the Rural Rehabilitation Division of the F.E.R.A. in the Washington office. This I have verified. Colonists have also come in and talked to me and without any prompting from me have verified the fact that these figures were represented to them as being the total cost to them of their property and obligations up here on the project. Similar information left the Washington office for Wisconsin and Michigan. From Exhibit A you will see that the total debt, including real estate, was represented to be between three and four thousand dollars.

Exhibit B: The first page of Exhibit B shows the deductions which the Board of Directors authorized at their April meeting and took up with me upon my meeting with them shortly after my arrival here. The subsequent pages in Exhibit B represent a tabulated summary which I had made up in order to show the state of the net debt of each colonist after the deductions authorized by the Board were made. By going over this tabulated summary you will see that there is a very wide discrepancy as to most of the colonists between the representation made to them as to their debts by the SERA field workers (with the help of Washington data) and the net debt which the tabulated summary shows they have actually incurred, even after all deductions have been made which were authorized by the Board of Directors of the ARRC.

I am now having worked up Exhibit C which will represent a survey of the income return capacity of the land tracts on which the colonists live. . . . Among other factors which have to be considered is the cost of getting a sufficient number of acres of land in cultivation to yield an income return which will produce this "Ability to Pay," and under the third page of Exhibit A you will see that a representation was made that they should have the land with twelve acres cleared as a start.

Exhibit A

To:	STATE EMERGENCY RELIEF ADMINISTRATION OF MINNESOTA Division of Social Service
From:	Miss Mona Callister, Superviser, Field Work
Date:	March 13, 1935.
Re:	EXCERPT from Report on the Washington Conference on the Alaska Rural Rehabilitation Project

The Rural Rehabilitation Corporation of Alaska has been authized [*sic*] to buy two hundred forty-acre tracts of land. Each tract will be given a number. Two hundred families will be selected from the relief rolls in Wisconsin, Michigan and Minnesota. These two hundred families, after signifying a willingness to go to Alaska, will be allowed to choose by lot a number. The number which they have chosen will designate one plot of land they may contract for. The cost per family will amount to, not over $3500 and, undoubtedly, considerably less. A break down of this $3500 per family is listed below:

40 Acre Farm at $7.50 per Acre		$ 300.00
Community Plan covering clearance and cultivation per year		210.00
House and well		1600.00
Barn		200.00
Fences		60.00
Livestock and Poultry		345.00
Furniture and Household Articles (This item may be eliminated)		285.00
Farm equipment and Tools (This item may be eliminated)		75.00
Seed and Feed		130.00
Railroad and Boat Fare per family		300.00
Surveying charge		7.50
	Total	$3512.50

In addition to this outlay, an amount equivalent to $585* for subsistence for the first year must be provided for the family. A part of this amount will be taken care of by the RRC and a part will be taken care of by the SERA. The breakdown for the subsistence for the first year is as follows:

Food	$170.00	(ARRC)
Clothing	170.00	(SERA)

*Arithmetical inconsistency in the original copy.

Medicals	20.00	(ARRC)
Rentals	50.00	(ARRC)
School Tax	5.00	(AARC)*
Recreation	15.00	(AARC)*
Miscellaneous	25.00	(AARC)*
	$455.00†	

Subsistence is to be allowed for the first year on the average dize [*sic*] family. The first year's subsistence is to be taken care of by the Corporation as the individuals are working for them. As individuals they are getting a certain amount of land cleared and buildings constructed. All the property is listed under RRC until the loan is entirely liquidated. The second year enough food should be raised to make them self-supporting and after the fourth year the individuals begin paying on their property. The land is to be cleared on a basis of twenty-two acres in the four years. There are free grazing facilities as there are no grazing laws. A three percent interest is to be paid until the amortization period of thirty years has expired, but no interest is due for the first five years.

Cost Summary—Alaska Project

Buildings:	
200 houses, including wells and fencing @ $1,160 each	$232,000
200 barns @ $200 each	40,000
Implement Barn	1,080
Garage and Repair Shop	8,918
Creamery	15,750
Cannery	8,160
Poultry Houses for Community Hatchery	6,000
Manager's Home	4,360
Teacher's Home, equipped	34,200
2 Grain-Mill-Work Center Buildings	2,300
Warehouse 40′ × 120′ × 10′	4,284
Duplex Teachers' House	3,260
Trading Post	10,000
School and Community House	150,000
	$522,512‡
Equipment:	
Garage and Repair Shop	5,500
Implements for Rental and Construction	103,130
Work Center-Grain Mills	1,550
Creamery	6,200

*ARRC. Typographical error in the original copy.
†Arithmetical inconsistency in original copy.
‡This total for buildings should be $520,312, but one of the items in the column may have been miscopied from a worksheet.

	Cannery	7,200
	Poultry Houses	2,000
	Central Heating Plant	18,000
		$143,580
Supplies:		
	Livestock — 400 cows @ $85 each	54,000*
	5 Bulls @ $200 each	1,000
	3,000 hens	3,000
	100 horses @ $175 each	17,500
	50 sets Harness @ $38 set	1,750
	50 Army Wagons @ $55 each	2,750
	Furniture and Household Goods	57,000
	Seed	6,000
	Feed for Horses and 100 Cows—1st year	17,815
	Farm Tools and Equipment	15,000
		$155,815
Land:		
	Cost of accumulation	500
	Surveying and staking	5,000
	2200 A	23,000
	Deeds and Filing fees	1,500
		$ 30,000
		$851,907
	Transportation	60,000
	Operating Capital	60,000
	Supervision during construction	10,000
		$981,907†

Alaskan Project

It is of prime importance that the families be carefully chosen with the viewpoint of building a community uppermost in mind. The building of a community means not merely the throwing together of numerous stranded families, but the thorough fitting together of such personalities as will go to make up a vigorous and progressive life.

The essential thing is that a community is being built, and that this community must be made so attractive as to assure that families will not choose to leave, even were prosperity to return in other districts. The purpose of these communities is to combine the advantages of city life with the advantages of farm life. Although legally these families are quite able to receive in return a portion of their equity, the advantages such as security, independence, friendships, enjoyment, etc., to be gained from continuing in the community, should be of such significance to them, that they will take the longer time point of view.

*This figure should be $34,000, but the subtotal is correct for $34,000.

†The grand total is consistent with the subtotals.

Experience at Woodlake, Texas, has demonstrated, that the method of statistically analyzing the family as to this qualification and that qualification and rejecting on such a basis is not sound, since it does not consider the family as an organic unit, and does not balance exceptional virtue against relatively lesser weakness. The case method which considers each family as a whole and tends to visualize the possibility of that individual family's adjustment to the community in question, is a more sound approach. However, certain general qualifications ought to be kept in mind, at least for the first of these experiments.

It is preferable that there be three or four children, on the average, since a community is built around the joy and happiness of children, around the school and around the community play facilities. It is not wise that the families have over six children since with the plots of ground relatively small, the family may be almost certain, not only to live in crowded quarters, but to be relatively poor as compared to the neighboring families with less children. However, normal family of a husband, wife and child is necessary. It is wise in so far as possible, to choose people who have some form of specialized skill. Not only will such skills be valuable in a community of varied activity, but they also promise a superior ability on the part of those possessing them in adjusting themselves to suggestions for improvement and for cooperation.

It is necessary to choose people who will cooperate. Much of the success of a rural community must depend on voluntary disciplined cooperation. Producing similar crops in order to provide better markets is essential. Plans call for cooperative buying and selling as a basic requirement of a high form of farm economic life. The families must give evidence of being able and desirous of staying by an arrangement. The first few years will be difficult. The family must consider the proposition as the opportunity of a life time. It should not be presented to them as a way of meeting their present difficulties. In making their decision, they should choose between life in a rural community and a theoretically actual job in the city. They must be firmly convinced that they wish to see it through.

In other words, this program is not merely a program to take care of unemployed and stranded families. It is a program which, if successful, will have historical importance to American life in general. Therefore, not only is it important to so construct the community as to give it the proper physical organization to permit the spontaneous development of happy life; not only is it necessary to so thoroughly think through the problems of the economic basis of the community and of its facilities for cooperative action, in order to assure that want will never return but it is also crucial that in the first experiments, the most careful choice of personalities be made. This is not merely an attempt to temporarily take care of some families who now are penalized by the economic collapse of the early 1930s but it is an attempt to leave an instructive and permanent demonstration of what American life might produce.

Table 1

Estimated Cost under Plan of Using 400 Transients as a Work Relief Project, Clearing 12 Acres the First Year, the Balance to Be Cleared by the *Home Unit Owners* at the Rate of 5 Acres per Year

	1st Yr.	2nd Yr.	3rd Yr.	4th Yr.	5th Yr.
Land—40 a. @ $3.75, 12 a. cleared	$ 150.00*				
Clearing and cultivation—20 a. @ $36	720.00†	180.00	180.00	180.00	180.00
House, including well	1,100.00				
Barn	200.00				
Fencing, material only	60.00				
	2,230.00	180.00	180.00	180.00	180.00
Livestock					
2 cows	170.00†	170.00			
1/4 interest in team horses	110.00				
Furniture and household goods	285.00				
Farm equipment and tools	75.00				
Total	640.00	350.00	180.00	180.00	180.00
Seed and feed	130.00				
Total Cost	3,000.00	350.00	180.00	180.00	180.00
Transportation	250.00				
	3,250.00				
Amount to be spent 1st year	2,360.00				
AMORTIZATION (interest @ 3%; 30 years to pay out)					
Home unit	63.30‡	150.00	150.00	150.00	150.00
Transportation	7.30‡	55.00	55.00	55.00	55.00

SOURCE: Rural Rehabilitation Office, FERA, Washington, D.C.

*In the original source this figure is incorrectly given as $750.

†[Note in the original source] "The $720 charge for clearing represents rental of tractor clearing equipment at the rate for 4 years after the first year. The $170 livestock charge represents 2 cows to be furnished the second year.

‡In the first year, only the interest at 3% was to be paid on what had been spent in that year ($2,360 less $250 for transportation). The $7.30 for transportation should be $7.50.

Exhibit B

Alaska Rural Rehabilitation Corporation
Matanuska Valley Colonization Project

Palmer, Alaska

Excerpt from the Minutes of a Meeting of the Board of Directors of the Alaska Rural Rehabilitation Corporation held in Palmer, Alaska, on April 23 and 24, 1937.

After a general discussion covering the accounts of the different colonists, Director Hess offered the following resolution for the consideration of the Board.

Resolution

WHEREAS, a survey of the indebtedness of the colonists has been made as of January 31, 1937 after an appraisal as of 1936 of all property valued to each colonist, and

WHEREAS, these statements shows [*sic*] charges that are subject to adjustment, therefore,

BE IT RESOLVED, that the General Manager be authorized and directed to make the following deductions (or credits) on the colonists' indebtedness as of the date indicated, January 31, 1937.

1. All dental, doctor and hospital charges.
2. A feed allowance of $250 per colonist.
3. All well charges in excess of $25.00.
4. Five Hundred Dollars ($500.00) for material used on buildings.
5. Clothing charges for initial purchase, per statement, which is part of this file.
6. Subsistence and clothing allowances for June 1, 1935, to January 31, 1937, computed on the basis of the food and clothing budget schedule in effect on December 31, 1936, which schedule is hereby made a part of this file.
7. Labor for work performed on buildings by the colonists.
8. Credit for land cleared by the colonists according to the schedules established by the General Manager.

IT IS FURTHER RESOLVED, that after these deductions have been made, all amounts in excess of $8,000 shall be further deducted from the account as of January 31, 1937.

The resolution was seconded by Director McDonald and unanimously carried.

Appendix 2

Provisions of the Realty Contract
Purchaser John Doe
Homesite Number 220
Alaska Rural Rehabilitation Corporation
Contract for Sale and Purchase of Realty

THIS CONTRACT made and entered into by and between ALASKA RURAL REHABILITATION CORPORATION, an Alaskan corporation with offices at Palmer, Alaska, in the Cooperative Community known as the Matanuska Valley Colony, hereinafter called the Corporation, and the undersigned purchaser, a member of said Cooperative Rural community, whose post office address is Palmer, Alaska, hereinafter called the Purchaser, who is joined in the execution of the same by the undersigned wife of the Purchaser, WITNESSETH:

WHEREAS, the Cooperative Rural Community known as the Matanuska Valley Colony, has been established at and near Palmer, Alaska, by the Corporation, by the aid of grants of funds of the Government of the United States made through the Federal Emergency Relief Administration in pursuance of public policy and for the public purpose of assisting in promoting and establishing colonization and rural rehabilitation in Alaska by enabling worthy and well qualified persons and their families to:

(a) occupy family sized tracts of land with adequate improvements and a home thereon in a Cooperative Rural Community and thereby obtain employment and a gainful living in agricultural and allied activities and enjoy the benefits of said community under properly controlled conditions on a cooperative basis; and

(b) in due time to become the owners of said property on long time and low payment terms not ordinarily procurable through usual commercial channels, and thereby be placed in a position to enjoy the benefits referred to in sub-paragraph (a) herein permanently; and

WHEREAS, in the course of carrying out said public trust under the application of subparagraph (a) above the Purchaser and others have each been placed by the Corporation in occupancy of an improved family sized tract of land and in a home thereon in said Cooperative Rural Community and the economic advantages referred to in subparagraph (a) are afforded the Purchaser and his wife and family and said other occupants of said tracts of land by membership in Matanuska Valley Farmers Cooperating Association, organized through the sponsorship of the corporation under the Cooperative Association laws of Alaska and in conformity with "The Agricultural Marketing Act" of the United States to enable the Purchaser and other members of said Community and their successors to cooperatively market their agricultural products raised upon the land occupied and farmed by them and to cooperatively purchase and otherwise acquire needed supplies, commodities and services through said Association; and

WHEREAS, the Purchaser now wishes the benefits provided for in sub-paragraph (b) above to be extended to him and the benefits enjoyed under sub-paragraph (a) above to be thereby made permanent and wishes to enter into a contract of purchase, in pursuance of said desires, with the Corporation and the said Corporation approves the entering into said contract;

NOW, THEREFORE, in consideration of the above premises and the mutual convenants and considerations herein mentioned, as well as and including the low purchase price, low installment payments extended over a long time period and other terms which are greatly to the advantage of the Purchaser as a Colonist, the Corporation and the Purchaser as parties hereto for themselves, their respective successors, assigns, heirs, executors and/or administrators, AGREE AS FOLLOWS:

I. *Property and Purchase Price.* The Corporation in consideration of the principal sum of Three Thousand Seven Hundred & no/100 Dollars ($3, 700.00) as the purchase price thereof with credits thereon as herein allowed and applied, with interest on the unpaid portions thereof to be paid as hereinafter provided, and of the agreements, covenants, conditions and reservations herein contained, hereby agrees to sell to the Purchaser and the Purchaser agrees to buy upon the terms and conditions herein provided the following described property situated in the Palmer Recording Precinct of the Third Judicial District of the Territory of Alaska:

[DESCRIPTION OF PROPERTY AND IMPROVEMENTS]

together with all the tenements, hereditaments and appurtenances thereto belonging or in any wise appertaining.

II. *Use of Premises as Farm Home.* The Purchaser shall personally and continuously occupy and use said above described premises as a farm and as a home for himself and the members of his family living thereon unless the Corporation shall otherwise consent thereto in writing and shall not establish any mercantile or similar business thereon; shall follow and observe such production, crop and distribution control and practices, including soil conservation and windbreak methods and conduct such livestock, poultry and dairy and other enterprises on said property as are in accordance with approved farm organization, management, practices and good husbandry, under the advice and direction of the Corporation and in compliance with his contract or contracts with Matanuska Valley Farmers Cooperating Association; shall at all times maintain said premises in good condition and repair and free from weeds, brush, washes or gulleys detrimental to efficient farming operations or the value of said premises for agricultural use; and shall not commit or permit any unlawful acts or waste or nuisances upon said premises or any part thereof.

III. *Care and Preservation of Property.* The Purchaser shall not without the written consent of the Corporation: (a) demolish, altar [*sic*] or change the location of any of the buildings or structures or erect new ones on said premises; (b) in any way interfere with the easements or rights of way herein referred to or provided for; (c) lease or let any part of said premises; or (d) mortgage or encumber, other than to the Corporation or Matanuska Valley Farmers Cooperating Association, any crops or products of said premises or any machinery, equipment, tools or livestock used by him in farming on said premises.

IV. *Terms of Payment and Security.* The Corporation hereby allows and applies to the payment of the principal sum named in Section I hereof as the purchase price of said property the following credits:

leaving the total amount which the Purchaser agrees to pay to complete the payment of said purchase price thereof the sum of dollars ($3700.00) together with interest at the rate of three (3%) per cent per annum on the balance thereof from time to time remaining unpaid, the same being payable in the following installments and manner: the final payment of the last installment to be made on the 15th day of November , 19 69 ; *provided that,* if the date of any installment payment should fall on a legal holiday said installment payment, including the final payment, may be paid on the next business day following, and provided, also, that with the written consent of the Corporation the Purchaser shall have the privilege of making prepayments of any of said installments or portions thereof, and the privilege of making additional payments for the reduction or extinguishment of the principal debt and interest thereon on any installment date. Each and every installment not paid when due shall bear interest thereafter at the rate of three (3)% per annum until paid which amount shall be added to said installment when paid. The corporation expressly reserves a first lien and mortgage on the Purchaser's right, title and interest, now held or hereafter acquired in the above described land and improvements thereon and on said land itself to secure the payment of any and all sums due hereunder and the fulfillment of any and all terms of this Contract and upon the crops grown upon said lands each year to secure the payment of any sums which may become due hereunder and be unpaid at the time the crop for such year is gathered or harvested and the Purchaser and his wife hereby mortgage the same accordingly to the Corporation.

The proceeds of any installment of payment made to the Corporation shall be applied as follows: First—to payment of any interest on unpaid balances of the principal sum due hereunder at the date of such installment; Secondly—To the payment on account of the principal sum of this Contract; provided, however, that the Corporation may apply the proceeds of any installment or other payment made by the Purchaser hereunder to the payment of insurance, taxes and/or assessments due or delinquent and payable by the Purchaser hereunder on or in connection with the above described premises before applying the same to the payment of interest or principal due and payable as hereinabove provided, in which case the amount of the installment remaining unpaid shall bear interest at the rate of three per cent (3%) per annum until paid the same as an unpaid installment as provided herein. The Purchaser also agrees that the Corporation may at its discretion apply to the payment of any obligations due under this Contract any moneys in its hands as agent or otherwise, of or due the Purchaser from any source whatsoever, except as otherwise agreed upon, but it is expressly mutually understood and agreed that the Corporation is not obligated so to do.

V. *Taxes and Assessments*. The Purchaser covenants and agrees to pay all taxes including Territorial and local taxes and any and all installments of special improvement taxes and/or assessments, including road, levee and drainage taxes due and payable from time to time on the above described premises, except as he is relieved from doing so by the homestead tax exemption laws or other laws of the Territory of Alaska. It is mutually understood and agreed that in the event the Purchaser fails to keep up and pay said taxes and assessments as hereinabove provided the Corporation may pay the same itself and the Purchaser be obligated to repay the same to the Corporation with interest at the rate of three (3%) per cent per annum from the date of such payment with interest and the amount or amounts thus paid by the Corporation may be added to the principal sum representing the purchase price hereunder, or the Corporation may pay the same and take the amount thereof out of the installment payment or payments made by the Purchaser with which to do so as provided for in Section IV hereof or for repayment to itself.

VI. *Insurance*. It is mutually understood and agreed that the Purchaser together with his family is in occupancy and is in charge of the above described premises and that he is responsible for the safety and security thereof and must make good injuries or losses thereto. The Purchaser agrees upon written notice from the Corporation to take out fire, windstorm, hail and tornado insurance in the amount specified by the corporation, payable to the Corporation in trust for the Purchaser, covering improvements on said premises in a firm, company or association approved by the Corporation and pay the premiums thereon. In the event of loss or damages recovered upon the policies, the proceeds, or so much thereof as may be necessary, shall be used to repair or restore the property damaged or destroyed. It is also mutually understood and agreed that in the event the Purchaser fails to keep up and pay his premiums on said insurance the Corporation may pay the same itself and the Purchaser shall be obligated to repay the same to the Corporation at the rate of three (3%) per cent from the date of such payment until paid and the amount or amounts thus paid by the Corporation may be added to the principal sum representing the purchase price hereunder or the Corporation may pay the same and take the amount thereof out of the installment payment or payments made by the Purchaser with which to do so as provided for in Section IV hereof or for repayment to itself. It is mutually understood and agreed that until such time as the Purchaser is notified in writing to take out said insurance, the Corporation will take care of the protection of said property resulting from loss or damage by fire, which is not caused by the wilful or negligent act of the Purchaser or his servants; provided, however, that this paragraph shall not be construed to make the Corporation liable for any household goods, or other personal property belonging to the Purchaser.

VII. *Public Trust Impressed upon Land, and its Transfer.* It is mutually agreed and recognized that the above described premises are subject to the fulfillment of the public trust and purpose for which Federal grants of funds were made to purchase and acquire the same as part of the Cooperative Rural Community of Matanuska Valley Colony as set forth herein and more particularly in the "Whereas" provisions at the beginning of this Contract and that said trust and purpose include administrative regulations governing said Community and the occupancy and use of said premises according to and under the rules of Matanuska Valley Farmers Cooperating Association, and that said trust and purpose thus subjecting said premises constitute a condition running with the land and improvements thereon, adhere to and follow said premises continuously into the hands of all holders or owners thereof forever whether they or any of them hold by grant, gift, sale, devise, inheritance or otherwise. It is further mutually agreed and recognized that said premises or any right, title, interest or privilege therein is subject to purchase by the Corporation at its option at any time the same passes by death, operation of law or otherwise to any person or persons (natural, corporate or governmental), incapable, unable, unwilling or unfit to comply with and carry out the requirements and provisions of this Section of this Contract in reference to said trust and purpose or who refuse to do so as determined by the General Manager of the Corporation. The Purchaser agrees that he will not grant, make a gift of, bargain, sell, devise or otherwise convey, transfer, assign, or dispose of said premises or his interest therein or any part thereof or in this Contract or any part thereof or attempt to do so to anyone other than the Corporation who is not desirous and capable of complying with the requirements and conditions of this Section of this Contract and who does not sign a written agreement so to do and to become a bona fide member of said Community and of Matanuska Valley Farmers Cooperating Association on a farm furnished by the Corporation and who is not approved in writing as acceptable as such by the General Manager of the Corporation. Provided however, that the Purchaser may grant, make a gift of, bargain, sell, devise or otherwise convey, transfer, assign or dispose of said premises or his interest therein or any part thereof or in this Contract or any part thereof to the Corporation and the Corporation may buy the same at any time the Corporation and the Purchaser shall agree to do so as provided in this Contract and it is mutually agreed that the Corporation shall have the first right and option to buy the same and if the Purchaser desires to sell and receives a bona fide offer from a permitted prospective buyer hereunder the offer together with the terms thereof must be reduced to writing, signed by the offeror and properly acknowledged before a Notary Public and shown to the General Manager of the Corporation and if it is an enforcible [*sic*] offer at a higher price and on better terms than the Corporation agrees to pay and give, then the General Manager, in behalf of the Corporation, shall, at the request of the Purchaser herein, relinquish the Corporation's first right to buy by endorsement accordingly on the said written offer signed by him and properly notarized and then the Purchaser herein may sell to the said offeror on the terms of said offer only, all legal documents of sale thereunder being subject to inspection of the General Manager of the Corporation and attempted sales other than under the terms of said offer being null and void, subject to prevention by injunction and constituting a fundamental breach of this Contract.

It is mutually agreed and recognized that this Section of this Contract is in pursuance of public policy and the welfare of the Rural Cooperative Community of Matanuska Valley Colony and the members thereof and to assure the fulfillment of the purposes of said federal grants of funds as provided herein and for the protection of the continued use and occupancy of said premises in accordance therewith. It is also mutually agreed and recognized that this Section of this Contract is a principal part of the consideration thereof and of the Corporation entering into the same and its agreement to part with the title to the said premises for the low purchase price and is enforceable by specific performance, injunction and mandamus and that any attempt to sell or transfer said premises or interest therein or in this Contract in violation of the terms hereof shall be and is null and void.

VIII. *Corporation's Right to Buy.* In the event the Corporation shall purchase or exercise its right and option to purchase the Purchaser's interest in this Contract and the above described premises pursuant to Section VII hereof the Corporation shall pay the Purchaser and the Purchaser agrees to accept in full payment thereof an amount computed as follows, to-wit:

(a) There shall be added to the total amount of principal paid by the Purchaser prior to the date of the exercise of the above mentioned option (1) the then fair value of any crops planted by the Purchaser and then growing on said premises and (2) the then fair value of any improvements made by the Purchaser on said premises with the consent of the Corporation.

(b) From the amount calculated in (a) above there shall be deducted (1) any interest, insurance, taxes or assessments then accrued and unpaid and (2) any depreciation in the value of said premises caused by the use thereof, or by failure of the Purchaser to maintain said premises in good condition and repair, and (3) any debts due from the Purchaser to the Corporation on any obligations whatsoever.

In case the Corporation and the Purchaser shall not agree on the fair value of any such crops or improvements or the amount of any such depreciation the same shall be determined by the majority of three appraisers, one of whom shall be appointed by the General Manager of the Corporation, one by the Purchaser, and the third by the other two appraisers so appointed. The method of computation of purchase price provided in this Section shall be applied in all cases of purchases made by the Corporation from any person or persons under the authority of Section VII hereof, and when a portion of a right, title, interest or privilege in said premises is purchased, said method of computation of purchase price shall be applied proportionately according to the portion purchased.

IX. *Purchaser's Relationships with the Community, the Cooperative Association and the Corporation.* The Purchaser now agrees that he has entered into this contract with the purpose in view of establishing a permanent home for himself and family on the premises described herein in the Cooperative Rural Community of Matanuska Valley Colony and not for resale or speculation but to enjoy the benefits and to help fulfill the public trust and public policy and purpose for which Federal grants of funds have been made and have been and are being expended by the Corporation as more particularly set forth in the "Whereas" provisions at the beginning of this Contract as a part hereof, and that he and the members of his family will abide by all administrative directions and supervisions of the Corporation, its duly constituted agents and representatives properly authorized and keep and perform their obligations to and contract with the Corporation.

The Purchaser further agrees to accept and maintain membership in

Matanuska Valley Farmers Cooperating Association, on the terms provided by said Association, and to keep and perform his contract and membership obligations therewith, and that he and the members of his family will abide by and comply with its rules and regulations and cooperate with the other members of said Community and said Association and with the Corporation in all activities within the Community and in connection therewith for the success thereof.

The Purchaser further agrees that the Corporation and its duly authorized agents shall have the right of ingress and egress at all reasonable times, over, across, and upon said premises herein described for the purpose of inspection, supervision, maintenance and carrying out said rules and regulations and the public trust and public policy and purpose for which the Cooperative Rural Community of Matanuska Valley Colony has been established, and in order to protect, help improve, and to conserve said premises, its interest therein and in this Contract, and that the Corporation also has easement and right of way in, on and over said premises, for the construction, operation and maintenance of light, water, power, telephone and other utilities commonly known as public utilities (whether publicly or privately owned) which easement and right of way the Corporation hereby especially reserves.

X. *Violation of Contract.* In the event that the Purchaser violates any of the terms or conditions of this Contract, or is adjudicated a bankrupt or an insolvent, the Corporation shall have the right to terminate all of the rights of the Purchaser hereunder, by giving written notice addressed to the Purchaser that his rights hereunder shall cease and determine thirty (30) days subsequent to the date of such notice; and upon the expiration of the thirty (30) days specified in said notice, the rights of the Purchaser hereunder shall cease and determine absolutely, except as hereinafter otherwise expressly provided.

XI. *Termination Rights of Purchaser.* In the event the rights of the Purchaser under this Contract shall be terminated in accordance with the provisions of Section X, the Corporation shall, without waiving any of its other rights hereunder, cancel this Contract and pay to the Purchaser within sixty (60) days after the Purchaser shall have vacated possession in accordance with the provisions of Section XII, a sum equal to the amount which would be payable by the Corporation if it exercised right of purchase provided for in Section VIII above, computed as of the date the Purchaser vacates possession, less any expenses incurred by the Corporation, including all Court costs, Attorneys' fees, or other expenses necessitated by the Purchaser's breach or failure to comply with any of the provisions of this Contract, and/or in the Corporation regaining possession of the above described premises under Section XII of this Contract, by Court action or otherwise, and/or for the enforcement of any right of the Corporation hereunder.

XII. *Corporation's Right of Repossession.* In the event of the termination of the rights of the Purchaser under this Contract or the Corporation exercising its right to purchase or its acceptance of the offer of the Purchaser to sell his interest in this Contract and in the above described premises as provided in this Contract, the Purchaser shall, within thirty (30) days after receipt of notice from the Corporation of the same, vacate and surrender possession of said property. In the event the Purchaser fails to vacate and surrender possession of said property within such time, he shall remain in possession thereof only as a tenant at the sufference of the Corporation and the Corporation shall have the right and power immediately or at any time thereafter to re-enter upon and take possession of said property and remove therefrom the Purchaser or anyone whether claiming by, through or under him or otherwise and their property and effects without process of law and without being guilty of any manner of trespass either in law or in equity. Provided, however, that it is mutually understood and agreed by both parties to this Contract that if the above described land is public land occupied by the Purchaser by his lawful settlement and entry thereon and in fulfillment of other governmental requirements and not yet proved up by the Purchaser and he has not received a patent and title to said land from the Government at the time any violations of this Contract by the Purchaser should take place, then the Corporation, at its election shall exercise its right of repossession by removing the above described buildings and improvements from said land as personality [*sic*] and same shall in no wise be a trespass, and may foreclose the Purchaser's interest, if any, in the same as provided herein.

XIII. *Final Deed of Conveyance.* Upon the payment in full by the Purchaser of all sums due the Corporation under the provisions of this Contract and in the event that this Contract shall not have been heretofore terminated under the terms thereof by the Corporation, the Corporation shall execute and deliver to the Purchaser a deed of conveyance to the premises herein described, which shall recite the conditions of Section VII hereof continuously running with the land and improvements thereof, together with provisions for the reversion of title to said premises to the Corporation in case of breach thereof, as a part and condition of said deed of conveyance and warrant and convey a good and merchantible [*sic*] title to the premises herein described free of incumbrances to the Purchaser, his heirs and assigns forever.

XIV. *Effect of this Contract.* It is mutually agreed and understood that this Contract is binding upon and enures to the successors, assigns, heirs, executors, administrators and legal representatives of the respective parties hereto and that there are no oral or other conditions, promises, covenants, representations or inducements in addition to or at variance with any terms hereof and that this Contract expresses the voluntary and clear understanding of the parties hereto fully and completely, and that it goes into effect on the 15th day of November, 1937 .

Notes

Preface

1 Kirk H. Stone, "Alaska Group Settlement: The Matanuska Colony," (Ph.D. diss., University of Michigan, 1949); Evangeline R. (Mrs. Robert) Atwood, *We Shall Be Remembered* (Anchorage, Alaska: Alaska Methodist University Press, 1966). Her husband is publisher of the *Anchorage Daily Times* and trustee of Alaska Methodist University; she is the sister of Elmer E. Rasmuson, Anchorage banker and for many years president of the board of regents of the University of Alaska.

Introduction

1 *Anchorage Daily Times,* 15 May 1935, quoting from "On Receiving an Eagle's Quill from Lake Superior." The original reads "Of *nations* yet to be" and "The *rudiments* of empire here." The Anchorage newspaper may have intended the alteration, or perhaps it was bad memory.

2 An indication of how commonly the depression was related to the closing of the frontier is found in the statements of men in public life quoted by Curtis P. Nettels, "Frederick Jackson Turner and the New Deal," *Wisconsin Magazine of History* 17 (March 1934): 257–65. An interesting and unexpected example of the view is in Edmund Wilson, "An Appeal to Progressives," *The Shores of Light: A Literary Chronicle of the Twenties and Thirties* (New York: Farrar, Straus and Young, 1952), pp. 518–33, esp. p. 525. The essay appeared originally in the *New Republic,* 14 January 1931.

3 The predictions of a stabilized and eventually declining population persisted surprisingly far into the 1940s. See the National Resources Planning Board, *Estimates of Future Population of the United States, 1940–2000,* prepared by Warren A. Thompson and P. K. Whelpton (Washington, D.C.: U.S. Government Printing Office, 1943), pp. 29–35; U.S. Department of Commerce, *Forecasts of the Population of the U.S., 1945–1975,* prepared by P. K. Whelpton (Washington, D.C.: U.S. Government Printing Office, 1947), pp. 40–41, fig. 5 and table 28. (U.S. Government Printing Office hereafter cited as GPO.)

4 *The Public Papers and Addresses of Franklin D. Roosevelt,* ed. Samuel I. Rosenman, vol. 1, *The Genesis of the New Deal, 1928–1932* (New York: Random House, 1938), pp. 742–56.

5 Ibid., pp. 746–47.

6 Ibid., pp. 748–49, 751.

7 Ibid., pp. 750–51.

8 Carl N. Degler, "The Ordeal of Herbert Hoover," *Yale Review* 52 (summer 1963): 563–83, argues that neither the ideas nor the gloom of the speech was representative of Roosevelt. For the writing of the speech and its delivery with little or no prior examination, see Rexford G. Tugwell, *The Democratic Roosevelt* (Garden City,

N.Y.: Doubleday & Co., 1957), p. 246; Arthur M. Schlesinger, Jr., *The Crisis of the Old Order, 1919–1933* (Boston: Houghton Mifflin Co., 1957), pp. 424–26.

9 Daniel R. Fusfeld, *The Economic Thought of Franklin D. Roosevelt and the Origins of the New Deal* (New York: Columbia University Press, 1956), pp. 25–26; Frank Freidel, *Franklin D. Roosevelt,* vol. 1, *The Apprenticeship* (Boston: Little, Brown & Co., 1952), pp. 61, 72.

10 Tugwell, *The Democratic Roosevelt,* p. 56*n.*; Freidel, *The Apprenticeship,* chap. 4, on Roosevelt's career at Harvard, and p. 72.

11 Among the studies of forerunners of Turner and of the frontier thought "in the air" in the 1880s and 1890s are Herman C. Nixon, "Precursors of Turner in the Interpretation of the American Frontier," *South Atlantic Quarterly* 28 (January 1929): 83–89, and Lee Benson, *Turner and Beard: American Historical Writing Reconsidered* (Glencoe, Ill.: The Free Press, 1960), pts. 1 and 2. Two surveys and discussions of the huge literature on Turner and the frontier thesis are Robert E. Riegel, "American Frontier Theory," *Journal of World History* 3 (1956): 356–80, and Gene M. Gressley, "The Turner Thesis—A Problem in Historiography," *Agricultural History* 32 (October 1958): 227–49.

12 The collected essays are in Frederick Jackson Turner, *The Frontier in American History* (New York: Henry Holt & Co., 1920).

13 Ibid., p. 261.

14 E.g., James Bryce, *The American Commonwealth* (New York: Macmillan Co., 1899), vol. 2, p. 829 and pp. 830–32.

15 William J. Trimble, "The Influence of the Passing of the Public Lands, *Atlantic Monthly* 113 (June 1914): 763. Also, Frederic L. Paxson, *When the West Is Gone* (New York: Henry Holt & Co., 1930); C. W. Wright, "The Significance of the Disappearance of Free Land in Our Economic Development," *American Economic Review* 14, Supplement (1926): 265–71.

16 Benson, *Turner and Beard,* pt. 1, esp. pp. 21–33; Turner, *The Frontier in American History,* p. 11.

17 James C. Malin, "Space and History: Reflections on the Closed-Space Doctrines of Turner and Mackinder and the Challenge of Those Ideas by the Air Age," *Agricultural History* 18, pt. 1 (April 1944): 65–74.

18 Arthur M. Schlesinger, *New Viewpoints in American History* (New York: Macmillan Co., 1922), p. 1; Walter P. Webb, "History as High Adventure," *American Historical Review* 64 (January 1959): 265–81; idem, *The Great Frontier* (Boston: Houghton Mifflin Co., 1952), pp. 17–27 and passim.

19 William E. Leuchtenburg, *Franklin D. Roosevelt and the New Deal, 1932–1940* (New York: Harper & Row, 1963), pp. 29, 94, 142; Eric F. Goldman, *Rendezvous with Destiny* (New York: Vintage Books, 1956), p. 249; Carl N. Degler, *Out of Our Past* (New York: Harper & Row, 1962), pp. 131–32.

20 Alvin H. Hansen, "Economic Progress and Declining Population Growth," *American Economic Review* 29 (March 1939): 1–15; *Full Recovery or Stagnation?* (New York: W. W. Norton and Co., 1938), esp. pp. 28, 253, 313; *Fiscal Policy and Business Cycles* (New York: W. W. Norton and Co., 1941), pp. 38–44, 83, 344–61; *Business Cycles and National Income* (New York: W. W. Norton and Co., 1951), pp. 17–38, 72–75. To support his discussion of vanished frontiers, Hansen in all four of the above writings cited only the articles edited by Isaiah Bowman in *Limits of*

Land Settlement (New York, 1937). Webb used Bowman's *The Pioneer Fringe* (New York, 1931).

21 E. R. Eastman, "The Frontiers Are Gone, So Surplus Population Must Turn to the Land," *American Agriculture* 129 (1932): 163; O. E. Baker, "Rural–Urban Migration and the National Welfare," *Annals of the Association of American Geographers* 33 (June 1933): 59–126; O. E. Baker, "Rural and Urban Distribution of the Population in the United States," *The Annals* 188 (November 1936): 264–79; Bushrod W. Allin, "Migration Required for Best Land Use," *Journal of Farm Economics* 18 (August 1936): 493–99; Mordecai Ezekiel, "Population and Unemployment," *The Annals* 188 (November 1936): 230–42.

22 The scores of critical articles are surveyed in Riegel, "American Frontier Theory," pp. 356–80; Gressley, "The Turner Thesis—A Problem in Historiography," pp. 227–49; and Ray A. Billington, *The American Frontier* (Washington D.C.: Service Center for Teachers, 1958). For a chronological account of the criticism, Minnie Edith Cureton, "The History of the Criticisms of the Turner Thesis" (Ph. D. diss., Stanford University, 1949).

23 George W. Pierson, "American Historians and the Frontier Hypothesis in 1941," *Wisconsin Magazine of History* 26, pts. 1 and 2 (September and December 1942): 36–60 and 170–85.

24 Everett E. Edwards, ed., *References to the Significance of the Frontier,* U.S. Department of Agriculture, Bibliographical Contribution no. 25 (Washington, D.C.: GPO, 1935), p. 30, message of Governor Philip F. LaFollette to the Wisconsin legislature, 15 January 1931; Nettels, "Frederick Jackson Turner and the New Deal," pp. 257–65; Henry A. Wallace, *New Frontiers* (New York: Reynal and Hitchcock, 1934), pp. 3–5, 271–77, 285–86, and passim; Rexford G. Tugwell, "No More Frontiers," *Today* 4 (22 and 29 June 1935): 3–4, 21, and 8–9, 22–23.

25 Merle Curti, *Probing Our Past* (New York: Harper and Brothers, 1955), pp. 46–47.

26 E.g., Charles M. Wilson, *Backwoods America* (Chapell Hill: University of North Carolina Press, 1934), chap. 17; Wilson, "The Surviving American Frontier," *Current History and Forum* 34 (May 1931): 189–92; also, James West, *Plainville, U.S.A.* (New York: Columbia University Press, 1945), p. 136 n.

27 The agrarian creed is described in Clifford B. Anderson, "The Metamorphosis of American Agrarian Idealism in the 1920's and 1930's," *Agricultural History* 35 (October 1961): 182–88.

28 Earl H. Bell, *Culture of a Contemporary Rural Community: Sublette, Kansas,* Bureau of Agricultural Economics, Rural Life Studies no. 2 (Washington, D.C.: GPO, 1942); Edward O. Moe and Carl C. Taylor, *Culture of a Contemporary Rural Community: Irwin, Iowa* (Washington, D.C.: GPO, 1942).

29 Joseph Schafer, *The Social History of American Agriculture* (New York: Macmillan Co., 1936), pp. 271, 293.

30 Paul K. Conkin, *Tomorrow a New World: The New Deal Community Program* (Ithaca, N.Y.: Cornell University Press, 1959), pp. 1–36, describes the back-to-the-land movement and its contribution to the New Deal community building and resettlement program. On proposals for veterans' land settlement, see Bill G. Reid, "Franklin K. Lane's Idea for Veterans' Colonization, 1918–1921," *Pacific Historical Review* 33 (November 1964): 447–61. For the largely aesthetic objection to the city see Ralph Borsodi, *This Ugly Civilization* (New York: Simon and Schuster,

1929), and Borsodi, "One Way Out," *New Republic* 59 (17, 24, and 31 July 1929), pt. 1, pp. 223–25; pt. 2, 252–56; pt. 3, 281–83.

31 Arthur Pound, "Land Ho! The Trek Toward Economic Security," *Atlantic Monthly* 151 (June 1933): 714–21; Philip Curtiss, "They Are Moving to the Country," *Harper's Magazine* 171 (June 1935): 67–79; Harry R. O'Brien, "The New Stampede to the Land," *The Country Gentleman* 102 (October 1932): 3–5.

32 William B. Duryee, *A Living from the Land: How to Make a Small Farm Support You* (Cleveland: World Publishing Co., 1934); M. G. Kains, *Five Acres and Independence* (New York: Greenberg: Publisher, 1935); Charles M. Wilson, "Land for the Taking," *American Magazine* 113 (March 1932): 54–56.

33 "Lure of the Land," *Nation* 131 (8 October 1930): 366; Wheeler McMillen, "Back-to-the-Land Fallacies," *Outlook* 160 (20 January 1932): 81–82; "You Need More Than Land to Go Back to the Farm," *Literary Digest* 114 (9 July 1932): 26–28.

34 Russell Lord, "Back to the Farm?" *Forum* 89 (February 1933): 97–103, quote on p. 97.

35 *Public Papers and Addresses,* 1: 15, 21–23, 28–29, 79, 81; Cornell speech, pp. 141, 142–43.

36 Ibid., pp. 485–96, 505, 510–11; Roosevelt, "A New Rural Planning," in *Rural Planning,* Proceedings of the 14th American Country Life Conference, Ithaca, N.Y., 17–20, August 1931 (Chicago: University of Chicago Press, 1932); Roosevelt, "Back-to-the-Land," *Review of Reviews* 86 (Ocotber 1931): 63–64.

37 Freidel, *Franklin D. Roosevelt,* vol. 3, *The Triumph,* p. 266.

38 Tugwell, *The Democratic Roosevelt,* p. 158.

39 Ibid., pp. 158–59.

40 Discussions of resettlement programs and agencies or of specific projects are found in Conkin, *Tomorrow a New World;* Russell Lord and Paul H. Johnstone, eds., *A Place on Earth: A Critical Appraisal of Subsistence Homesteads* (Washington, D.C.: GPO, 1942); Russell Lord, *The Wallaces of Iowa* (Boston: Houghton Mifflin Co., 1947), pp. 409–23; James G. Maddox, "The Farm Security Administration" (Ph.D. diss., Harvard University, 1950); U.S. Congress, Senate, *The Resettlement Program, Report of the Administrator of the Resettlement Administration,* Senate Document 213, 74th Cong., 2d sess., 12, May 1936; Raymond P. Duggan, *A Federal Resettlement Project: Granger Homesteads* (Washington, D.C.: Catholic University, 1937); Paul W. Wager, *One Foot on the Soil: A Study of Subsistence Homesteads in Alabama* (University, Ala.: University of Alabama, Bureau of Public Administration, 1945); Edward C. Banfield, *Government Project* (Glencoe, Ill.: The Free Press, 1951).

41 Conkin, *Tomorrow a New World,* chap. 14.

42 E.g., see several short articles in *Rural Rehabilitation,* published by the FERA, vol. 1 (15 February 1935), O. E. Baker, "Rural–Urban Migration and the National Welfare," p. 25 (digest of 1933 article, see n. 4 above); an interview with George W. Russell (AE), p. 27; Lawrence Westbrook, "Culture Must Come from the Soil," p. 28.

43 Searle F. Charles, *Minister of Relief: Harry Hopkins and the Depression* (Syracuse, N.Y.: Syracuse University Press, 1963), pp. 33–43; Corrington Gill, "A Study of the Three Million Families on Relief in October, 1933," *The Annals* 176 (November 1934): 25–26.

44 For this and later developments in land studies see Lewis C. Gray, "The Social and Economic Implications of the National Land Program," *Journal of Farm Economics* 18 (May 1936): 257–73.

45 This summary is drawn from the following reports and studies, of which the first is the most inclusive and would supply the essential information if the others were unavailable: Carter Goodrich et al., *Migration and Economic Opportunity: The Report of the Study of Population Redistribution* (Philadelphia: University of Pennsylvania Press, 1936); National Planning Board, *Final Report, 1933–1934* (Washington, D. C.: GPO, 1934); National Resources Board, *A Report on National Planning and Public Works* (Washington, D. C.: GPO, 1934); P. G. Beck and M. C. Forster, *Six Rural Problem Areas: Relief—Resources—Rehabilitation* (Washington, D.C.: GPO, 1935); Berta Asch and A. R. Mangus, *Farmers on Relief and Rehabilitation* (Washington, D.C.: GPO, 1937); Dwight Sanderson, *Research Memorandum on Rural Life in the Depression,* Bulletin 34 (New York: Social Science Research Council, 1937); National Resources Committee, *The Problems of a Changing Population* (Washington, D.C.: GPO, 1938); A. R. Mangus, *Changing Aspects of Rural Relief* (Washington, D.C.: GPO, 1938); Carl C. Taylor, Helen W. Wheeler, and E. L. Kirkpatrick, *Disadvantaged Classes in American Agriculture,* Social Research Report no. 8 (Washington, D.C.: GPO, 1938); C. E. Lively and Conrad Taeuber, *Rural Migration in the United States* (Washington, D.C.: GPO, 1939); John N. Webb and Malcom Brown, *Migrant Families* (Washington, D.C.: GPO, 1938); Warren S. Thompson, *Research Memorandum on Internal Migration in the Depression,* bulletin 30 (New York: Social Science Research Council, 1937); National Resources Committee, *The Northern Lake States Region* (Washington, D.C.: GPO, 1939); Philip E. Ryan, *Migration and Social Welfare* (New York: Russell Sage Foundation, 1940).

46 Harry L. Hopkins, "Hope for the Millions," *Today* 4 (4 May 1935): 3–4, 20; Lawrence Westbrook, "The Program of Rural Rehabilitation of the FERA," *Journal of Farm Economics* 17 (February 1935): 89–100.

47 Rexford G. Tugwell, *The Battle for Democracy* (New York: Columbia University Press, 1935), pp. 156–57.

48 E. L. Kirkpatrick, *Analysis of 70,000 Rural Rehabilitation Families* (Washington, D.C.: GPO, 1938), pp. 33–46.

49 Conkin, *Tomorrow a New World,* pp. 332–37.

50 Sherman E. Johnson, Robert D. Davidson, and Russell W. Bierman, "Land Settlement in the United States," *International Journal of Agrarian Affairs* 1 (September 1935): 64–76.

Chapter 1

1 H. H. Bancroft, *History of Alaska* (San Francisco: Bancroft and Co., 1886); Jeannette Paddock Nichols, *Alaska* (Cleveland: Arthur H. Clark Co., 1924), p. 408; Ernest Gruening, *The State of Alaska* (New York: Random House, 1954).

2 The 1880 population of 430 whites is from Ivan Petroff's one-man census, and its accuracy has been questioned by Gruening, *The State of Alaska,* pp. 62–63. However, a correction by even a three- or four-fold increase would still make obvious the scanty interest of Americans in Alaska at that time.

3 William H. Dall, "Report Upon the Agricultural Resources of Alaska," *Report of*

the Commissioner of Agriculture, 1868 (Washington, D.C.: Department of Agriculture, 1868), pp. 172–89. George Sundborg, *Bibliography and Abstracts on the Subject of Agriculture in Alaska, 1867–1942* (Juneau: National Resources Planning Board, 1942), p. ix.

4 Sundborg, *Bibliography and Abstracts,* pp. ix–x.

5 U.S. Department of Agriculture, *A Report to Congress on Agriculture in Alaska, Including Reports by Walter H. Evans, Benton Killin, and Sheldon Jackson,* Bulletin no. 48, Office of Experiment Stations (Washington, D.C.: GPO, 1898).

6 Ibid., pp. 26, 34–35.

7 Ibid., pp. 7, 8, 23–25.

8 Ibid., p. 25.

9 A brief account of the establishment of the Sitka and other experiment stations is given in Sundborg, *Bibliography and Abstracts,* pp. x–xiii. On C. C. Georgeson, see *Who Was Who in America,* vol. 2 (Chicago: A. N. Marquis Co., 1942–50).

10 C. C. Georgeson, "Agricultural Experiments in Alaska," *Yearbook of the United States Department of Agriculture, 1898* (Washington, D.C.: GPO, 1899), p. 515.

11 For the establishment of the various stations and the reports on their work, see *Annual Reports of the Office of Experiment Stations, Fiscal Years 1903–1932* (Washington, D.C.: GPO).

12 Gruening, *The State of Alaska,* pp. 277–78.

16 C. C. Georgeson, "The Possibilities of Alaska," *National Geographic Magazine* 13 (March 1902): 81–85.

14 On soldiers' additional homestead entries, a relic of the Civil War, see Paul W. Gates, for the Public Land Law Review Commission, *History of Public Land Law and Development* (Washington, D.C.: GPO, 1968), pp. 281–83. For use of the scrip by cannery and other companies to obtain business sites, see Nichols, *Alaska,* p. 158 n. The annual issues of *Report of the Governor of Alaska* through the 1930s listed ten or a dozen such entries a year. For changes in the homestead regulations and requirements, mineral entries, and all public land regulations, see U.S. Department of the Interior, *Instructions Relating to Acquisition of Title to Public Lands in the Territory of Alaska,* General Land Office Circular no. 491 (Washington, D.C.: GPO, 1923).

15 Georgeson, "The Possibilities of Alaska," p. 85.

16 Middleton Smith, "Gardening in Northern Alaska," *National Geographic Magazine* 14 (September 1903): 355–57.

17 Henry Gannett, "Agriculture in Alaska," *National Geographic Magazine* 13 (March 1902): 85.

18 C. C. Georgeson, *Suggestions to Pioneer Farmers in Alaska* (Washington, D.C.: GPO, 1902). The guide was reissued, with revisions and some changes in form and title, in 1916, 1917, 1923, 1930, 1937 (two revisions in that same year), and 1941.

19 Georgeson, *Suggestions to Pioneer Farmers,* pp. 8–10.

20 Ibid., pp. 14–15.

21 C. C. Georgeson, "Agricultural Capacity of Alaska: What Population Can the Territory Support?" *National Geographic Magazine* 20 (July 1909): 676–79.

22 The Alaska game regulations of 1908 and the revisions of 1915 are given in C. C. Georgeson, *Information for Prospective Settlers in Alaska,* the 1916 revision of his 1902 bulletin for prospective farmers. Later versions of the game laws appear in revi-

sions of the bulletin. The seasons were long, the limits large, and the game taken in season could be sold. Natives and miners or explorers in actual need could take game out of season. In 1918 Governor Riggs complained that the regulations from outside threatened the game. The use of game meat, he said, was essential, especially in remote areas; the real threat came from trophy-hunting sportsmen and from the cannery operators who fed transient labor on game in or out of season. Riggs also complained that many market hunters were bringing in only the hind quarters. *Annual Report of the Governor of Alaska, 1918* (Washington, D.C.: GPO, 1918), pp. 59–60.

23 The early days in the district are described by James Wickersham, district judge and later territorial delegate, in *Old Yukon: Tales—Trails—and Trials* (Washington, D.C.: Washington Law Book Co., 1938).

24 *Annual Report of the Governor of Alaska, 1903,* pp. 12–13.

25 Territory of Alaska, *Session Laws, Resolutions, and Memorials,* 1st Territorial Legislature, 1913, House Joint Memorial no. 4.

26 *Annual Report of the Governor of Alaska, 1904,* p. 33.

27 Levi Chubbuck, *Possible Agicultural Development in Alaska,* U.S. Department of Agriculture Bulletin no. 50 (Washington, D.C: GPO, 1914), pp. 10–21.

28 *Alaska, Our Frontier Wonderland* (Seattle: Alaska Bureau, Seattle Chamber of Commerce, 1917), pp. 67–69.

29 The activities of the Fairbanks station are included in C. C. Georgeson's yearly versions of the *Annual Report of Alaska Agricultural Experiment Stations* (Washington, D.C.: GPO, 1907–27).

30 E.g., Alfred H. Brooks, "The Value of Alaska," *The Geographical Review* 15 (January 1925): 25–50.

31 *Alaska, Our Frontier Wonderland,* pp. 76–77.

32 U.S., Bureau of the Census, *Fourteenth Census of the United States: 1920,* "Agriculture, Reports for the States," 6, pt. 3, tables 7–11. The census report on Alaska is probably the only one listing dogs as work animals. In 1920 there were 17,625 working dogs, 363 of them on farms.

33 The early history of the region and of Knik is given in Hugh A. Johnson and Keith L. Stanton, *Matanuska Valley Memoir* (Palmer, Alaska: University of Alaska and Alaska Agricutlural Experiment Station, 1955), pp. 5–26.

34 Ibid., pp. 11–13.

35 Ibid., pp. 18–22; and C. C. Georgeson, *Report on Agricultural Investigations in Alaska in 1899,* Experiment Stations Bulletin no. 82 (Washington, D.C.: GPO, 1900).

36 Otto F. Ohlson to the Secretary of the Interior, 10 January 1929, Alaska Railroad, Anchorage, File 47.5 (Colonization). For pictures of Matanuska Valley homesteads, see the 1916 and 1917 editions of *Information for Prospective Settlers in Alaska.* Also, Lydia May Kellogg, "Early Matanuska Homesteading," *The Magazine Alaska* 5 (summer 1951): 8–11, and Gerrit Snider, "Sunny Old Knik," ibid., pp. 12–15, 53.

37 Gruening, *State of Alaska,* pp. 188, 225–26; *Annual Report of the Governor of Alaska, 1915,* pp. 35, 61.

38 U.S. Code, title 48, sec. 301.

39 For the development and the construction of the railroad, see Joshua Bernhardt, *The Alaska Engineering Commission,* Institute for Government Research, Service

Monographs of the United States Government no. 4 (New York: D. Appleton and Co., 1922).

40 *Report of the Governor of Alaska, 1917,* p. 48.

41 Hugh H. Bennett and Thomas D. Rice, *Soil Reconnaissance in Alaska, With an Estimate of the Agricultural Possibilities* (Washington, D.C.: GPO, 1915).

42 The Alaska Railroad's promotion of settlement and the work of the Land and Industrial Commission can be followed in the memoranda and publicity releases from Christensen's office, now in Alaska Railroad File 47.5 (Colonization), at the Anchorage office. See also the editions of the *Annual Report of the Governor of Alaska,* with some variation in title, for the years 1915–23.

43 *Annual Report of the Governor of Alaska, 1917,* pp. 6–12, 55–60, 1, 48–49, 7, and *Annual Report of the Governor of Alaska, 1918,* pp. 1, 10.

44 *Annual Report of the Governor of Alaska,* for the years 1919–22.

45 Ibid., 1923, pp. 1–2.

46 *Fourteenth Census of the United States: 1920,* "Agriculture, Reports for States—Alaska," 6, pt. 3, tables 1–3.

47 *Annual Report of the Governor of Alaska, 1923,* pp. 44–45.

48 *Fairbanks Daily News-Miner,* special annual edition, 1 July 1923.

49 U.S. Department of the Interior, *General Information Regarding the Territory of Alaska* (Washington, D.C.: GPO, 1931), pp. 36–37.

50 Mrs. Downes to Noel Smith, Alaska Railroad File 47.5, 1 August 1927; Smith to Mrs. Downes, 8 August 1927, ibid.

51 Smith to Alberts and Myers, April–June 1927, ibid.

52 Parks to Garfield, 3 May 1927, ibid.

53 Alaska Railroad File 47.5, an undated copy of the plan attached to a 27 July 1927 letter from Smith to Gasser referring to "your plan."

54 Ohlson's character and temperament can be gathered from his letters and memoranda in the Alaska Railroad and Alaska Rural Rehabilitation Corporation files. For biographical information, see *Who's Who in Alaska and Alaska Business Index* (Juneau: Tewkesbury Publishers, 1947). Ohlson's management of the Alaska Railroad is described in Edwin M. Fitch, *The Alaska Railroad* (New York: Frederick A. Praeger, 1967), pp. 70–76. For Ohlson's promotional pamphlet, see U.S. Department of the Interior, *The Resources of Alaska,* by O. F. Ohlson (Anchorage: Alaska Railroad, 1928).

55 Ohlson to West, 10 January 1929, Alaska Railroad File 47.5.

56 Ibid., letters between Snodgrass and settlers, 1927–29.

57 Letters between Snodgrass and Ohlson, 1929–34, refer to promotion of settlement. In a long letter to Jacob Baker, assistant administrator of the FERA, 10, August 1934, Ohlson summarized the colonizing work of the Alaska Railroad. See also *Annual Report of the Governor of Alaska, 1929,* p. 20, and ibid., *1930,* p. 26.

58 Ohlson to Eric Brattstrom, 7 August 1929, Alaska Railroad File 47.5.

59 *Report of the Icelandic Committee from Wisconsin on the Character and Resources of Alaska* (Washington, D.C.: GPO, 1875); *Fourteenth Census of the United States: 1920,* "Population (Alaska)," vol. 3, tables 1–5; "Agriculture (Alaska)," vol. 6, table 5.

60 In the northern cutover region of the Great Lakes states, where the rate of farm abandonment was high, the areas of most stable settlement were those of up to 90 percent foreign-born settlers, with the greatest stability in areas of predominantly Scandinavian and Finnish settlement. Finnish settlers had the lowest rate of

farm abandonment regardless of seemingly adverse soil and climatic conditions. See W. A. Hartman and J. D. Black, *Economic Aspects of Land Settlement in the Cut-Over Region of the Great Lakes States* (Washington, D.C.: GPO, 1931), pp. 66–69, 77–78.

61 Eugene Van Cleef, "The Finn in America," *Geographical Review* 6 (September 1918): 185–214; idem, "The Finns of the Pacific Coast of the United States, and Consideration of the Problem of Scientific Land Settlement," *Annals of the Association of American Geographers* 30 (March 1940): 25–38. For Finnish settlement in Minnesota, see D. H. Davis, "The Finland Community, Minnesota," *Geographical Review* 25 (July 1935): 382–94. The economic and political conditions that pushed Finns to America and the decades of toil required to make a decent farm are described in John I. Kolehmeinen and George W. Hill, *Haven in the Woods: The Story of the Finns in Wisconsin* (Madison: State Historical Society of Wisconsin, 1965).

62 Sherman Conrad, "The Matanuska Valley Colonization Project: Rural Rehabilitation in Alaska," *Monthly Report of the Federal Emergency Relief Administration* (April 1936), p. 34.

63 Harold L. Ickes, "Let's Open Up Alaska!" *This Week* (3 February 1946): 4–5, 18.

64 Snodgrass to Ohlson, 27 July 1929, Alaska Railroad File 47.5; Ohlson to B. C. Thomas, Los Angeles, Calif., undated, ibid. The *Alaska Weekly* (Seattle), 3 May 1929, praised the whole plan as a practical method of offering guidance to selected settlers, not incompetents.

65 Snodgrass to Ohlson, 3 September 1929, Alaska Railroad File 47.5.

66 Snodgrass to the Dodd Brothers (cattle dealers of Kirkland, Washington), 19 April 1930, Alaska Railroad File 47.5.

67 Ummel to James L. Devlin of *Detroit News*, 19 April 1930, ibid.

68 Snodgrass to Ohlson, 12 April 1930, ibid.

69 Ohlson to Jacob Baker (assistant administrator of the FERA), 10 August 1934, ibid.

70 *Annual Report of the Governor of Alaska*, for the years 1928–33.

71 *Fairbanks Daily News-Miner*, 9 November 1933.

72 *Annual Report of the Governor of Alaska, 1934*, pp. 1, 5, 20, 38–39.

73 *Anchorage Daily Times*, 11 September 1934.

74 *Daily Alaska Empire* (Juneau), Progress and Development edition, 31 March 1940, sec. 1, p. 6; sec. 2, p. 8, gives statistical summaries of Alaskan trade.

75 John J. Underwood, *Alaska, An Empire in the Making* (New York: Dodd, Mead and Co., 1920; first ed., 1913), p. xv. Underwood was a Seattle newspaperman closely connected with the chamber of commerce of that city.

Chapter 2

1 *Daily Alaska Empire* (Juneau), 16, 17, 18 July 1934.

2 *Anchorage Daily Times*, 28 July 1934.

3 Ibid., editorial, "Matanuska Colonization"; 30 July and 2 August 1934.

4 Ibid., 2 August 1934.

5 Ohlson to Baker, 10 August 1934 (copies of a letter and a radiogram), Alaska Railroad File 47.5.

6 E.g., Gruening, *State of Alaska*, pp. 299–300, 305–06, and 540*n.*, citing Hugh A.

Johnson and Don L. Irwin, *The Position of Agriculture in Alaska's Current Economy* (Palmer, Alaska: University of Alaska and the Agricultural Research Administration, U.S.D.A., 1953), p. 1.

7 The peasant and his values are described by Robert Redfield, "Peasant Society and Culture," the individually paged second half of *The Little Community and Peasant Society and Culture* (Chicago: University of Chicago Press, Phoenix Books, 1960), pp. 18–19, 60–64.

8 Sherman Conrad, "The Matanuska Valley Colonization Project: Rural Rehabilitation in Alaska," *Monthly Report of the Federal Emergency Relief Administration* (April 1936): 36. (Hereafter cited as Conrad, *Monthly Report, FERA*.)

9 Ohlson to Baker, 10 August 1934, Alaska Railroad File 47.5.

10 Copies of messages and letters between Ohlson, Baker, Ickes, and Roper in ibid., 11, 12, 29 August and 15 September 1934. For newspaper coverage, see *Anchorage Daily Times*, 28 August and 29 September 1934.

11 *Anchorage Daily Times*, 11 October 1934.

12 Editorial, *Seward Gateway*, reprinted in *Anchorage Daily Times*, 29 October 1934.

13 *Anchorage Daily Times*, news stories and editorials, 12–29 October 1934.

14 Sheely to Ohlson, 12 December 1934, Alaska Railroad File 47.5.

15 Ohlson's memorandum, 10 December 1934, ibid.

16 Snell to Ohlson, 26 November 1934, ibid.

17 *Anchorage Daily Times*, 4 December 1934.

18 *Anchorage Daily Times* and *Fairbanks Daily News-Miner*, 22 December 1934.

19 *Fairbanks Daily News-Miner*, 3 December 1934 and 27 February 1935.

20 For these activities early in 1935, see the *Anchorage Daily Times*, 10, 15, 16 January and 20, 23 February 1935; *Fairbanks Daily News-Miner*, 15 January and 27 February 1935; and Conrad, *Monthly Report, FERA* (April 1936): 30–37.

21 Interview with Irwin, 2 September 1960.

22 Kirk H. Stone, "Alaska Group Settlement: The Matanuska Valley Colony," mimeographed (Washington, D.C., Department of the Interior, Bureau of Land Management [1950]), pp. 8–8a. The study was originally a Ph.D. dissertation in geography, University of Michigan, 1949, and was then issued in mimeographed form during the postwar interest in Alaskan settlement. There are some differences in the preface and pagination. References here are to the mimeographed version.

23 Interviews with Irwin, 2 September 1960, and with Gasser, 22 August 1960.

24 Gruening, *State of Alaska*, p. 299. Also, Stuart R. Tompkins, *Alaska: Promyshlennik and Sourdough* (Norman: University of Oklahoma Press, 1945), pp. 289–92; C. L. Andrews, *The Story of Alaska* (Caldwell, Idaho: Caxton Printers, 1940), pp. 232, 236–38; J. B. Caldwell, *Introducing Alaska* (New York: G. P. Putnam's Sons, 1947), chap. 5.

25 Gruening to author, 11 July 1961.

26 Conrad, *Monthly Report, FERA* (April 1936): 30–37.

27 Lawrence Westbrook, "Rehabilitation of Stranded Families," *Annals of the American Academy of Political and Social Science* 176 (November 1934): 74–79; and "The Program of Rural Rehabilitation of the FERA" (Paper delivered at the annual meeting of the American Farm Economic Association, Chicago, 27 December 1934), reprinted in the *Journal of Farm Economics* 17 (1935): 89–100.

28 Westbrook to author, 10 July 1961.

29 The possible military significance of the colony was later mentioned in the press: *New York Times,* 25 April 1935, p. 20; *New Republic* 83 (29 May 1935): 61–62. In the last months of 1934 and in early 1935 Alaskan newspapers almost daily reported rumors of planned air and naval base and military highway construction.
30 Rudolph A. Christiansen, "The Wisconsin Resettlement Program" (M.S. thesis, University of Wisconsin, 1954), pp. 145–46.
31 *Anchorage Daily Times,* 4 December 1934.
32 *Time* 26 (1 July 1935): 14.
33 *Anchorage Daily Times,* 16 January 1935.
34 Ibid., 10 January 1935; 16 January 1935; 23 February 1935.
35 *Fairbanks Daily News-Miner,* 9 February 1935.
36 Ibid., 10 November 1934.
37 *Anchorage Daily Times,* 19 January 1935.
38 *Fairbanks Daily News-Miner,* 26 February 1935; *Anchorage Daily Times,* 26 February 1935; *House Journal of Alaska* (1935), p. 338; *Senate Journal of Alaska* (1935), pp. 175–76, 193, 200.
39 *Anchorage Daily Times,* 27 February 1935.
40 The Ruste and Ohlson letters and Ruste's "Plan for Social-Economic Reorganization" and his "Agricultural Engineering Phase of the Integral Social-Economic Unit Plan" are in Alaska Railroad File 47.5.

Chapter 3

1 Gruening, *State of Alaska,* p. 462, map and text.
2 Stone, "Alaska Group Settlement," p. 29, and map, fig. 15. The number of colonists (201) does not include the one additional family chosen from Oklahoma or one man who had been living at the time in Minnesota, but who had a homestead claim in the colony and returned to it.
3 U.S. National Resources Committee, *The Northern Lake States Region,* pp. 1–3. An earlier study included 113 counties in the cutover region: Hartman and Black, *Economic Aspects of Land Settlement in the Cut-Over Region,* p. 2.
4 Beck and Forster, *Six Rural Problem Areas,* summary, pp. 1–8; the problem and the cutover region defined, pp. 9–13. For other studies, see U.S. National Resources Board, *A Report on National Planning and Public Works;* U.S. National Resources Committee *The Northern Lake States Region;* C. P. Loomis, Joseph J. Lister, Dwight M. Davidson, Jr., *Standards of Living in the Great Lakes Cut-Over Area,* Social Research Report 13 (Washington, D.C.: GPO, 1938). For a nongovernmental study, see Carter Goodrich et al., *Migration and Economic Opportunity,* pt. 1, chap. 4.
5 A concise account of the whole region is Walter A. Rowlands, "The Great Lakes Cutover Region," in *Regionalism in America,* ed. Merrill Jensen (Madison: University of Wisconsin Press, 1952), pp. 331–46. For the general settlement of the region, see Ray A. Billington, *Westward Expansion* (New York: Macmillan Co., 1960), chap. 14, pp. 290–309. The development of mining, lumbering, and agriculture is described by Ralph H. Brown, *Historical Geography of the United States* (New York: Harcourt, Brace and Co., 1948), pp. 289–366.
6 Brown, *Historical Geography,* pp. 323–25, 333–36.
7 George A. Pond, *A Study of Farm Organization in Southwestern Minnesota,* U.S. Department of Agriculture, Bulletin no. 1271 (Washington, D.C.: GPO, 1924),

pp. 1–6. Also, Leonard S. Wilson, "Some Notes on the Growth of Population in Minnesota," *Geographical Review* 30 (October 1940): 660–64; Arthur Henry Moehlman, "The Red River of the North," *Geographical Review* 25 (January 1925): 79–91.

8 Merle Curti et al., *The Making of an American Community* (Stanford, Calif.: Stanford University Press, 1959), pp. 11, 239.

9 For the rise and decline of lumbering in the region, see R. V. Reynolds and Albert H. Pierson, *Lumber Cut of the United States, 1870–1920,* U.S. Department of Agriculture, Bulletin no. 1119 (Washington, D.C.: GPO, 1923), pp. 30–33; U.S. Department of Agriculture, *Timber Depletion and the Answer,* Circular 112 (Washington, D.C.: GPO, 1920), pp. 3, 4–9. Also, Brown, *Historical Geography,* pp. 308–09, and U.S. National Resources Committee, *The Northern Lake States Region,* pp. 1–5.

10 Charles M. Davis, "The Cities and Towns of the High Plains of Michigan," *Geographical Review* 28 (October 1938): 664–73; also, U.S. National Resources Committee, *The Northern Lakes States Region,* pp. 6–7.

11 John D. Black and L. C. Gray, *Land Settlement and Colonization in the Great Lakes States* (Washington, D.C.: GPO, 1925). Promotion and colonization in Wisconsin is described by Arlan Helgeson, State Historical Society of Wisconsin, *Farms in the Cutover: Agricultural Settlement in Northern Wisconsin* (Madison: University of Wisconsin Press, 1962).

12 Bertha Henderson, *Farm Lands Available for Settlement* (Washington, D.C.: GPO, 1922), pp. 44–48 and appendix; state immigration bureaus, pp. 49–51.

13 Black and Gray, *Land Settlement and Colonization,* pp. 2–5.

14 "Made to Order Farms," *National Real Estate Journal* 23 (January 1922): 41–44.

15 Black and Gray, *Land Settlement and Colonization,* p. l.

16 Ibid., pp. 20–28, 31.

17 Ibid., pp. 20–21, 48–55.

18 Ibid., pp. 62–63, 83–85, and Henderson, *Farm Lands Available for Settlement,* pp. 6, 46–47.

19 E.g., see R. E. Ammon and J. S. Bordner, *Farm Prospector's Guide to Northern Wisconsin,* Bulletin no. 121 (Madison: Wisconsin Department of Agriculture and Markets, 1931); W. A. Hartman, "State Policies in Regulating Land Settlement Activities," *Journal of Farm Economics* 13 (May 1931): 259–69; U.S. Department of Agriculture, *State Land Settlement Problems and Policies in the United States* (Washington, D.C.: GPO 1933).

20 Helgeson, *Farms in the Cutover,* pp. 80–95.

21 Ibid., pp. 96–104.

22 Black and Gray, *Land Settlement and Colonization,* pp. 68–69.

23 Ibid., pp. 83–85.

24 U.S. National Resources Board, *Report on National Planning,* pp. 156–57, 175–97; also, U.S. National Resources Committee, *The Northern Lake States Region,* p. 8.

25 O'Brien, "The New Stampede to the Land," pp. 3–5.

26 U.S. Department of Commerce, *Historical Statistics of the United States* (Washington, D.C.: GPO, 1960), pp. 39, 47.

27 Warren S. Thompson, *Research Memorandum on Internal Migration in the Depression,* pp. 21–25. Also, Lively and Taeuber, *Rural Migration in the United States,* pp. xv–xx (findings summarized).

28 Beck and Forster, *Six Rural Problem Areas,* pp. 52, 65–73.

29 Noble Clark, *Using Farm Lands for Unemployment Relief,* Wisconsin Agricultural Experiment Station Bulletin (Madison: University of Wisconsin Press, 1933).

30 *Making the Most of Taylor County Land,* University of Wisconsin College of Agriculture Special Circular (Madison: University of Wisconsin Press, 1931); Noble Clark, *What Chance Has a City Man on a Wisconsin Farm?* University of Wisconsin College of Agriculture Extension Service Radio Circular (Madison: University of Wisconsin Press, 1932).

31 E. C. Johnson and T. B. Manny, "Part-Time Farming in the Duluth Area," *Farm Business Notes,* no. 131 (Minneapolis: University of Minnesota Press, 1933).

32 R. W. Murchie, *Land Settlement as a Relief Measure,* no. 5, Day and Hour Series (Minneapolis: University of Minnesota Press, 1933), pp. 6–8, 16.

33 Ibid., pp. 1–17, 26–28.

34 Goodrich et al., *Migration and Economic Opportunity,* pp. 165–68.

35 Berta Asch and A. R. Mangus, *Farmers on Relief and Rehabilitation,* p. 124, table 17. The information is for June 1935 and was gathered in nine regions in which rural poverty, as indicated by relief rates, was extreme. The information for the northern cutover region was based on a sampling of 3,006 relief families, See also Loomis, Lister, and Davidson, *Standards of Living in the Great Lakes Cut-Over Area,* p. 6.

36 For national relief rates and local variations see Goodrich et al., *Migration and Economic Opportunity,* plate 4 and pp. 38–39, 46, 190–92.

37 Taylor, Wheeler, and Kirkpatrick, *Disadvantaged Classes in American Agriculture,* pp. 90–92.

38 Asch and Mangus, *Farmers on Relief and Rehabilitation,* pp. xviii–xx (rural relief trends summarized). For a general account of the rural relief problem, with attention to specific areas, see Mangus, *Changing Aspects of Rural Relief.*

39 Asch and Mangus, *Farmers on Relief and Rehabilitation,* pp. 45–47.

40 Goodrich et al., *Migration and Economic Opportunity,* pp. 191–92.

41 The study of the area was made by George S. Wehrwein of the University of Wisconsin in 1936 based on information for 1933–35—quoted by Goodrich et al., *Migration and Economic Opportunity,* pp. 168–70.

42 E. L. Kirkpatrick, *Needed Standards of Living for Rural Resettlement,* Wisconsin Rural Rehabilitation Division, Resettlement Administration (Madison: May 1936), pp. 1–40.

43 Oscar B. Jesness, Reynolds I. Nowell, and associates, *A Program for Land Use in Northern Minnesota* (Minneapolis: University of Minnesota Press, 1935), pp. 245–53.

44 Beck and Forster, *Six Rural Problem Areas,* pp. 15–16.

45 Ibid., p. 7.

46 U.S. National Resources Committee, *The Northern Lake States Region,* pp. 10–12; also, T. J. Woofter, Jr. and Ellen Winston, *Seven Lean Years* (Chapel Hill: University of North Carolina Press, 1939), pp. 121–32. For the persistence of marginal agriculture in cutover areas of Michigan, even during postwar prosperity, see Lauren H. Brown, *Michigan Farm Organization and Practices,* Michigan Agricultural Experiment Station, Special Bulletins nos. 336 and 337 (East Lansing: Michigan State College, February 1946 and June 1946).

47 V. Webster Johnson, Sidney Henderson, and James H. Marshall, *A Land Program*

for Forest County, Wisconsin, U.S. Department of Agriculture, Technical Bulletin no. 687 (Washington, D.C.: GPO, 1939). pp. 17–18.

48 Beck and Forster, *Six Rural Problem Areas* pp. 13–15; U.S. National Resources Committee, *The Northern Lake States Region,* pp. 5–7; Goodrich et al., *Migration and Economic Opportunity,* pp. 175–76, 186–88.

49 U.S. National Resources Board, *A Report on National Planning,* pp. 128–29; also, Goodrich et al., *Migration and Economic Opportunity,* pp. 179–85.

50 Jesness, Nowell, and associates, *A Program for Land Use in Northern Minnesota,* p. 253.

51 Ibid., pp. 84–85.

52 U.S. Department of Agriculture, *Farm Opportunities in the United States: Outlook, Problems, Policies* (Washington, D.C.: GPO, 1945), pp. 56–57.

53 Goodrich et al., *Migration and Economic Opportunity,* plate 3, "Plane of Living," and pp. 16–24.

54 The ARRC's personnel records on the Matanuska colonists verify this. In 1962 one typical colonist recalled that he had none of the conveniences in Minnesota and that his family's colony home had plumbing and electricity years before either his mother or his mother-in-law in Minnesota got them.

55 All the reports on the region include some discussion of the level of living. See, e.g., Taylor, Wheeler, and Kirkpatrick, *Disadvantaged Classes in American Agriculture,* pp. 17, 89, 110–21.

56 Johnson, Henderson, and Marshall, *A Land Program for Forest County, Wisconsin,* pp. 26–27.

57 U.S. National Resources Committee, *The Northern Lake States Region,* pp. 7–8.

58 U.S. National Resources Board, *A Report on National Planning,* pp. 177–80.

59. Goodrich et al., *Migration and Economic Opportunity,* pp. 170–74; Loomis, Lister, and Davidson, *Standards of Living in the Great Lakes Cut-Over Area,* p. 2, table 2. For a discussion of the public and private burden of isolated settlement, see George S. Wehrwein and J. A. Baker, "The Cost of Isolated Settlement in Northern Wisconsin," *Rural Sociology* 2 (September 1937): 253–65.

60 Jesness, Nowell, and associates, *A Program for Land Use in Northern Minnesota,* chap. 10, pp. 253, 262; also, L. C. Gray, "The Social and Economic Implications of the National Land System," pp. 257–73, esp. pp. 268–69.

61 U.S. National Resources Board, *A Report on National Planning,* p. 184.

62 Ibid.

63 C. I. Hendrickson, "Rural Zoning: Controlling Land Utilization under the Police Power," *Journal of Farm Economics* 18 (August 1936): 477–92; U.S. Department of Agriculture, *The Why and How of Rural Zoning,* Bulletin no. 196 (Washington, D.C.: GPO, 1958); Johnson, Henderson, and Marshall, *A Land Program for Forest County, Wisconsin,* pp. 60–71; Goodrich et al., *Migration and Economic Opportunity,* pp. 604–09.

64 Rudolph A. Christiansen, "The Wisconsin Resettlement Program" (M.S. thesis, University of Wisconsin, 1954).

65 Chester R. Wasson, "The Grubstake Plan for the Evacuation and Resettlement of the Inhabitants of Beltrami Island, Minnesota," *Social Science Review* 12 (June 1938): pp. 276–97.

66 Bushrod W. Allin, "Migration Required for Best Land Use," pp. 493–99; also,

Lawrence Westbrook, "The Program of Rural Rehabilitation of the FERA," pp. 89–100; and Westbrook, notes on rehabilitation in *Rural Rehabilitation*, newsletter of the FERA Rural Rehabilitation Division, vol. 1 (February 1935), p. 28.

67 U.S. Congress, Senate Document 213, *The Resettlement Administration Program, Report of the Administrator*, 74th Cong, 2d sess., 1936, pp. 2–10.

68 This is the argument running though Goodrich et al., *Migration and Economic Opportunity*.

69 Kolehmeinen and Hill, *Haven in the Woods*, chap. 3; George W. Hill and Ronald A. Smith, *Man in the Cut-Over: A Study of Family Farm Resources in Northern Wisconsin* (Madison: University of Wisconsin Agricultural Experiment Station and Rural Survey Section, W.P.A., 1941), pp. 11, 15–16, and passim. The studies on which the book is based were done in 1933–34 and 1938–39. For the decline of a once modestly successful rural area, see Darrell H. Davis, "Finland Community," pp. 382–94; also, Wasson, "Grubstake Plan," pp. 284–85.

70 In 1935 climatic data for the region had been taken for fourteen years at the Matanuska station, and there were seventeen years of records taken at Anchorage; see U.S. Department of Agriculture, *Climate and Man, Yearbook of Agriculture, 1941* (Washington, D.C.: GPO, 1941), pp. 1211–12 (Alaska climatic summary); on the distribution of permafrost, see *Evaluation of Soils and Permafrost Conditions in the Territory of Alaska by Means of Aerial Photographs*, prepared by Robert E. Frost and the Engineering Experiment Station, Purdue University (Corps of Engineers, U.S. Army, 1950), pp. 27–36; R. F. Legget, "Permafrost Research," *Arctic Research: Current Status of Research*, Special Publication no. 2 (Arctic Institute of North America, 1955), pp. 41–46. On Alaskan soils see U.S. Department of Agriculture, *Soils and Men, Yearbook of Agriculture, 1938* (Washington, D.C.: GPO, 1938), pp. 1148–51.

Chapter 4

1 In some form these criticisms are found in almost all writings on Alaska that make any reference to the colony. See Stone, "Alaska Group Settlement," pp. ii–vii, 10–25, 55–73; Gruening, *The State of Alaska*, pp. 299–300, 305–06; Johnson and Irwin, *The Position of Agriculture in Alaska's Current Economy*, p. 1; Clarence C. Hulley, "A Historical Survey of the Matanuska Valley Settlement in Alaska," *Pacific Northwest Quarterly* 40 (October 1949): 327–40.

2 Stone, "Alaska Group Settlement," pp. 37–38.

3 By 1935 final entries had been made on 1,072 Alaskan homesteads. Computed from the annual totals in *Homesteads*, Bureau of Land Management (Washington, D.C.: GPO, 1962).

4 John B. Holt, *An Analysis of Methods and Criteria Used in Selecting Families for Colonization Projects* (Washington, D.C.: GPO, 1937), p. 2; Marie Jasny, *Family Selection on a Federal Irrigation Project* (Washington, D.C.: GPO, 1938), pp. 10–11.

5 Goodrich et al., *Migration and Economic Opportunity*, chap. 10. See Erich Kraemer, three studies for the RA under the general title *Land Settlement Technique Abroad*, Land Policy Circular Supplement (Washington, D.C.: GPO, June 1935–July 1936).

6 Jesness, Nowell, and associates, *A Program for Land Use in Northern Minnesota*, pp. 240–42, 253–56; Goodrich et al., *Migration and Economic Opportunity*, pp. 612–13.

7 Lawrence Westbrook, "The Program of Rural Rehabilitation of the FERA," pp. 89–100.
8 A. M. Goodman, "Report of the Present, and Estimate of the Future, Agriculture of the Matanuska Valley of Alaska" (typescript report) ARRC File 2921–8, pp. 41–42. Goodman was a member of a special inspection group headed by Lt. Col. Leroy Hunt in July and August 1935.
9 Herbert C. Hanson, ARRC general manager, to James G. Maddox, F.S.A, ARRC File 2925, 17 April 1940.
10 Darrell H. Davis, "The Finland Community, Minnesota," pp. 382–94.
11 The people of the Ozarks described admiringly by Charles M. Wilson in *Backwoods America* in many ways resemble settlers chosen for the Matanuska Project and would have been equally unacceptable to professional agriculturists and others who wanted "real farmers." A similar area and population are studied in James West, *Plainville, U.S.A.* (New York: Columbia University Press, 1961).
12 Harry Hopkins, "Hope for the Millions," pp. 3, 4, 20.
13 Conversation with Irwin, 2 September 1960.
14 Announced for March 13, *New York Times* (9 March 1935), p. 17.
15 This and the following discussion of colonists' qualifications is based on Conrad, *Monthly Report, FERA* (April 1936): 30–37.
16 Ibid., p. 34.
17 Lawrence Westbrook, "Rural-Industrial Communities for Stranded Families," FERA, Division of Rural Rehabilitation and Stranded Populations (n.p., [1934]), p. 23.
18 Holt, *An Analysis of Methods and Criteria*, p. 40.
19 The selection process is described by Mrs. Winthrop D. Lane, an FERA social worker, quoted by Holt, *An Analysis of Methods and Criteria*, pp. 40–41. In interviews and questionnaires in 1960–62, original colonists who then remained in the valley recalled that they had taken the initiative in asking relief authorities to be included in the project, and several claimed that they had applied for relief simply to meet formal qualifications for the colony.
20 The information sought and the question are taken from the personnel forms in the ARRC files on the individual colonists.
21 The reports of the caseworkers are included in the individual colonists' files in the ARRC records. See also Holt, *An Analysis of Methods and Criteria*, pp. 18, 26–28.
22 The discussion is based on the tabulation of farm and nonfarm experience in Stone, "Alaska Group Settlement," pp. 31–33.
23 E.g., see Don L. Irwin and G. W. Gasser in the interviews already cited; Mrs. I. M. Sandvik, a colonist wife, interviewed 8 June 1962; Mrs. Lydia Fohn-Hansen, once home demonstration agent in the extension service at the colony, interviewed 7 June 1962; Stone, "Alaska Group Settlement," chap. 5; Hulley, "Historical Survey of Matanuska Valley Settlement," pp. 327–40.
24 *New York Times*, 21 April 1935, sec. 2, p. 10.
25 From a detailed account by F. S. Lee of his admission to the colony, attached to the October 1962 questionnaire circulated among the original colonists by the author.
26 ARRC files, records on individual colonists, the Burt Garton file. Also, the ARRC Tract Book, showing assignments and transfers of colony tracts, records Garton's assignment to Tract 188.

27 Notes added to the 1962 questionnaire by F. M. Henry.

28 All federal actions affecting public lands in Alaska from 1867 to 30 June 1958 are listed chronologically in brief form in *Orders Affecting Public Lands in Alaska*, U.S. Department of the Interior, Bureau of Land Management (Washington, D.C., 1959).

29 Executive Orders 7126-a and 7128, 5 and 6 August 1935.

30 *Anchorage Daily Times*, 3 June 1935; *Daily Alaska Empire* (Juneau), 4 June and 7 and 6 August 1935.

31 The description of the valley, its terrain, climate, and soils is drawn from material found in many bulletins and reports on Alaskan land and agriculture by federal, territorial, and state agencies, but it follows especially W. A. Rockie, *Physical Land Conditions in the Matanuska Valley, Alaska* (Washington, D.C.: GPO, 1946), and Rockie, "A Picture of Matanuska," *Geographical Review* 32 (July 1942): 353–71. See also Herbert C. Hanson, *Agriculture in the Matanuska Valley, Alaska* (Washington, D.C.: GPO [1934]) and G. W. Gasser, *Information for the Alaska Farmer–Settler*, Alaska Development Board, Circular no. 1 (Juneau, 1946).

32 Hugh A. Johnson and Keith L. Stanton, "Matanuska Valley Memoir: The Story of How One Alaskan Community Developed" (Palmer, Alaska: University of Alaska Agricultural Experiment Station, 1955), p. 51, and Ohlson to Jacob Baker, 10 August 1934, Alaska Railroad File 47.5.

33 *Anchorage Daily Times*, 2 and 4 April 1935.

34 Stone, "Alaska Group Settlement," p. 24; Johnson and Stanton, *Matanuska Valley Memoir*, p. 51.

35 ARRC Tract Book, descriptions and histories of each of the 208 tracts.

36 Rockie, *Physical Land Conditions*, p. 2.

37 ARRC files 1807-1, 1807-2.

38 ARRC Articles of Incorporation, 12 April 1935.

39 ARRC Amended By-Laws, 29 October 1935.

40 Copies of the "Alaska Rural Rehabilitation Corporation, Matanuska Valley Settlement Agreement" are in the individual colonists' files in the ARRC records.

41 *New York Times*, 9 March 1935, p. 17; *Fairbanks Daily News-Miner*, 11, 19, and 25 March 1935.

42 *Anchorage Daily Times*, 9, 16, and 23 April 1935; *Daily Alaska Empire*, 2 May 1935; *Fairbanks Daily News-Miner*, 15 April 1935.

43 ARRC files, inventories in individual colonists' records.

44 *Fairbanks Daily News-Miner*, 26 April 1935; ibid., 1, and 2 May 1935; *Daily Alaska Empire*, 1 May 1935.

45 *New York Times*, 2 May 1935, p. 43.

46 *Seward Gateway*, 7 May 1935.

47 *Anchorage Daily Times*, 8, 9, and 10 May 1935.

48 Ibid., 10 and 11 May 1935.

49 *Daily Alaska Empire*, 11 and 12 May 1935.

50 *Anchorage Daily Times*, 22, 23, and 24 May 1935.

51 Stone, "Alaska Group Settlement," fig. 14.

52 *Fairbanks Daily News-Miner*, 17 June 1935; *Daily Alaska Empire*, 20 June 1935.

53 *Anchorage Daily Times*, 13 May 1935.

54 Ibid., Scripps-Howard special feature article.

55 *New York Times*, 25 April 1935, p. 20; "Pioneers in 1935: New Homesteads in

Alaska," *New Republic* 83 (29 May 1935): 61–62, used the colony to defend the unemployed against charges of shiftlessness.

56 *New York Times,* 9 May 1935, p. 20. The lowest Matanuska temperature then recorded was −36°F.

57 Ibid., 14 May 1935, p. 16.

58 "Settlers Heed Call of Rich Soil," *Newsweek* 5 (16 March 1935): 9; "Alaskan Colonization," *Literary Digest* 119 (1 June 1935): 48.

59 "Transplanting," *Time* 25 (6 May 1935): 17.

60 *Daily Alaska Empire,* 17 May 1935; *Fairbanks Daily News-Miner,* 4 June 1935.

61 *Anchorage Daily Times,* 15 May 1935, letter to the editor. For letters agreeing with Snider, see ibid., 17 May 1935.

62 *Fairbanks Daily News-Miner,* 11 June 1935. "Radical" and "agitator" were terms often applied to unhappy transients and protesting colonists and often used by colonists themselves, but no one explained what the terms meant beyond cantankerous grumbling.

63 *Daily Alaska Empire,* 13 June 1935.

Chapter 5

1 *Anchorage Daily Times,* 13 May 1935.

2 U.S., Congress, Senate, *Congressional Record,* 74th Cong., 1st sess., 1935, 74, pt. 9: 7537–40; Cole's original remarks are quoted on p. 7538. (Hereafter cited as *Congressional Record.*)

3 *Time* 25 (20 May 1935): 4, letters to the editor; *Anchorage Daily Times,* 6 June 1935; also 7 June 1935, editorial reprinted from the *Seward Gateway,* "Sour Grapes to Christensen."

4 *Anchorage Daily Times,* 19 June and *Fairbanks Daily News-Miner,* 19 and 21 June 1935.

5 The transients' labor was not free in the sense that it was eventually calculated as part of the cost of building houses and barns or clearing land. However, the cost of building the community center facilities and roads was not charged to the colonists. When interviewed 8 June 1962, Mrs. Sandvik did not think of herself as a malcontent. She did not believe then that she and others had been misled by FERA officials, but that they had perhaps expected too much and been too enthusiastic. In 1962, Mrs. Sandvik thought of herself, in 1935, as having observed and reported the discontent of others.

6 *Fairbanks Daily News-Miner,* 24 June 1935.

7 *Daily Alaska Empire,* 19 June 1935.

8 Ibid., 20 June 1935.

9 *Fairbanks Daily News-Miner,* 20 and 21 June 1935; *Daily Alaska Empire,* 5 July 1935.

10 *Congressional Record,* 74th Cong., 2d sess., 1935, 74, pt. 9:9848–50.

11 Ibid., p. 9849.

12 Ibid., pp. 9849–50. The article was included in Senator Vandenberg's remarks.

13 Other colonists suggested mysteriously to reporters that officials had made promises and had broken them with the deliberate intention of creating discontent. *Fairbanks Daily News-Miner,* 21 June 1935.

14 *Congressional Record,* 74th Cong., 2d sess., 1935, 74, pt. 9: 9946–47.

15 Ibid., p. 9947

16 *Fairbanks Daily News-Miner,* 24 June 1935.

17 Arville Schaleben in the *Washington Star*, 20 June 1935, and quoted by Senator Vandenberg in the *Congressional Record, loc. cit.*, pp. 9947–48.
18 ARRC, Matanuska Valley Settlement Agreement, p. 2 n.
19 Telegram from Sheely to Westbrook, 25 November 1935 ARRC, unnumbered files; Westbrook's telegram in reply, 2 December 1935.
20 *Fairbanks Daily News-Miner*, 22 and 24 June 1935; *Daily Alaska Empire*, 24, 25, and 29 June and 3 July 1935.
21 *Fairbanks Daily News-Miner*, 28 June and 3 July 1935.
22 Ibid., 19 July 1935.
23 Ibid., 18, 25, 30, and 31 July 1935.
24 Ibid., 30 August 1935, and the *Anchorage Daily Times*, 26 June 1935.
25 *Fairbanks Daily News-Miner*, 6 February 1936.
26 Ibid., 11 June 1936.
27 *Congressional Record*, 74th Cong., 1st sess., 1935, 74, pt. 9: 10,285–86. Hopkins's report is included in the remarks of Senator Homer T. Bone, Washington. The Hopkins report and stories on measles and scarlet fever in the colony appeared in the *Fairbanks Daily News-Miner*, 26 and 28 June and 16 July 1935.
28 *Congressional Record, loc. cit.*, pp. 10,277–86.
29 Ibid., p. 10,278.
30 Ibid., pp. 10,278, 10,282, 10,284–85.
31 *Fairbanks Daily News-Miner*, 25 June 1935.
32 *New York Times*, 28 June 1935, p. 15.
33 Ibid., 7 July 1935, sec. 2, p. 1. Notices of departures appeared in Alaska newspapers through the summer and fall of 1935. The indebtedness appears in the ARRC balance sheet of 31 October 1935 in the Papers of Luther C. Hess, vice president of the reorganized ARRC. The papers, housed in Archives, Elmer E. Rasmuson Library, University of Alaska, are hereafter referred to as the Hess Papers.
34 The ARRC kept no records of colonists after departure but received a number of inquiries from the King County, Washington, relief officials. Stone, "Alaska Group Settlement," p. 37, estimates that thirty-seven original colonists who left the colony remained somewhere in Alaska in the late 1940s.
35 *Fairbanks Daily News-Miner*, 5 July and 7 and 10 August 1935.
36 *New York Times*, 13 August 1935, p. 10; 17 August 1935, p. 12.
37 Stone, "Alaska Group Settlement," pp. 42–43, 55–57; Hulley, "A Historical Survey of Matanuska Vally Settlement," pp. 327–40.
38 Mrs. I. M. Sandvik, interview, 8 June 1962.
39 F. S. Lee, in a memorandum attached to the questionnaire of October 1962, described the handling of materials and labor and the confusion in record keeping. See also General Manager's Annual Report to the Board of Directors, 17 August 1938, Hess Papers, in which Leo B. Jacobs reviews the colonists' debts and acknowledges the unreliability of the records.
40 ARRC File 2920–3, evaluation of colonists' real estate.
41 Ibid., and ARRC Tract Histories, Tract 99.
42 *Fairbanks Daily News-Miner*, 11 October 1935; *Matanuska Valley Pioneer*, 14 November 1935.
43 *Matanuska Valley Pioneer*, 10 October 1935.
44 The advertisement appears in the *Matanuska Valley Pioneer*, 21 November 1935.

45 *Fairbanks Daily News-Miner*, 5 November 1935.
46 Ibid., 28 October 1935.
47 Hess Papers, Minutes, Special Meeting and Meeting of the Reorganized Directors of the ARRC, 29 and 30 October 1935, Palmer. Also, *Fairbanks Daily News-Miner*, 15 and 25 October 1935.
48 In the Hess Papers, 1935–36, Ross Sheely's weekly reports by radio to Colonel Westbrook summarize the progress in construction and the development of the community center facilities.
49 *Fairbanks Daily News-Miner*, 7, 10, 24, and 26 September 1935; *Matanuska Valley Pioneer*, 29 August, 26 September, and 17 October 1935.
50 ARRC Organizational Chart and Ross Sheely, radio report to Westbrook on ARRC employment, 29 December 1935, Hess Papers, 1935.
51 *Report of the Commissioner of Education, Biennium Ended June 30, 1936* (Juneau, December 1936), p. 17; also, "School at Colony Kept Despite All Handicaps," by a Matanuska teacher, *Alaska Weekly* (Seattle), 5 June 1935, pp. 2, 6.
52 Conversation with Mrs. Fohn-Hansen, 7 July 1962; A. M. Goodman, "Report on the Present, and Estimate of the Future, Agriculture of the Matanuska Valley of Alaska," ARRC File 2921–8, pp. 21–22; ARRC File 652–4, Hunting, Trapping, and Fur Farming.
53 ARRC File 652–4.
54 E.g., Anthony Vickaryous, who had experience in commercial fishing on Lake Superior.
55 Allman died in 1953. Mrs. Ruth Allman supplied many biographical details in a conversation at Juneau, 20 August 1962.
56 Ross Sheely to L. C. Hess, 7 January 1936, Hess Papers, 1936, questioning the propriety of the political editorials in Allman's paper while the ARRC indirectly supported it. Hess's reply, 15 January 1936.
57 E.g., see *Matanuska Valley Pioneer*, 10 October 1935, for Allman's criticism of a syndicated newspaper article by Rex Beach.
58 Ibid., 14 November 1935. Mrs. Rotz's letter appeared in the *Detroit Times*, 26 October 1935.
59 *Matanuska Valley Pioneer*, 12 December 1935.
60 Ibid., 9 April 1936.
61 Ibid., 23 January 1936. On 4 June 1936, Allman printed a notice from the Wisconsin Public Welfare Department that, because a year had passed since colonization, Wisconsin no longer would assume any responsibility for the return of colonists originally from Wisconsin.
62 Ibid., 21 May 1936.
63 Ibid., 12 December 1935.
64 Ibid., 26 September 1935.
65 *Cordova Daily Times*, 17 September 1935.
66 Westbrook to Sheely, 26 August 1936, ARRC File 2630–12.
67 Westbrook to Sheely, 3 October 1936, ibid.
68 Sheely to Westbrook, 6 and 12 October 1936, ibid.
69 Westbrook to Sheely, 13 October 1936, ibid. There is no indication in the ARRC files or in the first printed version of Allman's paper that copies of the *Pioneer* were sent.

70 E. P. Conkle, *Two Hundred Were Chosen* (New York: Samuel French, 1937), pp. 45–46. Also, Burns Mantle, ed., *The Best Plays of 1936–1937* (New York: Dodd, Mead & Co., 1937); Florence L. Kellogg, "Two Hundred Were Chosen" (review), *Survey Graphic* 26 (January 1937): 41; *Newsweek* 8 (28 November 1936): 19–20; *Time* 28 (30 November 1936): 54.

71 *Congressional Record,* 74th Cong., 2d sess., 1936, 80, pt. 7:7715–21; also *Ketchikan Chronicle,* 19 July 1935.

72 Charles L. Smith, "The Matanuski [*sic*] Valley Project," *National Republic* (January 1936): 5, 32. The misspelling is consistent.

73 "Forty Acres in Alaskan Valley," *Literary Digest* 121 (9 May 1936): 8–9.

74 *Congressional Record,* 74th Cong., 2d sess., 1936, 80, pt. 6: 6111; ibid., 76th Cong., 1st sess., 1939, 84, pt. 1:2589.

75 W. B. Courtney, "Pilgrims' Progress: Matanuska Valley Project," *Collier's* 101 (7 May 1938): 12 ff., and reprinted in *Reader's Digest* 33 (July 1938): 71 ff.

76 Elsie McComick, "A Planned Economy Is Put to the Test," *New York Times Magazine* (8 September 1935), pp. 10, 19.

77 Arthur Stringer, "Red-Plush Pioneers," *Saturday Evening Post* 208 (28 December 1935): 8 ff.; reprinted under the title "Cold-Storage El Dorado," *Reader's Digest* 28 (March 1936): 29–32.

78 Hess to Governor Troy, 27 November 1935, Hess Papers, 1935.

79 Quoted in Dan Noonan, "Matanuska's a Good Thing," *Alaska Sportsman* 2 (February 1936): 8–11, 22. Noonan collected statements about the colony from Anthony Dimond, Bishop Joseph R. Crimont, Mayor D. C. Brownell of Seward, Rasmuson, former Governor Thomas Riggs, then living in New York, and others.

80 In November 1935 Westbrook authorized Sheely to include old settlers in cooperative marketing but advised delay in granting loans until after the expected transfer of the colony to the RA, which did not occur. However, credit had already been extended to some old settlers, and in May 1936 the ARRC allowed old settlers credit up to $2,500 for making improvements and for equipment and livestock. Such borrowers had to sign a cooperative marketing agreement. Westbrook to Sheely (telegram), 2 November 1935; M. D. Snodgrass to ARRC board, 4 December 1935, regarding his ARRC debt; and minutes of the ARRC board meeting, 16 May 1936, all in the Hess Papers, 1935–36.

81 Churchill Fisher, "Their Sun Still Rises," *Alaska Sportsman* 4 (July 1938): 10–11, 25–26.

82 Grace Caroline Stafford, "So This Is Palmer," *The Magazine Alaska* 5 (Summer, 1951): 16–17, 46. The magazine was an attempt to revive an old irregularly published periodical, and the articles in this issue were taken from a backlog of old pieces. The Stafford article was written in 1936. Also, Frank J. Cotter, "The Colony Is Bound for Success," *Alaska Weekly* (Seattle), 5 June 1936. Cotter, who had been a prospector and stampeder for over twenty years, speaks of the colony's bright future but reports the cautious, almost suspicious attitude of sourdough Alaskans.

83 See ARRC File 652-4 on attempted fur farming and Snider's offers of help.

Chapter 6

1 *Final Statistical Report of the Federal Emergency Administration* (Washington, D.C.:

GPO, 1942), pp. iii–v, 9–10. (Hereafter cited as *Final Statistical Report, FERA,*)
2 Conkin, *Tomorrow a New World,* pp. 142–44.
3 Ibid., p. 137; *Final Statistical Report, FERA,* pp. 68, 95, 115–17.
4 References to an expected transfer are found in letters and telegrams exchanged by Sheely, Westbrook, and L. C. Hess, November 1935 to January 1936, Hess Papers, 1935–1936.
5 Hess Papers, 1936, In March the manager's reports were addressed to Westbrook as assistant WPA administrator, but they came from "FERA, Palmer, Alaska." In May the reports were marked "WPA, Palmer."
6 H. M. Colvin, temporary WPA representative at Palmer, to Westbrook (telegram), 28 June 1937, Hess Papers. For Westbrook's reply see ibid., 29 June.
7 Harold L. Ickes, *The Secret Diary of Harold L. Ickes* (New York: Simon and Schuster, 1954), 2:443.
8 Ibid., pp. 441–44.
9 Ibid., p. 461. The transfer was made on 3 September and announced on 12 September 1938.
10 *Binghamton (New York) Press,* 14 Septmber 1938; *Philadelphia Bulletin,* 14 September 1938; *Reno* (Nevada) *Gazette,* 17 September 1938.
11 Conkin, *Tomorrow a New World,* pp. 163–64, 172–73, 177–82.
12 *Congressional Record,* 74th Cong., 2d sess., 1936, 80, 6:6110–11.
13 Ibid., 8:8191.
14 *Final Statistical Report, FERA,* table 43, p. 116.
15 Stone, "Alaska Group Settlement," table 9, p. 41.
16 E.g., see Corey Ford and Alastair MacBain, "Uncle Sam's Icebox," *Collier's* 107 (4 January 1941): 29–30, 40, giving the cost as $8 million.
17 Ted Leitzell, "Cabbages and Commissars: Matanuska Valley," *American Mercury* 46 (January 1939): 1–11; U.S., Congress, Senate, Subcommittee of the Committee on Territories and Insular Affairs, *Hearings, Settlement and Development of Alaska,* 76th Cong., 3d sess., 1940, p. 169 and passim.
18 *Binghamton* (New York) *Press,* 3 January 1939.
19 Conkin, *Tomorrow A New World,* pp. 332–37.
20 *Newsweek* 11 (23 May 1938): 10.
21 Hess Papers, 1937. The debt survey is attached to the ARRC board meeting minutes for 23 April 1937.
22 U. S. Department of Commerce, Bureau of the Census, *Fourteenth Census of the United States: 1920,* vol. 6, part 3, *Agriculture, Reports for States: Alaska,* tables 2, 3, 16, p. 369.
23 U.S. Department of Agriculture, *Some Economic Aspects of Farming in Alaska* (Washington, D.C.: GPO, 1950), p. 84; also, Walter U. Fuhriman, "The Possibilities of Profitable Farming in Alaska," in *Seminars on Alaska,* Bureau of Land Management, U.S. Department of the Interior (Washington, D.C.: GPO, 1950), pp. 22–29.
24 H. P. Gazaway, *Facts and Observations on Agricultural Development in Alaska,* Alaska Division of Lands, Department of Natural Resources (n.p., July 1960), p. 5.
25 *Fairbanks Daily News-Miner,* 2 April 1936.
26 Minutes of the ARRC board of directors, 16 May 1936, Hess Papers, 1936; *Anchorage Weekly Times,* 19 August 1937.

27 *The Valley Settler*, 30 September and 14 October 1938.

28 After 1944 the general managers' monthly reports in the ARRC files show a decrease in supervisory activities, fewer comments on "colonists' problems," and fewer and finally no remarks on general colony morale.

29 Annual Report of the General Manager. 11 August 1937, Hess Papers,

30 Annual Report of the General Manager, 17 August 1938, foreword, Hess Papers.

31 ARRC File 2630, with many subdivisions, contains public relations material.

32 ARRC Well Log.

33 ARRC file on George Connors, including correspondence.

34 ARRC unclassified files; ARRC File 658-1, correspondence, January–May 1936.

35 ARRC File 2921.

36 ARRC Bulletin no. 1, Educational Series, March 1940.

37 The comments on Irwin and the other managers are based on the general impressions gained from ARRC records and from interviews with some colonists still in the valley. For the cattle breeding see A. M. Goodman's memorandum, ARRC File 2921-8, p. 30, and his letter to Irwin, 29 August 1935.

38 On Ohlson and the railroad see Fitch, *The Alaska Railroad*, pp. 70–76; also his biographical sketch in *Who's Who in Alaska*.

39 Gruening, The *State of Alaska*, pp. 271–75.

40 *Fairbanks Daily News-Miner*, 4 and 13 November 1935. For a wholesale attack by the territorial legislature on Ohlson, the railroad, the Interior Department, and federal agencies generally, see *Senate Journal of Alaska*, 1939, Senate Joint Memorial no. 5, pp. 161, 607.

41 U.S., Congress, Senate, Subcommittee of the Committee on Territories and Insular Affairs, *Settlement and Development of Alaska, Hearings on S. 3577*, 75th Cong. 3d sess., 1949, pp. 26–61.

42 Withdrawals, admissions, and total colony populations are taken from the weekly, later monthly, reports of the general managers to Colonel Westbrook and the ARRC, included in the Hess Papers. The changes in the colony population given in Stone, "Alaska Group Settlement," pp. 35–36, table 7, show the result of changes by 1939, but the figures for specific dates do not agree with the managers' reports.

43 The withdrawal of Chris Anderson, Report of the General Manager, June 1938 in Hess Papers.

44 Minutes, ARRC board meeting, 16 May 1938, Hess Papers.

45 E.g, comments by Don Irwin and G. W. Gasser in interviews, 2 September and 22 August 1960; also, Johnson and Stanton, "Matanuska Valley Memoir," pp. 54–55.

46 *Matanuska Valley Pioneer*, 13 January and 27 February 1936.

47 The selection process is shown by the ARRC files on individual replacements, and the monthly reports of the general managers mention new arrivals by name and usually give brief background sketches. One of the interviewers was Stewart Campbell, an FERA and WPA employee who had been in the colony with Colonel Hunt's group and was later for a time administrative assistant to Leo Jacobs.

48 Minutes, annual meeting, ARRC Board of Directors, 17 August 1938, Hess Papers.

49 Such conditions were described in a bulletin intended to answer inquiries about

settlement, undated but attached to the February 1942 monthly report of the general manager, ARRC files. Also, Herbert C. Hanson, *Agriculture in the Matanuska Valley, Alaska* (Washington, D.C.: Department of the Interior [1944]), pp. 9–10; C. W. Peters, *Questions and Answers on Agriculture and Living Conditions in the Matanuska Valley of Alaska* (Palmer: ARRC, 1949); *Alaska: General Information Circular* (Anchorage: Alaska Railroad, 1947), pp. 25–28.

50 Correspondence of O. F. Ohlson and H. C. Hanson with F. P. Keppel and R. I. Nowell of the Equitable Insurance Company, 26 and 27 June, 2 August, and 4 October 1940, ARRC File 2630-21.

51 Johnson and Stanton, "Matanuska Valley Memoir," p. 55; Stone, "Alaska Group Settlement," p. 37.

52 Minutes, special meeting, ARRC Board of Directors, 28 September 1938, Hess Papers, at which the discontented colonists were interviewed.

53 The sampling is taken from the ARRC files on individual colonists, references in the general managers' reports, and conversations with their acquaintances.

54 ARRC individual file, references in ARRC board minutes, and *Who's Who in Alaska and Alaska Business Index.*

55 Johnson and Stanton, "Matanuska Valley Memoir," pp. 92–93.

56 Minutes, ARRC Board of Directors, 16 May 1936, Hess Papers.

57 Sheely to Westbrook (telegram) 18 May 1936, and Westbrook to Sheely (telegram), 25 May and letter, 3 June 1936, Hess Papers,

58 ARRC File 1807-1, 1807-2, dealing with colonist homesteading.

59 ARRC, General Manager's Monthly Report, June and July 1941.

60 Ibid., December 1941.

61 Ibid., June and July 1938, and Annual Report, 17 August 1938.

62 Act of 17 October 1940, 54 stat. 1191, secs. 1 and 2.

63 Johnson and Stanton, "Matanuska Valley Memoir," p. 51.

64 U.S. Department of the Interior, Circular no. 1563, General Land Office, Washington, D. C., 23 August 1943, describing the department's cooperation with the ARRC, requiring certification of settlers by the ARRC, and granting the ARRC the right to buy needed land. Also, H. C. Hanson, *Agriculture in the Matanuska Valley,* p. 10.

65 Act of 9 March 1942, 56 stat. 150.

66 Public Land Order 272, 11 April 1945; 393, 15 August 1947; 847, 27 June 1952; 1275, 14 March 1956. Veterans were given preference for ninety days after the opening of each area.

67 Prospective settlers were informed of the general characteristics of the region, agricultural opportunities, and land regulations in a number of publications; e.g., *Homestead Opportunities on Public Land in the Matanuska Valley,* Alaska Leaflet no. 2 (Washington, D.C.: GPO, 1947) and *Information Relative to the Use and Disposal of Public Lands and Resources in Alaska* (Washington, D.C.: GPO, 1957).

68 Burke Riley, *Federal Land Policy and Its Effect on Development and Settlement in Alaska* (Juneau: Alaska Development Board, 1948), pp. 1–5, 44; Gruening, *The State of Alaska,* pp. 299–300, and chap. 23; Hugh A. Johnson and Don L. Irwin, *The Position of Agriculture in Alaska's Current Economy,* pp. 1–2, 15; Stone, "Alaska Group Settlement," pp. 25, 58–59; Johnson and Stanton, "Matanuska Valley Memoir," pp. 53–54, 56–57.

Chapter 7

1 Such views appear in many comments on the colony and are concentrated in Stone, "Alaska Group Settlement"; the list of things undone is on pp. 10–11.

2 *Fairbanks Daily News-Miner,* 16 January 1936; Sheely to Hess, 15 January 1936, Hess Papers.

3 The term was an old one for poker or other gambling chips, and the presence in the community of the Presbyterian minister, Bert J. Bingle, was coincidental. *Fairbanks Daily News-Miner,* 28 January 1936; Harold Wentworth and Stuart Berg Flexner, *Dictionary of American Slang* (New York: Thomas Y. Crowell Co., 1960), p. 38; James J. Hurley, *Twenty Years of Progress in the Matanuska Valley, Alaska* (Palmer: ARRC, 1955), pp. 10–11; Maurice M. Gould and Kenneth Bressett, *Alaska's Coinage Through the Years* (Racine, Wisconsin: Whitman Publishing Co., 1960), pp. 9–12. *Matanuska Valley Pioneer,* 27 February 1936.

4 General Manager's Weekly Reports, June–September 1936, Hess Papers; report to the general manager by Roland Snodgrass, "field man in charge of rural development," 20 September 1940, ARRC unnumbered file.

5 *Fairbanks Daily News-Miner,* 3 September and 4 and 9 November 1936.

6 Report by Anton Anderson, the "location engineer," to Ross Sheely, 1 August 1936, on typical clearing during the past winter, ARRC unnumbered file.

7 Land Clearing, 22 December 1936, ARRC File 2923–1.

8 Anderson to Sheely, 13 July 1936, memorandum outlining the "Colonist Work Credit Program," ARRC File 2924.

9 Telegrams, Sheely to Westbrook, 8 January 1937, and Westbrook to Sheely, 15 January 1937, ARRC unnumbered file.

10 Report by Anton Anderson, 10 April 1937, ARRC File 2924.

11 "Report of the First Month of Operation of the Work Credit System," by Ross Sheely to the ARRC, 11 March 1937, Hess Papers.

12 Form 104, 2 June 1937, ARRC File 2924.

13 Report on the work credit system by Stuart C. Campbell to Leo Jacobs, 10 August 1937, Hess Papers.

14 The system was suggested by Campbell in his August 1937 report to Jacobs; see also ARRC File 2924-1, notices to colonists, 17 September 1937.

15 ARRC File 2923, Summary of Land Improvements; summary report by J. V. Chapman to the general manager, 1 February 1938, Hess Papers.

16 Minutes, ARRC Board of Directors, 23 and 24 April 1937, Hess Papers, at which the policy was discussed and rejected.

17 The grange representative, Victor J. Falk, appeared at the same directors' meeting at which the employment policy was voted down.

18 Report of the Rural Development Department to the general manager, 1 January 1938, and the general manager's January 1 report to Colonel Westbrook, Hess Papers.

19 Annual Report of the General Manager, 17 August 1938, Hess Papers.

20 ARRC, unnumbered file on land clearing and rural development, report by J. V. Chapman to the general manager for October 1938.

21 *Historical Statistics of the United States* p. 166, G118-130. The 6.7 million farm families in 1935–36 had an average family income of $951, including the value of

products consumed. The 23.7 million nonfarm families averaged $2,020 annually.

22 The various reports of the general managers and the discussions of the board of directors refer regularly to colonist complaints and usually describe colony morale as low or poor, only occasionally as fair.

23 Lord and Johnstone, *A Place on Earth,* pp. 191–92, 196.

24 Minutes, Special Meeting, ARRC Board of Directors, 23 and 24 April 1937, Hess Papers.

25 The background of the cooperative is found in ARRC File 658-1, MVFCA, Original Plan and General Organization, and File 658-2, Articles of Incorporation and By-Laws; emendations found in Minutes, Stockholders' Meeting, 26 May 1937, ARRC File 658–3.

26 MVFCA Bulletin no. 1, 12 June 1937, ibid.

27 Minutes, Civic Association, 8 November 1937, ARRC File 657-4.

28 Westbrook to Sheely, 5 March 1937, ARRC unnumbered file.

29 ARRC File 2630-21. The telegram is dated 27 September 1937. Colvin's letter to Westbrook is undated. The article in *Time* 30 (13 September 1937): 10, refers to "costly failures" and incorrectly identifies the Matanuska project with Tugwell and the RA.

30 H. M. Colvin to O. F. Ohlson, 23 June 1937, Hess Papers, enclosing a copy of Colvin's June 18 letter to Colonel Westbrook and copies of the exhibits he included.

31 Sheely to Westbrook (telegram), 25 November 1935, and Westbrook's telegram reply, 2 December 1935, Hess Papers.

32 The estimate of the average debt was made by Leo Jacobs in his annual report, 17 August 1937, Hess Papers. It seems rather high, well over $2,000 above the January 31 figure.

33 Report of the Debt Adjustment Committee to the ARRC Board of Directors, Hess Papers.

34 Jacobs's memorandum to Colvin, 11 November 1937, Hess Papers.

35 ARRC files on Henning Benson, Tract 95.

36 General Manager's Report to the ARRC Board of Directors, August 1938, Hess Papers. Leo Jacobs reviewed the debt reduction, the colonists' objections to the contract, and the management's efforts to persuade them of its fairness and advantages.

37 A lawyer reading the contract thirty years later would be struck by the moralizing tone, the murkiness of the language, and the opportunities for possible litigation that it raised.

38 Beck and Forster, *Six Rural Problem Areas,* p. 7.

39 Bill G. Reid, "Proposed American Plans for Soldier Settlement During the World War I Period" (Ph.D. diss., University of Oklahoma, 1963), pp. 42–43, and U.S. National Resources Board, *Report on National Planning,* p. 201.

40 Ibid., pp. 182, 202; Robert England, *The Colonization of Western Canada: A Study of Contemporary Land Settlement (1896–1934)* (London: P. S. King and Son, Ltd., 1935), pp. 93–105.

41 ARRC File 658–1, a commentary by Jacobs on the contract, 14 March 1938, intended for distribution to the colonists.

42 From interviews in the summers of 1960 and 1961 and answers to questionnaires in September–October 1962.

43 ARRC Forms 246 and 248, dated 23 April 1940.

44 Colony Council Meeting, 28 March 1938, ARRC File 657.

45 ARRC File 2925-3, on the LUPC, and letter from Howard Estelle to H. C. Hanson, 10 January 1941, and Hanson's reply, 21 January 1941.

46 LUPC memorandum to Hanson, 26 December 1940, ibid.

47 Emerson's memorandum to Ickes, with Ohlson's recommendations, 24 February 1941; Ickes's approval, 18 April 1941; Emerson's letter to Ohlson, 19 April 1941, all in ibid.

48 ARRC unnumbered file, Land Clearing Supplemental Contract.

49 Minutes, Annual Meeting, ARRC Board of Directors, 17, 18, and 19 August 1938, Hess Papers. Westbrook's telegraphic order was dated 5 August.

50 Leo Jacobs's memorandum on the clearing programs, 6 July 1938, ARRC unnumbered file.

51 J. V. Chapman, Rural Development Department, monthly report, 1 November 1939, ibid.

52 Sheely to Ohlson, 12 January 1940, ARRC File 2923; MVFCA board of directors to the ARRC, 22 January 1940, and Hanson's reply, 24 January 1940, ibid.

53 MVFCA Bulletin no. 1, 12 June 1937, ARRC File 658–2.

54 Westbrook to Jacobs, 24 February 1938, and Jacobs's report to the ARRC board, 16 August 1938, Hess Papers.

55 ARRC File 658–2, Agreement for Transfer and Management of Facilities; Minutes, ARRC Board of Directors, 12 August 1940, Hess Papers, with a review of the steps in the transaction; *Annual Report of the Governor of Alaska, 1940,* p. 67.

56 Resolution of the ARRC board, 6 April 1940, ARRC File 2923; Minutes, Adjourned Meeting, ARRC Board, 14 August 1940, Hess Papers.

57 General Manager's Monthly Report for October 1940, Hess Papers.

58 From interviews, summers of 1960 and 1961, and colonists' answers to questionnaires, September–October 1962.

59 Memorandum to the colonists, 16 December 1936, ARRC File 658–1.

60 *Annual Report of the Governor of Alaska, 1940,* pp. 66–67; George W. Gasser, *The Matanuska Valley* (Juneau: Alaska Development Board, 1946), p. 17.

61 O. L. Mimms, J. L. Paschal, and W. U. Fuhriman, *Some Economic Aspects of Farming in Alaska, with Chief Attention to the Matanuska Valley* (Washington, D.C.: GPO, 1950), p. 27.

62 *Milwaukee Journal,* 10 April 1938, a feature on the Matanuska project by Jack Allman, former publisher of the *Matanuska Valley Pioneer* and no longer a defender of the colony.

63 *Cleveland News,* feature articles by Bradley Stack, 4, 5, and 6 December 1939.

64 Editorial, *Anchorage Daily Times,* 20 June 1938, and news story on the same day.

65 Colvin to Ray, 15 April 1939, ARRC File 658-1.

66 Hanson, *Agriculture in the Matanuska Valley,* p. 12; Gasser, *Information for the Alaskan Farmer-Settler,* p. 29; Gasser, *The Matanuska Valley,* pp. 16–17; *Alaska Farm Facts,* Bulletin 27 (Palmer: University of Alaska Agricultural Experiment Station, 1961), pp. 10–12.

67 Memorandum by the ARRC accountant analyzing the debts, 1 August 1939,

ARRC File 2924. Minutes, ARRC board meeting, 21 August 1939, Hess Papers.

68 Memorandum 2 July 1940, ARRC File 2925.

69 Minutes, ARRC board meeting, 14 August 1940, Hess Papers.

70 ARRC General Manager's Monthly Reports, October 1940–February 1941.

71 ARRC General Manager's Monthly Reports, July 1942.

72 ARRC General Manager's Monthly Reports, January 1941 (summary of colonist employment and earnings).

73 The changes during the war years can be traced in the ARRC file, General Manager's Monthly Reports, 1940–44.

74 Ibid., February 1942, with an attached copy of a standard mineographed reply to letters of inquiry.

75 ARRC unnumbered file, "Something Should Be Done," a typescript sketch of the colony's origins. The title refers to the depression background.

76 ARRC, General Manager's Monthly Reports, July and November 1941.

77 For the attack on the FSA and the death of the agency see Grant McConnell, *The Decline of Agrarian Democracy* (Berkeley: University of California Press, 1953), chap. 9; also, James G. Maddox, "The Farm Security Administration" (Ph.D. diss., Harvard University, 1950), chap. 20.

78 Paul W. Wager, *One Foot on the Soil,* pp. 146–47.

79 Palmer Recording District, deed to Virgil Eckert for Tract 100, 1 May 1944.

80 McConnell, *Decline of Agrarian Democracy,* chap. 9.

Chapter 8

1 The Palmer office accumulated a file of several thousand press clippings from newspapers outside Alaska for the years 1935–41. ARRC Files 2630-9 to 2630-38 contain bulletins, press releases, replies to inquiries, information sent to journalists and politicians, etc.

2 E.g., see a letter from Leo B. Jacobs to R. A. Gunnison of the *Christian Science Monitor,* 20 July 1938 (ARRC File 2630–15), painfully explaining that the colonists who had been described as "going on their own" were independent only because they were employed by the ARRC or were being paid to clear their own land.

3 Not all special articles were unfriendly. A full and generally favorable treatment of the colony was given by Ernie Pyle in seven syndicated articles, *Washington* (D.C.) *News,* 26, 28, and 31 August and 1, 2, 3, and 4 September 1937.

4 E.g., feature articles mentioning Virgil Eckert, Joseph Puhl, and Victor Johnson; see also, in ARRC File 2630, correspondence between the ARRC, Mr. and Mrs. Victor Johnson, and Barrett Willoughby, who wrote a number of feature articles on the Johnsons, collected in "I'm A Cream Puff Pioneer," *Alaska Holiday* (Boston: Little, Brown, & Co., 1940), pp. 227–60.

5 The following account is based on the ARRC's file on Pippel and on scores of news stories about him appearing in Alaska newspapers as well as in the outside press. In the ARRC file alone he appeared in over a hundred features and editorials from the outside press.

6 An exception was the feature in the *Ladysmith* (Wisconsin) *News,* 15 September 1939, giving a realistic account of Pippel's activities.

7 Minutes, ARRC board of directors meeting, 23 and 24 April 1937, with exhibit

showing colonists' debts and the proposed reduction; ARRC board meeting, 11 August 1937, approving the reduction principle; report of the Debt Adjustment Committee to the ARRC board, 9 August 1938, explaining the further 20 percent reduction, all in Hess Papers.

8 ARRC File 2921-9, a typescript summary by Joseph Flakne of the estimated profits for various crops and for dairy, hog, and poultry farming. In contrast, the average of several grains yielded only $29.76 an acre.

9 In newspaper editorials the gross income became the net income and there were no references to the debt Pippel contracted in establishing himself or to the cancellation of about half the debt. *New Orleans Item Tribune*, 4 December 1938; *Macon Telegraph*, 7 December 1938.

10 *Anchorage Daily Times*, 15 May and 3 August 1939.

11 *Daily Alaska Empire* (Juneau), 26 August 1939; *Minneapolis Tribune*, 10 September 1939; *Washington Star*, 17 September 1939.

12 *Fairbanks Daily News-Miner*, 16 March 1941.

13 Reported in ARRC General Manager's Monthly Report, April 1945, when Pippel visited the valley.

14 Herbert H. Hillshire, "Vision of Utopia Revised at Matanuska," *Nation's Business* 26 (November 1938): 17–18, 54; reprinted in *Alaska Life* 1 (December 1938): 6–7, 14, 15, 19.

15 A sampling of the echoes of the article: *Time*, 2 December 1938, p. 13; *Cleveland News*, 2 December 1938; *Boise News*, 23 December 1938; *Sacramento Union*, 16 December 1938; *Seattle Times*, 17 December 1938.

16 Ted Leitzell, "Cabbages and Commissars: Matanuska Valley," *American Mercury* 46 (January 1939): 1–11. This article was also echoed in the press, often with direct quotations—e.g., *Santa Fe New Mexican*, 29 December 1938; *Binghamton* (New York) *Press*, 3 January 1939; *Muncie Star*, 9 January 1939; *Terre Haute Star*, 16 January 1939; *Davenport Times*, 16 January 1939; *Indianapolis Star*, 4 January 1939.

17 *The Valley Settler*, 10 and 17 February 1939; the installment of February 24 was omitted, but the article was completed in the third installment in an extra issue of the paper on 28 February 1939.

18 *American Mercury* 47 (July 1939): 376–77.

19 The account of Ruddell's background and career in the colony is based on the large Ruddell file in the ARRC's records of individual colonists and on many references to him in ARRC correspondence, memoranda, board meetings, etc.

20 Advertisement by Ruddell, *Matanuska Valley Pioneer*, 21 November 1935.

21 *Seattle Daily Times*, 10 February 1937.

22 Dimond to Sheely, 18 February 1937. Copies of the letters and telegrams between Sheely, Dimond, Westbrook, and Ohlson on the Ruddell matter are included in the ARRC file on Ruddell.

23 *Fairbanks Daily News-Miner*, 22 May 1937, a feature article with photographs carried to the press elsewhere.

24 News stories on his departure referred to him as the colony's one-man grievance committee. *Daily Alaska Empire* (Juneau), 25 January 1938.

25 ARRC, Ruddell file, letters from the King County Welfare Department, 23 February and 15 July 1938.

26 ARRC, Ruddell file, copy of a letter by Leo B. Jacobs to Congressman Engel, undated but in the summer of 1938.
27 The following discussion of LeDuc is based on his individual ARRC file, six thick folders.
28 LeDuc to Eisenhower, 17 June 1936, ARRC LeDuc file.
29 *The Valley Settler,* 24 February 1939.
30 Copy of a letter by Ernest Gruening to Senator Burton K. Wheeler, 28 April 1939, ARRC LeDuc file. Gruening slightly understates LeDuc's income by giving the total as before rather than after payment of small accounts with the ARRC. In addition to free rent, use of the land, and any non-ARRC employment, Le Duc had, in the fifteen months of 1938 and the first quarter of 1939, an income from the ARRC of $1,205, and he paid to the ARRC $123.
31 Information on the organization is contained in an unnumbered ARRC file labeled "Ice Worms," and additional information is in ARRC file 650-9, Mass Meetings and Colonists' Problems.
32 However, of the more than twenty original colonists who were interviewed in the summers of 1960 and 1961 or who answered questionnaires in 1962, only one cautiously showed some sympathy for the Ice Worms. The others usually described the group as people who "wanted something for nothing."
33 Rasmussen to Senator Downey, 28 April 1939, ARRC Rasmussen file.
34 The materials on these activities are collected in ARRC file 650-9 under the heading Mass Meetings and Colonists' Problems.
35 Ibid., and *Daily Alaska Empire* (Juneau), 23, 25, and 27 February 1939; *The Valley Settler,* 24 February 1939; *Anchorage Daily Times,* 25 and 27 February 1939.
36 Anthony E. Karnes, Commissioner of Education, to A. A. Johnson, Palmer School Board (telegrams), 27 and 28 February and 1 March 1939, ARRC File 650-9.
37 Ibid, reports on conditions in the colony by William W. Head, acting general manager; letter of 4 March to Ross Sheely, then in Washington; an undated copy of a March telegram to Sheely, originally sent in code; a decoded copy of a telegram of 13 March to Colonel O. F. Ohlson in Washington.
38 Copies of the sheet are in the ARRC miscellaneous file. References in the text allow approximate dating.
39 Rasmussen to Hanson, 2 April 1940, ARRC Rasmussen file.
40 ARRC, Rasmussen file.
41 ARRC General Manager's Monthly Reports, October, November, and December 1940; January and February 1941.
42 *Fairbanks Daily News-Miner,* 3 and 6 December 1940; also the *New York Times,* 6 December 1940, p. 28.
43 LeDuc to Hanson, 12 February 1941, ARRC LeDue file.
44 Phil R. Curran, "Matanuska Colony and Defense Unity Plans," United Press special article, *Fairbanks Daily News-Miner,* 30 December 1940.
45 ARRC Miscellaneous File. A note attached by H. C. Hanson dates the news letter. Emphasis added.
46 ARRC General Manager's Monthly Reports, October 1941 through April 1942; also, District Court, Territory of Alaska, Third Division, file nos. S-2526, S-2527, S-2528, S-2529, S-2530, S-2531.
47 ARRC General Manager's Monthly Report, July 1942 and January 1947; also, Palmer Recording District, Deed Records, book 4, p. 233.

48 ARRC General Manager's Monthly Report, June, 1946; Deed Records, Palmer Recording District, book, 12, p. 97.
49 Carl R. Rasmussen, "Matanuska Valley Farmers Cooperating Association: The Valley's Greatest Industry," *Matanuska Valley Record* (July 1951), 1: 1–2, 8.
50 *Fairbanks Daily News-Miner,* 9 January 1965.
51 *Seward* (Alaska) *Gateway,* 2 November 1937.
52 *Detroit Free Press,* 2 July 1937; also, *Atlanta Constitution,* 16 July 1937.
53 *Reno Gazette,* 28 June 1937; *New York Herald-Tribune,* 16 May 1938; *Baltimore Sun,* 11 May 1938.
54 *Richmond* (Virginia) *Times-Dispatch,* 25 July 1939.
55 *Detroit Free Press,* 22 July 1939.
56 *Philadelphia Ledger,* 13 October 1939; *Springfield* (Illinois) *Journal,* 15 October 1939.
57 *New York World-Telegram,* 11 October 1939; *Schenectady Gazette,* 19 October 1939.
58 *St. Louis Globe Democrat,* 21 October 1939; *San Diego Union,* 22 October 1939; *Oklahoma City Oklahoman,* 23 October 1939.
59 *Chicago Tribune,* 26 October 1939.

Chapter 9

1 U.S. Bureau of Land Management, *Homesteads* (Washington, D.C.: GPO, 1962), gives the number of final entries and the number of acres patented annually by states since 1868.
2 E.g., *Fairbanks Daily News-Miner,* 15 April 1936, reporting a supposed plan for a federal colony in the Tanana Valley and pointing out the advantages of the local experiment station, the soil, climate, and market. Ibid., 22 April 1936, reporting 3,000 applicants for openings in the Matanuska Colony and predicting that 500 families would be added there by the end of the summer. *Annual Report of the Governor of Alaska,* 1937, pp. 1, 47–48.
3 *Fairbanks Daily News-Miner,* 12 October 1939, reporting the position taken by the territorial chambers of commerce at a time when further colonization was rumored. References to the cost of the colony to the territory are scattered through the Hess Papers.
4 *Fairbanks Daily News-Miner,* 6, 7, 11, and 13 May 1936.
5 Ibid., 29 October 1936.
6 Ibid., 2 November 1938. The ARRC files for 1938–40 contain many memoranda, reports, etc., in which offhand references were made to the possibility of Mormon colonization. See also *Anchorage Daily Times,* 22 August 1938.
7 ARRC Miscellaneous File, memorandum, Lorin T. Oldroyd to Ross Sheely, undated, but apparently late 1939.
8 *Anchorage Daily Times,* 27 November 1939.
9 U.S. National Resources Committee, *Regional Planning; Part VII, Alaska—Its Resources and Development* (Washington, D.C.: GPO, 1938).
10 Ibid., *Part I, Report of the Alaska Resources Committee.* The committee's views and recommendations are given here, pp. 9–31. The references and quotations are from these pages.
11 Robert Marshall, *Arctic Village* (New York; Harrison Smith and Robert Haas, 1933).

12 Harold L. Ickes, *The Secret Diary of Harold L. Ickes* (New York: Simon and Schuster, 1954), 2:440–53. *Fairbanks Daily News-Miner,* 11, 12, and 13 August 1938.

13 Arthur G. Thompson (Anchorage Chamber of Commerce), "Is It Time to Develop Alaska?" *Anchorage Daily Times,* 23 February 1939; Herbert H. Hilscher, "The Dealer Demands the Pot," *Alaska Life* 3 (May 1940): 4–5, 8.

14 The reply was published serially in the *Fairbanks Daily News-Miner,* 11, 12, 13, 14, 16, and 17 January 1939. For articles praising the council, see ibid., "Good Work by Planning Council," 12 January 1939; "Let's Keep Alaska a Wilderness—Oh, Yeah!" 16 January 1939; "Exclusive Reindeer Pasture Menace," 17 January 1939.

15 E.g., *Anchorage Daily Times,* 25 June 1935.

16 *Fairbanks Daily News-Miner,* 23 November 1938.

17 George L. Warren, "The Prospect for New Settlers," *Survey Graphic* 30 (March 1941): 167–68, is a brief summary of the organizations and conferences dealing with international migration and refugee settlement.

18 E.g., Herbert Heaton, "Migration and Cheap Land—The End of Two Chapters," *Sociological Review* 26 (July 1934): 231–48; Isaiah Bowman, ed., *The Limits of Land Settlement;* Bowman, *The Pioneer Fringe,* Special Publication no. 13, American Geographical Society (New York: American Geographical Society, 1931); Goronwy Rees, "The Unpeopled Spaces," *The Spectator* 149 (19 November 1937): 883–84, a review article based on *The Limits of Land Settlement.*

19 "The Organization of Migration for Settlement," *International Labor Review* 37 (May 1938): 561–83.

20 The refugee problem, the Evian Conference, and American participation in planning for refugee migration are treated from the State Department position in Cordell Hull, *The Memoirs of Cordell Hull* (New York: Macmillan Co., 1948), 1: 578–79, 713–14; 2: 1537, 1540. Arthur D. Morse gives chief attention to development in Europe while tracing American policy on refugees in *While Six Million Died* (New York: Random House, 1968); David S. Wyman focuses on the State Department and on American nativist and anti-Semitic tendencies in *Paper Walls: America and the Refugee Crisis, 1938–1941* (Amherst: University of Massachusetts Press, 1968).

21 "New Attempts to Colonize the Northland," *Fairbanks Daily News-Miner,* 3 November 1938. The men were Robert G. F. Tallman, Judge Ben Lindsey, C. Hilliard, Jr., and Ira L. Quist.

22 "Alaska's Newest Colonization Project," *Fairbanks Daily News-Miner,* 5 November 1938; "Alaska's Place in the Colonization Picture," ibid., 17 November 1938.

23 Ibid., 19 and 21 November 1938.

24 *New London* (Connecticut) *Day,* 29 November 1938; *Quincy* (Illinois) *Herald-Whig,* 26 November 1938; *Birmingham* (Alabama) *News,* 28 November 1938; *Seattle Times,* 4 November 1938.

25 *Fairbanks Daily News-Miner,* 23 and 29 November 1938. Quote from ibid., 26 November 1938.

26 Ibid., 23 June 1939, news story and editorial. *Congressional Record,* 76th Cong., 1st sess., 1939, 84, pt. 7: 7759, 7833.

27 Slattery's name was not actually attached to either of the two issues of the report—first the press release of 14 August 1939, and then *The Problem of Alaskan Develop-*

ment (Washington, D.C.: GPO, 1940). For a digest of the plan, see Emily C. Davis, "Alaska and European Refugees," *Science Supplement* 90 (27 October 1939): 10–11.

28 For Slattery's career in the conservation movement, J. Leonard Bates, "Fulfilling American Democracy: The Conservation Movement, 1907 to 1921," *Mississippi Valley Historical Review* 44 (June 1957): 29–57; for his interest in veteran's land settlement, Bill G. Reid, "Proposed American Plans for Soldier Settlement During the World War I Period" (Ph.D. diss., University of Oklahoma, 1963), pp. 27–28; on the origins of the anti-Pinchot attitude in Alaska, J. P. Nichols, *History of Alaska*, pp. 369, 370 n., 378–80.

29 *Anchorage Daily Times, Fairbanks Daily News-Miner,* and *Daily Alaska Empire* of Juneau all ran three or four news stories, feature articles, or editorials on the Slattery Plan from mid-August through October 1939.

30 ARRC, Minutes, adjourned meeting of the board of directors, 21 August 1939, p. 14, in Hess Papers.

31 The following discussion is based on the April 1940 version of *The Problem of Alaskan Development.*

32 *New York Times,* 22 August 1939.

33 *Fairbanks Daily News-Miner,* 12 February 1940.

34 E.g., *New York Post,* 16 August 1939; *Sioux Falls Argus-Leader,* 17 August 1939; *El Paso Times,* 17 August 1939; *Boston Post,* 18 August 1939; *St. Louis Star-Times,* 17 August 1939; *Chicago Times,* 18 August 1939; *Philadelphia Bulletin,* 17 August 1939; *San Antonio Express,* 30 August 1939; *Charlotte* (North Carolina) *Observer,* 27 August 1939; *Portland Journal,* 6 September 1939.

35 *Cincinnati Enquirer,* reprinted in the *Daily Alaska Empire* (Juneau), 31 August 1939.

36 *Daily Alaska Empire,* reprinted in the *Anchorage Daily Times,* 20 November 1939.

37 Robert Marshall, "Should We Settle Alaska?" *New Republic* 102 (8 January 1940): 49–50. Marshall was the son of Louis Marshall, constitutional lawyer, leader in Jewish affairs, and long president of the American Jewish Committee. See *DAB* for Robert Marshall's Alaskan experience, his exploration, mapping, and studies in the Brooks Range; see also his papers collected in *Alaska Wilderness* (Berkeley: University of California Press, 1970). Ernest Gruening, as director of the Division of Territories and Island Possessions, just before his appointment as territorial governor of Alaska, also opposed Jewish refugee settlement in Alaska.

38 Ibid., pp. 54–55.

39 The Anchorage and Fairbanks chambers' resolutions were published in the *Fairbanks Daily New-Miner,* 12 and 19 October 1939. The Juneau chamber's resolution was inserted by Senator Arthur Vandenberg in the *Congressional Record,* 76th Cong., 3d sess., 1940, 86, pt. 5:5520. For an exchange between the Valdez chamber of commerce and A. J. Wirt of the Interior Department, *Fairbanks Daily News-Miner,* 6 April 1940.

40 *Congressional Record,* 76th Cong., 3d sess., 1940, 86, pt. 16:4066–70, extension of remarks by Dimond, including the text of a 20 March 1940 letter to Senator Millard Tydings.

41 *Fairbanks Daily News-Miner,* 14, 15, 23, and 25 March and 5, 6, and 9 April 1940.

42 U.S. Congress, Senate Subcommittee of the Committee on Territories and Insular Affairs, *Hearings on S. 3577, The Settlement and Development of Alaska,* 76th Cong.,

3d Sess., 13, 15, and 18 May 1940. (Hereafter cited as Senate Subcomittee, *Hearings, Settlement and Development*).

43 Ibid., pp. 172–79, 95–108.

44 Alvin Johnson, *Pioneer's Progress* (Lincoln, Nebraska: University of Nebraska Press, 1960), chaps. 28, 31, 33.

45 Senate Subcommittee, *Hearings, Settlement and Development*, pp. 108–18.

46 Ibid., pp. 179–94.

47 Ibid., pp. 210–18.

48 Corey Ford and Alastair MacBain, "Uncle Sam's Ice Box," pp. 29–30, 40.

49 *Fairbanks Daily News-Miner*, 6 April 1940.

50 Alaska Planning Council, *A Study of the "Slattery Plan" for Alaska's Development* (Juneau, January 1940), pp. 14–32, 7.

51 *Anchorage Daily Times*, 2 November 1939.

52 Senate Subcommittee, *Hearings, Settlement and Development*, pp. 163–71; also, Trevor's letter to Senator Tydings, pp. 113–14.

53 Ibid., pp. 118–20.

54 Ibid., pp. 84, 212, 216; *Congressional Record*, 76th Cong., 3d sess., 1940, 86, pt. 16: 4172–73.

55 "Fortune Quarterly Survey," *Fortune* 18 (July 1938): 80; *Fortune* 19 (April 1939): 102. Also, "Open Our Doors to German Refugees?" *Reader's Digest* 34 (May 1939): 82–88.

56 Herbert H. Hilscher, "Alaska—Little Siberia," *Alaska Life* 3 (June 1940): 6, 19, 21, an attack on the Interior Department and a prediction of additional future proposals for refugee settlement.

57 *Galveston News*, 23 March 1940; *New York Times*, 13 April 1940, p. 16; "Where Shall We Put the Finns?" *Alaska Life* 3 (June 1940): 10–11, an editorial quoting a protest from the Juneau Chamber of Commerce to Maverick that used the Matanuska Colony as an example of failure of sponsored settlement and of a "shocking waste of public funds." At the end of the war the proposal for Finnish extra-quota settlement was renewed and the Alaska legislature protested in a joint memorial to Congress, *Congressional Record*, 79th Cong., 1st sess., 1945, 91, pt. 3:3360.

58 *Fairbanks Daily News-Miner*, 5 and 7 March 1941. Territory of Alaska, *Senate Journal*, 15th Legis., 1941, pp. 17, 58; *House Journal*, pp. 77, 103. Roosevelt answered with a letter to the legislature asking for a truce between Alaskans and Ickes, *News-Miner*, 28 March 1941.

59 *Congressional Record*, 77th Cong., 1st sess., 87, pt. 10:A419–A421. Oddly, and disturbing to confidence in the value of oral histories, in tape recording his recollections for the Columbia Oral History Collection in 1949 and 1950, Congressman Dickstein was confused about even some of the broad aspects of the refugee problem and made no mention at all of his bill for refugee immigration and settlement.

60 *Daily Alaska* (Juneau) *Empire*, 23 March 1941.

61 Hull, *Memoirs*, 1:713–14; *Fairbanks Daily News-Miner*, 18 October 1939.

62 W. D. Forsyth, *The Myth of Open Spaces: Australian, British and World Trends of Population and Migration* (Melbourne: Melbourne University Press, 1942); C. Hartley Grattan, "Postwar Migration: A Mirage," *Harper's Magazine* 188 (December 1943): 24–33.

63 Refugee Economic Corporation, *Quest for Settlement: Summaries of Selected Economic and Geographic Reports* (New York: Refugee Economic Corporation, 1948); Sir Bernard Binns, *Land Settlement for Agriculture* (Rome: Food and Agriculture Organizations, U.N., 1951).

64 Maurice R. Davie, "Recent Refugee Immigration from Europe," in *Postwar Problems of Migration: Papers Presented at the Roundtable on Population Problems* (New York: Milbank Memorial Fund, 1947), pp. 110–23.

65 D. B. Turner, "The Resources Future," in *The Canadian Northwest: Its Potentialities*, ed. Frank Underhill, Symposium of the Royal Society of Canada (Toronto: University of Toronto Press, 1948), p. 83; also, Murray Cooke, Regional Settlement Supervisor, Department of Immigration and Citizenship, "Population and Development and the Place of Immigration," in *Proceedings, Northern Development Conference* (Edmonton: Edmonton Chamber of Commerce, 1957).

66 Edna Scofield, "Finland's Farm-Refugee Problem," *The Geographical Review* 31 (January 1941): 148–50; Raye R. Platt, ed., *Finland and its Geography* (New York: Duell, Sloan and Pearce, for the American Geographical Society, 1955), pp. 130–33, 137–38. For an earlier study of the urban drift in Sweden, see Dorothy Swaine Thomas, "Internal Migrations in Sweden: A Note on the Extensiveness as Compared with Net Migration Gain or Loss," *American Journal of Sociology* 42 (November 1936): 345–57.

67 For a variety of agrarian attitudes, see O. E. Baker, Ralph Borsodi, and M. L. Wilson, *Agriculture in Modern Life* (New York: Harper and Brothers, 1939). For a Catholic view, the National Catholic Rural Conference, *Manifesto on Rural Life* (Milwaukee: Bruce Publishing Company, 1939).

68 Baker, Barsodi, and Wilson, *Agriculture in Modern Life*, pp. 255–62, 265–66.

69 M. L. Wilson, "The Problem of Surplus Agricultural Population," *International Journal of Agarian Affairs* 1 (October 1939): 37–48.

70 E.g., the *Sacramento Union*, 16 December 1938, praised the initiative and individualism of Walter Pippel in the midst of the mismanaged and regimented Matanuska Colony; the *Union*, 26 February 1939, called for more settlement projects like a recent one in Minnesota and like the Matanuska Colony, which it called a success; and the *Union*, 2 March 1940, suggested that the Matanuska Colony could serve as a model for similar colonies, which it thought should be established both in Alaska and elsewhere.

71 E.g., "An enlightened planning in respect to Alaska might well make it a place for settlement of American refugees from the American depression. It is not a waste area for which we cannot find use in solving our own problems" (*Moscow* [Idaho] *Star Mirror*, reprinted in the *Anchorage Daily Times*, 28 September 1939). Also, *Hoquiam Washingtonian* and *Centralia* (Washington) *Chronicle*, reprinted in the *Anchorage Daily Times*, 23 and 26 September 1939; also, *Portland* (Oregon) *Journal*, 6 September 1939; *Philadelphia Bulletin*, 17 August 1939; *Boston Post*, 18 August 1939; *New York Evening Post*, 17 August 1939; *Minot* (North Dakota) *News*, 25 March 1940.

72 "Frontier Frustration," *Commonweal* 29 (April 1939): 704–05.

73 Richard L. Neuberger, "The Public Domain: The West Needs People," *Survey Graphic* 30 (February 1941): 72–78.

74 Neuberger, "Highballing at Sixty Below," *Saturday Evening Post* 216 (23 November

1943): 15; "Yukon Adventure," ibid. (19 February 1944): 20–21 ff.; "Eskimo Guerillas," ibid. (17 February 1945): 6 ff.; "For Pioneers of the Years Ahead," *New York Times Magazine*, 17 September 1944, pp. 16–17 ff.

75 Neuberger, "Alaska: Sanctuary for Europe's Homeless," *Alaska Life* 10 (September 1947): 8–9, 22.

76 Lord and Johnstone, *A Place on Earth*, assumed in 1942 that there would be a revival of interest in the back-to-the-land movement and quoted the *Boston Post* on the desirability of making such provisions against future depression. The contributors in Elmer T. Peterson, ed., *Cities Are Abnormal* (Norman: University of Oklahoma Press, 1946), supported land settlement and decentralization with the familiar arguments of falling birthrate, slowing population increase, threatened depression, and the unwholesomeness of urban life. Joseph W. Eaton, *Exploring Tomorrow's Agriculture: Cooperative Group Farming, A Practical Problem of Rural Rehabilitation* (New York: Harper and Bros., 1943), took the remarkably mistaken view that after the war cooperative group farming might play a part in correcting the ills associated with the system of individually operated farms.

Chapter 10

1 George W. Rogers, *The Future of Alaska: Economic Consequences of Statehood* (Baltimore: The Johns Hopkins Press, for Resources for the Future, Inc., 1962), pp. 63, 80, 92.

2 *Congressional Record*, 75th Cong., 1st sess., 1937, 71, pt. 4:4055–56, and 3d sess., 1938, 83, pt. 10:1949–50; also, *Anchorage Daily Times*, 4 and 5 December 1939, and Rogers, *Future of Alaska*, p. 92.

3 George W. Rogers and Richard A. Cooley, *Alaska's Population and Economy: Regional Growth, Development and Future Outlook*, vol. 2, *Statistical Handbook*, Division of State Planning, Office of the Governor (Juneau, 1962), table P-4, p. 8.

4 *Fairbanks Daily News-Miner*, 6 September 1939; 12 June 1940; 28 and 30 December 1940; 16 and 29 January 1941.

5 *Dayton* (Ohio) *News*, 16 February 1940; *New York Sun*, 14 May 1940; *Oakland* (California) *Tribune*, 23 May 1940.

6 *Daily Alaska* (Juneau) *Empire*, 23 March 1941.

7 *Fairbanks Daily News-Miner*, 23 February 1957.

8 E.g., Ernest P. Walker, *Alaska: America's Continental Frontier Outpost* (Washington, D.C.: Smithsonian Institution, 1943), is superficial, routine, and contains a number of factual errors; Beka Doherty and Arthur Hepner, "Alaska: Last American Frontier," *Foreign Policy Reports*, 18 (1 December 1942), pp. 238–47, includes a simplified, rosy view of the Matanuska Colony as a supposed example of what could be done on a larger scale; Joseph Driscoll, *War Discovers Alaska* (Philadelphia: J. B. Lippincott Co., 1943), and Harold Griffin, *Alaska and the Canadian Northwest: The New Frontier* (New York: W. W. Norton & Co., 1944), are standard commercial journalism. "Bridge to Asia," *Fortune* 25 (March 1942): 94–101, calling Alaska "long forgotten," rediscovers it.

9 Alaska Regional Planning Office, *Postwar Economic Development of Alaska*, Region 10 (Juneau: 1942). The report had been prepared in the early autumn of 1941 under the title *Post Defense Economic Development in Alaska*. After 7 December 1941, some minor revisions were made and the title was appropriately changed.

10 James C. Rettie, *The North Pacific Study* (Portland, Oregon, June 1944). There are four volumes containing fifteen sections or monographs individually paginated. Vol. 4 contains monographs 13, 14, 15, and is titled *Agricultural Development, Land Resources and Population Trends*. The Canadian report is *Canada's New Northwest*, The North Pacific Planning Project, Charles Camsell, Director (n.p., 1947). The background of the whole project is given in the preface and foreword, pp. 5–9.

11 Benjamin H. Kizer, *The U.S.–Canadian Northwest*, Institute of Pacific Relations (Princeton, N.J.: Princeton University Press, 1944), pp. 8–14.

12 *Public Papers and Addresses of Franklin D. Roosevelt*, 1944–45 (New York: Harper & Bros., 1950), items 57, 58, pp. 213–16, 223.

13 Ernest Gruening, "Go North, Young Man," *Reader's Digest* 44 (January 1944), pp. 53–57, condensed from *Future*, December 1943. Richard L. Neuberger, as a captain who served with the army in construction of the Alaska Highway, boosted Alaska's postwar attractions in the same manner as Gruening in articles in *Collier's*, *The Progressive*, and in the *St. Louis Post-Dispatch* and other newspapers. These articles were used by congressional champions of Alaskan development (*Congressional Record*, 79th Cong., 1st sess., 91, pt. 10: A-96, A-98, A-949–50). A consciously restrained yet inviting view of Alaska is given by George Sundborg, later administrative assistant to Senator Gruening, in *Opportunity in Alaska* (New York: Macmillan Co., 1945), especially on land opportunities and agriculture, pp. 76–80.

14 William Gillman, "Colonists for Alaska," *Yale Review* 34 (Summer, 1945): 666–82.

15 Land Settlement Work Group of the Interbureau Committee on Postwar Agricultural Programs, *Farm Opportunities in the United States: Outlook, Problems, Policies* (Washington, D.C.: GPO, July 1945). A review of past settlement plans for veterans is given in Davis T. Rowlands, "Land and Homes for Returning Servicemen," *The Annals* 227 (May 1943): 143–51. Those who spoke with assurance of thousands of veterans eager to settle in Alaska explained the lack of actual settlement by charging the federal government and especially the Interior Department with failure to "open up the country" in some unspecified manner. *Congressional Record*, 79th Cong., 2d sess., 92, pt. 9: 628–29, extension of remarks, Congressman Homer D. Angell, Oregon.

16 General Land Office, U.S. Department of the Interior, *Answers to Questions by Servicemen About Land Settlement in Alaska* (Washington, D.C.: GPO, March 1944). This bulletin was also mailed by the Juneau field office of the National Resources Planning Board to those who made inquiries there.

17 Division of Territories and Island Possessions, U.S. Department of the Interior, *Alaska* (Washington, D.C.: GPO, 1945), foreword by Harold L. Ickes.

18 Harold L. Ickes, "Let's Open Up Alaska!" pp. 4–5, 18.

19 *Congressional Record*, 79th Cong., 1st sess., 91, pt. 1:1209, and pt. 3 : 3360.

20 *Fairbanks Daily News-Miner*, 15 February 1946, p. 1.

21 *Annual Report of the Secretary of the Interior, 1945* (Washington, D.C.: GPO, 1945), pp. 251–52.

22 U.S. Congress, House, *Report, Subcommittee of Committee on Appropriations*, 79th Cong., 1st sess. (Washington, D.C.: GPO, 1945), p. 1.

23 Ibid., pp. 2–8, and *Annual Report of the Secretary of the Interior, 1945*, pp. 253, 258. Comment on release of the subcommittee report in *Fairbanks Daily News-Miner*, 15 February 1946, pp. 1–2.

24 *Annual Report of the Secretary of the Interior, 1947* (Washington, D.C.: GPO, 1947), pp. 362–65; and *Congressional Record*, 79th Cong., 2d sess., 92, pt. 12: A-4209-210, Extension of Remarks, Delegate E. L. Bartlett. Bartlett was happy to say that Congress had apppropriated more money for Interior Department use in Alaska than ever before, but he quickly pointed to the need for even larger expenditures for Alaskan development.

25 U.S. Department of the Interior, Bureau of Land Management, *Papers Presented at Seminars on Alaska, February 2, 3, 6, 7, 1950* (Washington, D.C.: GPO, 1950), pp. 5–6. See also pp. 1–2, opening statement by William E. Warne, Assistant Secretary of the Interior. The department issued a mimeographed and bound version of Kirk H. Stone's study of the colony, "Alaska Group Settlement."

26 U.S. Department of the Interior, Bureau of Land Management, *Agricultural Settlement Opportunities in Alaska: Anchorage Area* (Washington, D.C.: GPO, 1947), and *Areas Suitable for Group Agricultural Settlement in Alaska*, rev. ed. (Washington, D.C.: GPO, 1948). In contrast, much larger estimates of settlement and farming opportunities, accompanied by assurances that the figures were conservative, were given in George Sundborg, *Opportunity in Alaska*, pp. 76–80. The Bureau of Land Management estimated that in the whole Tanana Valley 160 farms could be added, but Herbert H. Hilscher, *Alaska Now* (Boston: Little, Brown, & Co., 1948), chaps. 9, 10, claimed that there was an immediate need in the Fairbanks region alone for 500 added farms and painted a rosy picture of a homesteader gaining his subsistence in the first year and enjoying cash sales of from $3,000 to $5,000 in the second year—a local development that would have more than doubled the whole Alaskan agricultural production. Hilscher regarded the Matanuska project as a failure and referred to it as the "neo-Communistic colony" (p. 156).

27 U.S. Department of the Interior, *Papers Presented at Seminars on Alaska*, p. 6; *Congressional Record*, 81st Cong., 1st sess. 95, pt. 8:10,803. U.S. Department of the Interior, Bureau of Land Management, *Orders Affecting Public Lands in Alaska* (Washington, D.C.: GPO, 1959), Public Land Order 487, 16 June 1949, and Public Land Order 585, 14 April 1949.

28 Walt Pedersen, "Hold That Land," *The Alaskan Agriculturist* 2 (June 1949): 4–6, and Pedersen, "An Open Letter to Politicians and Planners," *The Alaskan Agriculturist* 2 (April 1950): 4; also, *The Valley Settler* (Palmer, Alaska), 6 August 1948, p. 4.

29 The withdrawals were revoked in twenty-two Public Land Orders given in U.S. Department of the Interior, *Orders Affecting Public Lands in Alaska*, pp. 105–36, and *Papers Presented at Seminars on Alaska*, pp. 6–7. On the effects of heaving or hummocking caused by permafrost, see W. A. Rockie, "Pitting on Alaska Farm Lands: A New Erosion Problem," *Geographical Review* 32 (January 1942): 128–34.

30 Information and quote in this paragraph taken from O. S. Aamodt, C. E. Kellogg, I. J. Nygard, et al., *Report on Exploratory Investigation of Agricultural Problems in Alaska*, U. S. Department of Agriculture, Agricultural Research Administration, Miscellaneous Publication no. 700 (Washington, D.C.: GPO, 1949), pp. 2–9, 52–78.

31 Hugh A. Johnson and Wendell Calhoun, *Markets for the Products of Alaska Cropland*, U.S. Department of Agriculture, Bureau of Agricultural Economics and the Alaska Agricultural Experiment Station (Washington, D.C.: GPO, 1950); and O. L. Mimms, J. L. Paschal, and W. U. Fuhriman, *Some Economic Aspects of Farming*

in Alaska, with Chief Attention to the Matanuska Valley, U. S. Department of Agriculture, Bureau of Agricultural Economics and the Alaska Agricultural Experiment Station (Washington, D.C.: GPO, 1950).

32 There were some exceptions, e.g., I. M. C. Anderson, "Livestock in the Aleutian Islands," in *Proceedings of the Sixth and Seventh Alaska Science Conferences, 1955 and 1956*, ed. H. E. Slotnick and L. H. Salisbury [University of Alaska, 1958], pt. 2, pp. 1–8.

33 Allan H. Mick and Hugh A. Johnson, "Soil Resources and Agricultural Development in Alaska," *Arctic Research: The Current Status of Research*, ed. Diana Rowley, The Arctic Institute of North America, Special Publication no. 2, (1957), pp. 124–36, esp. pp. 131–32.

34 Hugh A. Johnson, "The Social Cost of Isolated Settlement" (Paper presented at the Sixth Alaska Science Conference, College, Alaska, 1–4 June 1955).

35 Alaska Development Board, *Biennial Report, 1945–1947* (Juneau, January 1947), pp. 31–33. (Hereafter cited as *Biennial Report.*)

36 Richard F. Gorman, *Fur Farming Opportunities in Alaska*, Alaska Development Board (Juneau, February 1947).

37 Johnson and Irwin, *The Position of Agriculture in Alaska's Current Economy*, p. 7.

38 G. W. Gasser, *Information for the Alaska Farm–Settler*, Circular no. 1; *The Tanana Valley*, Circular no. 2; *The Matanuska Valley*, Circular no. 3; *Livestock in Alaska*, Circular no. 4, Alaska Development Board (Juneau, 1946).

39 *Biennial Report, 1946–47*, p. 31.

40 U. S. Congress, House, Subcommittee on Public Lands of the Committee on Public Lands, *Hearings on the Alaska Veterans' Homesteading Act of 1947, H.R. 868, 1548, 4059*, 80th Cong., 1st sess., 1947, pp. 126–28.

41 Ibid., pp. 158–83, letters and resolutions opposing the bill from Alaskan organizations, through Delegate E. L. Bartlett. A semi-official statement of the Forest Service's position on the bill is in Erle Kauffman, "Timber Homestead in Alaska," *American Forests* 53 (November 1947): 488–91, 527.

42 Hearings before the Subcommittee on Public Lands, written statement by Don L. Irwin to Delegate E. L. Bartlett, pp. 160–63.

43 Ibid., references to the Matanuska Colony throughout and pp. 117, 122, 135. The ARRC had originally been named as the agency to finance veterans, but objections to the ARRC caused the substitution of the Reconstruction Finance Corporation (pp. 208, 258–59). Kauffman, "Timber Homestead in Alaska," discusses forest management, sustained-yield lumbering, and the impracticality of small-scale operations in that region.

44 *United States Code*, title 43, sec. 279. The conditions described were in effect until 1959.

45 Gruening, *The State of Alaska*, chap. 28, describes the campaign for statehood in great detail.

46 Robert Atwood, "Who Owns Alaska?" *Anchorage Daily Times*, 22 May 1947; reprinted in extensions of remarks by E. L. Bartlett, *Congressional Record*, 80th Cong., 1st sess., 93, pt. 1: A2523–24.

47 U. S. Congress, House, *Hearings Before the Subcommittee on Territorial and Insular Possessions of the Committee on Public Lands*, 80th Cong., 1st sess., 1947, p. 37.

48 Ibid., pp. 8–9, 50–52, 82–84.

49 Copy of chamber of commerce telegram to the members of the legislature, 17 March 1949, ARRC unnumbered file, renewing old offers of land. *Anchorage Daily Times*, 16 and 17 March and 6 April 1949.

50 Copies of letters sent to the members of the legislature, January 1949, ARRC unnumbered file; T. A. Moyer, "Palmer, Future Capital of Alaska," *Matanuska Valley Record*, April 1951, pp. 1–2.

51 *The Valley Frontiersman*, 8 November and 3 December 1947.

52 William T. Zabradnicek, "Problems and Plans of the Palmer School," *Matanuska Valley Record*, August 1951, p. 4; Lucille K. Mick, "The Growing City of Palmer," *Alaska Record and Matanuska Valley Record*, August 1953, pp. 1, 10–13; September 1953, p. 12; October 1953, p. 12.

53 M. D. Snodgrass, "Give Us Statehood," *Alaska Record and Matanuska Valley Record*, December 1953, pp. 5, 14.

54 E. W. Liebenthal, "The Outlook on Kenai," *Matanuska Record* 2 (May 1952): 2–3.

55 *Anchorage Daily Times*, 9 February 1948; *The Valley Frontiersman*, 20 and 27 September 1947.

56 *The Valley Frontiersman*, 21 and 24 January and 12 May 1948; also, T. A. Moyer, "The Plight of the Homesteader," *Matanuska Valley Record*, October 1951, pp. 1–2.

57 Evangeline R. (Mrs. Robert B.) Atwood, *Alaska's Struggle for Self-Government—83 Years of Neglect* (Privately reprinted from a series in the *Anchorage Daily Times*, 24 March–19 April 1950), p. 19. See also preface, n. 1.

58 William E. Warne, Assistant Secretary of the Interior, "Alaska, Far-from-Forgotten-Land," *The Reclamation Era* 35 (January 1949).

59 U.S. Congress, House, *Alaska: A Reconnaissance Report on the Potential Development of Water Resources in the Territory of Alaska for Irrigation, Power Production, and Other Beneficial Uses*, 82nd Cong., 1st sess., January 1952, House Doc. 197. Prepared under the direction of the Bureau of Reclamation and presented to the secretary of the interior in 1949, the report was several times revised before publication in 1952. (Hereafter cited as *Alaska: A Reconnaissance Report.*)

60 Ibid., pp. 4–5, 12–13, 55–62, 107–108. The assumptions and the argument of the report are conveniently summarized in the opening pages.

61 The low estimate by the task force was supported by another study putting the tillable area at one million acres or less and pointing out that, before Alaska's cropland would be needed, 150 to 200 million acres would have been added to the cultivated areas of the States. Charles E. Kellogg and Iver J. Nygard, *Exploratory Study of the Principal Soil Groups of Alaska*, U.S. Department of Agriculture, Agricultural Monograph no. 7 (Washington, D.C.: GPO, 1951), pp. 124, 135.

62 After a campaign by the Presbyterian missionary Sheldon Jackson, the reindeer, European and Asian cousin of the caribou, was introduced in Alaska as a substitute for the depleted game on which the Eskimo of northern and western Alaska had depended. Vilhjalmur Stefansson, *The Northward Course of Empire* (New York: Macmillan Co., 1924), pp. 60–70, predicted that the Arctic would become the world's great source of meat. Also, Stefansson, "The Resources of the Arctic and the Problem of Their Utilization," in *Problems of Polar Research*, ed. W. L. G. Joerg, Special Publication no. 7 (New York: American Geographical Society, 1928), pp. 209–33; Alfred H. Brooks, "The Value of Alaska," pp. 25–50; U.S.

Department of the Interior, *General Information Regarding the Territory of Alaska* (Washington, D.C.: GPO, 1931), pp. 40–44; *Congressional Record*, 76th Cong., 1st sess., 1939, 84, pt. 3: 2600–04, Delegate Anthony Dimond's historical summary of the reindeer industry in connection with the debate on the appropriations to carry out the 1937 bill for buying out white owners and restoring the Eskimo monopoly; Margaret Lantis, "The Reindeer Industry in Alaska," *Arctic* 3 (April 1950): 27–44; and A. E. Porsild, "Land Use in the Arctic," *Canadian Geographical Journal*, Part I, vol. 48 (June 1954): 232–43 and Part 2, vol. 49 (July 1954): 20–31.

63 *Alaska: A Reconnaissance Report*, pp. 102–03.

64 ARRC General Manager's Monthly Reports, June 1942, and January–February 1943.

65 *Alaska: A Reconnaissance Report*, p. 62, table 28.

66 G. W. Gasser, *The Matanuska Valley* (Juneau: Alaska Development Board, 1946), p. 17.

67 Johnson and Calhoun, *Markets for the Products of Alaska Cropland*, pp. 19–24.

68 ARRC General Manager's Monthly Reports, February and April 1946.

69 *Alaska: A Reconnaissance Report*, p. 4, letter of transmittal, Michael W. Straus to Secretary of the Interior Julius A. Krug.

70 "A New Frontier," *New York Times*, 25 April 1935, p. 20; *Congressional Record*, 75th Cong., 1st sess., 1937, 71, pt. 4: 4056.

71 *Pressing Scientific Problems of the North* (New York: Arctic Institute of North America [1955],), pp. 1–2.

72 Arctic Institute of North America, *Arctic Bibliography*, 10 vols. (Washington D.C.: GPO, 1953–1961). Additional volumes were in preparation in 1961; by 1971 there were 15 volumes and over 100,000 entires.

73 E.g., Robert E. Frost, *Evaluation of Soils and Permafrost Conditions in the Territory of Alaska by Means of Aerial Photographs* (Purdue University Engineering Experiment Station, Corps of Engineers, Department of the Army, 1940).

74 Lt. Gen. Arthur G. Trudeau, "Significance of Research and Development in the Arctic," *Man Living in the Arctic*, Conference Proceedings, Quartermaster Research and Engineering Center, Natick, Mass. (Washington, D.C.: National Academy of Sciences–National Research Council, 1961), pp. 7–14.

75 Col. Willard Pearson, "Alaska—Gibraltar of the North," in *Man Living in he Arctic*, pp. 35–57. The importance assigned the paper by the military is shown by its later appearance in public addresses, briefings, and promotional activity, as described in Rogers, *Future of Alaska*, p. 231 n.

76 Trevor Lloyd, "Human Society in the Arctic Today," ibid., pp. 125–34, quotation, p. 126 (Lloyd is professor of georgaphy at McGill University); also, Steven M. Horvath, "Summation: Man's Future Conquest of the Arctic," ibid., pp. 115–18.

77 Kirk H. Stone, "Some Geographical Bases for Planning New Alaska Settlement," *Science in Alaska: Selected Papers, Alaska Science Conference, November 9–11, 1950*, ed. Henry B. Collins (Arctic Institute of North America, 1952), pp. 136–50; and Kirk H. Stone, "Populating Alaska: The United States Phase, *Geographical Review* 42 (1952): 384–404.

78 Kirk H. Stone, "Human Geographic Research in the Northern North American Lands," *Arctic Research: The Current Status of Research and Some Immediate Problems*

in the North American Arctic and Subarctic, ed. Diana Rowley, Special Publication no. 2 (Arctic Institute of North America, 1955), pp. 209–33.

79 *Canadian North,* Technical Assistant to the Chief of Naval Operations for Polar Projects, prepared by contributors at Georgetown University, Paul R. Sullivan, Director (Department of the Navy, 1956), pp. 3–5.

80 Ibid., p. 20.

81 Kirk H. Stone, "The Norwegian Edges of Settlement: Measures of Permanence," abstract, *Annals of the Association of American Geographers* 47 (June 1957): 179.

82 Kirk H. Stone, *High Latitude Fringes of Settlement,* Annual report, third year, to Geography Branch, Office of Naval Operations (Madison: University of Wisconsin, 1960), "Research Objectives," p. 1.

83 F. Gerald Ridge, "General Principles for the Planning of Subarctic Settlements" (Ph.D. diss., McGill University, 1953); Roy Jackson Fletcher, "Potential Settlement Sites in the Central Arctic Archipelago" (M.A. thesis, University of Minnesota, 1959); Robert L. Monahan, "The Development of Settlement in the Fairbanks Area, Alaska: A Study of Permanence" (Ph.D. diss., McGill University, 1959).

84 U.S. Congress, House, Committee on Banking and Currency, *Report to Accompany H. R. 3615, Alaska Housing Act, Report No. 396,* 81st Cong., 1st sess., 1949, p. 2. Also, The Alaska Public Works Act, 24 August 1949, chap. 504, sec. 3, 63 *Stat.* 627, Title 48 *Federal Code Annotated,* sec. 486–486j.

85 In the summers of 1960 and 1961 this attitude was common among the homesteaders and others in the area of new settlement around the village of Willow and beyond, along the Alaska Railroad and Susitna River. An estimated population of one million by 1980 is given Herb and Miriam Hilscher, *Alaska, U.S.A.* (Boston: Little, Brown, & Co.: 1959), pp. 209–10. This was originally *Alaska Now* (1948) by Herbert H. Hilscher, revised and with the frontier quality improved by the change to "Herb."

86 *Fairbanks Daily News-Miner,* 16 November 1961; 19 September 1963; 18 March 1964; 12 June 1964. U.S., Congress, Senate, Merchant Marine and Fisheries Subcommittee of Committee on Interstate and Foreign Commerce, *Hearings on S. 1899, To Authorize the Establishment of the Arctic Wildlife Range, Alaska,* 86th Cong., 1st sess., pt. 1, June, 1959; pt. 2, October 1959–April 1960.

87 Various population forecasts are given in Rogers and Cooley, *Alaska's Population and Economy,* vol. 2, *Statistical Handbook,* pp. 54–55, table P-45.

88 U. S. Congress, House, *Transport Requirements for the Growth of Northwest North America,* vol. 2, *Research Report by Battelle Memorial Institute on an Integrated Transport System to Encourage Economic Development of Northwest North America,* House Document no. 176, vol. 2, 87th Cong., 1st sess., 1961 (hereafter cited as the *Battelle Report*). The gist of the report is in preliminary sec. 1, pp. I-1 to I-26 and tables I-1, I-2, VI-1, VI-2. The *Battelle Report* is discussed throughout Rogers, *The Future of Alaska.*

89 Similar assumptions about federal spending and the growth of agriculture appear in Arthur D. Little, Inc., *Possibilities for Agricultural Industry in Alaska: Report to the State of Alaska* (Cambridge: Arthur D. Little, Inc., 1961), p. 1. The report describes difficulties but refers to Alaska's "tremendous agricultural potential," seemingly on the ground that so little had been developed by 1961.

90 *Battelle Report,* p. I-2.

91 Ibid., p. I-26. "Area" refers to Alaska plus Yukon Territory, northern British Columbia, northwestern Alberta, and that part of the Northwest Territories west of the Mackenzie River.

Chapter 11

1 E.g., in the *New York Times*, in addition to news stories, feature articles and editorials appeared 4 January 1959, sec. 4, pp. 3, 10; 12 January 1959, p. 41; 18 January 1959, p. 76; 19 January 1959, pp. 1, 14; 20 January 1959, p. 34; 1 February 1959, sec. 4, p. 10; 15 February 1959, sec. 6, p. 8. Alaskan newspapers made the frontier theme a standard daily item.

2 The discussion of Alaska's population, resources, and economy generally follows Rogers, *The Future of Alaska*, which deals with the economic and social problems of the period of transition to statehood; statistics are from Rogers and Cooley, *Alaska's Population and Economy*, vol. 1, *Analysis*, and vol. 2, *Statistical Handbook*.

3 Rogers and Cooley, *Alaska's Population and Economy*, 2:203, table NR-19; *Battelle Report*, 2:V-217-18. Alaskan wild furs other than the Pribilof fur seals through the 1950s had an annual commercial value fluctuating between one and two million dollars, which was divided among some thousands of white, Eskimo, and Indian trappers.

4 U.S., Bureau of the Census, *Sixteenth Census of the United States: 1940, Agriculture in Alaska*, tables 1, 2, 15. No agriculture report for 1960 showed any fur farm in operation.

5 Institute of Business, Economic and Government Research, *Alaska Monthly Review of Business and Economic Conditions* (College, Alaska: University of Alaska, May 1964), 1:5–6, on the pulp industry; on the petroleum and gas industry, see the August 1964 special issue on oil and gas.

6 Rogers and Cooley, *Alaska's Population and Economy*, 2:64A.

7 U.S. Department of Commerce, Office of Business Economics, *Income in Alaska, Supplement to Survey of Current Business* (Washington, D.C.: GPO, June 1960), p. 4. (Hereafter cited as *Income in Alaska*.)

8 Ibid., pp. 5–6.

9 The importance of continued federal spending is shown by the interest in advance estimates of federal budgets for Alaska. E.g., a newsletter of Seattle-First National Bank 15 February 1962 estimated the budget for fiscal 1963 at more than $368 million, and Senator E. L. Bartlett's Washington newsletter, 4 January 1964, estimated federal spending in Alaska in fiscal 1965 at $518 million (pp. 8–13).

10 Calculated from U.S. Bureau of the Census, *U.S. Census of Population: 1950*, vol. 2, *Characteristics of the Population*, pt. 51, Alaska (Washington, D.C.: GPO, 1952), tables 6, 14, 15.

11 Rogers and Cooley, *Alaska's Population and Economy*, 2:33, table P-25.

12 Ibid., table P-38. *U.S. Census of Population: 1960*, vol. 1, *Characteristics of the Population*, pt. 3, Alaska, sec. D, Detailed Characteristics, table 98, shows 217,940 U.S.-born Alaskans, 68,796 of them born in Alaska, and of those, 43,081 were of aboriginal stock, leaving 26,715 Alaska-born whites. No statistics on the southern influx are available. The *U.S. Census of Population: 1960*, table 98, shows 148,144 white Alaskans born in other states but gives only a listing by undefined regions—South, 38,920; West, 42,223. However, the impression of such an influx is supported by

observation and attention to accents and other evidence. In Fairbanks before World War II, there were three churches—Episcopal, Presbyterian, and Roman Catholic—but by 1960 there were eighteen, ten of them Baptist, with additional Holiness and Pentecostal groups not included in the survey. The changes in Anchorage were similar, and in Alaska as a whole there were more than sixty Baptist churches, most of them associated with the Southern Baptist Convention. Edward Scott Gaustad, *Historical Atlas of Religion in America* (New York: Harper & Row, 1962), pp. 154 (fig. 125) and 155.

13 U.S. Bureau of the Census, *U.S. Census of Population: 1960, Number of Inhabitants, Alaska*, Final Report PC(1)-3A (Washington, D.C.: GPO, 1960), tables 6, 8. Rogers and Cooley, *Alaska's Population and Economy*, vol. 2, tables P-12, P-15–19.

14 The bonanza was limited to construction workers and others in the "defense oriented economy," with per capita incomes averaging 75 percent above the U.S. level. Workers in resource-based industries were at the national level, the military 12 percent below it, and the native economy 40 percent below it. For Alaska all average per capita incomes were 17 percent above the U.S. level, but in the Anchorage and Fairbanks areas the cost of living was 35 to 45 percent above that of Seattle. *Income in Alaska*, pp. 14–18.

15 Rogers and Cooley, *Alaska's Population and Economy*, vol. 2, estimated monthly civilian and military population of Alaska between 1949 and 1960 (pp. 9–13, table P-5) and estimated components of net change in Alaska's population between 1950 and 1960, p. 15, table P-7.

16 *Historical Abstract of the United States, 1960*, p. 188, table 239. One-third figure calculated from the number of patents and acreage patented, 1945–1961; given in U.S. Department of the Interior, *Homesteads*, pp. 24–28.

17 Rogers and Cooley, *Alaska's Population and Economy*, 2:15, table P-7. The figures represent only the gain by migration. Many others came to Alaska, found no jobs or only temporary employment, exhausted their funds, and returned home. See U.S. Department of the Interior, *Statistical Abstract of the United States, 1960* (p. 188, table 239) and *Statistical Appendix to the Annual Report of the Director, Bureau of Land Management* (p. 47, table 15) (Washington, D.C.: GPO, 1960).

18 The Fifty-niners' preparations, departure, and journey to Alaska were reported almost daily in Associated Press news stories. This account was based on news items and feature stories in the *New York Times*, 6 March 1959, p. 18; 10 March, p. 38; 14 March, p. 11; 27 March, p. 10; 30 March, p. 33; 10 May, p. 25; 7 June, p. 68; 26 June, p. 25; also, the *Anchorage Daily Times*, in almost daily coverage from 27 January through April 1959.

19 *Anchorage Daily Times*, 31 January 1959, editorial; also, news items and editorials, 5 and 6 February. On the estimate of 600 more Fifty-niners to follow, see the *Anchorage Daily Times*, 1 April 1959.

20 *Anchorage Daily Times*, 27 and 28 March 1959.

21 Ibid., 30 March 1959.

22 Ibid., 30 March and 2 and 14 April 1959.

23 Ibid., 15 April 1959.

24 *Anchorage Daily Times*, 14, 15, and 16 April 1959.

25 Ibid., 22 and 28 April 1959. O'Carroll Colvin, "Factory Hands in the Wilderness: Alaska's '59ers," *The Nation* 189 (26 September 1959): 166–69.

26 *Anchorage Daily Times*, 28 April 1950; *New York Times*, 7 June 1959, p. 68.

27 *Anchorage Daily Times*, 27 March 1959.
28 "America's Durable Frontier," *Life* 36 (6 April 1959): 40.
29 *Anchorage Daily Times*, 31 January 1959; 6 March 1959; and 30 March 1959.
30 *New York Times* 30 March 1959, p. 33 and 10 May 1959, p. 25; *Anchorage Daily Times*, 3 and 4 April 1959.
31 *New York Times*, 26 June 1959, p. 25.
32 Colvin, "Factory Hands in the Wilderness," pp. 166–69.
33 *Time* 75 (25 April 1960): 25.
34 *Fairbanks Daily News-Miner*, 15 November 1962.
35 By the late summer of 1964 a bridge across the Susitna near Talkeetna was nearing completion. When opened, it would allow the homesteaders to travel by road to Anchorage.
36 Rogers, *The Future of Alaska*, pp. 196–97; on the importance to Alaska of the federal highway program as an employment factor, see pp. 205–13, 220–21.
37 In the twenty years from 1942 through 1961, original entries were made on 862,047 acres in Alaska, the equivalent of 5,387 160-acre homesteads; in the same period there were 1,906 completed or final entries. *Statistical Abstract of the United States*, 1964, p. 199, table 265.
38 Later an attempt was made to require methods "reasonably calculated to produce profitable results" and to require the planting of crops other than native grasses. Regulations summarized from the *Federal Register* of 2 May and 29 May 1963, in Senator Gruening's weekly newsletter, *From the Nation's Capital*, ed George Sundborg, no. 21, 1963, p. 4.
39 Institute of Business, Economic and Government Research, *Alaska Monthly Review of Business and Economic Conditions* (College, Alaska: University of Alaska, July 1964), 1:1. (Hereafter cited as the *Alaska Monthly Review*.)
40 The most misleading figures have been for total land in farms and average farm size. The inclusion of fur farms (now disappeared) on large leases and a few very large but partially used grazing leases from the BLM has made the data almost useless and has given a wholly unrepresentative average farm size of 1,500 to 2,800 acres even though the 160-acre quarter section had been standard for all but a few farms. The 1959 *Census of Agriculture*, cited in the *Alaska Monthly Review*, gives 880,000 acres in Alaska farms, but over 90 percent of that was in a few large, sparsely stocked grazing leases, mainly on Kodiak Island. Rogers and Cooley, *Alaska's Population and Economy*, 2:195, table NR-6, gives the average farm size as 2,420 acres. For a comment on agricultural statistics in Alaska, see Johnson and Irwin, *The Position of Agriculture in Alaska's Current Economy*, pp. 6–7.
41 Gazaway, *Facts and Observations*, p. 34, table 3, gives, by 1959 census definition, 24,342 acres of cropland, including grasses for hay or silage, but only 17,148 acres harvested. Also, for clearing, cropland, and harvested area, 1949–57, see University of Alaska Agricultural Experiment Station and U.S. Department of Agriculture, *Alaska Farm Facts*, Agricultural Research Service Bulletin no. 27 ([Palmer], 1961), p. 11, table 4.
42 Rogers and Cooley, *Alaska's Population and Economy*, vol. 2, tables NR-1 through NR-7.
43 Varying totals are given by the BLM's *Homesteads* and in a later worksheet prepared by the Fairbanks office of the BLM, the latter showing 378,747 acres.
44 Gazaway, *Facts and Observations*, p. 13.

45 The account of farming activity in the various areas is based on the *Alaska Monthly Review* survey and *Alaska Farm Facts,* both cited above, and Alaska Division of Agriculture and U.S. Department of Agriculture, *Farm Production, Alaska—1959* ([Palmer], 1960). The number of part-time and full-time farming and current homesteaders in December 1959 is from Gazaway, *Facts and Observatons,* p. 13.

46 Fairbanks office, Bureau of Land Management, typescript summary of homesteading in Alaska through 1961, by land office regions, Fairbanks, Anchorage, and Juneau. There were 730 patented homesteads in the Fairbanks district, which included the whole of Alaska north of the Alaska Range. However, 80 or 90 percent of all homesteading in that district had been in the Tanana Valley close to Fairbanks. Elsewhere large areas were held under patented or unpatented mineral claims or in smaller parcels as trade and manufacturing sites, headquarters sites, homesites, or under the 1938 Small Tract Act.

47 Act of 11 June 1906, c. 3074, sec. 1, 34 *Stat.* 233, 16 *U.S.C.* sec. 506. Repealed, Act of 23 October 1962, P.L. 87-869, 76 *Stat.* 1157. However, forest homesteads had not been opened for several years before the repeal.

48 Riley, *Federal Land Policy,* p. 5.

49 The following account of homesteading and the development of the Kenai Peninsula is based on Hugh A. Johnson and Robert J. Coffman, *Land Occupancy, Ownership, and Use on Homesteads in the Kenai Peninsula,* Alaska Agricultural Experiment Station, Bulletin 21 (Palmer: 1956).

50 *Farm Production, Alaska—1959,* table 1.

51 Ibid., p. 1, for percentage of total sales by area; also, *Alaska Monthly Review,* July 1964, p. 4, and *Alaska Farm Facts,* pp. 4–34. For the number of farmers, see Gazaway, *Facts and Observations,* p. 13.

52 Stone, "Alaska Group Settlement," pp. 70–71.

53 A list of the original colonists still in Alaska has been kept by the committee for the celebration of the annual Colony Day. In 1962, questionnaires were sent to the colonists on the 1961 list, and seventeen replied. In addition, the writer at various times interviewed six colonists in the valley who were not among those replying to the questionnaire.

54 Mick and Johnson, *Arctic Research: The Current Status of Research,* pp. 131–32.

55 Gazaway, *Facts and Observations,* p. 56, table 20, Farm Sale Prices; also, conversations in 1960 and 1961 with Mr. James Hurley, ARRC manager.

56 *Alaska Monthly Review,* July 1964, p. 2 .The figure appears too high. There are 250- to 300-acre farms in the valley, but most farms are smaller. The figure probably results from adding together all land included in any farm and dividing by only 177, a figure that would exclude some small part-time farms. The Gazaway estimate of 225 farms would give an average farm size of 176 acres, which appears more realistic.

57 Gazaway, *Facts and Observations,* p. 33, table 2. The average 58 percent equity and the $27,500 indebtedness may fail to convey the solid success of some farmers, who, according to the ARRC manager, allowed old colony debts to run on at the low 3 percent interest rate while making substantial investments elsewhere.

58 Edward Higbee, *Farms and Farmers in an Urban Age* (New York: The Twentieth Century Fund, 1963), p. 155, table 1.

59 Ibid., p. 157, table 3.

60 U.S. Bureau of the Census, *Sixteenth Census: 1940, Territory of Alaska, Population: Composition and Characteristics,* table 2, and *U.S. Census of Population, 1960, Alaska,* PC (1) 3A, Number of Inhabitants, tables 6 and 8. The populations for the earlier years are in the 1940 census, those for 1950 in the 1960 census. The region from Palmer to Talkeetna was variously divided in census districts; some manipulation of district populations was required for comparisons. The 1940 census listed separately the "Alaska RR colony, Alaska RR colony community center," and Palmer. Palmer, when originally incorporated, was a first-class city, that is, in Alaska a community having 400 or more permanent inhabitants. A second-class city has 50 or more permanent inhabitants.

61 State of Alaska, Department of Commerce, Division of Tourism and Economic Development *The Incorporated Towns and Cities of Alaska: Financial Data* (Juneau, October 1960), tables 1 and 7.

62 The Tanana Valley Cooperative Association merged with the MVFCA in 1955, but the Matanuska cooperative later dropped its Fairbanks branch.

63 H. P. Gazaway, "Cooperatives in the New State," mimeographed bulletin, Alaska Experiment Station, Extension Service (n.p. [1958]).

64 Rogers, *Future of Alaska,* p. 139; U.S. Department of Commerce, *Income in Alaska,* p. 7.

65 Alaska Department of Agriculture and University of Alaska Agricultural Experiment Station, *Information for Prospective Settlers Concerning Agriculture in Alaska,* (Palmer: September, 1958).

66 U.S. Department of the Interior, Bureau of Land Management, *Establishing a Farm in Alaska* (Washington, D.C.: GPO, 1961).

67 72 *Stat.* 339, Public Law 85-508, 85th Cong., 7 July 1958, sec. 6. Part of the selection, 400,000 acres, was to be from reserved land, that is, the national forests, in areas near established communities.

68 Ibid., sec. 10.

69 Hugh A. Johnson and Harold T. Jorgenson, *The Land Resources of Alaska* (New York: University Publishers, for the Conservation Foundation and the University of Alaska, 1963), pp. 480–81, 494–500.

70 Ibid., pp. 481, 484 (table 39), 443–44 (table 42).

71 *Session Laws of Alaska, 1959,* chap. 169, Alaska Land Act, secs. 1 and 3. For all the activities of the Division of Lands, see State of Alaska, Division of Lands, Department of Natural Resources, *Report, 1963* (Anchorage, 1964).

72 Johnson and Jorgenson, *The Land Resources of Alaska,* pp. 402–03; Bureau of Land Management, *Establishing a Farm in Alaska,* pp. 6–7.

73 Division of Lands, *Report, 1963,* and announcement of sales issued by the local offices of the division.

74 *Fairbanks Daily News-Miner,* 19 and 21 September 1963.

75 "An Open Letter to Planners and Politicians," *Alaskan Agriculturist* 2 (April 1950): 4, denounces the refusal of the territory to establish a school for the six children in one region of the Kenai Peninsula and regards that refusal as a barrier to the supposedly desirable settlement of the area. Years later, settlers northwest of Fairbanks petitioned that their road, normally closed in winter, be kept open

and that buses be operated on two 62-mile round trips daily for the children of nine families (*Fairbanks Daily News-Miner,* 3 September 1964).

76 The comments on the region and the settlers are based on the writer's travel through the area by truck and on foot in the summers of 1960 and 1961 and on conversations with a number of settlers.

77 Louise Potter, *A Study of a Frontier Town in Alaska: Wasilla to 1959* (Hanover, New Hampshire: privately printed, n.d.), pp. 41–46. By 1961 the number of children and the area to be covered had increased so that the longest bus routes required three hours both morning and evening.

78 Similarly, Australians, concentrated in a few urban areas and employed in an industrial and commercial economy, find the real Australia and the explanation of national character in the past and in the great unsettled areas which they, like Alaskans and Canadians, call "the bush." See Russel Ward, *The Australian Legend* (Melbourne: Oxford University Press, 1958), chap. 1; and in chap. 9 see a discussion of Turner and the Australian frontier myth that suggests a number of parallels with Alaska. See also, Denis W. Brogan, "Implications of Modern City Growth," in *The Historian and the City,* ed. Oscar Handlin and John Burchard (Cambridge: M.I.T. Press and Harvard University Press, 1963), pp. 163–64 n., on the conscious preservation of the trappings and lore of an imagined past by the dwellers of suburban Sydney and Adelaide.

79 A book-jacket appreciation by Evengeline R. Atwood of Gerrit Snider, *So Was Alaska* (Anchorage: privately printed, 1961).

80 C. Earl Albrecht, M.D., Commencement Address, University of Alaska, 25 May 1964.

81 Tugwell, *The Battle for Democracy,* p. 157.

Chapter 12

1 Turner, *The Frontier in American History,* p. 296.

2 Frederick Jackson Turner Papers, Henry E. Huntington Library and Art Gallery, TU File Drawers 18B and 19A.

3 Turner Papers, 19A, Arthur Stringer, "If Canada Should Come In," *Hampton's Magazine,* April 1911, pp. 402–13.

4 Stringer, "Red-Plush Pioneers," *Saturday Evening Post* 208 (28 December 1935): 8 ff.; reprinted as "Cold-Storage El Dorado," *Reader's Digest* 38 (March 1936): 29–32.

5 Marcus Lee Hansen and John B. Brebner, *The Mingling of the Canadian and American Peoples* (New Haven: Yale University Press, 1940), chap. 10; Paul F. Sharp, "The American Frontier and the 'Last Best West'," *Agricultural History* 21 (April 1947): 65–75.

6 England, *Colonization of Western Canada;* Charles A. Dawson and R. W. Murchie, *The Settlement of the Peace River Country: A Study of a Pioneer Area,* vol. 6, *Canadian Frontiers of Settlement* (Toronto: Macmillan Co. of Canada, 1934); F. H. Kitto, *The Peace River Country, Canada: Its Resources and Development* (Ottawa: Department of the Interior, 1930); Henry M. Leppard, "The Settlement of the Peace River Country," *Geographical Review* 25 (January 1935): 62–78.

7 Kitto, *Peace River Dountry,* p. 14; Leppard, "Settlement of the Peace River Country," p. 62.

8 England, *Colonization of Western Canada,* chaps. 5, 6, pp. 116–35; England, "Land Settlement in Northern Areas of Western Canada," *Canadian Journal of Economics and Political Science* 1 (November 1935): 578–87; C. A. Dawson, *Group Settlement, Ethnic Communities in Western Canada* (Toronto: Macmillan Co. of Canada, 1936), pp. 377–80.

9 Evon Z. Vogt, *Modern Homesteaders: The Life of a Twentieth-Century Frontier Community* (Cambridge: Harvard University Press, 1955); James West, *Plainville, U.S.A.*; Kenneth MacLeish and Kimball Young, *Culture of a Contemporary Rural Community: Landoff, New Hampshire,* U.S. Department of Agriculture, Bureau of Agricultural Economics, Rural Life Studies no. 3 (Washington, D.C.: GPO, 1942); Walter M. Kollmorgan, *Culture of a Contemporary Rural Community: The Old Order Amish of Lancaster County, Pennsylvania,* U.S. Department of Agriculture, Bureau of Agricultural Economics, Rural Life Studies no. 4 (Washington, D.C.: GPO, 1942); Kollmorgan, "A Reconnaissance of Some Cultural–Agricultural Islands in the South," *Economic Geography* 17 (October 1941): 409–30. On the supposed possibility of creating a million or more such prosperous small farms, see Alvin Johnson, "Homesteads and Subsistence Homesteads," *Yale Review* 24 (March 1935): 433–47.

10 Karel Denis Bicha, "The American Farmer and the Canadian West, 1896–1914: A Revised View," *Agricultural History* 38 (January 1964): 43–46.

11 W. A. Mackintosh, "Some Aspects of a Pioneer Economy," *Canadian Journal of Economics and Political Science* 2 (November 1936): 457–63; R. W. Murchie, *Agricultural Progress on the Prairie Frontier* (Toronto: Macmillan Co. of Canada, 1936).

12 England, *Colonization of Western Canada,* chaps, 11–14; Dawson, *Group Settlement,* pp. 377–80.

13 S. Adler-Rudel, "Moritz Baron Hirsch: Profile of a Great Philanthropist," *Yearbook 7* of the *Leo Baeck Institute of Jews from Germany* (London, 1963), pp. 29–69. Elsewhere the Baron's name is spelled Maurice. Jewish Colonizing Association, *The Jewish Colonizing Association: Its Work in the Argentine Republic, 1891–1941* (Buenos Aires: JCA, [1941]).

14 *Jewish Colonizing Association,* pp. 10–19, 39–46; Jacob Beller, *Jews in Latin America* (New York: Jonathan David Publishers, 1969), pp. 161–69, 190–203.

15 Statistical and other information is taken from ICEM bulletins such as *Review of Achievements* (Geneva: ICEM, 1972) and *Twenty Years Dedicated to the Free Movement of People* (Geneva: ICEM, 1972). *International Migration,* a trilingual quarterly published jointly by the ICEM and the Research Group for European Migration Problems, publishes articles on migration and on land settlement and provides a summary of migration statistics in each issue.

16 Herzl G. Weizmann, "Progress Report on Land Settlement Scheme in the Rhodesias with European Migrants," a mimeographed report for the ICEM at Salisbury, Rhodesia, April 1956, in the files of the ICEM, Geneva, p. 9. Also, Weizmann, "A Preliminary Plan for Immigrant Land Settlement in Latin America," mimeographed, February 1955, ICEM files, Geneva. Similar comments on European agricultural migration were made by Dr. G. Beijer, advisory editor of *International Migration,* at The Hague, 18 April 1972.

17 Eric Hoffer, "The Role of the Undesirables," *Harper's* 205 (December 1952):

79–84, suggests that the migratory workers and tramps in California transients' camps of the 1930s most nearly resembled the old pioneer generation.

18 Charles P. Loomis and Dwight M. Davidson, Jr., *Standards of Living of the Residents of Seven Rural Resettlement Communities,* U.S. Department of Agriculture, FSA and Bureau of Agricultural Economics (Washington, D.C.: GPO, 1938); Charles P. Loomis, *Social Relationships and Institutions in Seven New Rural Communities,* U.S. Department of Agriculture, FSA and Bureau of Agricultural Economics (Washington, D.C.: GPO, 1940).

19 Conkin, *Tomorrow a New World,* pp. 137–38, 140, 334; Loomis, *Social Relationships,* p. 11.

20 Banfield, *Government Project.* See especially the foreword by R. G. Tugwell, pp. 9–13, and the final chapter, "Why They Failed," for comments on the settlers' psychology, their irrational struggles, and the belief that the spirit of cooperation and community organization could be engineered in such a sproject.

Epilogue

1 U.S. Department of Commerce, Bureau of the Census, *1970 Census of Population, Preliminary Reports, Alaska.* In the following discussion the sources of statistical and specific factual information are given, but much of the general view is based on my travel, observation, and general acquaintance with Alaskan conditions.

2 *1970 Census, Alaska,* table 2, Population of Incorporated Places of 1,000 Inhabitants or More.

3 U.S. Department of Commerce, Bureau of the Census, *1969 Census of Agriculture, Part 49, Alaska,* table 1, Farm and Land in Farms, 1935–1969.

4 Ibid., p. vii, summary, highlights, 1969 and 1964.

5 *1970 Census, Alaska,* table 2.

6 Alaska Crop and Livestock Reporting Service, *Alaska Agriculture: Alaska Farm Facts*([Palmer], May 1972), pp. 45–42, "Alaska Equine Census, 1971."

7 *1970 Census, Alaska,* table 2.

8 *1969 Census of Agriculture, Alaska,* p. 3, table 4.

9 "It's Not Kansas—But Alaska!" *Agroborealis* 4 (November 1972): 15–17; *Alaska Agriculture: Alaska Farm Facts,* Crop Summary, p. 16; Cropland Utilization, p. 17.

10 *Fairbanks Daily News-Miner,* Oil and Resources Supplement, 19 June 1973, p. A-4.

11 *1969 Census of Agriculture, Alaska,* p. x, chart 2.

12 "From the Director's Desk," *Agroborealis* 4 (November 1972): 2. Another and typically inflated claim of agricultural opportunity in Alaska appears in Mary Beth Buza, "Agrarian Alaska—There's a Vast Farming Potential in the 49th State," *Alaska Today* 1 (May 1973): 42–43.

13 Arlon R. Tussing, "When the Alaska 'Land Freeze' Ends," pamphlet report for the Federal Field Committee for Development Planning in Alaska, November 1969, pp. 1 ff. Public Land Order 4582, 17 January 1969.

14 Public Land Orders 4962, 8 December 1970; 5081, 17 June 1971; and 5146, 7 December 1971.

15 U.S. Congress, *An Act to Provide for the Settlement of Certain Land Claims of Alaska Natives, and for Other Purposes,* Public Law 92–203, 92nd Cong. 18 December 1971.

16 Public Land Order 5185, 9 March 1972.

17 *Fairbanks Daily News-Miner*, 29 November 1972.

18 Ibid., 2 December 1972.

19 Ibid., 27 June 1972.

20 Ibid., 29 September 1972.

21 Inquest 72-11 (February 1972), District Court, Fourth Judicial District, Fairbanks, Alaska. An Associated Press feature story was widely published in March.

22 The desire is not limited to white Alaskans. Spokesmen for native groups join in demands for oil production and construction of the pipeline and in protesting the possible setting aside of 80 million acres in wilderness and wildlife areas with no provision for multiple use—that is, mining, lumbering, and the like. There has been some opposition to the pipeline from the regional association of interior Indians, Doyon, Incorporated, but that has appeared to be a strategy intended to win guarantees of employment for Indians in pipeline construction and other work related to oil production. *Fairbanks Daily News-Miner*, 24 July 1973, and 25 July 1973.

23 The movement was regularly reported by press, radio, and television as straight news, and in June 1973, the originator of the petition claimed 14,000 signatures and predicted a total of 60,000 or more. *All-Alaska Weekly* (Fairbanks), 22 June 1972, pp. 1, 13.

Selected Bibliography

Bibliographies and Collections

Alaska Railroad (General Offices, Anchorage, Alaska). File 47.5. Correspondence and memoranda on the colonizing efforts of the railroad, 1915–1935, especially in the period 1929–1933.

Alaska Rural Rehabilitation Corporation (ARRC), Palmer, Alaska. The available records of the corporation cover approximately 1935–1945; most later records are in the current files of the corporation. The files cover all aspects of the colony's development and include folders on the individual colonists, original and replacement. There is also an extensive collection of nationwide newspaper items on the colony gathered for the ARRC by a clipping service.

Bercaw, Louise O., and A. M. Hannay. *Bibliography on Land Utilization, 1918–1936*, U.S. Department of Agriculture Miscellaneous Publication no. 284. Washington, D.C.: GPO, 1938.

———; Hannay, A. M.; and Colvin, Esther. *Bibliography on Land Settlement With Particular Reference to Small Holdings and Subsistence Homesteads*, U.S. Department of Agriculture Miscellaneous Publication no. 172. Washington, D.C.: GPO, 1934.

Edwards, Everett E., ed. *References to the Significance of the Frontier in American History*, U.S. Department of Agriculture, Bibliographical Contribution no. 25. Washington, D.C.: GPO, 1935.

Luther C. Hess Papers. University of Alaska Library, College, Alaska. Six folders of materials relating to the Matanuska Colony gathered by the vice-president of the ARRC board of directors.

Sundborg, George, ed. *Bibliography and Abstracts on the Subject of Agriculture in Alaska*, National Resources Planning Board, Region 10. Juneau: 1942.

U.S., Department of the Interior, Bureau of Land Management. *Public Lands Bibliography*. Washington, D.C.: GPO, 1962.

U.S., Library of Congress, Division of Bibliography. *Alaska: A Selected List of Recent References*. Comp. Grace Hadley Fuller, under the direction of Florence S. Hellman. Mimeographed. Washington, D.C.: 1943.

Who's Who in Alaska and Alaska Business Index. Juneau: Tewkesbury Publishers, 1947.

Wickersham, James. *A Bibliography of Alaskan Literature, 1724–1924*, Alaska Agricultural College and School of Mines. Cordova, Alaska: Cordova Times Printers, 1927.

Public Documents

United States

Asch, Berta, and Mangus, A. R. *Farmers on Relief and Rehabilitation.* Works Progress Administration, Division of Social Research. Research monograph 8. Washington, D.C.: GPO, 1937.

Beck, P. G., and Forster, M. C. *Six Rural Problem Areas: Relief—Resources—Rehabilitation.* Federal Emergency Relief Administration, Division of Research, Statistics, and Finance. Research monograph 1. Washington, D.C.: GPO, 1935.

Bell, Earl H.. *Culture of a Contemporary Rural Community: Sublette, Kansas.* U.S. Department of Agriculture, Bureau of Agricultural Economics, Rural Life Studies no. 2. Washington, D.C.: GPO, 1942.

Black, John D., and Gray, L. C. *Land Settlement and Colonization in the Great Lake States.* U.S. Department of Agriculture, with the Agricultural Experiment Station of the University of Minnesota. Department bulletin no. 1295. Washington, D.C.: GPO, 1925.

Chubbuck, Levi. *Possible Agricultural Development in Alaska.* U.S. Department of Agriculture bulletin no. 50. Washington, D.C.: GPO, 1914.

Conrad, Sherman. "The Matanuska Valley Colonization Project: Rural Rehabilitation in Alaska." *Monthly Report of the Federal Emergency Relief Administration.* April, 1936, pp. 30–37.

Gaer, Joseph. *Toward Farm Security: The Problem of Rural Poverty and the Farm Security Administration.* Washington, D.C.: GPO, 1941.

Georgeson, C. C. *Information for Prospective Settlers in Alaska.* Alaska Agricultural Experiment Stations circular no. 1. U.S. Department of Agriculture. Washington, D.C.: GPO, 1916. (Revised editions by Georgeson in 1917, 1923, and by others in 1930, 1937, 1941, and 1958.)

———. *Suggestions to Pioneer Farmers in Alaska.* Alaska Agricultural Experiment Stations, bulletin no. 1. Washington, D.C.: GPO, 1902.

Hartman, William A., and Black, John D. *Economic Aspects of Land Settlement in the Cut-Over Region of the Great Lakes States.* U.S. Department of Agriculture circular no. 160. Washington, D.C.: GPO, 1931.

Henderson, Bertha. *Farm Lands Available for Settlement.* Farmers' bulletin no. 1271, U.S. Department of Agriculture. Washington, D.C.: GPO, 1922.

Hill, George W., and Smith, Ronald A. *Man in the "Cut-Over": A Study of Family-Farm Resources in Northern Wisconsin.* University of Wisconsin, Agricultural Experiment Station, cooperating with Rural Survey Section, WPA. Research Bulletin 139. Madison, 1941.

Holt, John B. *An Analysis of Methods and Criteria Used in Selecting Families for Colonization Projects.* U.S. Department of Agriculture, Farm Security Administration and Bureau of Agricultural Economics. Social research report no. 1. Washington, D.C.: GPO, 1937.

Intergovernmental Committee for European Migration. *Review of Achievements*. Geneva, Switzerland, 1972.

Intergovernmental Committee for European Migration. *Twenty Years Dedicated to the Free Movement of People*. Geneva, Switzerland, 1972.

Jasny, Marie. *Family Selection on a Federal Irrigation Project—Tule Lake Division of the Klamath Irrigation Project, Oregon–California*. U.S. Department of Agriculture, Farm Security Administration and Bureau of Agricultural Economics. Social research report no. 5. Washington, D.C.: GPO, 1938.

Johnson, Hugh A., and Calhoun, Wendell. *Markets for the Products of Alaska Cropland*. U.S. Department of Agriculture, Bureau of Agricultural Economics and the Alaska Agricultural Experiment Station. Washington, D.C.: GPO, 1950.

Johnson, Sherman E. *Changes in American Farming*. Bureau of Agricultural Economics miscellaneous publication no. 707, U.S. Department of Agriculture. Washington, D.C.: GPO, 1949.

Johnson, V. Webster, Henderson, Sidney, and Marshall, James H. *A Land Program for Forest County, Wisconsin*. Technical bulletin no. 687, U.S. Department of Agriculture. Washington, D.C.: GPO, 1939.

Jones, Ronald W., and Goodsell, Wylie D. *Typical Family-Operated Farms, 1930–1945*. U.S. Department of Agriculture, Bureau of Agricultural Economics. Washington, D.C.: GPO, 1946.

Kellogg, Charles E., and Nygard, Iver J. *Exploratory Study of the Principal Soil Groups of Alaska*. Agricultural monograph no. 7, U.S. Department of Agriculture. Washington, D.C.: GPO, 1951.

Kirkpatrick, E. L.. *Analysis of 70,000 Rural Rehabilitation Families*. U.S. Department of Agriculture, Farm Security Administration and the Bureau of Agricultural Economics. Social research report no. 9. Washington, D.C.: GPO, 1938.

Kollmorgan, Walter M. *Culture of a Contemporary Rural Community: The Old Order Amish of Lancaster County, Pennsylvania*. U.S. Department of Agriculture, Bureau of Agricultural Economics, Rural Life Studies no. 4. Washington, D.C.: GPO, 1942.

Kraemer, Erich. *Land Settlement Technique Abroad: Financing of Full-Time Farming Settlement in England, Germany, Denmark, Norway, and Sweden*. Resettlement Administration, Land Policy circular supplement. Washington, D.C.: GPO, 1935.

———. *Land Settlement Technique Abroad: Organization of Activities in England, Germany, and Italy*. Resettlement Administration, Land Policy circular supplement. Washington, D.C.: GPO, 1935.

———. *Land Settlement Technique Abroad: Selection of Settlers in Agricultural Settlement of Several European Countries*. Resettlement Administration, Land-Use Planning Publication no. 5. Washington, D.C.: GPO, 1936.

Lively, C. E., and Taeuber, Conrad. *Rural Migration in the United States*. Works

Progress Administration. Research monograph 19. Washington, D.C.: GPO, 1939.

Loomis, Charles P. *Social Relationships and Institutions in Seven New Rural Communities.* U.S. Department of Agriculture, Farm Security Administration and the Bureau of Agricultural Economics. Social research report no. 18. Washington, D.C.: GPO, 1940.

———, and Davidson, Dwight M., Jr. *Standards of Living of the Residents of Seven Rural Resettlement Communities.* U.S. Department of Agriculture, Farm Security Administration and Bureau of Agricultural Economics. Washington, D.C.: GPO, 1938.

———; Lister, Joseph J; and Davidson, Dwight M., Jr. *Standards of Living in the Great Lakes Cut-Over Area.* U.S. Department of Agriculture, Farm Security Administration and the Bureau of Agricultural Economics. Social research report no. 13. Washington, D.C.: GPO, 1938.

Lord, Russell, and Johnstone, Paul H., eds. *A Place on Earth: A Critical Appraisal of Subsistence Homesteads.* U.S. Department of Agriculture, Bureau of Agricultural Economics. Washington, D.C.: GPO, 1942.

MacLeish, Kenneth, and Young, Kimball. *Culture of a Contemporary Rural Community: Landoff, New Hampshire.* U.S. Department of Agriculture, Bureau of Agricultural Economics, Rural Life Studies no. 3. Washington, D.C.: GPO, 1942.

Mangus, A. R. *Changing Aspects of Rural Relief.* Works Progress Administration, Division of Social Research. Research monograph 14. Washington, D.C.: GPO, 1938.

Maris, Paul V. *The Land Is Mine: From Tenancy to Family Farm Ownership.* Farmers Home Administration, U.S. Department of Agriculture, Agricultural monograph no. 8. Washington, D.C.: GPO, 1950.

Mimms, O. L.; Paschal, J. L.; and Fuhriman, W. U. *Some Economic Aspects of Farming in Alaska, with Chief Attention to the Matanuska Valley.* U.S. Department of Agriculture, Bureau of Agricultural Economics and the Alaska Agricultural Experiment Station. Washington, D.C.: GPO, 1950.

Moe, Edward O., and Taylor, Carl C. *Culture of a Contemporary Rural Community: Irwin, Iowa.* U.S. Department of Agriculture, Bureau of Agricultural Economics, Rural Life Studies no. 5. Washington, D.C.: GPO, 1942.

Rockie, William A. *Physical Land Conditions in the Matanuska Valley, Alaska.* U.S. Department of Agriculture, Soil Conservation Service. Washington, D.C.: GPO, 1946.

Stone, Kirk H. "Alaska Group Settlement: The Matanuska Valley Colony." Bureau of Land Management. Mimeographed. Washington, D.C.: GPO, 1950. (This is a somewhat abridged version of Stone's 1949 Ph.D. dissertation.)

Taylor, Carl C.; Wheeler, Helen W.; and Kirkpatrick, E. L. *Disadvantaged*

Classes in American Agriculture. U.S. Department of Agriculture, Farm Security Administration and Bureau of Agricultural Economics, Social Science report 8. Washington, D.C.: GPO, 1938.

U.S., Bureau of the Census. *Census of Agriculture, 1969*, pt. 49, *Alaska.*

———. *Fourteenth Census of the United States: 1920.*

———. *Fifteenth Census of the United States: 1930.*

———. *Sixteenth Census of the United States: 1940.*

———. *Seventeenth Census of the United States: 1950.*

———. *Eighteenth Census of the United States: 1960.*

———. *Nineteenth Census of the United States: 1970.*

U.S., Congress, House. *Alaska: A Reconnaissance Report on the Potential Development of Water Resources in the Territory of Alaska for Irrigation, Power Production, and Other Beneficial Uses.* 82nd Cong., 1st sess., 1952, House Document 197. Washington, D.C.: GPO, 1952.

———. *Alaska Veterans' Homesteading Act of 1947, Hearings Before the Subcommittee on Public Lands of the Committee on Public Lands*, 80th Cong., 1st sess. Washington, D.C.: GPO, 1947.

———. *Hearings Before the Subcommittee on Territorial and Insular Possessions of the Committee on Public Lands, August 30–September 12, 1947.* 80th Cong., 1st sess. Washington, D.C.: GPO, 1947.

———. *Transport Requirements for the Growth of Northwest North America: Final Report of the Alaska International Rail and Highway Commission.* 3 vols. 87th Cong., 1st sess., 1961, House Document No. 176. Washington, D.C.: GPO, 1961.

U.S., Congress, Senate. *The Resettlement Administration Program: Report by the Administrator of the Resettlement Administration.* Senate Document 213; 74th Cong., 2d sess. Washington, D.C.: GPO, 1936.

———. *Settlement and Development of Alaska: Hearings Before a Subcommittee of the Committee on Territories and Insular Affairs, May 13, 15, 18, 1940.* 76th Cong., 3d sess. Washington, D.C.: GPO, 1940.

U.S., Department of Agriculture. *Climate and Man: Yearbook of Agriculture, 1941.* Washington, D.C.: GPO, 1941.

———. *Farmers in a Changing World: Yearbook of Agriculture, 1940.* Washington, D.C.: GPO, 1940.

———. *Farm Opportunities in the United States: Outlook, Problems, Policies.* Land Settlement Work Group, Interbureau Committee on Postwar Agricultural Problems. Washington, D.C.: GPO, 1945.

———. *Report on Exploratory Investigations of Agricultural Problems in Alaska.* Agricultural Research Administration, Miscellaneous Publication no. 700. Washington, D.C.: GPO, 1949.

———. *A Report to Congress on Agriculture in Alaska*, including reports by W. H. Evans, B. Killin, and S. Jackson. Office of Experiment Stations, Bulletin no. 48. Washington, D.C.: GPO, 1898.

———. *Soils and Men: Yearbook of Agriculture, 1938.* Washington, D.C.: GPO, 1938.

———. *State Land Settlement Problems and Policies in the United States.* Technical Bulletin no. 357. Washington, D.C.: GPO, 1933.

U.S., Department of Commerce. *Forecasts of the Population of the United States,* prepared by P. K. Whelpton. Washington, D.C.: GPO, 1947.

———. *Historical Statistics of the United States, Colonial Times to 1957.* Washington, D.C.: GPO, 1960.

———. *Statistical Abstract of the United States, 1960.* Washington, D.C.: GPO, 1960.

———. *Statistical Abstract of the United States, 1964.* Washington, D.C.: GPO, 1964.

———. Office of Business Economics. *Income in Alaska.* Washington, D.C.: GPO, 1960.

———, Weather Bureau. *The Climate of the Matanuska Valley,* prepared by Robert F. Dale. Technical Paper no. 27. Washington, D.C.: GPO, 1956.

U.S., Department of the Interior. *Alaska.* Washington, D.C.: GPO, 1945.

———. *Annual Report of the Governor of Alaska to the Secretary of the Interior.* Washington, D.C.: GPO, 1928–58.

———. *Answers to Questions by Servicemen about Land Settlement in Alaska.* Pamphlet prepared by General Land Office. Washington, D.C.: GPO, 1944.

———. *The Problem of Alaskan Development.* Washington, D.C.: GPO, 1940.

———. *Report of the Secretary of the Interior.* Washington, D.C.: GPO, 1896–1902, 1935–45.

———. Bureau of Land Management. *Agricultural Settlement Opportunities in Alaska: Anchorage Area.* Washington, D.C.: GPO, 1947.

———. Bureau of Land Management. *Areas Suitable for Group Settlement in Alaska.* Washington, D.C.: GPO, 1948.

———. Bureau of Land Management. *Establishing a Farm in Alaska.* Washington, D.C.: GPO, 1961.

———. Bureau of Land Management. *Homesteads.* Washington, D.C.: GPO, 1962.

———. Bureau of Land Management. *Information Relative to the Use and Disposal of Public Lands and Resources in Alaska.* Washington, D.C.: GPO, 1957.

———. Bureau of Land Management. *Orders Affecting Public Lands in Alaska.* Washington, D.C.: GPO, 1959.

———. Bureau of Land Management. *Papers Presented at the Seminars on Alaska, February 2, 3, 6, 7, 1950.* Mimeographed. Washington, D.C.: GPO, 1950.

———. Bureau of Land Management. *Statistical Appendix to the Annual Report of the Director, Bureau of Land Management, 1960.* Washington, D.C.: GPO, 1961.

———. General Land Office. *Information, Laws, and Regulations Relating to Public Lands in the Territory of Alaska.* Circular no. 491. Washington, D.C.: GPO, 1928.

U.S., Joint Economic Committee, United States and Canada. The North Pacific Planning Project, *North Pacific Study.* 4 vols., 15 secs. Mimeographed. Prepared by the staff of Region X, National Resources Planning Board, Portland, Oreg., 1944.

U.S., National Planning Board. *Final Report, 1933–1934.* Washington, D.C.: GPO, 1934.

U.S., National Resources Board. *A Report on National Planning and Public Works.* Washington, D.C.: GPO, 1934.

U.S., National Resources Committee. *The Northern Lake States Region.* Washington, D.C.: GPO, 1939.

———. *The Problems of a Changing Population.* Washington, D.C.: GPO, 1938.

———. *Regional Planning: Part VII, Alaska—Its Resources and Development.* Washington, D.C.: GPO, 1938.

U.S., National Resources Planning Board. *Estimates of Future Population of the United States.* Prepared by Warren A. Thompson and P. K. Whelpton. Washington, D.C.: GPO, 1943.

———. *Post War Economic Development of Alaska: Report of the Alaska Regional Planning Office, Region 10.* Juneau, 1942.

Webb, John N., and Brown, Malcom. *Migrant Families.* Works Progress Administration, Research Monograph 18. Washington, D.C.: GPO, 1938.

Westbrook, Lawrence. "Rural–Industrial Communities for Stranded Families: An Outline of Suggested Procedures for the Guidance of State and County Relief Administrations and Cooperating Public Agencies," Federal Emergency Relief Administration, Division of Rural Rehabilitation and Stranded Populations [1934]. On the cover sheet is a notice, "This copy is for official consideration only. Not approved for general use or distribution."

Wynne, Waller. *Culture of a Contemporary Rural Community: Harmony, Georgia.* U.S. Department of Agriculture, Bureau of Agricultural Economics, Rural Life Studies no. 6. Washington, D.C.: GPO, 1943.

Alaska

Alaska Planning Council. *General Information Regarding Alaska.* Juneau, 1941.

———. *A Study of the "Slattery Plan" for Alaska's Development.* Juneau, 1940.

Cooley, Richard A. *Fairbanks, Alaska: A Survey of Progress.* Alaska Development Board. Juneau, 1954.

Gasser, George W. *Information for the Alaska Farmer–Settler.* Alaska Development Board, Circular no. 1. Juneau, 1946.

———. *The Matanuska Valley.* Alaska Development Board, Circular no. 3. Juneau, 1946.

———. *The Tanana Valley*. Alaska Development Board, Circular no. 2. Juneau, 1946.

Gazaway, H. P. *Facts and Observations on Agricultural Development in Alaska*. Prepared for the Alaska Division of Lands, Department of Natural Resources. [Anchorage], 1960.

Johnson, Hugh A., and Coffman, Robert J. *Land Occupancy, Ownership and Use on Homesteads in the Kenai Peninsula*. Bulletin 21, Alaska Agricultural Experiment Station. Palmer, 1956.

———, and Irwin, Don L. *The Position of Agriculture in Alaska's Current Economy*. University of Alaska Agricultural Experiment Station and the U.S. Department of Agriculture, Agricultural Research Administration, Special Report no. 1. Palmer, 1953.

Riley, Burke. *Federal Land Policy and Its Effect on Development and Settlement in Alaska*. Alaska Development Board. Juneau, 1948.

Rogers, George W., and Cooley, Richard A. *Alaska's Population and Economy: Regional Growth, Development and Future Outlook*. Vol. 1, *Analysis*. Vol. 2, *Statistical Handbook*. Division of State Planning, Office of the Governor. Juneau, 1962.

State of Alaska, Department of Commerce, Division of Tourism and Economic Development. *The Incorporated Towns and Cities of Alaska: Financial Data*. Juneau, 1960.

———, Department of Natural Resources. *Annual Report of the Division of Lands, 1963*. [Anchorage], 1963.

———, University of Alaska Agricultural Experiment Station. *Alaska Farm Facts*. Prepared in cooperation with the U.S. Department of Agriculture, Agricultural Research Service. Palmer, 1961.

———, University of Alaska Agricultural Experiment Station. *Farm and Consumer Research in Alaska*. Prepared in cooperation with the U.S. Department of Agriculture, Agricultural Research Service. Palmer, 1959.

Territory of Alaska. *Biennial Report of the Alaska Resource Development Board, 1955–1957*. Juneau, 1957.

———, Department of Agriculture. *Information for Prospective Settlers Concerning Agriculture in Alaska*. Prepared jointly with the University of Alaska Agricultural Experiment Station. Palmer, 1958.

Canada

Canada. *Final Report of the Royal Commission on Canada's Economic Prospects*. Ottawa, 1957.

Canada. *The Northwest Territories: Its Economic Prospects*. A brief to the Royal Commission on Canada's Economic Prospects, by R. G. Robertson, Commissioner, Northwest Territories. Ottawa, 1955.

Canada, Department of the Interior. *The Yukon Territory: Its Resources and Development*. Ottawa, 1916.

Canada, Department of Mines and Resources. *The Northwest Territories: Administration, Resources, and Development.* Ottawa, 1943.

Canada, Dominion Experimental Station, Fort Simpson, Northwest Territories. *Progress Report, 1947–1953.* Ottawa, 1953.

Canada, Dominion Experimental Station, Whitehorse, Yukon Territory. *Progress Report, 1945–1952.* Ottawa, 1952.

Canada, North Pacific Planning Project, Charles Camsell, director. *Canada's New Northwest.* 1947.

Kitto, F. H. *The Peace River Country, Canada: Its Resources and Opportunities.* Department of the Interior. Ottawa, 1930.

Lothian, W. F. *Yukon Territory.* Bureau of Northwest Territories and Yukon Affairs. Ottawa, 1947.

Books and Periodicals

Adams, John Q. "This Is Matanuska." *Alaska Sportsman* 4, pt. 1 (April, 1938): 16–18, 24; pt. 2 (May, 1938): 14–15, 20–21, 25–26.

"Alaskan Colonization," *Literary Digest* 119 (June 1, 1935): 48.

Albright, W. D. "An Economic Land-Settlement Policy." *Canadian Journal of Economics and Political Science* 2 (November, 1936): 550–55.

Alexander, Will W. "Rural Resettlement." *Southern Review* 1 (1936): 528–39.

Allin, Bushrod W. "Migration Required for Best Land Use." *Journal of Farm Economics* 18 (August, 1936): 493–99.

Anderson, Clifford B. "The Metamorphosis of American Agrarian Idealism in the 1920's and 1930's." *Agricultural History* 35 (October, 1961): 182–88.

Baker, O. E. "Rural and Urban Distribution of the Population in the United States." *The Annals* 188 (November, 1936): 264–79.

———. "Rural–Urban Migration and the National Welfare." *Annals of the Association of American Geographers* 33 (June, 1933): 59–126.

———; Borsodi, Ralph; and Wilson, M. L. *Agriculture in Modern Life.* New York: Harper and Brothers, 1939.

Banfield, Edward C. *Government Project.* Glencoe, Ill.: The Free Press, 1951.

Beard, Charles A. "The Frontier in American History." (Review) *The New Republic* 25 (February 16, 1921): 349–50.

Benson, Lee. *Turner and Beard: American Historical Writing Reconsidered.* Glencoe, Ill.: The Free Press, 1960.

Bernhardt, Joshua. *The Alaska Engineering Commission.* Institute for Government Research, Service Monographs of the United States Government no. 4. New York: D. Appleton and Co., 1922.

Bicha, Karel Denis. "The American Farmer and the Canadian West, 1896–1914: A Revised View." *Agricultural History* 38 (January, 1964): 43–46.

Black, John D. "Agricultural Population in Relation to Agricultural Resources." *The Annals* 188 (November, 1936): 205–17.

Bladen, V. W., ed. *Canadian Population and Northern Colonization.* Symposium presented to the Royal Society of Canada. 1961. Toronto: University of Toronto Press, 1962.

Bogue, Allan G. "Social Theory and the Pioneer." *Agricultural History* 34 (January, 1960): 21–34.

Bowes, Gordon E., ed. *Peace River Chronicles.* Vancouver: Prescott Publishing Co., 1963.

Bowman, Isaiah, ed. *Limits of Land Settlement: A Report on Present-Day Possibilities.* New York: Council on Foreign Relations, 1937.

———. *The Pioneer Fringe.* Special Publication no. 13. New York: American Geographical Society, 1931.

———. "The Pioneering Process." *Science* 75 (May 20, 1932): 521–28.

Brooks, Alfred H. *Blazing Alaska's Trails.* Ed. Burton L. Fryxell. University of Alaska and the Arctic Institute of North America, 1953.

———. "The Value of Alaska." *The Geographical Review* 15 (January 1925): 25–50.

Brunner, Edmund de S., and Lorge, Irving. *Rural Trends in Depression Years: A Survey of Village-Centered Agricultural Communities, 1930–1936.* New York: Columbia University Press, 1937.

Burnette, O. Lawrence, Jr., ed. *Wisconsin Witness to Frederick Jackson Turner: A Collection of Essays on the Historian and the Thesis.* Madison: State Historical Society of Wisconsin, 1961.

Caldwell, J. B. *Introducing Alaska.* New York: G. P. Putnam's Sons, 1947.

"The Call of the Land." *Commonweal* 20 (May 25, 1934): 85–86.

Campbell, J. M. "In the Country." *Commonweal* 15 (February 3, 1932): 378–80.

Careless, J. M. "Frontierism, Metropolitanism, and Canadian History." *Canadian Historical Review* 35 (March, 1954): 1–21.

Carstensen, Vernon, ed. *The Public Lands: Studies in the History of the Public Domain.* Madison: University of Wisconsin Press, 1963.

Chicanot, E. L. "Canada's Back-to-the-Land Movement." *Empire Review* 36 (1936): 159–64.

Clark, Henry W. "Resettlement of the Last Frontier." *Commonweal* 28 (July 1, 1938): 266–68.

Clark, Noble, *What Chance Has a City Man on a Wisconsin Farm?* Madison: University of Wisconsin, Extension Service, 1932.

Clawson, Marion; Held, R. Burnell; and Stoddard, Charles H. *Land for the Future.* Baltimore: The Johns Hopkins Press for Resources for the Future, 1960.

Colvin, O'Carroll. "Factory Hands in the Wilderness: Alaska's '59ers." *The Nation* 189 (September 26, 1959): 166–69.

Conkin, Paul K. *Tomorrow a New World: The New Deal Community Program.* Ithaca: Cornell University Press, 1959.

Courtney, William B. "Pilgrims' Progress: Matanuska Valley Project." *Collier's* 101 (May 7, 1938): 12.

Curti, Merle. "Intellectuals and Other People." *American Historical Review* 70 (January, 1955): 259–82.

———. *Probing Our Past.* New York: Harper and Brothers, 1955.

———; Daniel, Robert; Livermore, Shaw, Jr.; Van Hise, Joseph; and W. Curti, Margaret. *The Making of an American Community: A Case Study of Democracy in a Frontier County.* Stanford, Calif.: Stanford University Press, 1959.

Curtiss, Philip. "They Are Moving to the Country." *Harper's Magazine* 171 (June, 1935): 67–79.

Davis, Charles M. "The Cities and Towns of the High Plains of Michigan." *Geographical Review* 28 (October, 1938): 664–73.

Davis, Darrell H. "The Finland Community, Minnesota." *Geographical Review* 25 (July, 1935): 382–94.

Davis, Kingsley. "The Unpredicted Pattern of Population Change." *The Annals* 305 (May, 1956): 53–159.

Dawson, C. A., *Group Settlement, Ethnic Communities in Western Canada.* Vol. 7, *Canadian Frontiers of Settlement,* ed. W. A. Mackintosh and W. L. G. Joerg. Toronto: Macmillan Co. of Canada, 1936.

———, ed. *The New North-West.* Toronto: University of Toronto Press, 1947.

———, and Murchie, R. W. *The Settlement of the Peace River Country: A Study of a Pioneer Area.* Vol. 6, *Canadian Frontiers of Settlement,* ed. W. A. Mackintosh and W. L. G. Joerg. Toronto: Macmillan Co. of Canada, 1934.

Doherty, Beka, and Hepner, Arthur. "Alaska: Last American Frontier," *Foreign Policy Reports* 18 (December 1, 1942): 238–47.

Duggan, Raymond P. *A Federal Resettlement Project: Granger Homesteads.* School of Social Work, Catholic University of America, Monograph no. 1. Washington, D.C.: Catholic University of America, 1937.

Duryee, William B. *A Living from the Land: How to Make a Small Farm Support You.* Cleveland: World Publishing Co., 1934.

Edmonton Chamber of Commerce. *Northern Development Conference, Proceedings.* Edmonton: Chamber of Commerce, 1957.

Edwards, Everett E., ed. *The Early Writings of Frederick Jackson Turner.* Madison: University of Wisconsin Press, 1938.

England, Robert. *The Colonization of Western Canada: A Study of Contemporary Land Settlement (1896–1934).* London: P. S. King and Son, Ltd., 1936.

———. "Land Settlement in the Northern Areas of Western Canada (1925–1935)." *Canadian Journal of Economics and Political Science* 1 (November, 1935): 578–87.

Ezekiel, Mordecai. "Population and Unemployment." *The Annals* 188 (November, 1936): 230–42.

Fisher, Churchill. "Their Sun Still Rises." *Alaska Sportsman* 4 (July, 1938): 10–11, 25–26.

Fitch, Edward M. *The Alaska Railroad.* New York: Frederick A. Praeger Publishers, 1967.

Fitzpatrick, Brian. "The Big Man's Frontier and Australian Farming." *Agricultural History* 21 (January, 1947): 8–12.

Ford, Corey, and MacBain, Alastair. "Uncle Sam's Icebox." *Collier's* 107 (January 4, 1941): 28–30, 40.

Forsyth, W. D. *The Myth of Open Spaces: Australian, British and World Trends of Population and Migration.* Melbourne: Melbourne University Press, 1956.

"Fortune Quarterly Survey." *Fortune* 18 (July, 1938): 80, and 19 (April, 1939): 102.

"Forty Acres in Alaskan Valley." *Literary Digest* 121 (May 9, 1936): 8–9.

Freidel, Frank. *Franklin D. Roosevelt*, vol. 1, *The Apprenticeship.* Boston: Little, Brown & Co., 1952.

"Frontier Frustration." *Commonweal* 29 (April 21, 1939): 704–05.

Fusfeld, Daniel R. *The Economic Thought of Franklin D. Roosevelt and the Origins of the New Deal.* New York: Columbia University Press, 1956.

Gallaher, Art, Jr. *Plainville Fifteen Years Later.* New York: Columbia University Press, 1961.

Gard, Wayne. "America's Desolate Acres." *Current History* 42 (June, 1935): 259–64.

Gast, Ross H. "The Subsistence Homesteads Program." *The Annals* 175 (September, 1934): 240–43.

Georgeson, C. C. "Agricultural Capacity of Alaska: What Population Can the Territory Support?" *National Geographic Magazine* 20 (July, 1909): 676–79.

———. "The Possibilities of Alaska." *National Geographic Magazine* 13 (March, 1902): 81–85.

Gill, Corrington. "A Study of the Three Million Families on Relief in October, 1935." *The Annals* 176 (November, 1934): 25–36.

Gilman, William. "Colonists for Alaska." *Yale Review* 34 (Summer, 1945): 666–82.

Goodrich, Carter. "Internal Migration and Economic Opportunity." *The Annals* 138 (November, 1936): 260–63.

———, and Davison, Sol. "The Frontier as Safety Valve: A Rejoinder." *Political Science Quarterly* 53 (June, 1938): 268–71.

———; Allin, Bushrod W.; Thornthwaite, C. Warren; Brunck, Hermann K.; Tryon, Frederick G.; Creamer, Daniel B.; Vance, Rupert B.; Hayes, Marion; and others. *Migration and Economic Opportunity: The Report of the Study of Population Redistribution.* Philadelphia: University of Pennsylvania Press, 1936.

Grattan, C. Hartley. "Postwar Migration: A Mirage." *Harper's Magazine* 188 (December, 1943): 24–33.

Gray, Lewis C. "The Resettlement Land Program." *American Forests* 42 (August, 1936): 347–49.

———. "The Social and Economic Implications of the National Land Program." *Journal of Farm Economics* 18 (May, 1936): 257–73.

Gressley, Gene M. "Colonialism: A Western Complaint." *Pacific Northwest Quarterly* 54 (January, 1963): 1–8.

———. "The Turner Thesis—A Problem in Historiography." *Agricultural History* 32 (October, 1958): 227–49.

Gruening, Ernest. "Go North, Young Man." *Reader's Digest* 44 (January, 1944): 53–57.

———. *The State of Alaska.* New York: Random House, 1954.

Gwin, J. Blaine. "Subsistence Homesteads." *Social Forces* 12 (May, 1934): 522–25.

Hansen, Alvin H. *Business Cycles and National Income.* New York: W. W. Norton and Co., 1951.

———. "Economic Progress and Declining Population Growth." *American Economic Review* 29 (March, 1939): 1–15.

———. *Fiscal Policy and Business Cycles.* New York: W. W. Norton and Co., 1941.

———. *Full Recovery or Stagnation?* New York: W. W. Norton and Co., 1938.

Hartman, William A. "State Policies in Regulating Land Settlement Activities." *Journal of Farm Economics* 13 (1931): 259–69.

Heaton, Herbert. "Migration and Cheap Land—The End of Two Chapters." *The Sociological Review* 26 (July, 1934): 231–48.

Helgeson, Arlan. *Farms in the Cutover: Agricultural Settlement in Northern Wisconsin.* Madison: State Historical Society of Wisconsin, University of Wisconsin Press, 1962.

Herrick, John. "Back on the Land." *Scientific American* 153 (July, 1935): 24–26.

Hillshire, Herbert H. "Vision of Utopia Revised at Matanuska." *Nation's Business* 26 (November, 1938): 17–18, 54.

Hilscher, Herbert H. "Alaska—Little Siberia." *Alaska Life* 3 (June, 1940): 19, 21.

———, and Hilscher, Miriam. *Alaska, U.S.A.* Boston: Little, Brown & Co., 1959.

Holt, John R. "Our Last Frontier—Alaska." *Quartermaster Review* 14 (May–June, 1935): 19–26.

Hopkins, Harry L. "Hope for the Millions." *Today* 4 (May 4, 1935): 3–4, 20.

Huber, Louis R. "What Price Frontier?" *Alaska Life* 4 (February, 1941): 4–5, 15.

Hulley, Clarence C. "A Historical Survey of the Matanuska Valley Settlement in Alaska." *Pacific Northwest Quarterly* 40 (October, 1949): 327–40.

Ickes, Harold L. "Let's Open Up Alaska!" *This Week* (February 3, 1946); 4–5, 18.

Irwin, Don L. "Agriculture in the Matanuska Valley of Alaska." *The Scientific Monthly* 60 (March, 1945): 203–12.

Jarrett, Henry, ed. *Perspectives on Conservation: Essays on America's Natural Resources.* Baltimore: The Johns Hopkins Press, 1958.

Jensen, Merrill, ed. *Regionalism in America.* Madison: University of Wisconsin Press, 1952.

Jesness, Oscar B.; Nowell, Reynolds I.; and associates. *A Program for Land Use in Northern Minnesota: A Type Study in Land Utilization.* Minneapolis: University of Minnesota Press, 1935.

Joerg, W. L. G., ed. *Pioneer Settlement.* Special Publication no. 14. New York: American Geographical Society, 1932.

Johnson, Alvin. "Homesteads and Subsistence Homesteads." *Yale Review* 24 (March, 1935): 433–47.

Johnson, E. C., and Manny, T. B. "Part-Time Farming in the Duluth Area." Farm Business Notes no. 131. Minneapolis: University of Minnesota Agricultural Extension Service, 1933.

Johnson, Hugh A., and Jorgenson, Harold T. *The Land Resources of Alaska.* New York: University Publishers for the University of Alaska, 1963.

———, and Stanton, Keith L. *Matanuska Valley Memoir: The Story of How One Alaskan Community Developed.* Palmer, Alaska: University of Alaska Experiment Station, 1955).

Johnson, Sherman E.; Davidson, Robert D.; and Bierman, Russell W. "Land Settlement in the United States." *International Journal of Agrarian Affairs* 1 (September, 1953): 64–76.

Johnsone, Paul H. "Somewhere Else." *Land Policy Review* 2 (November–December, 1939): 1–9.

Kains, M. G. *Five Acres and Independence.* New York: Greenberg Publishers, 1935.

Kellogg, Charles E. "Soils of Alaska." *Proceedings, Alaska Science Conference of the National Academy of Sciences, Washington, D.C., November, 1950.* Bulletin no. 122, National Research Council (April, 1951): 37–38.

Kirkpatrick, E. L. *Needed Standards of Living for Rural Resettlement.* Resettlement Administration, Wisconsin Rural Rehabilitation Division. Madison, 1936.

Kolehmeinen, John I., and Hill, George W. *Haven in the Woods: The Story of the Finns in Wisconsin.* Madison: State Historical Society of Wisconsin, 1965.

Kollmorgan, Walter M. "A Reconnaissance of Some Cultural–Agricultural Islands in the South." *Economic Geography* 17 (October, 1941): 409–30.

"Land Settlement for Unemployed." *Monthly Labor Review* 35 (September, 1932): 512–23.

Lantis, Margaret. "The Reindeer Industry in Alaska." *Arctic* 3 (April, 1950): 27–44.

Leitzell, Ted. "Cabbages and Commissars: Matanuska Valley." *American Mercury* 44 (January, 1939): 1–11.

Leppard, Henry M. "The Settlement of the Peace River Country." *The Geographical Review* 25 (January, 1935): 62–78.

Loehr, Rodney C. "Self-Sufficiency on the Farm." *Agricultural History* 26 (April, 1952): 37–41.

Lord, Russell. *The Agrarian Revival: A Study of Agricultural Extension.* New York: American Association for Adult Education, 1939.

———. "Back-to-the-Farm?" *Forum* 89 (February, 1933): 97–103.

———. *The Wallaces of Iowa.* Boston: Houghton Mifflin Co., 1947.

Lovett, Robert Morss. "Reply to 'Should We Settle Alaska?'" *The New Republic* 102 (January 8, 1940): 54.

"The Low-Down Truth of Alaska." *Fairbanks Daily News-Miner,* special annual edition. July 1, 1923.

"Lure of the Land." *The Nation* 131 (October 8, 1930): 366.

McConnell, Grant. *The Decline of Agrarian Democracy.* Berkeley and Los Angeles: University of California Press, 1953.

McCormick, Elsie. "A Planned Economy Is Put to the Test." *New York Times Magazine* (September 8, 1935): 10, 19.

Mackintosh, W.A. "Some Aspects of a Pioneer Economy. *Canadian Journal of Economics and Political Science* 2 (November, 1936): 457–63.

McMillen, Wheeler. "Back-to-the-Land Fallacies." *Outlook* 160 (January 20, 1932): 81–82.

Maddox, James G. "Suggestions for a National Program of Rural Rehabilitation and Relief." *Journal of Farm Economics* 21 (November, 1939): 881–96.

Making the Most of Taylor County Land. University of Wisconsin, College of Agriculture, Extension Service. Madison, 1931.

Malin, James C. "Space and History: Reflections on the Closed-Space Doctrines of Turner and Mackinder and the Challenge of Those Ideas by the Air Age." *Agricultural History* 18, pt. 1 (April, 1944): 65–74; (July, 1944): 107–26.

Marshall, Robert. "Should We Settle Alaska?" *The New Republic* 102 (January 8, 1940): 49–50.

Murchie, R.W. *Agricultural Progress on the Prairie Frontier.* Vol. 5, *Canadian Frontiers of Settlement,* ed. W. A. Mackintosh and W. L. G. Joerg. Toronto: Macmillan Co. of Canada, 1936.

———. *Land Settlement as a Relief Measure.* No. 5, Day and Hour Series. Minneapolis: University of Minnesota, 1933.

Nettels, Curtis P. "Frederick Jackson Turner and the New Deal." *Wisconsin Magazine of History* 17 (March, 1934): 257–65.

Neuberger, Richard L. "Alaska: Sanctuary for Europe's Homeless." *Alaska Life* 10 (September, 1947): 8–9, 22.

———. "Public Domain: The West Needs People." Survey Graphic 30 (February, 1941): 72–78.

Nichols, Jeannette Paddock. *Alaska.* Cleveland: Arthur H. Clark Co., 1924.

Noonan, Dan. "Matanuska's a Good Thing." *Alaska Sportsman* 2 (February, 1936): 8–11, 22.

O'Brien, Harry R. "The New Stampede to the Land." *The Country Gentleman* 102 (October, 1932): 3–5.

O'Callaghan, Jerry A. "The War Veteran and the Public Lands." *Agricultural History* 28 (October, 1954): 163–68.

"Open Our Doors to German Refugees?" *Reader's Digest* 34 (May, 1939): 82–88.

"The Organization of Migration for Settlement." *International Labor Review* 37 (May, 1938): 561–83.

Paxson, Frederic L. *When the West Is Gone.* New York: Henry Holt and Co., 1930.

Peffer, E. Louise. *The Closing of the Public Domain.* Stanford, Calif.: University Press, 1951.

Pierson, George Wilson. "American Historians and the Frontier Hypothesis in 1941." *Wisconsin Magazine of History* 26, pt. 1 (September, 1942): 36–60; pt. 2 (December, 1942): 170–85.

"Pioneers in 1935: New Homesteads in Alaska." *The New Republic* 133 (May 29, 1935): 61–62.

Porsild, A. E. "Land Use in the Arctic." *Canadian Geographical Journal* 48, pt. 1 (June, 1954): 232–43; 49, pt. 2 (July, 1954): 20–31.

Postwar Problems of Migration: Papers Presented at the Round Table on Population Problems, 1946 Conference, Milbank Memorial Fund. New York: Milbank Memorial Fund, 1947.

Potter, Louise. *A Study of a Frontier Town in Alaska: Wasilla to 1959.* Hanover, N. H.: privately printed, 1960.

Pound, Arthur. "Land Ho! The Trek Toward Economic Security." *Atlantic Monthly* 151 (June, 1933): 714–21.

Rees, Goronwy. "The Unpeopled Spaces." *The Spectator* 149 (November 19, 1937): 883–84.

Refugee Economic Corporation. *Quest for Settlement: Summaries of Selected Economic and Geographic Reports on Settlement Possibilities for European Immigrants.* New York: Refugee Economic Corporation, 1948.

Reid, Bill G. "Franklin K. Lane's Idea for Veterans' Colonization, 1918–1921." *Pacific Historical Review* 33 (November, 1964): 447–61.

Richardson, Elmo R. *The Politics of Conservation: Crusades and Controversies, 1897–1913.* Berkeley and Los Angeles: University of California Press, 1962.

Riegel, Robert E. "American Frontier Theory." *Journal of World History* 3 (1956): 356–80.

Rockie, William A. "A Picture of Matanuska." *Geographical Review* 32 (July, 1942): 353–71.

———. "Pitting on Alaska Farm Lands: A New Erosion Problem." *The Geographical Review* 32 (January, 1942): 128–34.

Rogers, George W. *Alaska in Transition: The Southeast Region.* Baltimore: The Johns Hopkins Press, 1960.

———. *The Future of Alaska: Economic Consequences of Statehood.* Baltimore: The Johns Hopkins Press for Resources for the Future, 1962.

Roosevelt, Eleanor. "Subsistence Homesteads." *The Forum and Century* 91 (April, 1934): 199–201.

Roosevelt, Franklin D. "A New Rural Planning." *Rural Planning.* Proceedings of the 14th American Country Life Conference, Ithaca, N.Y., August 17–20, 1931. Chicago: University of Chicago Press, 1932.

———. "Back-to-the-Land," *Review of Reviews* 136 (October, 1931): 63–64.

———. *The Public Papers and Addresses of Franklin D. Roosevelt,* ed. Samuel I. Rosenman. Vols. 1, 2, 3, 4, 13. New York: Random House, 1938–1950.

Rowlands, David T. "Land and Homes for Returning Servicemen." *The Annals* 227 (May, 1943): 143–51.

Ryan, Philip E. *Migration and Social Welfare: An Approach to the Problem of the Non-Settled Person in the Community.* New York: Russell Sage Foundation, 1940.

Sanderson, Dwight. *Research Memorandum on Rural Life in the Depression.* Bulletin 34, Social Science Research Council, Committee on Studies in Social Aspects of the Depression. New York: SSRC, 1937.

Schafer, Joseph. "Concerning the Frontier as Safety Valve." *Political Science Quarterly* 52 (September, 1937): 407–20.

———. *The Social History of American Agriculture.* New York: Macmillan Co., 1936.

———. "Some Facts Bearing on the Safety-Valve Theory." *Wisconsin Magazine of History* 20 (December, 1936): 215–32.

Schaleben, Arville. "Matanuska Takes Root." *Christian Science Monitor Magazine* (December 2, 1936): 3, 18.

———. "Our New Pioneers." *American Magazine* 121 (January, 1936): 22–23, 90–94.

Scofield, Edna. "Finland's Farm-Refugee Problem." *The Geographical Review* 31 (January, 1941): 148–50.

Seeman, A. L. "Regions and Resources of Alaska." *Economic Geography* 13 (October, 1937): 334–36.

Sharp, Paul F. "The American Frontier and the 'Last Best West.'" *Agricultural History* 21 (April, 1947): 65–75.

Smith, Charles L. "The Matanuski [*sic*] Valley Project." *National Republic* (January, 1936): 5, 32.

Snider, Gerrit. *So Was Alaska.* Anchorage: privately printed, 1961.

Stanley, George F. G. "Western Canada and the Frontier Thesis." *Report of the Annual Meeting, Canadian Historical Association, May, 1940* (Toronto: University of Toronto Press, 1940), pp. 105–17.

Stanton, William J. "The Purpose and Source of Seasonal Migration to Alaska." *Economic Geography* 31 (April, 1955): 138–48.

Stefansson, Vilhjalmur. *The Northward Course of Empire.* New York: Macmillan Co., 1924.

Stone, Kirk H. "The Norwegian Edges of Settlement: Measures of Perma-

nence." Abstract, *Annals of the Association of American Geographers* 47 (June, 1957): 179.
———. "Populating Alaska: The United States Phase." *The Geographical Review* 42 (1952): 384–404.
———. "Some Geographical Bases for Planning New Settlement in Alaska." *Science in Alaska: Selected Papers of the Alaskan Science Conference of the National Academy of Sciences*. Washington: Arctic Institute of North America, 1952.
Stringer, Arthur. "Red-Plush Pioneers." *Saturday Evening Post* 208 (December 28, 1935): 8.
Sundborg, George. "Alaska Agriculture." *Alaska Life* 5 (August, 1942): 11–14.
———. *Opportunity in Alaska*. New York: Macmillan Co., 1945.
Taylor, Carl C. "Social And Economic Significance of the Subsistence Homestead Program—From the Viewpoint of a Sociologist." *Journal of Farm Economics* 17 (November, 1935): 720–31.
Thomas, Dorothy Swaine." Internal Migrations in Sweden: A Note on the Extensiveness as Compared with Net Migration Gain or Loss." *American Journal of Sociology* 42 (November, 1936): 345–57.
Thompson, Warren S. *Research Memorandum on Internal Migration in the Depression*. Bulletin 30, Social Science Research Council, Committee on Studies in Social Aspects of the Depression. New York: SSRC, 1937.
Tompkins, Stuart Ramsey. *Alaska: Promyshlennik and Sourdough*. Norman; Okla.: University of Oklahoma Press, 1945.
Trimble, William J. "The Influence of the Passing of the Public Lands." *Atlantic Monthly* 113 (June, 1914): 755–67.
Tugwell, Rexford G. *The Battle for Democracy*. New York: Columbia University Press, 1935.
———. "Cooperation and Resettlement. *Current History* (reprint) (February, 1937): 71–76.
———. *The Democratic Roosevelt*. Garden City, N.Y.: Doubleday and Co., 1957.
———. "The Planned Use of the Land." *Today* 1 (January 20, 1934): 6–7, 23–24.
———. "The Progressive Orthodoxy of Franklin D. Roosevelt." *Ethics* 64 (October, 1953): 1–23.
———. "The Sources of New Deal Reformism." *Ethics* 64 (July, 1954): 249–76.
———, and Banfield, Edward C. "Governmental Planning at Mid-Century." *Journal of Politics* 13 (May, 1951): 133–63.
Turner, Frederick Jackson. *The Frontier in American History*. New York: Henry Holt and Co., 1920.
Underhill, Frank H., ed. *The Canadian Northwest: Its Potentialities*. Symposium of the Royal Society of Canada, 1958. Toronto: University of Toronto Press, 1959.

Van Cleef, Eugene. "The Finn in America." *Geographical Review* 6 (September, 1918): 185–214.

———. "The Finns of the Pacific Coast of the United States, and Consideration of the Problem of Scientific Land Settlement." *Annals of the Association of American Geographers* 30 (March, 1940): 25–38.

Vogt, Evon Z. *Modern Homesteaders: The Life of a Twentieth-Century Frontier Community*. Cambridge: Harvard University Press, 1955.

Wager, Paul W. *One Foot on the Soil: A Study of Subsistence Homesteads in Alabama*. University of Alabama, Bureau of Public Administration. University, Ala., 1945.

Walker, Ernest P. *Alaska: America's Continental Frontier Outpost*. Washington, D.C.: Smithsonian Institution, 1943.

Wallace, Henry A. *New Frontiers*. New York: Reynal and Hitchcock, 1934.

Ward, Russel. *The Australian Legend*. Melbourne: Oxford University Press, 1958.

Ware, Harold M., and Powell, Webster. "Planning for Permanent Poverty: What Subsistence Farming Really Stands For." *Harper's Magazine* 170 (April, 1935): 513–24.

Warren, George L. "The Prospect for New Settlers." *Survey Graphic* 30 (March, 1941): 167–168.

Wasson, Chester R. "The Grubstake Plan for the Evacuation and Resettlement of the Inhabitants of Beltrami Island, Minnesota." *The Social Science Review* 12 (June, 1938): 276–97.

Webb, Walter Prescott. *The Great Frontier*. Boston: Houghton Mifflin Co., 1952.

Wehrwein, George S., and Baker, J. A. "The Cost of Isolated Settlement in Northern Wisconsin." *Rural Sociology* 2 (September, 1937): 253–65.

Westbrook, Lawrence. "The Program of Rural Rehabilitation of the FERA." *Journal of Farm Economics* 17 (February, 1935): 89–100.

———. "Rehabilitation of Stranded Families." *The Annals* 176 (November, 1934): 74–79.

"Where Shall We Put the Finns?" *Alaska Life* 3 (June, 1940): 10–11.

Willoughby, Barrett. *Alaska Holiday*. Boston: Little, Brown & Co., 1940.

———. "Log of the New Pioneers." *Saturday Evening Post* 207 (June 29, 1937): 23.

Wilson, Charles M. *Backwoods America*. Chapel Hill: University of North Carolina Press, 1934.

———. "Can We Go Back to the Land?" *Commonweal* 17 (November 2, 1932): 9–12.

———. "Land for the Taking." *American Magazine* 113 (March, 1932): 54–56.

———. "The Surviving American Frontier." *Current History and Forum* 34 (May, 1931): 189–92.

Wilson, Milburn L. "The Place of Subsistence Homesteads in Our National

Economy." *Journal of Farm Economics* 16 (February, 1934): 73–84.

———. "The Problem of Surplus Agricultural Population." *International Journal of Agrarian Affairs* 1 (October, 1939): 37–48.

Withers, Carl [James West]. *Plainville, U.S.A.* New York: Columbia University Press, 1945.

"Woe in the Wilderness." *Time* 26 (July, 1935): 14.

Wood, G. L. "Pioneer Settlement." *Economic Record* 9 (June, 1933): 49–57.

Wright, C. W. "The Significance of the Disappearance of Free Land in Our Economic Development." *American Economic Review, Supplement* 16 (1926): 265–71.

Wyman, Walker D., and Kroeber, Clifton B., eds. *The Frontier in Perspective.* Madison: University of Wisconsin Press, 1957.

"You Need More Than Land to Go Back to the Farm." *Literary Digest* 114 (July 9, 1932): 26–28.

Zeuch, William E. "The Subsistence Homestead Program from the Viewpoint of an Economist." *Journal of Farm Economics* 17 (November, 1935): 710–19.

Zon, Raphael; Cooper, William S.; et al. *Conservation of Renewable Natural Resources.* University of Pennsylvania Bicentennial Conference. Philadelphia: University of Pennsylvania Press, 1941.

Unpublished Works

Christiansen, Rudolph A. "The Wisconsin Resettlement Program." M.S. thesis, University of Wisconsin, 1954.

Cureton, Minnie Edith. "The History of the Criticisms of the Turner Thesis." Ph.D. dissertation, Stanford University, 1949.

Feldman, Theodore Charles. "The Federal Colonization Project in the Matanuska Valley, Alaska." M.A. thesis, University of Washington, 1941.

Halldorson, Marvin A. "The Matanuska Valley Colonization Project." M.A. thesis, University of Colorado, 1936.

Maddox, James G. "The Farm Security Administration." Ph.D. dissertation, Harvard University, 1950.

Monahan, Robert L. "The Development of Settlement in the Fairbanks Area, Alaska: A Study of Permanence." Ph.D. dissertation, McGill University, 1959.

Reid, Bill G. "Proposed American Plans for Soldier Settlement During the World War I Period." Ph.D. dissertation, University of Oklahoma, 1963.

Stone, Kirk H. "Alaska Group Settlement: The Matanuska Valley Colony." Ph.D. dissertation, University of Michigan, 1949.

Index